North Korea's Mundane Revolution

ASIA PACIFIC MODERN

Takashi Fujitani, Series Editor

North Korea's Mundane Revolution

SOCIALIST LIVING AND THE RISE
OF KIM IL SUNG, 1953–1965

Andre Schmid

UNIVERSITY OF CALIFORNIA PRESS

University of California Press
Oakland, California

Library of Congress Cataloging-in-Publication Data

Names: Schmid, Andre, author.
Title: North Korea's mundane revolution : socialist living and the
    rise of Kim Il Sung, 1953-1965 / Andre Schmid.
Other titles: Asia Pacific modern ; 19.
Description: Oakland, California : University of California Press, [2024] |
    Series: Asia pacific modern ; 19 | Includes bibliographical references and index.
Identifiers: LCCN 2023018632 (print) | LCCN 2023018633 (ebook) |
    ISBN 9780520392830 (cloth) | ISBN 9780520392847 (paperback) |
    ISBN 9780520392861 (ebook)
Subjects: LCSH: Kim, Il-sŏng, 1912-1994—Political and social views. |
    Social change—Korea (North)—Citizen participation—20th century. |
    Socialism—Korea (North)—20th century. | Sex role—Korea (North)—
    20th century. | Korea (North)—Social life and customs—20th century. |
    Korea (North)—Politics and government—1948-1994.
Classification: LCC HN730.6.A8 S45 2024 (print) | LCC HN730.6.A8 (ebook) |
    DDC 306.095193—dc23/eng/20230901
LC record available at https://lccn.loc.gov/2023018632
LC ebook record available at https://lccn.loc.gov/2023018633

33 32 31 30 29 28 27 26 25 24
10 9 8 7 6 5 4 3 2 1

A la familia Paradinas

CONTENTS

FIGURES

NOTE ON KOREAN ROMANIZATION
AND USAGE

The romanization of modern Korean is the subject of much acrimony, due to the politics of colonialism and national division. I choose not to use the romanization system developed by the South Korean Ministry of Education for a book about North Korea and instead follow another, still not controversy-free romanization system known as the McCune–Reischauer system. This system, based on English-language pronunciation and created by foreigners, has experienced its own attacks, especially in South Korea, yet has long been standard in most anglophone library collections. Whenever possible, I try not to convert North Korean orthography to southern practice (the North's *nyŏsŏng* stands for "women" rather than the South's *yŏsŏng*; *rodong* for "labor" rather than *nodong*); employ North Korean usage (*chosŏn'ŏt* for the traditional female dress the South calls *hanbok*); and follow official North Korean translations of terms into English when they are available. Finally, when I use the term *Korea*, contrary to typical English usage, it signifies the Democratic People's Republic of Korea, North Korea, or the North. Otherwise, I specify the Republic of Korea, South Korea, or the South.

ACKNOWLEDGMENTS

Years ago, I had an argument about the possibilities of doing North Korean history. I was less than optimistic: too much Kim Il Sung, too much propaganda, not enough sources—or so I thought. In this book, I try to prove myself wrong.

Along the way, I owe a debt to a succession of motivated students. They pestered me about North Korea because they knew enough not to believe the caricatures in our media. Textbooks on Korean history in my own student days simply stopped talking about the North after the civil war—half the peninsula erased. My own studies provided me with no better answers. I preferred simply to avoid the topic altogether, as it is always easier to critique than to offer alternatives. My students were unfazed by my frowns, however. Their irksome questions kept coming. This book is, ultimately, a cantankerous teacher's attempt to make amends and offer something of an answer, however belated, to those pesky yet valuable queries.

Along the way, I've received much prodding from a wide array of colleagues and scholars, who have made this work possible and much richer. All the shortcomings remain my own. I have the good fortune to study at a university devoted to thinking globally about East Asia, the University of Toronto. I'm grateful to my colleagues who have presented formal seminar critiques of chapters of this work—Yi Gu and Lisa Yoneyama—and to others who have taken the time to read and discuss specific issues and comparative approaches, including Linda Feng, Anup Grewal, Tom Keirstead, Tong Lam, Yoonkyung Lee, Meng Yue, Janet Poole, Shiho Satsuka, Nhung Tuyet Tran, Y. Yvon Wang, Yiching Wu, and Yurou Zhong. Also, Tak Fujitani has been gracious with both his comments and his time in guiding the manuscript to press. Ken Kawashima first pushed me to think about housing. Beyond my own institution, I have been the beneficiary of colleagues across three continents who have asked me sharp questions and made pointed recommendations. At a conference in Moscow, Kim Seong Bo and Pak Myonglim shared their knowledge about the early postwar Party-state, which helped shape the direction of my project. I'm particularly grateful to Ruth Barraclough, Charles Kim, Suzy Kim, and Theodore Jun Yoo for commenting on a draft of the manuscript. Katherine H. S. Moon's smart laugh always steered me away from my silliest ideas. Valérie Gelézeau shared her ideas about apartments in Pyongyang. Friends in 1980s-era Tianjin gave me clues to the art of reading socialist newspapers. The Sedivy-Horvath clan shared insightful stories from older days back home and were always my hardest audience. Conversations with Hyun Ok Park were always learning opportunities for me. Olga Fedorenko suffered my linguistically challenged questions about Russian. I received additional helpful advice and thoughts from Nancy Abelmann, E. Taylor Atkins, Gregg Brazinsky, Hyaeweol Choi, Steven Chung, Koen de Ceuster, Henry Em, Sheldon Garon, Karl Gerth, Todd Henry, Nanzhi Jin, Jiyoung Jung, Cheehyung Harrison Kim, Elli Kim, Jisoo Kim, Dong-choon Kim, Sungjo Kim, Nancy Kwak, Heonik Kwon, Thomas Lahusen, Steven Lee, John Lie, Jie-Hyun Lim, Kimberley Manning, Natalia Matveeva, Owen Miller, Laura Nelson, James F. Person, Jooyeon Rhee, Sonia Ryang, Youngju Ryu, Schamma Schahadat, Zhihua Shen, Naoko Shimazu, Moe Taylor, Julia Adeney Thomas, Lynne Viola, Benjamin R. Young, and Dafna Zur. I derived valuable lessons about this project from a professor who asked me, "Why do you want to normalize North Koreans?"; from another who asked me suspiciously, "What are your political motivations for studying North Korea this way?"; and from a Korean businessman sitting beside me on a plane, who got up from his seat after seeing the "red" materials I was reading.

Over the years, wonderful research assistants have helped track down sources and taught me a great deal, including Sanghun Cho, Sungjo Kim, Derek Kramer, Sungsoo Lee, who was especially helpful in the final stages of proofreading, and Juwon Kim. I'm especially grateful to a number of librarians, who helped make this project possible with their on-the-spot guidance and knowledge. At my own university, in the Cheng Yu Tung East Asian Library, Hana Kim and Julia Chun provided regular and reliable advice; at the Library of Congress, Sonya Lee forged support for the North Korean collection, deserving a "model worker" story of her own, and was generous with her advice; at the Harvard-Yenching Library, Mikyung Kang opened the world of North Korean sources to me in an unforgettable first research trip;

and at the Russian State Library, Natasha Ahn took much time out of her calendar to showcase to me this bibliographic center of the socialist world.

All images are from the Library of Congress, Asian Division, Korean collection unless otherwise specified.

I've benefited from presenting portions of this manuscript in university-based lectures, when I received questions that shaped my research, often from unfamiliar audience members whom I regret being unable to identify here. These institutions have included Sogang University, University of Hawai'i, SOAS University of London, Princeton University, Northern Illinois University, University of Chicago, University of California–Berkeley, University of California–San Diego, Birkbeck–University of London, Stanford University, University of Pennsylvania, York University, McGill University, Free University of Berlin, University of Wisconsin–Madison, University of Illinois at Urbana-Champaign, Columbia University, and University of Michigan.

This project received financial support from the Social Sciences and Humanities Research Council of Canada and from the Dean's Office of the Faculty of Arts and Science, University of Toronto. No funding for this project was received from Seoul, Pyongyang, Washington, or Moscow.

Parts of this book were published in "Historicizing North Korea: State Socialism, Population Mobility, and Cold War Historiography," *The American Historical Review* 123.2 (2018): 439–462; "'My Turn to Speak': Criticism Culture and the Multiple Uses of Class in North Korea," *International Journal of Korean History* 21.2 (2016): 121–153; and "The Gendered Anxieties of Apartment Living in North Korea, 1953–65," in Schamma Schahadat and Thomas Lahusen, eds., *Postsocialist Landscapes: Real and Imaginary Spaces from Stalinstadt to Pyongyang* (Berlin: Transcript, 2020: 281–304).

My greatest debt goes, as usual, to Sonia, BB, and Paddy, who kept me off-center when needed and centered when necessary.

Cruiser Lake
Spring 2023

Introduction

NORTH KOREA'S MUNDANE REVOLUTION

PHOTOGRAPHED ON THE BALCONY OF THEIR APARTMENT, a family of four dressed in their finest look out over their newly constructed neighborhood.[1] The trundling buses and multistory buildings reveal they are in the "heroic capital," as North Korea's largest city, Pyongyang, was coming to be known (see figure 1). The photograph presented this specific family as a generic "any" family, offering none of the conventional identifiers—names, workplaces, and political affiliations were nowhere to be found. Such details were unnecessary because, by the year the portrait emerged in a 1959 monthly magazine, every reader would have recognized the iconography—a smiling conjugal couple with children in front of their apartment home—as representing an ideal vision of what was being widely touted as the "New Living."[2]

In 1959 the New Living represented a still vibrant dream for a mass utopia.[3] This was the promise of revolution, offered after more than three decades of colonial rule (1910–45) and reinitiated after the devastations of the first hot war (1950–53) of the Cold War. The New Living was an ideal rooted in Marxist-Leninist theories of material dialectics, motivated by the desire to overcome colonial capitalism, and shaped by Cold War rivalries. It offered a fantasy shared by both the North Korean Party-state and many Korean women and men about the plainest of desires: a quest for a better modern life, imagined as being possible only through socialism.[4]

Of course, the family's happy smiles also worked to shunt aside the existence of inequities, providing a visual version of the grandest of twentieth-century fictions: work hard and do what's necessary and the abundance of modernity can be enjoyed by you, your family, and everyone else. Just what was necessary and how these conditions would be made was hardly straightforward, remained elusive for many, and was replete with anxieties. Along

FIGURE 1. An ideal family under the "New Living." Anonymous, untitled, 1959.

the way, the Party-state and ordinary Koreans deployed various forms of memory politics, mixed with ideas about ideology and culture, to rationalize the disjunction between the photograph's ideal and the unevenness that continued to shape their gendered socioeconomic lives.

Like Europeans, Japanese, and North Americans after World War II, inhabitants of both halves of the Korean Peninsula marked the end of fighting in 1953 by struggling to reconstitute their families.[5] So, too, in the North, did the Party-state prioritize the family as a means of laying the basis for its political-economic vision, burnish its nationalist credentials, and show that it was serious about gender reform. Torn apart by nearly seventeen years of colonial and Cold War conflict, the social unit of the family was a key realm in which the Party-state would engage with popular aspirations and reestablish its postwar power. This turn to the family, on the part of both the Korean population and the Party-state, provides the subject of this book—not as a study of the family per se, but as a means to examine the historical processes that enabled this self-proclaimed socialist regime to consolidate its power. For most Korean men and women, who historically had little exposure to socialism, this was an unknown experiment. Yet by 1965, in the twelve years after the end of fighting, these processes had established the contours for much of the North's gendered political economy, social fabric, and ideological world.

I begin with this family portrait because the photograph's very simplicity suggests how the New Living opened up basic questions about labor, domesticity, consumption, and the modern individual in the newly rebuilding cities—all subjects shaped by gender. These questions ran deeply through Korean history, making the New Living a part of the peninsula's long twentieth century,[6] which itself unfolded on regional and global stages. For those familiar with the way North Korean history has been told both inside and outside the country, it may seem unusual to raise these questions. After all, our histories of North Korea have focused almost exclusively on the man credited with single-handedly establishing the most powerful political dynasty of the twentieth century: Kim Il Sung.

For my purposes, the New Living offers an alternative by providing a nexus to prioritize analysis of the localized processes of gendered socioeconomic and cultural change in cities—what I call the mundane histories of North Korea. This is not the same as either bottom-up history or an examination of intellectuals' use of the category of everyday life to reflect on the nature of socialist modernity. Instead, it examines the participation of Korean men and women in the many state-derived projects that together constituted the New Living.[7] It is often forgotten that millions of men and women fought in the Korean War against the United States, South Korea, and the United Nations, often at terrible personal cost. When the fighting finished, people redirected their wartime energies—whether they were loyal to the regime, committed to socialism, saw North Korea as the best locus for their patriotism, or simply dreamed of a better life in a system they did not choose—to rebuilding their country and their personal lives. War-weary in 1953, equipped with liberatory narratives of the promises of sovereignty, and experienced with the modern state and economy under colonialism, vast segments of the population had many motivations for participating in the New Living in the hopes of recreating a semblance of the life captured in the image of a family on their balcony. The New Living, then, was where popular aspirations met, negotiated, and mediated Party-state plans and goals. It was a realm where forms of knowledge that historically had circulated nationally, within the socialist bloc, and globally came to be translated and used—whether deliberately, unconsciously, or unwillingly—by Korean women and men in reconstituting their families in the security of their apartments and workplaces after the horrific violence of the mid-twentieth century. These widespread and decentered processes of negotiation—taking place in conjunction with the Party-state's determination to reestablish, expand, and stabilize its power—are the main subject of *North Korea's Mundane Revolution*. During this era, Pyongyang received more investment than any other city and became nationally celebrated as the "heart" of the country. While I examine these processes across the peninsula's many urban spaces, the focus of my research leans heavily toward Pyongyang.

In the following pages, I trace how the New Living helped push for a radical transformation in much of North Korea's economic and ideological life, while at the same time serving to depoliticize the two main categories originally used by the Party to criticize contemporary society: gender and class. At the same time that the New Living refocused energies into the self-reform necessary to push individuals along the transition to socialism, it also worked to create and legitimize gendered socioeconomic hierarchies, which were arising from the very changes it helped spur. The New Living glossed over the tensions and contradictions emerging out of a growing economy and elicited the participation of the population in ways that made the central plan "work," so to speak. This process of depoliticization became key to the consolidation of the Party-state's power. These were not conditions created by Kim Il Sung, as his personality cult would eventually claim. Rather, his personal rise to power depended on them, not vice versa.

THE CONCEIT OF THE "NEW," REVOLUTIONARY NARRATIVES, AND PARTY-STATE TIME

Every revolution claims the mastery of time for itself. The New Living featured various types of historical narrative that shaped the Party-state's policies as well as popular expectations and experiences. My account regularly returns to the uses of three narratives, each of which was invoked to frame the historical meaning of building socialism. None of them were mere rhetoric. Nor were they restricted to history books. These three narratives formed the mainstays of a memory politics that—sometimes loudly, sometimes quietly—became insinuated into the New Living to answer that most basic of revolutionary questions, first raised by Lenin: "What is to be done?"[8]

The first was the revolutionary narrative of the "new" in the New Living, which ultimately denied its own historicity. Against the backdrop of liberation from colonialism in 1945 and survival of civil war in 1953, *new* became the most common of adjectives. "New society," "new humanity," "new culture," "new era," and "new family"—all these phrases and more littered the pages of the media. The idea of "new" provided the fundamental conceit to the Korean Workers' Party's (KWP) claim to revolution: they had made a break with the past, one that severed the collective era from the feudal, colonial, and capitalist pasts.

Despite this emphasis on the novelty of the era, older viewers would not have been surprised by the 1959 family portrait. But for the architecture, much of the photograph would have appeared familiar to them. This was because the photograph's vision arose out of a long history of debate about the individual and family relations dating back at least to the 1890s. Across the century, Korea's compressed modernity included virtually every form of modern political regime and economy. Starting with the more than five-hundred-year-old royal dynasty that ended in 1910 (1392–1910), Korean men and women lived through the final throes of a feudal economic system, colonialism, fascism, capitalism, formal liberal democracy, military occupation, and a self-proclaimed socialist regime. Ever since the first nationalist reformers questioned the nature of the extended family and presented it as one of the primary traditions against which to measure their much-desired modern progress, women and men had pondered the gendered, class, sexual, and national potential of competing proposals for the modern family. That the ideal of a heteronormative nuclear family—blissful in its home—and its gendered social relations traveled across the tumultuous twentieth century and outlasted any single regime testifies to the remarkable fluidity of this vision, its hold over popular imagination even as it continued to be debated, and its centrality to modern governing rationalities.

The New Living, in short, was not so new. Indeed, the expression itself had a pre-collective-era history, when it also emerged as a common phrase in China as part of nationalist reformers' agendas.[9] Its simultaneous, if more short lived, appearance in 1950s South Korea exemplified this shared genealogy across the demilitarized zone.[10] Yet this history—transcending the nation-state and in circulation for decades—was precisely what the New Living disavowed in order to trumpet its own uniqueness. The constant assertion of novelty accompanied by a denial of the past was itself symptomatic of modernist conceptions of time—what Harry Harootunian has described as the "new in the ceaseless flow of change."[11] Such an arrangement of time, which worked by discovering the new through a negation of the past, had long been familiar to Korean writers, as Janet Poole has shown.[12] *New*, in short, was an old adjective, a favorite witness to continuous, contemporary change. The New Living was a dream of mass utopia created not from a blank slate or by Korean socialists alone. It was a coming together of decades-old activisms, layered upon each other, circulating among the population, never monopolized by a single state, and adapted to the exigencies and particular Cold War ecosystem of the latter half of Korea's long twentieth century. Within this context, *new* was often a substitute for *socialist*.

The second narrative, which I refer to as "Party-state time," was also prominent in the New Living and had Party ideologues explaining that socialism had not yet been achieved.[13] According to the Party's assessment of the stages of its revolution, the material basis for socialism was met in 1958. In that year, the final step to collectivize the economy had been taken by eliminating private commerce and completing the cooperativization of agriculture.[14] In theory, every person in the country had become working class, or proletarianized. Although a mechanistic interpretation of material dialectics might conclude that ideology, as a reflection of the material basis of the economy, would necessarily follow suit, this was not the KWP's position. Instead, KWP ideologues explained that under the conditions of colonialism and war, Korean men and women had remained largely unschooled in Marxism, and so their ideology lagged behind the now socialized material conditions.

Historians rarely give much credence to Party self-assessments. Yet what interests me is not so much the theoretical basis of the Party's evaluation, but the fact that this decision deeply shaped Party-state policies and the population's experiences of the postwar period. Enormous consequences flowed from the "transition to socialism" evaluation. Collectivization of the material meant there was no theoretical basis for a writer to explain existing socioeconomic problems as rooted in the material economy. The burden of causal explanations fell completely on ideology. The leading Party newspaper explained: "As is well known, to complete the task of socialist revolution successfully, it is not enough only to socialize the relations of production. Together with this . . . consciousness must be socialized."[15] One corollary of this position was that responsibility for elevating ideological levels lay with the people themselves. Yet responsibility easily blurred into blame, as if the people themselves were to be culpable for any remaining problems. The Party-state, in this conception of time, exonerated itself.

The call to raise ideological levels had begun as soon as the country had been liberated from colonialism.[16] Only now there was a greater urgency, underpinned by the historical task of catching up to material conditions. Yet I hasten to point out that what constituted ideology in these years was not fixed, but in flux and ill-defined. "Kim Il Sung Thought" had yet to rise to dominance.[17] Party ideologues evangelized on ideological needs, yet the parameters of the ideology were still evolving. One thing was sure, however: ideology extended well beyond the study of the Marxist texts on which Party-state time rested. The New Living would be subsumed within this campaign. Marxist dialectics and proper personal hygiene, Party history and punctual attendance, wage labor and unpaid domestic labor all became targets of the effort to elevate ideology.

Nonetheless, the very nebulousness of New Living only accentuated the indeterminacy of the ideology everyone was supposedly pursuing. No Party resolution ever set the New Living's bounds, nor did Kim Il Sung ever fully address this question. Ultimately, the New Living became one means through which the Party's already unclear definition of *sasang* (ideology) blurred into an even more capacious category, *munhwa* (culture). For the most part, the former represented Party ideology, or what would be studied in political study sessions, even as this changed significantly over time.[18] Everything that did not neatly fit into ideology was relegated to culture. The relationship between the two remained under-theorized and was never taken up by the main theoretical journal.[19] Issues, terminology, and content drifted between the two. In the following pages, I use the terms *ideology* and *culture* in line with Party-state practice. But in rejecting the Party's claim about its own ideological and cultural mastery and its conceit of a break, I use the term *discourse* to account for the wider range of language and practices beyond the Party-state's own usage of those two terms. If the KWP saw ideology as nestled within the broader category of culture, this book positions both ideology and culture as nestled within the era's discourse, which itself was part of the flow of Korea's long twentieth century.

Party-state time's tenet that popular ideological levels lagged came with a presumption that past beliefs and values—feudal, colonial, and bourgeois—continued to circulate among the population as what they called "remnants." This was one of the few ways the Party-state acknowledged continuities across the 1945 "break" that was so central to its revolutionary narrative about the "new." In these cases, the locus of continuity was almost always deemed to be in culture, however loosely defined, and not in state institutions or the Party itself. This narrative enabled the Party-state to present itself as the curator of potentially dangerous cultural forms received from the past. In a common expression of the era, the Party-state alone knew how "to inherit and develop" (*kyesŭng paljŏn*) those past beliefs—it had an all-knowing ability to understand, reject, and/or reform these beliefs and practices.

This, of course, was fantasy. Despite the Party-state's claims, there remained much that was invisible to the Party-state. It is one of the often-noted ironies of many postcolonial movements that however much they saw themselves as anticolonial and anticapitalist, after liberation they frequently turned to some of the same governing techniques on which their political adversaries had once rested their own power. This dynamic shaped North Korea as well. Many examples exist, but my research regularly returns to three rationalities that predate the regime and that became interwoven in the New Living. Chief among these was biopolitics: the political economy of health as captured in an array of practices and ideas that sought to manage and improve the health, discipline, and well-being of both individual bodies and the population as a whole.[20] Second was the reintroduction of the Fordist factory system—with its endless appetite for labor, technology, and capital—as the engine of the political economy, to reach socialism through enhanced production.[21] Third was the repurposing of previous forms of nationalism into socialist patriotism. All three were resurrected through specific forms of class and/or anticolonial critique that made them, in the eyes of authorities, reusable. Party-state authorities believed that biopolitical services could be extended, beyond their previous domination by the bourgeoisie and colonial Japanese, to all the people. Factories, stripped of class relations, could be made exploitation free. And old brands of nationalism could be purged of their bourgeois character. These rationalities were not part of the Party-state's definition of what to overthrow, or the direction in which gender equality policies pointed. *North Korea's Mundane Revolution* shows how all three transcended regimes, were under-critiqued, and shaped the New Living in ways beyond the imagination of the Party-state's views of its relationship to the past. A key dynamic of this inheritance centered on how, among the class-based critiques, much less was said about the feminization of domesticity in biopolitics, the gendered division of labor in the factory system, or the masculinist nature of nationalism.[22]

The third and final type of narrative in my analysis was the repeated use of classic developmentalist conceptions of time. This vision of time backed what James Scott has described as the overconfidence of modern states in their ability to renovate and redesign society—a description well suited to North Korea.[23] Part of the power of this Enlightenment-style narrative was that it had a long history prior to the collective era and did not need to be invented anew. Because developmentalism was so familiar to everyone, the Party-state's efforts to plot a policy along such a timeline always risked exceeding its grasp. Officials did everything they could to insert the Party-state into this narrative. And by grafting revolutionary and Party-state time onto this basic developmentalism, authorities hoped their narratives would reinforce each other and work to the regime's advantage. Developmentalism also served to explain away problems. It preached patience, asking ordinary men and women to postpone their gratification and to keep struggling to create the appropriate conditions for the Party-state's promises to be realized. Results were imminent, it sought to convince people, and would come somewhere in an ill-defined future.

These memory politics were central to the Party-state's consolidation of power and the formation of the New Living. These various narratives merged in one of the most significant urban projects of the postwar period, the 1958 campaign to rebuild Pyongyang. What was significant about this mass campaign, aside from the physical transformation of the cityscape, was that everyone—the producers of cement and glass; truck drivers delivering materials; architects drawing up plans; crane operators hoisting panels; Ri Myŏngwŏn, the organizer of a women's team of cement pargers; and the eventual residents—had their participation framed as advancing toward the teleological end of these three narratives, a better modern life under socialism. Through the construction of housing, women and men developed stakes in the success of the New Living and came to understand their participation on a grand historical scale. Prefabricated blocks, in short, materialized these narratives.

DEPOLITICIZATION AND THE
COLLECTIVE INDIVIDUAL

The Party-state's growing emphasis on ideology and culture after 1958 meant that enormous pressure was placed on individuals to "work on" and reform themselves. Historical studies of the individual Soviet subject have transformed the study of Stalinism,[24] but, with the exception of Suzy Kim's study on the period 1945–50, this has largely been ignored by historians of Korea.[25] One argument of this book is that the New Living's sense of the unfolding of individual consciousness ultimately depoliticized the two conceptual categories that had always been central to the Party's revolutionary narrative: gender and class. By depoliticization, I mean that both gender and class were stripped of their radical potential to analyze contemporary social relations or changes arising from the postwar political economy. This focus on the individual—together with the notion of raising one's "cultural levels"—as the route to collective ideals arose in the years immediately following the war, when tensions in the political economy, rooted in rapid growth, became more acute. The depoliticization of gender and class as sites of critiques in these years segued neatly with the consolidation of Party-state power and, eventually, the rise of Kim Il Sung.

My argument about depoliticization derives from a comparison with North Korea's two socialist neighbors and biggest wartime allies, the Soviet Union and the People's Republic of China. Although all three emphasized individual ideological reform, in neither of these neighbors did this emphasis translate into a similar depoliticization in their early postrevolutionary years. Class categories remained a central part of early Soviet and Chinese political culture, providing a central sociopolitical focus around which to define major campaigns. Not so in North Korea. There was no equivalent in Korea of Stalin's anti-Kulak purges, to cite one Soviet example. Nor was anyone in the KWP about to let a "Hundred Flowers" bloom, as in China's campaign of that name. For all of the continuing discussions of class struggle in Korea, Kim Il Sung was never interested in unleashing the social power of the people against established institutions or social formations. The class politics behind Maoist slogans like "Bombard the Headquarters" and "It's Right to Rebel" remained unimaginable in Korea.

That the Party-state refrained from such destabilizing campaigns and positioned itself as national protector had much to do with contemporary geopolitics surrounding the divided peninsula. All-out fighting in the

Korean War had ended in 1953 with an armistice, not a peace treaty. Roughly seventy thousand American troops were still barracked in the South, less than two hundred kilometers from Pyongyang. In 1958, the last Chinese PLA soldiers returned home. In that same year, the United States introduced nuclear weapons to the peninsula. Under these security conditions, the KWP likely did not want to risk the instability that might result from a class-based campaign not tightly controlled by the center.

This did not mean that class talk disappeared as part of the New Living—on the contrary, depoliticization led to its proliferation. The pragmatic desire for stability, due to geopolitical anxieties, also came with theoretical concerns. Most importantly, Party-state time assumed that because everyone had been proletarianized with the completion of collectivization in 1958, class struggle had been marginalized as a contemporary challenge. True, the authorities admitted, there remained antirevolutionary elements in what were often called the the "cracks," but these were no longer seen as class formations per se—rather, they were the detritus of history. Kim Il Sung repeated on many occasions that unlike European socialist parties, the KWP did not need to deal with a leftover domestic bourgeoisie, most of whom had escaped to the South. Instead, Party ideologues displaced class struggle from contemporary internal politics, moving it largely onto the past as a historical phenomenon; onto the South, as an obstacle to reunification; and onto the global stage, as manifest in imperialism.[26] Many of the most radical political statements emanating from Pyongyang institutions looked outward at international politics and were often made by delegates to various international events and not at domestic events.[27]

It is important to make clear that while I analyze contemporary discourse on class, my research makes no empirical claims about actual class formations or social stratification after the war. There is simply not enough data.[28] Arguably, the fact that authorities did not openly collect data on class reflected this emptying-out effect. It simply was not a relevant category in the eyes of officials who believed that the material basis for class differences had been eliminated. It should be noted, however, that it was precisely in these years that the economy grew rapidly. Wage scale hierarchies were established, Party membership and state bureaucracies grew, the *sŏngbun* (political loyalty) system was unrolled, and postsecondary universities and technical colleges were established—in short, numerous developments normally associated with class formation took place. Moreover, Party-state ideologues constantly admonished against what they called "equalism" (*py'ŏnggyunjuŭi*), meaning that not everyone should receive equal pay. One of the arguments in this book is that the dynamics of postwar social changes reverberated through the discursive environment—and thus, despite the lack of data, are visible to historians in areas as diverse as advice literature and modes of speech, the gendered division of labor, and discussions about interior décor, to name a few. More than this, it was not just that the New Living reflected these social changes but that the New Living helped constitute, legitimate, and naturalize them, even as it displaced class as a conceptual category of critique. In this sense, the depoliticizing power of the New Living was to deny any conceptual space in which to raise criticisms of the social relations that the New Living was itself partly responsible for forming.

Depoliticization also shaped the gender dynamics of the New Living, though with a less straightforward politics. This took place in the context of implementing what were, when they were passed in 1946, the first series of gender equality laws in Asian history. Many studies have shown how these laws were never fully realized and that the position of women remained unequal.[29] Although these studies rightly capture continuing inequities, they nevertheless often underplay the way women from around the country used these laws to advance into new social and political arenas in the face of often difficult circumstances, both structural and personal.[30] It should not be forgotten that much changed in the socioeconomic spheres between 1953 and 1965 at the behest of women entering formerly masculine domains such as construction, biological sciences, administrative positions, and the military.

Nevertheless, it is also clear that the gender equality laws provided cover for what I refer to throughout this study as the masculinist Party-state and for the local social power of men. The Party-state reinforced the local social power of men, and vice versa. This interrelationship was key to disadvantaging women, even as the Party-state promoted gender equality. It became central to the New Living, insofar as gender equality was pursued only so long as it did not directly question the way local male social power reinstantiated itself, in part, through the Party-state itself. This relationship determined how and in what realms gender equality would be deemed necessary—or not—by the Party-state and what policies would be implemented. As Catherine MacKinnon has described in her study of law and the state, "the law sees and treats women the way men see and treat women."[31] This statement can be expanded beyond North Korean family law, as will become obvious in the following pages, to include the various ensemble of institutions that made up the Party-state.[32]

In this sense, it was not just that there continued to be gender inequities but that these inequities were fundamental to the New Living, the organization of the political economy, and the expansion of the power of the Party-state itself. The mutually reinforcing power of local men and Party-state power made it all the more challenging for the Women's Union to advance its arguments for—and expand the definition of—equality. They certainly did so, but always carefully. In this sense, any analysis of North Korean authoritarianism must attribute this power not just to Party-state institutions alone but also to the simultaneous entrenchment of masculine power. Gender organizes political power—and vice versa. My study is animated by this dynamic insofar as the specific ways in which gender came to be depoliticized were connected to the relationship between the individual subject, ideology, and socialism. This line of inquiry reshapes a question asked by Wendy Brown: How did claims to socialist universal subjecthood re-inscribe male dominance as a part of the changes made in its name?[33]

The answer to this question rests in the KWP's imbalanced vision of its three main emancipatory subjects—the working class, the nation, and women. For the first two, the Party-state's task was unambiguous: the nation was to be liberated from the colonizer, and the working masses would be rescued from the bourgeoisie. In theory, both these goals had already been achieved: the nation was liberated with the end of colonialism in 1945, and the working class was freed with collectivization in 1958. Yet for the third subject, women, the Party-state could not quite bring itself to enunciate in dialectical terms what needed to be overthrown. Stock phrases like "liberation from the kitchen" showed just how difficult it was for the Party-state to name men, masculinism, patriarchy, or any other substitute as the target. It was far easier to slip women's emancipation into the catchall categories of antifeudalism and anticolonialism or identify specific policies—the end of childhood marriages, for example—as a way of directing energies toward specific issues of inequality, rather than deal conceptually or in practice with the implications of gender revolution. The New Living, despite all its attention to the relations between domesticity and factory life, did little to nudge aside, let alone overthrow, the power of men in their local social worlds, even though it supported and encouraged the entrance of women into wage work and education.

The uneven conception of emancipatory subjects meant that liberation— of the nation and of the working class—defined the sovereign power of the postcolonial state as resting primarily with men. As can be seen in the New

Living, now that Korean men grasped the levers of state power that had been denied them for over thirty years of colonial rule, any advancements of the interests of women were expected to abide by and not ruffle the simultaneous reassertion of localized male social power that came with decolonization. The fact that decolonization represented a reassertion of masculinity under the guise of national and proletarian sovereignty remained unspoken among all the discussions of equality and the universal socialist subject. The lack of a gendered critique of biopolitics, the Fordist factory system, and nationalism all reinforced this gendered arrangement. The advancement of women's liberation, while still a loudly and consistently announced goal of the Party-state, had to be pursued within this context and, in classic developmentalist fashion, could easily be deferred to an undefined future.

The Party-state's uneven vision of liberation did not rest easily with the Korean Democratic Women's Union. As a mass organization, the Women's Union was tasked with creating the conditions for the successful carrying out of Party-state policies. Yet unlike the General Federation of Trade Unions, which had been stripped of any power to represent workers' interests outside the Party, the Women's Union still served as an institutional site from which to push back, however carefully in the authoritarian environment, against policies that negatively affected their membership.[34] Yet even as its monthly magazine, *Women of Korea* (*Chosŏn nyŏsŏng*), expressed disgruntlement with certain policies, especially changes in divorce laws, its writers also produced a wide assortment of representations of new femininities—in the realms of speech, work styles, and consumption, to identify a few—that simultaneously reproduced gendered hierarchies, contained the social effects of their members' many advances, and even served to provide cultural justifications for the growing stratifications among women. *Women of Korea*'s writers indirectly critiqued specific Party-state policies, yet in other areas their representations often worked to depoliticize gender as a category of critique.

The depoliticization of gender and class was neither absolute nor complete. Their radical potential arose in instances of what I call "flashes of criticism." Appearing piecemeal in the press, these flashes suggested possible critiques of contemporary developments. They did so ambiguously, and left it up to readers to interpret on their own. A photograph might raise questions of commodity fetishism, a reproduction of a Mao speech could hint at contradictions between the people and leadership, a cartoon might question the appropriateness of material incentives or spoof the very idea of a "cooperative husband." These flashes re-politicized what had been depoliticized, pointing obliquely to the possibility of a different socialism. Most such flashes of criticism likely went unnoticed and were, of course, never taken up by the Party-state, yet I argue they were an important part of the New Living's discursive range.

My emphasis on depoliticization and ignored radical alternatives will lead some to ask why I still use the word *socialism* to describe the North Korean system in this era. This question arises in the context of a long tradition of critique, beginning with Trotsky, that has challenged the socialist bona fides of such regimes, arguing that what was built in the name of socialism was in fact nothing more than another type of capitalism, usually state capitalism.[35] Recently, Hyun Ok Park, Cheehyung Harrison Kim, and Owen Miller have taken this approach to North Korea.[36] Another form of critique, especially common in Seoul, takes socialism's anticapitalism as absolute: any idea or practice found at any other time or place in the peninsula's history—usually in the colonial period or in South Korea—is seen as evidence that North Korea was not really socialist, as if ideas and practices cannot change meaning as they travel across time and space. Both approaches demand an ahistorical purity on the part of North Korea and ultimately privilege South Korea, or capitalism more generally, as the norm for modernity against which a socialism must articulate its complete uniqueness to merit its claim to being genuine. While my own research has benefited from these approaches, especially state capitalism's emphasis on surplus value, my work is ultimately less oriented toward ideal-type definitions or arguments about regime types.

Instead, *North Korea's Mundane Revolution* examines the ways in which North Korean men and women themselves imagined socialism in the specific context of the New Living during years when basic socialist concepts needed to be learned and put into practice. In this sense, I do not offer necessary and sufficient criteria to define terms like *collective property* and *socialist value*, to see whether North Korea fit the definition, but aim to trace how these expressions came to be used in specific socioeconomic settings by Korean men and women. Often socialism was explained at the most general level, as seen in the sense of revolutionary and Party-state time. This allowed writers to add the adjective *socialist* to virtually any phenomenon. But as the New Living showed, more often than not people just got on with their lives, without reflecting on the socialist nature of specific practices and beliefs. Increasingly, by the 1960s, writers could even address issues that had only the vaguest connection to the Party's resolutions and pronouncements. Not everything in the 1950s and '60s, as much as the Party would hate to admit it, was reducible to that single word *socialist*. Nor did the word have a unitary meaning or consistent usage. The fact that there was an urge, at times, to define specific practices—motherhood, for example, or apartment spaces—as specifically socialist testified to the basic fact that there was no simple, clear dividing line. The struggle to define, more than the final conclusions, is what was most revealing. The New Living, despite its revolutionary claims, often blurred boundaries between capitalism and socialism, between the present and the past, between the Korean and the global, even as it proclaimed its uniqueness in political, temporal, and spatial terms. It is a residue of Cold War labeling practices that we continue to demand clear distinctions and a purity of form when, in fact, many of the New Living's practices were as familiar to older Koreans as others were alien.

NORTH KOREA AS HISTORY AND IDEOLOGY

In highlighting North Korea's mundane revolution, my study also shifts beyond the single, often seamless story lines presented by the tightly curated, high-level propaganda of art, speeches, movies, and posters. It turns to the materials Koreans read in their day-to-day lives, primarily print media such as magazines and newspapers published in Pyongyang. Monographs have also been included, ranging from worker memoirs to political study-session manuals and homemaking guides. After 1958, a surge of publications—especially magazines—emerged in line with the ideological pivot. In these pages, a wide variety of women and men appear, often ephemerally, who mostly were not famous and would no doubt be shocked to discover their presence in this book. These sources do not give an unmediated access to their voices, of course, but they often offer insight into the excitement and anxieties urban men and women faced in an era of immense change.

On occasion, I supplement these sources with the observations of foreign diplomats, usually Soviet and Eastern European officials, whose reports have become partially available in English.[37] This largely male cohort of diplomats constantly complained about their own limited access and often depended for information on the same sources I am using. Yet often their reports provide valuable insights and unique nuggets of information. Their reports about how North Korean economic planning shaped (or did not shape) standards of living are most useful. While Soviet and Eastern European reports often criticized North Korean policies and conditions, Korean publications were constrained by the Party-state dictatorship.

All the Korean publications were Party-state sanctioned. In such a situation, there is a tendency to consider as genuine opinion only those records that clearly do not reiterate the Party-state line.[38] Such an approach risks leading to a search for oppositional or out-of-line statements—a perennial problem in the study of state socialism.[39] That approach also mistakenly assumes that the Party-state line was always clear and distinct. On many matters, there was no doubt; on other matters, the line was murkier.

One of the arguments of this book is that there was no single author of this era's discourse. Discourse was neither univocal nor uniform. Eventually, by 1972, the KWP would announce Kim Il Sung Thought as the "unifying and uniform ideology" (*yuil sasang*) of the country. This was illusory. The rhetoric of ideological unity never translated wholesale to the much more variegated ideological and cultural worlds of the population. Even the most dedicated propaganda workers, who themselves were constantly berated for their lack of ideological discipline, would not have mistaken an aspirational claim of uniformity for the way ideology and culture actually worked.[40] The Party-state faced a challenge in meeting the overwhelming demand for reading materials while curating their content. The sheer number of publications, people, and organizations involved made the task unmanageable.

Although I cite over thirty magazines, journals, and newspapers in the following pages, many more existed. These publications were not censored like their predecessors in the colonial period, when officials blacked out offending portions of text. Rather, supposedly loyal and ideologically rigorous editors and writers took on the mission of using their writing to create the conditions for the proper implementation of Party-state policies. They did not always excel at this task. Nor were they always rigorous. Indeed, the central news agency's monthly journal *Korean Reporter* (*Chosŏn kija*) constantly complained about publications' reporting—about how they did not understand the qualities necessary for a proper political photograph, did not publish enough stories about Kim's Il Sung's partisan history, or overused statistics at the expense of personal narratives.[41] Obviously, this is not the same as oppositional voices, yet *Korean Reporter* demonstrates that editors and writers worked without specific guidelines on numerous matters and that much remained unsettled.

Individual magazines and journals differed. They often reflected the distinctive purview and interests of their sponsoring institution, be it a mass organization, a state bureaucratic unit, or one unit of the Party. When the leading economic journal wrote about the reserve of women's labor—which, tellingly, it did not do very often—it did so from a very different perspective than *Women of Korea*, which published incessantly on the topic and in ways that would not always have met with the approval of central economic planners. These distinctions were not presented by writers as oppositional or antagonistic to one another, given the official encouragement of what was called a "revolutionary optimism" (*hyŏngmyŏngjŏk nakkwanjuŭi*). Yet there are plenty of signs, when these texts are read closely together, that writers played on these differences even as they did not call attention to them. The claims of ideological and cultural concord glossed over the complexity of the discursive terrain in these years. This repetitive insistence on unity, rather than representing the state of affairs, was itself ideological and merely one of the ways ideology and culture worked—and everyone knew it.

This dynamic can be seen at play in a piece of criticism by Ŏ Hongt'aek of two provincial newspapers.[42] The subject of these newspapers' offending articles was one of the single most politically sensitive issues of the era: South Korea. What upset Ŏ was that the two newspapers had reproduced the central news agency's stories on the South, repeating them word for word in their own papers. At first glance, the criticism seems strange—was unity and the reproduction of the center's message not desirable? It is easy to imagine that the editors sought to play it safe on this fraught topic by replicating already approved text. But this was their mistake. They were not supposed to merely parrot the words of the center. As Ŏ admonished, they needed to do independent research to find issues that related southern conditions to the provincial circumstances of their own readership and write up their own interpretations. His point was to urge a proactive attitude and original writing. This was the "creative initiative" (*changbaljŏk palgi*)—a common term that will make repeated appearances in the following pages—that was generally expected of writers.

The easiest response to Ŏ's call for initiative would be to scoff, point to the editors' inability to challenge the Party-state line, and dismiss Ŏ's criticism as just more propaganda—especially since criticism in *Korean Reporter* demonstrated central surveillance over the media and provinces at play. Yet the strategy of my research is to take seriously Ŏ's enjoinment as an indication that, while opposition was not an option for editors and writers, there was in fact a degree of latitude for them to explore. Even in such a politically fraught area as intra-peninsular affairs, rote imitation remained unacceptable and writers were expected—pressured even—to riff on central themes. And as any fan of jazz music knows, to riff on standard repertoire is to mediate, reinterpret, and translate. To riff is even to risk originality. It is in this sense that writers across the contemporary mediascape can be seen as acting as producers of discourse in their own right. In less politically charged areas such as the New Living—where surveillance was not as tight, where Party-state ideological lines were not so well defined, and where writers were often working with issues and narratives that had a pre-collective-era or socialist-bloc history—they often rearticulated and expanded Party-state-approved utterances in ways not imagined by higher authorities. It is also in this context of a more variegated approach to discourse that, however politically restricted, the flashes of critique and the pushback on the part of the Women's Union must be understood. In this sense, *North Korea's Mundane Revolution* is also a study of official Party ideology and culture, only rather than seeing a single, clear Party "line" (*nosŏn*), I allow for more blurred contours and wiggle room than those at the top of the Party preferred to admit.

Within these archival limits (further explored in the appendix), this book tells a story divided into four parts. Each part focuses on a basic issue central to the New Living and to the twentieth-century world: the modern individual, labor, family, and consumption. Each was deeply gendered, and none received straightforward, uniform treatments. In each part, I separate out a "flash of criticism" suggestive of ultimately unpursued alternative possibilities. Chapter 1 lays out how the New Living was interwoven in a demographic crisis and the Party-state's reconstruction of a centrally planned economy and its membership. The chapters in part 1 ask the question from which the others flow: "How to self-improve?" Against the backdrop of a massive effort to house the population in apartment buildings, part 2 asks the question "How to build more efficiently?" Once these apartment buildings opened their doors, the question of lifestyle in domestic spaces arose, which I capture in the question posed by part 3, "How to make a happy family home?" With these apartments as the primary space for urban consumption, and as some people brought much-sought-after objects, particularly radios and sewing machines, into their domestic spaces, part 4 continues this line of inquiry by asking, "How to consume properly?"

At an earlier stage of this project, my plan had been to complete this book without once mentioning Kim Il Sung by name. His absence would be the argument—a North Korean history without the man and his ego.[43] As my work evolved, however, it became apparent that to write a non-Kim history left unchallenged, and arguably reinforced, a key claim of his personality cult: that Kim transcended history itself. Instead, this book's conclusion shows how Kim and his personality cult were shaped by, and built on, the era's discourse. The conclusion returns to Kim, not as climax but as denouement, to show how even the Great Leader's megalomania emerged out of the era's gendered social and political-economic challenges, and not the other way around.

ONE

The Anxieties of Socialist Transition

FOUR YEARS AFTER THE WAR, Wŏn Kwangsu published a two-panel cartoon that reflected a sense of the tumultuous changes transforming the country. The first panel showed a male worker, briefcase in hand, leaving his neighborhood for a day at the office (see figure 2). The second panel showed the end of the day, as the man returned home. With a shocked expression—accentuated by a question mark over his head and his hat flying off in astonishment—he looked down at his neighborhood and exclaimed, "Ah! I can't find where my home is!" The few simple houses he had left behind in the morning had mushroomed into a subdivision of identical houses neatly arrayed in rows, subsuming his own abode. In these two frames, Wŏn captured what he knew all his readers shared: a sense of the era's unsettling and dizzying change.

The cartoon played on the era's common trope for successful postwar recovery—what had come to be celebrated as the "changing face" of cityscapes. Yet, in Wŏn's hands, this triumphant image of buildings rising out of the destruction of war came with an undertone of uneasiness. The shock registered in the body of the male worker reflected a sense of anxiety experienced by modern city dwellers around the world in response to the speed of change in their lives—what the title of the cartoon labeled "The Rapid Rate of Construction." That Wŏn expected his readers to recognize, if only to laugh at, this discomfort indicates better than any contemporary statistic— the increase in cement production from 27,000 to 895,000 tons in four years, for example, or the 2.5-fold increase in the number of socks produced in Pyongyang in 1960—how urban men and women experienced the New Living as hat-flying-off-head levels of tumult.[1]

The broader visual culture of the era typically used photographs to represent reconstruction as a material process—the erection of housing, to be sure,

FIGURE 2. Wŏn Kwangsu, "The Rapid Rate of Construction," 1957.
First panel: "Off to work and back home soon." Second panel: "Ah!
I can't find where my home is!"

but also railways, dams, movie theaters, factories, children's palaces, and sports facilities. Yet the uneasiness in the cartoon signaled that much more was at play than mere physical infrastructure. The unspoken yet widespread anxieties arose out of enormous uncertainties and pressures in pursuing socialist transition in the face of the many challenges left by colonialism, war, and division. These anxieties were themselves rooted in the tensions that structured the rebuilding of the political economy and the growing institutional capacity of the Party-state. Faced with a demographic crisis, shortages in labor and capital, and an inexperienced membership, the Party-state could not resolve the tensions that it had in part inherited, but also created in its prioritization of breakneck economic growth. These tensions would ultimately be worked out in the local social worlds, where the New Living promised solutions, but often at high cost to subsegments of the population. Officially presented loudly, in an upbeat fashion, as striding confidently toward socialism, the New Living also—unofficially and much more quietly—was riven by anxieties.

DEMOGRAPHIC CRISIS AND THE "COMPLEX POPULATION PROBLEM"

August 15, 1953, marked the end of what in English is called the Korean War. For most Korean women and men, however, the direct and indirect experience of military conflict extended back earlier than the North's attack on the South on June 25, 1950. The postwar period is usually defined against these three years of conflict. Yet, as Yun Haedong has argued, the usual periodization of Korean history, with its emphasis on 1945–50 as a time of liberation before war, distracts from the fact that large segments of the population had been rallied for war at least as early as 1937, when Japanese authorities mobilized the colony for the invasion of China.[2] These seventeen years of nearly incessant warfare—from 1937 to 1953—bequeathed a twofold demographic crisis.

At its most basic, the demographic crisis was one of mass death. Somewhere between two and four million died during the Korean War alone—a figure that has tended to lean toward the upper end as more research has been conducted. The northern side suffered disproportionately, due primarily to the ferocity of American bombing campaigns. Kim Pyŏngno has estimated that the war dead in the South numbered 852,000—compared to 1.75 million in the North.[3] As proportions of the prewar population, these numbers represent 5 percent and 18 percent, respectively. When deaths are combined with wounded casualties, Kim estimates that nearly 35 percent of the North suffered, representing more than half of all families. Kim's figures may be on the high side—North Korean yearbooks show a smaller yet still massive loss of around 12 percent between 1949 and 1953.[4] Both figures, when compared to those for participants in World War II, put North Korea second on the list of deaths as a proportion of population. Only Poland suffered proportionately more. Personal memories of these losses lasted generations and did not need state propaganda to sustain them.

Wartime deaths skewed along gender lines. One postwar survey placed the male to female population ratio at 46.9 to 53.1.[5] For years afterward, the media featured widows and orphans as living reminders of the tolls of war. Wartime deaths were also experienced unevenly across space. Some rural areas, such as the Pugang Cooperative in Sinch'ŏn County, famous for its repeated battles, lost virtually their entire working-age cohort of men.[6] Cities quickly depopulated to avoid aerial bombardment.

Another side of the demographic crisis was what contemporaries called the "complex population problem." The peninsula's coerced integration into the Japanese imperial political economy had regularly led to the forcible displacement of Koreans—whether as porters in the Russo-Japanese War (1904–5); as "surplus" populations, pushed off their land as a result of early land surveys (1910–18); as construction workers, dislocated for precarious labor in the home islands; or, perhaps most famously, as coerced sex workers, known by the euphemism "comfort women."[7] As the empire expanded, colonial bodies became more important to the empire than agricultural produce and natural resources. At the height of World War II, somewhere between 13 percent and 20 percent of the population had been mobilized outside the peninsula, and most of them were likely men—an unprecedented mobilization of a colonial population in the comparative history of empires.[8] With Japan's surrender on August 15, 1945, and the dissolution of what at the time was the world's second largest empire, Koreans began what Lori Watt has called the "return home."[9]

But where was home—North or South? By agreement of the victors, the peninsula's liberation from colonialism took the form of a twin occupation, by the Soviet Union in the North and the United States in the South. In this divided environment, no matter on which side of the parallel one's hometown rested, the decision to repatriate to one side or the other assumed political overtones. No reliable statistics exist for how many people chose North as opposed to South. The American military government admitted it had no effective administrative apparatus to track returnees, whether from the North or other parts of the former Japanese empire. Still, its first rough survey estimated that the South's population rose by 22 percent in the single year of 1946.[10] People also moved between the two halves in this period. Somewhere between 45,000 and 650,000 had moved south by 1950. Smaller numbers headed north, with most estimates hovering around a quarter of a million.[11] As Bruce Cumings has noted, this exchange winnowed and polarized the population politically, as many of the more conservative groups—in particular, landlords and businesspeople—headed south, whereas more progressive segments of the population, including leading intellectuals and performers, often headed north.[12] This winnowing made the postwar class situation more straightforward than in European socialist states, where the bourgeoisie had less in the way of ready escape valves—a comparative advantage of the Korean political landscape not lost on Party authorities.[13]

War-induced population movement only accelerated when North Korea attacked the South in the summer of 1950. In a war in which the largest city, Seoul, changed hands four times and in which another major city, Kaesŏng, ended up on the opposite side from where it began, the toll on civilians was high. The rolling nature of the first year and a half, when soldiers from over twenty countries pushed down and then up, and again back down, led to refugee flows that, according to Janice Kim, included one of every three South Koreans.[14] The North Korean figure, if we had it, would likely be higher.

The demographic crisis was also marked by innumerable family separations. In South Korea, accounts are common of families unable to locate relatives, whom they presumed to be dead or in North Korea, only to discover, when national identity cards were rolled out in the 1960s, that their lost relatives were actually living in the South. In North Korea, a special information center opened in the Chunggu district to help people locate relatives and friends.[15] The hardened dividing line—incongruously named the "demilitarized zone," or DMZ—separated somewhere between 350,000 and 1.2 million people, depending on the estimate.[16] For years after the war, in both North and South, the act of writing an undeliverable letter to a family member on the other side of the DMZ symbolized familial frustration with division—a pathos both regimes eagerly exploited for their own purposes.[17]

In the seventeen years between 1937 and 1953, these conflict-induced disruptions—mobilization for two major wars, the collapse of the Japanese imperial political economy, the division of the peninsula into two antagonistic halves, and the establishment of two separate Cold War states—resulted in repeated demographic upheavals.[18] Decolonization and the establishment of Cold War structures were violent, unsettling processes. Korean men and women were on the move, unlike at any other time in the peninsula's history. It was only after 1953 that people could, within a still tense and politically bipolarized environment, begin rebuilding their lives and country. As one Polish diplomat observed a few months after the armistice, there was "growing stabilization of political and economic life in the DPRK."[19] Although the armistice did not end the war with a peace treaty, the effect of the elimination of martial law and fighting cannot be overestimated.

As Korean men and women began to resettle within these more stable conditions, both Korean regimes faced a fundamental challenge: determining who lived where. The destruction of state infrastructure, together with the mobility of people, meant that both states lacked basic information about the population within their territories as well as the means to gather it effectively. Moreover, in a divided peninsula under the conditions of the global Cold War and after decades of political strife, the question of who lived where took on an urgent political tone—who was loyal to whom? Both states launched biopolitical measures to register populations, to classify their loyalties, and to repress groups perceived as antagonistic. Much more is known about the use of violence in South Korea and its implementation of the *yŏnjwaje* system, or what Heonik Kwon has called a system of "guilt by association."[20]

North of the DMZ, the loyalty question led to the implementation of the sŏngbun system, a political labeling project like those in other socialist states. Background checks as a means of measuring loyalty had a long history prior to the war. Kim Chaeŭng has shown that as part of the Party's class politics, this system began what he calls the "systemization of discrimination."[21] Following Soviet examples, Party members had been required to write auto-biographies that were used to identify their class and family origins, as well as their political activities during and after the colonial period.[22] Thus, the Party already had experience in social labeling and categorization of popula-tions that would serve them well after the war.[23] At the end of 1958, the prac-tice was extended to the entire population: in December, teams of officials headed out to the provinces, working with local officials to classify every person according to a series of criteria meant to determine political loyalty to the Party. The process, which lasted into 1960, involved self-reporting and confessions. Some reports indicate that public punishments were used to encourage self-reporting.[24] While an individual's class background was one criterion, more important was the individual's, and their extended family's, conduct during the war and in the colonial era. Had someone in their family worn a Republic of Korea military uniform or collaborated with the enemy, Japanese or American? Had they supported the Party during the war? Family members found themselves grouped according to their relatives' pasts, regardless of their own individual history—one way the extended family remained relevant as a bureaucratic category in an era when the nuclear fam-ily rose to prominence. In this sense, the bottom, enemy category was the most expansive—a single doubted person in a family could result in a string of relatives, regardless of their personal loyalties, falling into this classifica-tion. By the end of the following year, the assessment had rotated through the entire country, with Pyongyang and Kaesŏng receiving special attention given their security importance and the number of relocated refugees.[25]

The implementation of the sŏngbun system was not discussed overtly in the media. Yet its rationale came through in stories that recounted the achievements and sacrifices of "patriotic martyr families" (*aeguk yŏlsa kajok*), who emerged as a means of remembering the war as a continually lived phe-nomenon.[26] Through this reward-for-service system, not just veterans but also widows and orphans received benefits—plum work assignments and school slots, superior rations, and subsidies to buy goods.[27] The KWP pushed the line that their wartime experience would naturally lend itself to greater loyalty to the Party and hatred of "enemies"—though still they were warned against complacency.[28] The enemies placed at the bottom of the sŏngbun system were not covered in the media through personal stories. For the most part, stories about enemies were abstract—they were presented as a category rather than as real individuals.[29] According to one study, by Kim Namsik, the top category consisted of Party members, together with workers in key heavy industries, ideological enthusiasts, farmers, and leaders in the collectivization of agriculture. The bottom consisted largely of antirevolutionary groups.[30]

Little is known about the social history of the implementation of these political labels—and what is known comes from dubious sources.[31] Judging from loyalty systems in other socialist settings, the unruly lives of families rarely fit the neat classification schemes dreamed up by security personnel and ideologues. That this was likely true in the DPRK is suggested by the fact that the entire system was restructured only seven years later—a hint that perhaps too many people had gamed the system and that classification had not been sufficiently rigorous. The revamped system divided the three categories into fifty-one subclassifications. Even the leadership publicly recognized that problems existed in the system's implementation. None other than Kim Il Sung himself worried that overly eager officials risked alienating people, including former enemies who were now willing to support the Party.[32]

In the same years that the sŏngbun classifications were rolled out, the Party-state eliminated colonial-era census practices, which had registered the population by families through their ostensible hometowns. Now local authorities developed a system to register people according to where they worked and lived. It quickly became clear, however, that many local administrative units were not up to the task. According to a 1962 report by one official, An Chaebok, local authorities in rural areas had been less than diligent in keeping accurate records of every resident in their districts. Names were missing. In particular, he cited the problem of not recording the names of children. When they grew up and were ready to join the workforce, there were no records of them—and this offered them the perfect moment to leak out of the system. An did not quantify the extent of the problem, yet he revealed how nearly a decade after the war, effective institutions for registering local rural populations were still lacking—at least, they were insufficient to stop young laborers from heeding the call of cities.[33] An's frustration was just one indication of how the demographic crisis and "complex population problem" would both shape and be shaped by the challenges of labor and capital in the Party's call to increase production.

In the pursuit of socialism, the Party-state had announced that the preeminent objective was to increase production. Even after 1958, the emphasis on ideological renovation remained, ultimately, in service to enhancing aggregate output levels. Yet as the Party-state developed its central economic planning and implementation apparatus across the 1950s, it faced two key shortages: investment capital and labor. Where would the money and the laboring bodies for all the growth plans come from? The struggle to deal with these shortages shaped livelihoods and the local social worlds of women and men in every city. The Party-state had no solution of its own.

Similarly to such discussions in other countries, early debates about economic priorities centered on where to allocate what little capital the Party-state controlled. After much dispute, the group that included Kim Il Sung and promoted heavy industry won the day. The industries of steel, chemicals, construction materials, machine building, electrical energy generation, and mining received the bulk of investment.[34] The Three-Year Plan (1954–56) allocated 40.2 percent of total capital investments to heavy industry, and only 9.3 percent and 9.2 percent to light and agricultural industries, respectively.[35]

At first, Pyongyang's socialist allies helped ease the scarcity of capital. As Balàzs Szalontai has reported, China and the Soviet Union postponed or canceled repayment of much of the war debt racked up by Korea.[36] Other forms of aid, offered in the spirit of socialist solidarity, quickly came pouring in, including cash donations, preferential trade deals, and technical assistance in the form of advisors and educational materials.[37] During the Three-Year Plan, according to an estimate by Kim Yŏnch'ŏl, 22.6 percent of the national budget consisted of foreign assistance.[38] Yet the overall value of assistance is difficult to confirm, because many donations were in kind. Turnkey factories such as the Pyongyang Wood Furniture Factory were donated by the Soviets outright.[39] East Germany provided funding, materials, and expertise for the reconstruction of Hamhŭng. The Chinese People's Liberation Army, present until 1958, turned their soldiers over to rebuilding infrastructure projects, including roads, buildings, and irrigation works.[40] Smaller countries such as Bulgaria and Romania made more specialized contributions, including brick-making equipment and fishing boats, respectively.[41] In the early postwar years, the print media gave publicity to many donations, such as when one magazine carried two-page photo spreads of goods received from the Soviet Union.[42]

Party authorities wanted to maximize assistance for as long as possible, even at the risk of alienating some of the donor nations. Political differences over how closely Korea's economy should be aligned and integrated with the socialist bloc dimmed donor enthusiasm. Over time, donor fatigue set in. Though smaller donations continued to be negotiated into the early 1960s, the heyday of postwar assistance did not last long. As a percentage of the national budget, assistance trended downward, dwindling to 12.2 percent in 1957, and to 2.7 percent in 1959. The decline was not unexpected. Economic planning authorities openly predicted in the media that assistance would eventually subside and warned that soon planning would rely on domestic capital accumulation alone.[43] The most obvious source in the 1950s was agriculture. For centuries, the land tenure system had been the source of rural grievances, with many calls by both farmers and scholars for reform, often radical in nature.[44] The Party-state took up the land issue in 1946, launching the first thoroughgoing redistribution from owners to tillers in Korean history. After the war, a question that bedeviled many other socialist countries arose: How quickly should agricultural lands be collectivized? In 1954, roughly 90 percent of all industry was nationally owned, but only 21.5 percent of farming households belonged to collectives. The Party decided to move quickly.[45] Over the next four years, farmers who had just been granted their own land a few years earlier now saw that same land folded into collectives—a process that Kim Seong Bo has shown met with varying degrees of support and opposition, largely depending on the wealth of the individual farming family.[46] There was little of the spectacular violence for which the Soviet and Chinese collectivizations are so famous; nevertheless, foreign reports of beatings and intense pressure to turn over harvests show that collectivization was coerced in many cases.[47] When completed in 1958, a radical form of social organization had transformed rural life.

Yet collectivization, rather than mitigating urban-rural disparities, arguably exacerbated them. Collectivization reinforced the same logic of capital flow characteristic of the colonial era, which was simultaneously being worked out in South Korea—namely, rural labor produced wealth that was whisked away from local communities by central institutions that, in turn, reinvested the capital in the state's priority industries, largely located in urban areas.[48] As Sŏ Tongman has shown, the early central economic plans barely discussed the possibility of investing in agricultural sectors.[49] Collectivization was a reorganization of local social worlds—both farming communities and local state organs—to maximize capital extraction for the Party's nonagricultural priorities. Even in the late 1950s, efforts to decentralize light and medium industry by creating at least one factory—later increased to five—in each rural county did not change this fundamental relationship.[50]

The scarcity of capital resulted in intense competition for funds at every level of the Party-state and among all economic enterprises. It led cadres and managers, whose interests did not always align with those of the center, to undermine central planning directives—in part by their lack of discipline. In the first half of 1956, the construction industry reached only 89 percent of their overall plan, with the provinces managing only 67 percent. In one publicized case, the Ministry of Light Industry diverted funds away from the centrally approved allocation in Pyongyang to its own priority project in Hamhŭng. Such incidents, according to one writer, made a mess of the central planning process and undermined central control.[51] The ability of enterprises to implement or circumvent the plan in sectors such as construction became a source of concern for economists.[52]

In this context of scarcity, central planners frequently adopted one strategy: shifting responsibilities onto lower levels of administration. But while responsibilities devolved, funding did not follow suit. Local authorities had to make do—in other words, scrounge in their local vicinities for funds remaining outside the central plans to finance their responsibilities. Not being self-sufficient risked public censure, as happened to the authorities in charge of the Sunch'on paper factory, who were ridiculed in a cartoon by Hong Chongho for constantly "stretching out" to the center for resources (see figure 3).[53] This devolution to lower levels was repeated by lower officials who often turned to local populations, especially women deemed not engaged in productive labor, to form ad hoc, underfunded organizations to achieve central goals—a phenomenon that will arise repeatedly in the following pages.

Aggregate data is often used to demonstrate the growth of the economy in these years, without attention to this unevenness. The American CIA—hardly known to favor North Korea—estimated that growth rates exceeded those of the South until the 1970s.[54] Diplomatic reports from Pyongyang by Soviet diplomats regularly noted how such aggregate figures did not translate into equal living standards. Such reports had their own cross-cultural biases—reflecting what Quinn Slobodian has called the "second world's third world." Many highlighted, in the words of one Soviet official, the "excessive forcing of the development of heavy industry to the detriment of the development of agriculture, and also light industry."[55] Reports constantly urged more investment in light industry.[56] Yet their complaints still acknowledged the

FIGURE 3. A cartoon ridiculing factory authorities for not being self-sufficient. Hong Chongho, untitled, 1960.

upswing in living standards—as one delegation put it, despite continued poverty, "people are living better than during the Japanese times."[57]

The exacerbation of unevenness between rural and urban areas by the extraction of capital during this period of macro-level growth also impacted the second major shortage facing economic planners: the labor supply. Already severe in 1955, the labor shortage only worsened. As the economy began, first, to recover and, by 1955, to grow beyond prewar levels, there were simply not enough bodies to meet the labor demands of the booming industrial sectors. Individual enterprises reported difficulties hiring enough workers, and Polish technical consultants reported that the lack of workers meant that tools remained idle and unused.[58] In 1958, reports indicated that the shortage had become "more severe than in any other period" and was expected to get worse, following the continued growth of the economy.[59] It did get worse. By 1965, the economist Kim Chongil noted that this still unresolved problem rested with two fundamentals: there was no surplus labor force, and natural population growth remained insufficient to ease immediate pressures.[60] His list of causes did not mention the demographic crisis of mass death in war. Nor did he discuss the inefficient allocation of labor within factories, where managers hoarded workers for potential future use, knowing they were in short supply. Yet the severity of the shortage got to the point where authorities looked upon international marriages through the lens of labor: in cases where a Korean and a Chinese married, efforts were made to get the Chinese spouse to come to Korea, in order to gain a single extra laboring body—a priority the Chinese government endeavoured to respect.[61]

Given the skewed gender ratios of the postwar population, and the need to continue conscripting men due to the tensions of the peninsula's division, the demands on women's labor were unrelenting. If, in many countries after World War II, women who had been employed in wage work during the war were expected to make way for returning male workers, it was not so in Korea. As economists pointed out, continued growth would be difficult indeed without female labor.[62] Once the few remaining merchants were brought into the central planning process with the collectivization of their businesses in 1958, the single largest labor reserve was those women not engaged in wage labor. The result, as we will see, led to much scrutiny and celebration of one of the premier figures of the New Living, the so-called mother-worker (*mosŏng rodongja*). She would be seen by many as the solution for tensions in the political economy.

The labor shortage shaped the implementation of the sŏngbun system. Recent studies have presented sŏngbun as a type of caste system in which the bottom group had little chance for advancement.[63] Yet the discriminating features of sŏngbun were countered by the pressures of the labor shortage. Party-state leaders regularly harped on how individuals in the "enemy" category needed to be included in the labor pool. The head of the Women's Union, Pak Chŏngae, urged sympathy and understanding of how people had often been manipulated by the Americans and South Koreans.[64] If now they were willing to return to the "bosom of the republic," she argued, then they should be allowed to freely take part in social labor. Her speech did not call for equality among the classifications but hinted at the wiggle room remaining—and that, ultimately, the labor of those in the lowest rung was still needed.[65] This was no criticism of sŏngbun itself. But it did lay out priorities.

The capital and labor shortages gave workers and factory managers considerable wiggle room. They had to make do outside of central economic plans, as became evident with the Party-state's inability to slow rural-urban migration. Urban enterprises, under pressure to increase production, skirted regulations to get the laborers they needed from the countryside—despite injunctions not to do so. Statistics for people evading central controls are obviously difficult to pin down. Yet we do have clues. In a 1959 article about labor issues in the premier economic journal, *Economic Construction* (*Kyŏngje kŏnsŏl*), Kim Unjong wrote that fully 30 percent of the 380,000 laborers who had newly joined the labor force in 1958 had come from the countryside—a figure of about 114,000 workers.[66] Kim offered the statistic out of frustration at the center's inability to balance rural and urban needs. He also noted that Kim Il Sung's instructions in this regard had been ignored. Five years after the war, large numbers of people were on the move. If the complicated population problem had been created by the conditions of the war, now the reorganization of the political economy created its own challenges as rural individuals, who experienced the disruptions of agricultural collectivization and were attracted by the possibilities of higher urban wages, moved to the cities despite prohibitions. Mobility was just one of the many issues where the tensions between different central planning policies and priorities worked against each other, giving contrary incentives to different segments of the population.

PARTY-STATE POWER AND ITS LIMITS

As much as the Party-state created the conditions for these tensions in the political economy, its own power was also limited by them. The war had been a disaster for the Party-state, if not for Kim Il Sung personally. It had only barely survived. During the war the leadership had scattered, was constantly on the move, and often hid in caves to escape American bombing. Operational control of the fighting had been transferred to the People's Liberation Army, which provided the main fighting force. The Party itself was in disarray, as many members died or defected southward. With the governing apparatus virtually dissolved, swaths of territory, especially in rural areas, shook off central rule. Economic production declined precipitously, as did the ability of central planners to control the economy. Major infrastructure—from roads to housing, dams to electrical networks—had been destroyed. Communicable diseases raged. Cities depopulated. The only institution to grow was the military. When fighting stabilized at the end of 1951, the Party-state finally had the respite to begin reestablishing its governance.[67] Nonetheless, when the armistice was signed in 1953, the Party-state that emerged remained remarkably weak. Recovery would take years and faced countless challenges.[68] The three years of fighting wiped out many of the accomplishments achieved between 1945 and 1950.

As it prepared to reassert itself when the fighting finished, the KWP faced a quandary: Who should make up the Party-state? In his study of Party membership, Yi Chuch'ŏl notes that rapid membership expansion aimed to gain the solidarity of the people—in short, a mass-based Party bringing in large segments of the population.[69] From the earliest recorded figure in October 1945, when the KWP's predecessor party had barely a thousand adherents, membership grew to 366,000 in 1946 and reached 1,164,945 in 1956—more than a threefold increase within ten years, despite the devastating toll the war had on its members, which according to his estimate was 22.4 percent of the membership.[70] Growth continued, reaching 1,166,359 members in 1961.[71] Beginning in 1965, the KWP announced that its membership was 1.6 million—a figure that it reported without change for many years. As a percentage of the population, the growth was impressive: in 1948, membership represented 8 percent, and it had climbed to 12.2 percent by 1961. Authorities did not publish figures breaking down this growth by gender, yet extant lists of at least the upper leadership remained predominantly male.[72] These were the personnel who would establish the Party-state's rule, whether as cadres or through their assignment to state institutions, mass organizations, media, the military, or economic enterprises.

The new members represented a startling turnover in the social basis of Korea's leadership. If there was any realm that the KWP could, without question, point to as revolutionary, it was in the social composition of the personnel who would fill and lead the wide spectrum of new institutions. Criteria for membership were focused primarily on socioeconomic background and records of Party sympathies. The KWP enlisted farmers and workers regardless of their political training or educational levels. With its roots in the intelligentsia, the Party quickly made inroads among farmers, especially poor farmers—a continual source of recruitment through the land reform and collectivization projects. As the emphasis on heavy industry began to reap results, increases in the total number of workers created a larger pool from which to identify potential Party members.[73] Specific policies designed to grow the economy both fashioned and identified potential recruits—who, with their status arising out of these policies, had personal stakes in the success of the Party-state. In this way, the Party created the conditions for its own renewal and expansion both institutionally and personnel-wise, the reinvigorated Party membership ensuring a deep association between the Party-state and their own personal advancement.[74]

Never before in Korean history had there been such a radical transformation of the social order or such a surge in upward mobility for broad segments of the working-class population. Rapid expansion also came at a cost. Education levels were often woeful. Many new Party members were illiterate. Complaints about the quality of political meetings abounded.[75] Within the bureaucracy, many overstepped their boundaries while others did little, confusing the articulation of institutional hierarchies and responsibilities. Partly, these were the challenges of inexperience. One leading official, Pak Kŭmch'ŏl, in describing how quickly the Party had changed, revealed that half of its members in 1958 had yet to experience "Party life" for more than five or six years.[76] Not surprisingly, once the wartime crisis settled, the KWP institutionalized formal training—not just ideological but basic education—for its recruits.

These measures aimed to regain the governing capacities severely damaged by the war. Party members became key because, following Soviet dual-track methods, they were appointed to head Party committees in each state, economic, and mass organization unit. As Sŏ Tongman has argued, one priority was to ensure control over the military, which had ballooned in size during the war and become more autonomous.[77] Party members were appointed as political officers throughout its units to guarantee adherence to Party guidance. Retired soldiers were appointed to factories, to mines, and to rural collectives, in the belief that their military discipline would strengthen central control. Similar strategies were adopted for rural communities, which—during the war, with the destruction of central administration—had become more autonomous by default. The reorganization of local administration to undercut traditional village structure also established perpendicular lines of control. The cities experienced a surge in local organizations. A single neighborhood had a local hygiene committee; committees for the General Federation of Trade Unions, the Women's Union, and the Youth Association, if not all five of the mass organizations; an *inminban* (neighborhood committee); homefront committees of various workplaces; and apartment building committees—let alone the ever-present local Party cells. While these units also worked to follow guidelines set out by the higher-ups in their organizations, central authorities constantly harped about how the units did not hold meetings, did not carry out their responsibilities, or, worse, simply went through the motions to give the appearance that they attended to their duties. These units were charged, at the local level, with taking care of the ideological and cultural well-being of their members and surveying the results.[78] They were the local sites in which the conditions for Party-state policies were to be implemented and where the New Living was to take shape. In these units and through their activities in local social worlds, central desires for the New Living came to be realized, mediated, and translated anew against the tensions of the political economy. The dual role of these organizations in surveilling and encouraging their members ensured a constant focus on the behaviors and culture of the individual as a means toward achieving collective ideals.

Translating Mao Zedong's Contradictions

It was not unusual for a major Korean newspaper to publish a speech by a visiting foreign leader, but in this particular case the leader had never set foot in the peninsula. Nevertheless, the Chairman of the Chinese Communist Party, Mao Zedong, had two and a half of the six pages of the national Party newspaper devoted to a translation of his speech, entitled "On the Correct Handling of Contradictions among the People."[a] The newspaper did not try to predetermine interpretations of the speech by providing any explanations or editing out any passages. What did the speech's reproduction mean in the Korean context—was it merely a nod of respect for the Great Helmsman and his support during the war? Or, given the shifting political situation in Pyongyang, did its publication suggest the need for an alternative, more radical politics?

At first glance, the speech's relevance to Korea is clear: both communist parties had recently come to power and were figuring out how to deal with class issues after decades of civil war. Ever the committed dialectician, Mao spelled out two sets of contradictions facing his country: those between the enemy and "ourselves" and those existing among the people. The former contradictions involved looking back in time, classifying people by their political loyalty during the anti-Japanese struggle and the Chinese Civil War. The latter contradictions were contemporary, having to do with issues that the Korean Workers' Party also faced, such as the cooperativization of agriculture, the termination of private commerce, the need for constant self-reformation of one's ideological outlook, and problems with bureaucratism. In these areas, Mao's speech confirmed decisions and directions already underway in Korea and fit neatly with the classifying logic of the sŏngbun system. Even some of the rhetoric—"We must learn from the Soviet Union"—was shared.

Yet Mao's speech went much further. His analysis of the second set of contradictions—those among the people—saw contemporary class struggle as much more antagonistic and widespread than did Kim Il Sung or the KWP's line on class relations. Mao specified contradictions between the workers and what he called the national bourgeoisie (*minjok chabon*). He addressed the contradictions between the state and the people as well as between the leadership and the led. And he talked about the contradictions among centralism and democracy—all lines of analysis that were not part of the KWP's views on contemporary politics.

For Mao, all these contradictions provided the theoretical basis for his call to "Let a Hundred Flowers Bloom and a Hundred Schools Contend." The speech signaled Mao's intent to deal with his listed contradictions by unleashing the criticism of the people. He confidently predicted that "implementing the policy of letting a Hundred Flowers Bloom and a Hundred Schools Contend" would not weaken, but make stronger the leading position of Marxism. Quickly, though, Mao's confidence would prove to be hubris. An outpouring of criticism, which neither promoted socialism nor was unifying as Mao expected, shook the Chinese Communist Party.

The translation appeared at a politically delicate time in Pyongyang. Only the year before, Kim Il Sung had made his major move to consolidate power in his own hands by eliminating key rivals. The Party's enrollment of new cadres was expanding rapidly, as were state institutions. And despite earlier calls for the de-Stalinization of leadership modes, Kim Il Sung and his allies had begun to explore and lay the groundwork for his personality cult. With U.S. troops still in the South, the emphasis was on stability—never one of Mao's political priorities.

Was the appearance of the translated speech an attempt to use Mao's authority to question these trends? Was Mao's inclusion of leadership issues and state-populace relations within his definition of class struggle being used to suggest that Korea, too, needed a more radical politics to question the particular form the Party leadership was taking? Did the reproduction of the speech indicate that the unnamed people who sponsored the translation believed that Korea, too, needed a hundred flowers to bloom?

Of course, by the time the speech appeared in Korea, Mao had launched the anti-Rightest campaign against the very critics his speech had produced. There was little follow-up to the Korean translation's publication. This was the first and last time *Rodong sinmun* translated one of Mao's speeches word for word. And although the term *contradiction* continued to appear in the lexicon of Party ideologues, it neither had the same analytical bite it had for Mao, nor was it ever applied to analyze the growing hierarchies ushered in by the Party's own policies. Little is known about the intent of this republication or how it may have been interpreted by readers. But whatever critique of the contemporary political situation and whatever more radical directions Mao's speech may have raised in the Korean context, their implications for the KWP and class analysis withered rather than bloomed.

a. Mo T'aektong, "Inmin naebuŭi mosun munjerŭl chŏnghwakhi chŏrihal te gwanhayŏ" [On the correct handling of contradictions among the people], *Rodong sinmun*, June 23, 1957: 2–4. Mao had given the speech in February 1957, but it was first printed in the Chinese Party newspaper *Renmin ribao* in the summer of that year, occasioning the Korean translation of the published text.

PART ONE

Cultural Living and the Ever-Striving Socialist Self

HOW TO SELF-IMPROVE?

This was a question that faced both men and women in the years after the guns went silent in the summer of 1953. The question took many forms: How should one contribute to the building of socialism? What was a good proletarian? How could one be a good socialist? All these questions emerged as challenges, opportunities, and burdens. They would shape the lives of everyone north of the DMZ. But with the whirlwind of answers rushing forth in response to these seemingly simple questions came a quandary: there were no neat, straightforward answers. Solutions emerged from the diverse institutions that made up the Party-state, from writers in the expanding newspaper presses, from cartoonists in magazines, and from leaders at all levels. They were all eager to offer behavioral norms—if not always uniform or consistent ones—for people to model. For their audiences, there was a surge of dos and don'ts—all designed to get them to take up the task of improving themselves as new socialist subjects in pursuit of the collective goal of transitioning to socialism.

As part of this grand didactic endeavor, a 1956 cartoon in a youth magazine offered its view on how *not* to be a good socialist (see figure 4).[1] With a few simple lines, the unknown illustrator captured two slovenly men, their shirts unbuttoned, revealing undershirts and not-so-subtle paunches, walking down the street with what seemed like not a care in the world. The pair wore ill-fitting clothes, one with his hat askew, the other with ruffled hair, reflecting a sense of nonchalance about their public appearance. Captioned with a sardonic half-question, half-exclamation, "Dressed like this . . ." the comic sought to elicit a chuckle or two from readers, who likely had witnessed similar scenes on city streets in the topsy-turvy postwar years.

옷차림이 이쾌서야……

FIGURE 4. Chŏn Sŏnggŭn, "Youth and Propriety," 1956. "Dressed like this…"

Beyond its humor, the cartoon had a serious purpose. It sought to make readers reflect on their own personal comportment as one gauge of their commitment to the grander project of constructing socialism. This was quite literally a pedestrian version of the socialist subject, an illustration that sought to inspire, cajole, or embarrass people into becoming self-scrutinizing and self-motivated individuals. Creating a good builder of socialism was certainly about heroic workers attacking a coalface with zeal; yet it was also about keeping the collective property of one's worker dormitory free of the smell of old cigarette butts. Being a good socialist subject was certainly about laboring in the dangerous conditions of a steel furnace; yet it was also about speaking with proper decorum and diction. As conditions stabilized after seventeen years of fighting, memories of the sacrifices and derring-do from the war and the colonial era continued to be invoked for building socialism, yet revolutionary impulses simultaneously came to be routinized, made part of a governing order that promised less drama and more stability.[2] This fusing of the heroic and the banal in ways that created space for the most ardent enthusiast of revolution while also exerting pressures—whether discursive, interpersonal, or institutional—on the full range of the population was fundamental to the New Living.

How to self-improve? was a question that rendered the much-vaunted proletarian consciousness into an activist disposition able, if rightly cultivated, to transform the world. The New Living held out the possibility that becoming a good socialist subject was, at least theoretically, attainable by all, regardless of one's work, gender, location, or sŏngbun status. This universalist creed came with another presumption: anybody, however good their sŏngbun, could just as easily slip up. Self-reflection, self-progression, and vigilance were key.

Yet the New Living, glossed as proletarian consciousness and presented as universal, was not as inclusive as it announced itself to be. Produced in an era of immense challenges to received gender hierarchies and at a time of rapid urbanization, the New Living often naturalized norms for the socialist subject that were coded as urban and masculine. In this sense, there was much more afoot in the New Living than just socialist transformation. It built on notions of individual self-cultivation that predated the collective era, absorbed anxieties about changing gender relations, and responded to the impact of the large numbers of newcomers to the cities. In realms as diverse as advice literature, promotion of feminine speech, modes of self-criticism, and dormitory surveillance, the New Living's individuating impulse reinforced rather than challenged the social stratification and gender hierarchies on which the postwar political economic order were being built. As a result, the New Living became a realm for reconfigurations of social distinctions, not just between men and women, but within genders as well. Proletarian consciousness, glossed as a form of culture centering on the individual, also emptied out gender and class as the potential conceptual categories for critiquing contemporary socioeconomic developments. In the developing postwar authoritarian environment, the New Living depoliticized rather than radicalized.

TWO

An Era of Advice

THE CLAIM TO UNIVERSALITY

"Comrades, you don't live alone!" Thus wrote Hwang Yŏngsik to offer a rationale for why, in 1965, seventeen years after the foundation of the DPRK, he deemed it necessary to provide guidance on how to behave in specific social settings.[1] Over the hundred pages of his book, Hwang gave instructions on how to shake hands, the proper forms for addressing a letter, how to behave on a bus, and the best ways to act as a host for guests.[2] He explained how a person's character could be detected from the tidiness of their clothes and berated the louts who sat in someone else's seat in a movie theater.[3] He told his readers to cultivate a keen sense of time and ensure punctual attendance at meetings, work, and engagements with friends.[4] Entitled *A Guide to Living*, his book of advice was nothing other than a treatise on proper etiquette for a socialist society. "If you read this book through," he counseled, "you'll come to know how you must act." For Hwang, these were to be the behavioral norms for "social life"—one long list of recommendations, in short, on how to be a good builder of socialism.

Hwang was not alone in offering his views on behavior. Published in 1965, *A Guide to Living* was, in many ways, the distillation of more than a decade of widespread writing about the mores needed for the creation of the New Living. An array of magazines with broad circulation featured columns such as "People with Cultivation," "Let's Correct These Tendencies," and "This Is Not Working Class–Like Behavior," in which proper manners for eating might be urged or speaking ill of others discouraged.[5] Cartoonists delighted in poking fun at ill-mannered rubes. These illustrations—a worker warming his bare feet by a stove, unaware of the stench he was forcing his colleagues to endure;[6] wastrel workers convincing friends to take them out for drinks[7]—constituted a significant part of the visual culture of the era. "Without Embarrassment" showed a well-dressed man emerging from a public toilet, his feet tracing tracks of wetness as he fastens his zipper.[8] "Let's Get Rid of These Phenomena," a general exhortatory column with rotating pieces of advice, showed how the postwar era was, in short, an era of advice.[9]

As scholars of advice literature in many national settings and times have shown, advice books such as Hwang's often seek to establish norms of social behavior at times of political and socioeconomic turmoil.[10] This was certainly the case in Korea after the dislocation and mass death of seventeen years of warfare, the establishment of a new postcolonial Party-state, and the upheavals of collectivization. In an environment of perceived behavioral insufficiency or inadequacy, moral advice literature flourished. The sense, on the part of these urban-based writers, that people were not behaving the way they *should* fit the presumptions of Party-state time that ideological levels needed to be elevated. The two reinforced each other. Hwang's promotion of good manners was subsumed into the Party's project.

Advice literature glossed over how its working-class readers actually behaved. The proletarian consciousness it aimed to help create was not a matter of ethnographically examining the customs and mores of real workers and how they lived in order to promote their non-elite lifestyles more widely. Advice literature was about ideal behaviors mediated by writers who set goals for reform. Moreover, their exhortations were rarely followed up with any consideration of the impact of their advice. That writers repeated the same pieces of advice again and again throughout the 1950s and '60s suggests that not everyone welcomed their advice and, arguably, that it did not have its intended effects. Why constantly repeat the call for orderly bus lines if everyone was, in fact, patiently waiting their turn to enter the bus or letting the elderly go first? The point was that people did not line up properly—and so the hectoring continued, as did the comics (see figure 5).[11] Yet the regular repetition, the constant disgruntlement of writers, and their ability to find new dislikable traits reflected as much on the writers themselves as on their readers. With its focus on "levels," advice literature stratified individuals according to a loose array of behavioral ideals—all determined by the writers themselves. Those speaking loudly at the theater, spitting on the street, or not cherishing the labor of others were slotted toward the bottom or were told, more harshly, that they had no "culturedness" (*munhwasŏng*). The very writing of such judgments privileged the purveyors of advice. Their own acts of

FIGURE 5. An advice cartoon calling for orderly bus lines. Anonymous, untitled, 1958.

advice giving claimed for themselves cultural and ideological mastery, even if this remained unacknowledged. Advice literature, with all its attention to cultural levels and its claim to universalism, thus helped articulate, constitute, and legitimize the unspoken but emerging postwar social hierarchies.

Hwang's advice derived largely from two directions—one from the socialist world and the other domestic. Advice literature in Korea shared much with Stalinist efforts to create the "New Man," a subject of wide-ranging research in comparative socialist studies.[12] In Korea, the language of the "New Man," though generally translated in the more gender-neutral expression "New Person" (*sinsaram* or *sae saram*), remained an uncommon usage.[13] Instead, Stalinist notions of "cultural life" (*kulturnost*) and "everyday life" (*byt*) seem to have translated better to the Korean context and were likely familiar to the many Koreans who had resided in the Soviet Union or who had engaged in various cultural exchanges.[14] Soviet advice manuals and etiquette guides sought, in the words of Catriona Kelly, much like Hwang's work, to "refine" behavior—or what Koreans would more commonly call "cultivate" (*kyoyang*).[15] As part of the transnational circulation of socialist texts, some of these manuals and guides—together with movies, art exhibitions, architectural designs, and the like—were taken up by Korean translators, published in Pyongyang, and discussed in the press. Mikhail Kalinin's famous essays on communist morality occasioned much commentary in the

Korean media.[16] Other, less noted authors such as A. S. Makarenko had their guidebooks on motherhood translated and made the subject of reading groups in the Women's Union.[17] Soviet authors took up such topics as love, marriage, and family in socialist societies.[18] Nor did this advice come from the Soviet Union alone. Chinese cartoons and commentaries on love and courtship were finding a place in the Korean press.[19] But by the time Hwang published his work in 1965, ties within the socialist bloc had become more complicated and relations with the Soviet Union had soured. What had been a near-ubiquitous slogan in the 1950s, "Learn from the Soviet Union!," began to wane by the late 1950s and had virtually disappeared by 1965. As a result, Hwang made no nod in this direction. It had become too politically sensitive to contextualize *A Guide to Living* as part of the circulation of socialist texts and practices, let alone as norms that constituted some notion of a transnational socialist culture. This cleared room to frame these norms as national.

Advice literature also looked back to the peninsula's past. While Hwang did cautiously bring up manuals from the Chosŏn dynasty (see "Flash of Criticism" later in this chapter), his real intellectual debt was to similar modes of advice given during the more recent, colonial past. Indeed, he did not need to coin new terminology because that work had already been done. The term *cultural living* (*munhwa saenghwal*), as much as it was adapted and expanded to incorporate Soviet notions of *kulturnost*, still had its origins in the colonial-era expression. This was part of what Travis Workman has described as a culturalism of colonialism.[20] As Harry Harootunian has argued, in the 1920s the Japanese equivalent of "cultural life" or "cultural living" (*bunka seikatsu*) emerged as a discourse on everyday life that was "futuristic and anticipatory of a different kind of society."[21] And as Mark Jones has pointed out, by the 1930s this expression served as a means for the upper middle class to distinguish and separate itself from the growing numbers of middle-income earners.[22] In colonial Korea, "cultural living" had become a key way for the newly arising urban bourgeoisie, particularly intellectuals, to envision, within the constraints of colonialism, a reform project for the future. It would continue to carry this stratifying, imaginative power after 1945.

This domestic genealogy was about much more than terminology, of course. Many of the practices espoused by purveyors of advice extended and amplified early reform efforts stretching back to the last years of the royal dynasty. Nowhere was this more evident than with biopolitical practices. Beginning in the 1890s, projects as varied as the management of waste, hair-cutting campaigns, the promotion of physical exercise, and the publication of nutritional information were launched as part of an attempt to rethink governance and national reform.[23] Taken up by the colonial government in 1910, as well as by nationalist leaders, biopolitics became fundamental to colonial rule.[24] The use of biopolitics only intensified as Japan's invasion of China expanded, becoming central, as Takashi Fujitani has argued, to the mobilization of the population for war.[25] Yet, too often, studies of biopolitics emphasize a top-down process of state and expert control over the population. While this was undoubtedly part of its politics, Foucault saw biopolitics as an alternative mode of power, not restricted to the sovereign coercive power of the state, but one that generated enthusiasm and participation on the part of regular people. By 1945, Korean women and men had already had decades of experience with biopolitics. If anything, most urban dwellers came with expectations from these colonial experiences for how sovereignty should translate into superior conditions—and they were willing to work for it. The Korean War also created specific conditions for the promotion of biopolitics. More civilians died during the war from communicable diseases than from combat, and after the war the movement of people back to the bombed-out urban centers led to the spread of communicable diseases.[26]

This outpouring of attention to public health was generated not just by the Party-state, but by the widespread initiatives of ordinary men and women. When a cartoonist in 1960 spoofed a mother for using her son as a lookout to avoid a home hygiene inspection, the shared humorousness of her fumbled attempt was derived not from resistance to the Party-state, but from families' decades-long experience with biopolitics, which most supported, even if they poked fun at some of its annoying, intrusive features (see figure 6).[27] People had learned—some, clearly, better than others—how to hide from inspectors. When magazines explained the special needs for summer hygiene or when health authorities dispensed advice on how to help stop the spread of communicable diseases and parasites,[28] these exhortations were made within the context of a wide-ranging biopolitical project that, while used for statist purposes, engaged the participation of urbanites in multiple ways and with likely varying degrees of enthusiasm. Projects such as investment in hospitals, expansion of free health care, promotion of postnatal care, and massive housing projects—featuring apartments with running water and flush toilets—were all means, in Foucault's felicitous phrase, of power "to make live" after the mass death of war, but they were also both popular and expected.[29]

Whether popular participation was in line with state goals or men and women used state goals for their own purposes, or some combination of the

〈만화〉

우리 엄마가
그랬어요

어머니—얘 길남아, 위생 검열
원이 오면 집에 있지
말라.

길남—온다! 온다! 뛰자!

위생 검열원—얘 너 어데로
가니.
길남—우리 엄마가 위생 검열
원이 오면 뛰라고 했
어요.

평남 순천 사전 부속
중학교 교원 박 용식 안

FIGURE 6. Pak Yongsik, "My Mother Said This," 1960. First panel: "Mother says, 'Hey Kilnam, if the Hygiene Inspector comes, be sure not to be at home.'" Second panel: "Kilnam says, 'She's coming, she's coming, let's go!'" Third panel: "The Hygiene Inspector asks, 'Hey, where are you going?' Kilnam responds, 'My mother said to run away if the Hygiene Inspector comes.'"

two, is impossible to discern from historical sources available to us.[30] This was what Alf Lüdtke has shown for other authoritarian settings: that people could simultaneously pursue their own self-interests while, outwardly, appearing to be doing just what the central state powers expected of them.[31] This engagement, as Jie-Hyun Lim has argued, remained crucial for the maintenance of a mass dictatorial regime, yet it did not, on its own, necessarily constitute consent—let alone address the legitimacy of the Party-state.[32]

In these many ways, advice literature became one field through which biopolitics transcended regime types. New notions of collective property would offer a political dynamic specific to socialism, yet as Foucault pointed out in reference to the Soviet Union, socialism had no theoretical critique of biopolitics.[33] Sure enough, there was always an anticolonial and class critique of biopolitics focused on the unequal distribution of services and benefits. But this critique offered a rationale for widening and intensifying the scope of biopolitics, not overthrowing it. By 1965, hygiene and sanitation had risen to become one of the most widely featured issues not just in advice literature like *A Guide to Living*, but in the media more generally.[34] It became one more way of judging an individual's cultural levels in ways that made the introduction of socialism less alien and more familiar.

While advice literature denied its genealogy back to the pre-collective era, many other practices and values were, in fact, novel. Prominent among these was the socialist ideal of collective property. Hwang's guide used what was a common distinction in the era, pitting "Our Things" and "My Things" against each other, only to collapse the distinction to show how, under socialism, all property was common. "The country's factories and enterprises are all the people's as well as mine," wrote Hwang.[35] However distant this ideal understanding of property may have been from the daily lives of workers, there were consequences to how one behaved. Now any action—good or bad—that impacted facilities reflected on an individual's appreciation of caring for collective property, which was seen as the product of labor. "To value, save, and preserve one's own goods is to repay the industrious labor of the workers who made them," Hwang concluded.[36] Anyone involved in ideological work—whether purveyors of advice or propaganda workers—were told to make this appreciation of collectivity one of their priorities.[37]

This contrastive use of collective property hinted at the ambivalent relationship of advice literature to class. With its emphasis on the individual and cultural levels, advice literature provided an alternative discourse that only vaguely connected with the Marxist understanding of class, insofar as it was often glossed as proletarian or "red" consciousness. At the same time, the core Marxist belief that an individual's workplace or socioeconomic background determined class and class consciousness—her relationship to the means of production, in other words—had no traction in advice literature. In effect, Party-state time's presumption that, since 1958, everyone belonged to the proletariat marginalized class struggle as a contemporary challenge. True, it admitted, there remained some antirevolutionary elements in the cracks of society, but these were no longer seen as class formations per se. Two prominent exceptions were the literary world, where writers from the colonial era were criticized for being bourgeois, and the film industry.[38] Even these cases, however, were frequently framed as remnants from the past.

Instead, advice literature became one of the many ways that class struggle was displaced from internal politics. Most obviously, class struggle was historical. The contrast with past ruling-class values was a point Hwang raised in his book's introduction. This followed the broader pattern of historical analysis that explained how the Party emerged out of the class contradictions of colonial society. So, too, did this historical emphasis get reproduced in most novels and movies that featured class politics. Another direction in which advice literature displaced class analysis was southward. Although Hwang did not address the issues of southern behavior and values in his guide, this was a prominent subject that eventually resulted in the publication of an entire journal, called *South Korean Problems* (*NamChosŏn munje*). Often, commentators used collective property to draw a contrast with the class relations of the South, an easy marker for distinguishing socialism from capitalism. Just as frequently, commentators wrote about the corrupting influence of the relationship between U.S. imperialism and the bourgeoisie of the South, lamenting how family relations in Seoul had been reduced to monetary ties.[39] Accordingly, reunification meant not just territorial unity but also the final resolution of the national class problem. This lack of certitude—that no necessary correlation existed between an individual's material relationships and her ideology—posited a remarkably flexible approach to ideology.

The displacement of class struggle meant that the immediate task targeted what came to be called *outmoded thought* (*nalgŭn sasang*)—a term present in virtually every contemporary work dealing with ideological or cultural reform. This again matched the presumptions of Party-state time, insofar as "outmoded thought" stood in for those parts of an individual's ideology that, due to the war and the speed of collectivization, they had not had the necessary time to reflect on and eliminate.[40] Now was the time to play catch-up. Hwang and the other purveyors of advice sought to guide part of that process. Outmoded thought served as a vague stand-in for the non-socialist or non-proletarian. It was a catchall term for that which had been inherited from the past—sometimes labeled feudal, Confucian, or traditional—ideological and cultural forms that interfered with the transition to social-ism. Perhaps surprisingly, outmoded practices and values were rarely labeled bourgeois, and antibourgeois class rhetoric was seldom invoked in order to create an Other against which to define what constituted socialist practices. In this cultural mode of reckoning, even an individual who worked in the factories of colonial Seoul, joined the people's army to fight in the war, and now worked in a chemical fertilizer plant—in other words, someone of ideal proletarian and sŏngbun backgrounds—harbored elements of outmoded thought. *Everyone* had to self-reform. As in Hwang's exhortation— "Comrades, you don't live alone!"—the language was universalist.

This centering of the individual, with a redefinition of struggle as self-reform, dominated the era's discourse. Expressions capturing this self-dynamism followed suit. Terms such as *chabal*, often translated as "spontane-ous" but more akin to "self-propelling," appeared in countless stories demonstrating the initiatives taken by individuals. The term for "host," *chuin*, came to be used as a noun, adjective, and adverb in describing how some individuals became the "master" of the situation confronting them, solving problems without resorting to anything but their own mental and material resources. *Charipsŏng*, denoting the ability to take care of matters fully—literally to stand up by oneself—could be used to judge a person's ability to work independently to get the job done. Most simple and direct was the term *chaegimsŏng*—a sense of responsibility toward collective tasks. Paramount among these terms was *ch'angbal*—creative initiative and dynamic effort. Less common was another associated term, which would rise spectacularly in the 1960s and will be discussed later, *juche*.[41] As Foucault has taught us, power does not just stop people from doing things. Nor is it merely repressive. As the proliferation of advice literature demonstrates, these terms reflected the sense that men and women should energize themselves to pur-sue socialist construction. Advice literature was, to use a term beloved by both Foucault and Party ideologues, *productive*. The fundamental vision of advice literature intersected with the presumptions of Party-state time, only here translated into a mundane realm where the explicit presence of the Party-state was unnecessary—the desire was for an activist population of individuals who would carry out with dynamism the policies and decisions made by the Party-state. An anonymous writer in an otherwise unremarkable piece put the logic this way: "At this time when we are struggling with all our strength to peacefully unify our ancestral land and construct socialism in the northern republic, how is it acceptable for us to stubbornly hang on to out-moded customs?"[42] This was the not-quite-heroic and hardly radical language of standing in line, arriving on time, and not spitting on the streets, which stood in for building a class-free socialist utopia at the vanguard of history and was rendered into a cultural revolution carried on within the self by every individual.

The mission of advice literature to participate in the self-improvement of an entire population was not as inclusive as its rhetoric proclaimed. Within its universal aspirations, advice literature often presumed norms for everyone to emulate, patterned on urban and masculine practices. The result was a wide range of texts, well beyond *A Guide to Living*, that worked hard to gloss over their urban bias while doing much work to create diverse ideals of proper femininity that intersected with the new political-economic realms into which women were entering.

SHOWCASE CITYSCAPES

After the fighting of the Korean War ended, cities began to grow—dramatically. The depopulation of urban centers due to American bombing campaigns was quickly reversed. As the economy continued to grow, better work and living conditions drew migrants from rural areas—despite the decrees and efforts of the central Party-state to stem the flow.[43] In less than a decade, between 1953 and 1960, the proportion of the population living in cities grew from 17.7 percent to 40.6 percent—a faster rise than in South Korea.[44] Many of the migrants were first-generation urbanites. Although official statistics did not provide generational breakdowns of urban residents, countless biographical stories in the media showed that many young workers left their parents behind for the opportunities of the city—a pattern later to be reproduced in South Korea.[45] This made cities more youthful than the countryside.

These demographic shifts were not fully reflected in the media and cer-tainly were not celebrated. Insofar as the influx of young workers to urban centers represented a gap between urban and rural living standards, it created an awkwardness in the coverage. Official ideology critiqued the historical unevenness between rural and urban as a legacy of colonial capitalism. In ideal visions of the socialist future, often offered in abstract essays on political economy, the new central economic plan would flatten these differences by shedding the profit motive.[46] In fact, economic planners could do little more than pay lip service to this vision of equal opportunities for rural and urban spaces.[47] The frequent, laudatory press reports about the smallest of rural advances—the electrification of a town or the opening of a rural medical clinic—testified to the eagerness to show that the countryside, too, was advancing, even as these reports hid the remaining unevenness across the country.[48]

For all the differences between South and North Korea, in terms of the structuring of domestic capital flows, there has always been one grand similarity: rural labor produced wealth that the central government reallocated to their urban-based priorities, such as factories. Central planning always favored the cities. Nevertheless, the theoretical aspiration for urban-rural evenness shaped media coverage. Reportage on the countryside tended to shun the style of denigrating representations of rural areas so common to industrializing societies. *Backward*, *superstitious*, and *unmodern* were adjectives rarely ascribed to the rural in public—unlike in contemporary South Korea.[49] Nor, by 1965, did media coverage come to be instilled with a romanticism or nostalgia for the countryside—unlike their contemporary Chinese counterparts.

The economic bias in favor of cities came together with a public celebration of urban spaces, particularly Pyongyang. It was the capital city that took pride of place. Called the "city of heroes," Pyongyang celebrated its 1,530th anniversary with grand hoopla in 1957. The celebration extolled the city's long history, especially its resistance to foreign invaders over the ages. The capital was designated the revolutionary epicenter, or "the key to our people's revolutionary struggle to build socialism."[50] This was about the now and the future—or, as a headline cried out the following year, Pyongyang was "the heart for the creation of the new history of the Korean people and the heroic city ... the political, economic, and cultural center."[51] Whatever calls emerged in the coming years to further reform and beautify the city, and whatever the vagaries of Party-state elite politics, Pyongyang always remained a "heroic" and "revolutionary" site[52] and a city of wonders, where one could ride in an air-conditioned bus[53] or, by 1964, visit the lion cubs at the zoo.[54]

This presentation of Pyongyang as a visual showcase of revolution was carefully curated through the creation of tourism in the capital city. Work units rewarded model workers with holidays, bringing them up to the capital city. Tour groups of as many as four hundred workers made the rounds,[55] and tour buses began to operate every Sunday in 1957.[56] Reports show visitors ogling the city's spectacles.[57] However ironically, these accounts reinforced the contrast between Pyongyang and the rest of the country. One elderly participant, Yi Pulban, came down from her mountain village to visit Pyongyang in 1957. "Back in my village I had, of course, heard from propagandists and radio the news about the recovery of Pyongyang," she was reported to have explained, "but standing here, looking at it with my own eyes, everything looks miraculous."[58] Yi listed the tall buildings, the constant movement, the fresh colors, and the variety of goods—all reflecting classic tropes in modernist descriptions of city space. These stories, in recording the genuine sensations of people like Yi, sought to show how far the country had come since the war and presented the city as being at the forefront of history, where the future of the entire nation could be glimpsed.

As their work proliferated in the wake of urbanization, cartoonists paid little heed to the countryside.[59] It was the raucous and undisciplined city that provided their best material, especially the new multiunit apartment buildings. Messily hanging laundry to dry outside one's window for everyone to see, men sitting semi-clothed in a window to avoid the summer heat, neighbors talking so loudly from one window to another that yet other neighbors became enraged at their "singing"—all were themes of the urban disarray that became fair game.[60] The visual culture of the era's cartoons was an urban one.

Hwang's *Guide to Living* also harbored this city bias. Like the media coverage of the countryside, he took care not to criticize rural areas for what they lacked. And like the cartoonists, he focused on the upheaval of city life that came with such rapid urbanization. Hwang devoted an entire chapter to what he called "On the Street," treating the appropriate mores for the new public spaces of the city.[61] He concentrated on parks, theaters, movie houses, buses—all places where, he believed, people did not know how to behave. When Hwang urged his readers to enjoy parks and contribute to making them even more beautiful, he also warned not to use them as hunting grounds—implicitly assuming that many of his readers were newcomers to the city.[62] There was, by contrast, no section of his book titled "In the Field" or "On the Collective Farm." For the most part, he simply ignored the countryside. His target, like that of almost all advice literature, was the flood of new and younger people. Of course, what remained unspoken was the fact that among the flood of new arrivals were many Party members, recruited during rural collectivization and brought to the cities to take up positions in the growing bureaucracies. In this sense, advice literature was a product of urbanization. Under the rubric of proletarian consciousness, its purveyors sought to acculturate rural newcomers to the city. Put differently, "cultural levels" privileged certain urban norms, defensively protecting a vision of the city under rapidly changing demographics. The question of how to self-improve absorbed longer-term questions that had originated in the urbanization of the 1920s. It prompted similar concerns, not just in the North but in the South as well. "How to self-improve?" translated, in an urban milieu, into "How to be a good modern urbanite?" This was a question that transcended regimes, but here it was interpellated into the creation of ideal socialist subjects. Answers may have varied, but similar demographic processes underlay the inquiry itself, which marked the peninsula's long twentieth century.

FEMININE SPEECH

In keeping with his universalist aspirations, Hwang maintained a gender-neutral tone in his writing. Still, when he was describing individual practices, his assumed reader—wearing pants, doffing a hat at the right moment, or hosting guests in a family home—was almost invariably male. As such, for Hwang and many other commentators, their answers to "How to be a good socialist builder?" seemingly transcended gender while doing much work to naturalize distinctions along an often essentialized male/female binary. At the very time the consequences of the gender equality laws were being worked out, advice literature—sometimes with nuance, sometimes not—proposed various ways in which the heterosociality of women entering the paid labor force in a wide array of settings would be defined. Gender, in short, was another tumultuous area of change, which advice literature sought to mediate. The various exhortations and injunctions about specifically feminine behaviors were often rooted in a reimagining of historical conventions that were naturalized as specifically Korean when masculinity was rarely represented as a repository of the nation-ness. Historians of China have often noted how similar processes led to the masculinization of women.[63] Not so in Korea, where a surge of advice about cultivating feminine qualities arose just as women were entering the wage workforce in massive numbers. This proliferation of attention to feminine qualities was powerfully reflected in the visual culture of the era, whether in discussions of what type of head scarves women might wear in the factory or of fashions for spiffy outfits beyond the factory (see figures 7 and 8). In part, this surge of cultural advice reflected male anxieties about the ramifications of the higher participation rate of women in wage work and desires to contain the consequences.

These tensions shaped discussions of language—one of the single most discussed subjects of advice literature—and especially of speech. The gendering of the spoken word was part of a more complex array of postcolonial language reforms. Immediately after liberation in 1945, Party ideologues and linguists began positing a relationship between language, sovereignty, and socialism. This association was hardly surprising, given that language had been fundamental to almost every reform project since as early as the 1890s. Under Japanese rule, the Korean language had been manipulated for colonial purposes until ultimately it became the object of extermination—what Janet Poole has called the disappearance of its future.[64] Yet with liberation a future reappeared, as the resurrection of Korean as the national language—however troublesome these categories—became one heralded means of reasserting the national and distancing the colonial. Language came to stand for sovereignty, a key moment in the peninsula's decolonization, both north and south.

Language remained very much in flux after 1945. Scholars, with the support of the Party-state, relaunched the type of standardizing linguistic projects that had been suppressed in the last years of colonialism. Publishers again began putting out dictionaries and grammar books. Dialects became the target of elimination, as uniformity became the key to simplifying language to heighten literacy rates.[65] Universal education and literacy movements supported this push. Linguistic conferences were held and journals published.[66] As in other decolonizing countries around the world, language became the object of much scrutiny, understood as a recoverable object that at once was a nationalist objective in its own right and was believed to be essential in order for other nationalist goals to be realized. The Korean language was both practical and, as many contemporaries opined in what was to become a standard expression, "beautiful."

For some, decolonization translated into a purge of Japanese terms, which had become interlaced throughout the Korean language. Ch'oe Wanho, a linguist in the Academy of Sciences, expressed his dismay that Japanese expressions still circulated a dozen years after liberation. "Our children who have grown up since liberation clearly don't even know that these are Japanese terms befouling our language." Appealing to long-standing tropes about mothers being less educated without actually saying it, he continued, "They are learning them from their mothers and using them. How

FIGURE 7. Feminine dress in the factory. Anonymous, untitled, 1965.

terrible is this?"[67] Another commentator, Han Chŏngjik, pointed out that there were ample expressions to capture meanings in Korean. He was bothered that on factory shop floors, expressions continued to "vulgarize" the language, citing the example of the Japanese "Let's *siage*," rather than the Korean "Let's *wansŏng*,"[68] both expressions meaning "Let's finish up." Yet Han's choice of examples would have displeased other language advocates, who resurrected an older nationalist politics of eliminating Sino-Korean expressions like *wansŏng*. Hwang's *Guide to Living* delved into this issue, targeting old speech-styles, often rooted in Chinese. He repeated the now decades-old argument that this style of literary expression interfered with the very purpose of language—the communica-

양복 차림

(1)   (2)   (3)   (4)

(이 페지를 참조 하세요)

FIGURE 8. Anonymous, "Western Suit Outfits," 1965.

tion of ideas among people. Why say "geostran," he asked, when a more current "yesterday" will do?[69] This winnowing of terms extended to other areas. The early use of Russian-derived expressions, prevalent in the mid-1950s, disappeared by the early 1960s, as relations with the Soviet Union soured. One national newspaper regularly highlighted "old words" (*yet'mal*), which often referred to phenomena it argued no longer existed under socialism. Under the Party's policy of collectivization, it pointed out, slash-and-burn farmers, called *hwajŏnmin*, had disappeared, meaning that the term itself was no longer necessary, as there was no social correlate.[70] By the 1960s, using Japanese, Chinese, Russian, or out-of-date expressions had come to be frowned upon.

The politics of language in this era was much more than a postcolonial-style recuperation and reinvention, however. The constant refrain that "words and thought cannot be separated"[71]—in other words, the inextricable relationship between language and ideology—guaranteed that the reassertion of Korean would look not just to the colonial past, but also to the socialist present and future. If, as the Party had declared and endless commentators explained, the population's ideological commitments lagged, then the assertion of a proper, socialist language served as one more means of raising their cultural level. As Hwang himself noted, "language was a vessel in which a person's thinking was poured" and from which one could discern a person's "level of cultivation."[72] Language, by this reckoning, became one more means of evaluating a person's official ideological and cultural commitments. One had to speak correctly, in other words. The building of socialism entailed forging steel *and* rectifying language.

At its simplest level, this consisted of explaining to most men and women, who had little prior exposure to Marxism, a wide assortment of alien vocabularies. Books such as a *Popular Dictionary of Political Terms* targeted wide audiences with near-encyclopedic treatments of the vocabulary they would need to participate in the newly developing political culture, whether reading the media, participating in political study sessions, or engaging in self-criticism.[73] The media often explained specific terms in separate articles, as did one Q&A column in *Worker* (*Rodongja*) magazine, which asked, "Explain to me what the 'independent property system' means,"[74] before explaining how not all property or capital was directly controlled by the state. Much of this vocabulary related to the economy. As various authorities bemoaned, Party and administrative leaders, factory managers, and workers simply did not understand socialist economic planning. An article asking, "What is meant by *togŭpche*?" (the wage-ranking system for workers) was more than a vocabulary lesson. It moved beyond the question of this single term to explain the whole panoply of concepts undergirding the socialist system of value and pricing to a population in which only the oldest members had ever experienced anything but a wartime economy. Books emerged explaining the complexities of getting prices "right"—a challenge experienced across the socialist bloc—beyond what the average reader needed to know. Yet the process started at the level of establishing a new language—the stepping-stone that everyone, it was believed, should understand, even if they did not need to comprehend the intricacies of macroeconomic planning.[75] Under the seeming simplicity of a technical economic term lay a profound series of assumptions about the ordering of the economy. The Party-state's political-economic plans could not be separated from the ideological purpose of language: establishing a shared conceptual vocabulary for all actors.

Hwang's concern with the manner of talking, not just the use of appropriate words, led him to address conversational etiquette. He hectored readers on their bad form. When asked a question by someone on the street, he insisted that to answer "Dunno" paled in comparison to "Don't know," which still fell short of what Hwang really wanted people to say: "I do not know. I will ask someone else for you."[76] The language section of *A Guide to Living* was full of don'ts: don't speak loudly in public, don't interrupt your interlocutors (especially one's elders), don't gesticulate with your hands when talking, don't whisper into someone's ear in front of another person, and don't use overly informal speech, since formal conjugations are superior. His list spread across five pages.[77] A sense that contemporary speech was uncouth suffused his cajoling, though Hwang never quite resorted to such harsh terms. Nor did he try to explain why he felt that speech was in such bad shape. Though overall his book privileged the urban, he was careful not to blame poor speech habits on new arrivals from the countryside. And while his assumed reader was male, he made no effort to distinguish gendered patterns of speaking. His language lessons were for everyone, equally—a national, standard language for all. This was the linguistic equivalent of the universal, inclusive subject as reflected in everyday spoken language.

Hwang may not have addressed gendered speech, but others did. In the fluid linguistic environment of the 1950s and '60s, when a national, socialist language was coming into being, the publications emerging out of the Women's Union emphasized the distinctiveness of feminine speech. As early as 1956, a book entitled *Women, Let Us Raise Our Cultural Levels* exhorted women to reflect on how they spoke. Much in the same way as did *A Guide to Living*, the book urged readers to eliminate dialects, overly loud talking, and coarse figures of speech. Its editors were less reticent than Hwang in pointing to the severity of the situation in the countryside, where the lack of "beautiful" and "refined" speech, they claimed, was especially pronounced "among aunties in rural villages" (*nongch'on ajumǒni*)—a rare instance of urban dismissiveness.[78] The book introduced a specifically gendered distinction: women should speak with what it called "modesty" and "humility." This ever-so-brief and tentative insinuation, little more than a couple of adjectives, describing a sought-after feminine quality of speech, would be more fully explored by other authors in years to come.

The term *kyŏmson* (modesty) took center place in imagining and exploring the distinctiveness of an idealized women's speech. Linguists, historians, and writers deployed this single word to call for changes that served to naturalize binary speaking patterns without any explicit discussion of masculine speech, which took on Hwang's universalist form. "Modest" speech, deemed as having roots in an ancient past, was declared a national tradition, not targeted for overthrow as feudal but to be inherited, developed, and made fundamental to the construction of socialism. As Ch'oe Wanho put it, "Our diligent and pure Korean women, from ancient times, have been proper in manners and modest in speech and conduct."[79] Historians, too often the most adept at naturalizing historical phenomena, plunged in. Chŏn Sŏnggŭn, a member of the history department at Kim Il Sung University, could write that "men value strong things, whereas women have a character that values soft things." Language, he went on to argue, should follow this distinction—a characterization, it will be seen, that was also carried through in official policies from the 1950s that classified jobs as suitable for women or not.

But how should these so-called feminine qualities be manifested in actual speech? Most commentators had difficulty explaining in written form what it was they expected. Some referred readers to the cinema and radio for models. Others resorted to stock phrases and adjectives expressing well-worn notions of femininity that predated the collective era. Beyond modesty, women should speak "beautifully," "with cultivation," "with decorum," or "gently." One female lecturer at Kim Il Sung University, Pak Yongsun, urged women to speak their thoughts not directly, but circuitously and in a humble fashion.[80] Ch'oe made comparisons as a matter of degree: not speaking in a loud voice was best for everyone, but especially for women.[81] Many commentators addressed the question of the use of levels of respect, telling women that, in Pak's words, only if they learned how to speak in a respectful manner would they "give off a feeling of their graciousness and tenderness."[82] Some offered advice for specific situations. "When speaking with another person," Chŏn Sŏnggŭn wrote in a demeaning mode, "she shouldn't just speak herself but be sure to give her conversational partner a sufficient chance to speak. She shouldn't just stubbornly insist on her own thoughts but must respect the words of her interlocutor." It is not difficult to imagine the gender of Chŏn's imagined interlocuter.[83]

Feminine speech became all the more pressing to these pundits precisely because of the advances of women after the revolution. "Today our Korean women are no longer 'inside the house' as they once were. Today all our women are actively participating in socialist construction in workplaces, in agricultural villages, and on the streets. Because of this, the proper and refined use of their mother language carries great meaning for the building of socialism." For the authors of these commentaries, the more public role of women meant more attention to speech and a greater need to perform properly this nationalized femininity when they spoke. Indeed, some commentators went so far as to suggest that only under socialism could the beauty of the Korean language be captured—or, as one put it, "In a socialist society, the cherished character of women is their modesty. . . . [T]heir modest behavior and modest nature are something to be cultivated and realized within collective life."[84] Yet left out of these celebratory accounts of realization—of the individual, of women as a whole, and of the nation—was how these ideal traits of feminine speech were differentiated from the universal speech, thus privileging the universal as masculine. Nor did these commentators question how "modesty" and its accompanying traits of indirectness, tenderness, and the like reinforced the very hierarchies the gender equality laws sought to undermine. These traits could just as easily have been rendered "feudal" or "outmoded thought" and targeted for elimination as part of the self-reform of the individual. They were not. While celebrating this newfound heterosociality, advice on feminine speech also sought to contain the meaning and social implications of shifting gender relations. It became one of the many ways that cultural arguments were used to reconfigure received gender hierarchies under socialism in the name of the nation.

Also not part of this conversation was the fact that this ideal feminine language, much like advice literature in general, had an urban bias. The proffered norms were patterned on ways that elite, educated, urban women might speak. Like any standard, this form of speech became key not just to the hierarchies between men and women but also to those among women, whether the distinctions drawn were between rural and urban or among women living in the cities. Little is known about social stratification or class formation after the war, let alone how the actual speech used by women in diverse social situations matched—or did not match—the characterizations of these writers. Yet the promotion of idealized feminine language, like other features of advice literature, preserved the cultural capital of its arbiters and elevated them above those who had not mastered or abided by its norms. This is perhaps one reason why the editors of *Women of Korea*, as promoters of feminine speech who benefited from the dynamics of "cultural levels," made no room in their pages for critiques of its gendering effects.

Over the course of the late 1950s and '60s, these newfound ideals of feminine speech received ever greater attention, as judged by the increase in the number of articles in a widening number of journals.[85] By 1964, the editors of *Women of Korea* deemed feminine speech sufficiently significant that they published a regular column entitled "Speaking Beautifully." In his 1965 *Guide to Living*, Hwang posed the challenge of language in a universalizing tone: "Using language beautifully and culturally together with developing its great potential is a patriotic duty for all of us."[86] For him, this was a socialist and nationalist project. Yet by 1965—amid the rapid growth of the economy, the growing size of Party-state institutions, and the advancement of women in both of these sectors—the widespread growth of commentaries on feminine speech had far more political significance than Hwang acknowledged. Ostensibly about the nation and socialism, language emerged as one key medium that reflected, constituted, and legitimated the gendered social differences emerging out of the establishment of a postwar political-economic order.

Socialist Morality as Ruling-Class Ideology?

Morality guidebooks had a long history in Korea. As the author of one such 1965 handbook, titled *A Guide to Living*, Hwang Yŏngsik worried that his work might be seen as an extension of this lineage. As he pointed out in the preface, Marxist historical interpretations saw feudal-era books—like the fifteenth-century compilation for elite women *Instructions for the Inner Chamber* (*Naehun*) and the late eighteenth-century *Small Manners for Scholars* (*Sasojŏl*)—as reflecting ruling ideologies. Was his book doing the same thing? Hwang hoped not. But he knew that anyone trained in basic historical materialism might see his work as serving a purpose similar to that of these old texts. Anxious about such criticism, he used his preface to imitate the voice of a hypothetical critic, writing, "Some comrades will say, 'We are living in a new socialist society, not in a feudal or capitalist society. What use are such morals and proprieties to us now?'"

Hwang answered not by claiming a revolutionary rupture or by highlighting the differences of his work. Perhaps counterintuitively, he answered by stressing continuities rather than change. The behavior and practices he called for in his text did have connections with past customs, only he drew a distinction between those of the ruling classes and the "beautiful customs" of the people (*inmin*). The point was not to abandon every received custom, he insisted, but to "inherit and develop" (*kyesŭng paljŏn*) those beautiful popular mores. He saw his book as performing a curatorial sorting-out of history—the good practices of the people to be preserved, and the bad customs of the ruling class to be discarded. On the national stage, this was a task that the Party assigned itself more generally. Hwang was only carrying it out, without any mention of material dialectics.

In a classic case of invention of traditions, Hwang drew up a list of his beautiful old mores to be preserved: "the love of country and people, respect of seniors and parents, mutual cooperation and amity among neighbors, simple and plain customs, diligence and honesty." The advice he offered to his readers later in the book—to line up neatly for a bus, not to speak loudly in the movie theater, and to respect collective property—aligned in Hwang's eyes with these long-held traits. In effect, the author saw residents of the modern, socialist city who worked in factories, offices, and schools as inheriting the popular mores of their rural and agricultural predecessors, though he was vague on how he saw this relationship.

For people like the hypothetical critic who found moral advice fussy or bothersome, Hwang had no patience. He dismissed them as people who did not abide by "our society's moral norms." They would be looked down upon as people without the abilities to maintain "noble" customs. He further blamed such people for being without "cultivation" (*kyoyang*), suggesting that these people did not appreciate the continued need for advice literature. Yet his rejection of these people drew the very style of moral and cultural distinctions that raised the doubts of his hypothetical critic in the first place. His rejection of his critics did not quite revert to the language of "cultural levels," yet his answer placed himself as in-the-know and any doubters as beneath him.

Was his book preserving the heritage of popular customs in an era of immense change? Or was his advice another form of ruling ideology that, like moral guidebooks of the past, hid the hierarchies it created? Hwang's manner of rejecting this criticism demonstrated, however ironically, that his hypothetical critic might just have a point.

THREE

The Politics of Criticism and Dormitory Surveillance

ADVICE LITERATURE WAS LARGELY UPBEAT. Its universalizing impulse assumed that readers shared, if not the enthusiasm, then at least the desire for self-improvement. Yet underlying this optimism about shared commitments was an anxiety: just like the two ill-dressed men walking down the street (in figure 4), not everyone shared the ability to self-reflect. It was still more worrisome, from the perspective of authorities, that while theoretically everyone had the potential to raise their "cultural levels," there was always the opposite dynamic too. Individuals might slip.[1] And improper behavior could be read not just as evidence of low cultural levels but as ideological danger—a much more serious proposition. To manage such possibilities, two additional forms of disciplinary techniques were brought into play: group- and self-criticism and surveillance of worker dormitories.

After the war, the Party extended to the entire population the self-criticism and small-group criticism that previously had been internal to its membership. Advice literature had a long history among the literate portion of the population; formal criticism sessions did not. This new practice came to be routinized in workplaces, neighborhoods, mass organizations, and political study sessions. Part of temporary campaigns, criticism also came to be regularized in review meetings in most organizations. A criticism culture quickly emerged.[2]

As propounded by Party ideologues, criticism constituted a fundamental element in the struggle to build socialism. An article published during the month of the armistice by Ri Hongjong explained criticism as a vehicle for change. Intended as a reference guide for others to adopt in their own small-group setting, Ri's article explained that mutual and self-criticism were weapons.[3] He recounted the long history of criticism, finding its original spirit in the critical nature of Marxism-Leninism itself, which "from its first day" had only developed due to its fearless criticism of others and self. This spirit needed to be continued today, he argued, taken up by the entire population. "Criticism and self-criticism are a decisive means of defeating all the outmoded and dying forces that harm our progressive movement. They are powerful and sharp weapons for uprooting all corruption and conservatism, stagnation, and passivity. They purge the vestiges of colonial and feudal thought, as well as the remains of Japanese bourgeois thought." Ri determinedly proclaimed that the Party "is not afraid of criticism and self-criticism."

While Ri may not have been afraid, others were. As the practice of criticism unrolled among the population, Party-state leaders grew anxious it would alienate people, propaganda workers grew concerned about best practices, and ordinary urban residents grew worried about its consequences. That the process generated fears at multiple levels became clear in 1955 after a Party meeting reiterated the need for pan-national implementation of criticism. The press followed with a flurry of articles that sought to assuage popular misgivings and demonstrate—often with Ri's style of rhetoric toned down and put in the form of first-person narratives—the benefits of criticism. People, the Party-state authorities were realizing, had to be not only told what to do, but convinced to do it.

Popular anxieties were, no doubt, stimulated in part by the vitriolic tenor of the criticisms of prominent political and intellectual figures, such as Pak Hŏnyŏng and Yi T'aejun.[4] The harsh language used to criticize Kim Il Sung's rivals also lingered in the press for years, as will became evident in the politics of apartment building. Aware of these concerns, propaganda workers accompanied the unrolling of criticism with an open examination, usually through personal accounts, of best practices. These accounts downplayed the antagonism of criticism, presenting it as yet another exercise in self-improvement. In one such case, Kim Ŭngsŏn wrote of his embarrassment at having his shortcoming exposed publicly—an experience, the story suggested, that was replicated widely. He soured on the practice and on his fellow workers. Yet ultimately—and this was the style of turn in all model stories—he turned around to appreciate that criticism had helped him learn about his own work practices. He wrote: "If I hadn't received and accepted sharp criticism and advice from my comrades, I probably would have made more mistakes and not gotten the results that I did. Criticism is certainly a powerful weapon for correcting shortcomings and advancing our goals [saop]."[5] Such stories were the ideal from the Party's perspective, of course, yet they also revealed both the discomfort of participants and the worries of the Party.

Part of the problem, from the perspective of Party-state leaders, hinged on the overzealousness of local propaganda workers and lower-level officials. According to multiple reports, these lower-level officials used criticism as a form of intimidation or coercion of workers. As a result, a flurry of reports arose discussing best practices. One report chided a group of schoolchildren who unilaterally established a hygiene inspection station at the front gates of their school, meting out criticism and punishments to those they deemed under the bar.[6] Cartoonists apparently received permission in this context to mock officials for not using more persuasive techniques to bring about healthier criticism practices.[7] Another mocked officials who aggressively criticized others but not themselves. One cartoon poked fun at authorities who, after receiving criticism from an underling, would find a setting in which to retaliate—what they called "repressing bottom-up criticism" (see figure 9).[8] The growing currency of the expression "comradely advice" was directed at ensuring that criticism would not devolve into personal bickering or gossip. This meta-criticism of criticism urged limits. The contrast between persuasive and coercive criticism arose to structure these concerns, an either-or proposition that ignored the difficulties in making these distinctions or assumed that everyone would be willing to accept properly communicated criticism.[9] Others urged that overheated political vocabulary should not be used.[10]

What became unavoidable, even when criticism fell under the rubric of "comradely advice," was the deeply personal nature of criticism. Criticism publicly singled out specific individuals in real-life settings, ostensibly with the same purpose as advice literature: to make them self-improve. This impulse became clear in a regular column called "My Turn to Speak" (*Nado han madi*), featured in the newspaper of the General Federation of Trade Unions in the late 1950s. Serving as a regular forum for workers to offer brief criticisms of a startlingly wide range of practices and behaviors, "My Turn to Speak" consisted of short outbursts of barely contained frustration and, in some cases, outrage. Selected and edited by the newspaper's staff, these criticisms assumed a more colloquial air than was the norm in the media. These criticisms were not from unmediated popular voices. They were selected and published in a paper run by one of the key mass organizations of the Party. Yet these minimal texts—as short as five lines or as long as two paragraphs— offered a type of fragmented insight into the general unruliness of postwar urban work life, one of the motivations for the Party to push for the

FIGURE 9. Anonymous, "What's Repressing Bottom-Up Criticism?,"
1954.

dissemination of criticism in the first place. That they were published gives
some sense of the approved realms as well as what was not typically included
as "comradely criticism."

Much like advice literature, these short critical pieces also emphasized the
individual. Yet whereas advice literature usually dealt with hypothetical
examples or generalized figures, criticism named names. Virtually every piece
identified the critic and the recipient of the critique, listing their workplace
and often naming other coworkers. There was no hiding. As in advice literature, biopolitical concerns appeared as regular topics. Hŏ Sŏngmun was
charged by one of his dormitory mates, Sŏ Yŏngbŏm, as having the messiest
of rooms, with clothes strewn around and the stench of sweat piercing the air.

"Every month when he gets his salary, he wastes it on gambling. He is uninterested in pursuing a cultural life. How is this OK?"[11] The pervasiveness of hygiene concerns made it safe for workers to criticize their immediate superiors, especially their factory leaders, for shortcomings in this regard. A worker in the eighth construction unit of the electricity bureau, Ri Sŏk, reported that workers had been complaining since the previous year about their broken bathing facilities, which were still not working. The situation reflected the fact that the leaders of the third unit, he charged, "were not sufficiently concerned about the livelihood of workers."[12] A similar situation existed at the Pyongyang Textile Factory, where arguments among the leadership of the factory had caused delays in the construction of bathing facilities. Noting that worker morale was sagging, Ch'oe Tŏkkil recalled, "Last time when the day care facilities were being built, there were the same problems. Has that lesson been forgotten?!"[13]

Workers often couched their complaints about work discipline—or the lack thereof—in the language of yet another value common to advice literature: cherishing the value and pleasures of labor. This is what made Ko Myŏngjin disgruntled about his construction coworker Yi Tongsŏp, a skilled musician who, according to Ko, claimed he had nothing to learn at the workplace, hated working, and often skipped off. Yi "is good at music," explained Ko, and keeps asking to be sent to music school rather than work. "How can a person who doesn't like to work play genuine music?"[14] Some criticisms stimulated responses from other readers. Hong Ŭngun became so infuriated by one six-line entry about a doctor, Kim Sunhŭi, who left work at the end of the day rather than stay late to treat a patient who was running a temperature above 40°C, that he sent in a response from Khaborovsk. "Comrade Kim Sunhŭi must quickly cast aside this kind of outmoded thinking," he wrote, before asking the editors to report back in the pages of the newspaper whether she had "corrected her ideological shortcomings" and was working sincerely.[15] Pak Manbong compounded his lackadaisical work with a fierce reluctance to receive criticism. "A few days ago," began the notice of Ri Hwanju, "Comrade Pak Manbong was processing an important component, but he failed to observe the proper standards. When the factory inspector pointed this out to him, instead of being grateful he got into a fistfight with the inspector. Comrade Pak Mongbong! Does this mean that even when you see something wrong, you think nothing should be said?"[16]

Comrade Pak's pugnaciousness may not have been explicitly linked to alcohol, but many other writers made the connection. One writer, in a rare case of someone retreating to anonymity, wrote about two named senior members of the Ch'ŏngjin Rubber Factory, who regularly showed up to work reeking of alcohol and causing problems. When another worker, Comrade Pae Yusaeng, told them to stop, rather than realize what they were doing, one of them, Comrade Chu Hwanju, a foreman, struck Pae with his fist. "How can you stay quiet about this behavior?" the writer complained.[17]

Umbrage at the absenteeism of coworkers had a special place in "My Turn to Speak." Comrade Kil Iru of Pyongyang Machine Manufacturing Factory may have been skilled at cut work, but, his colleague Kang Ch'ŏlju fumed, "Pretty much every day he just hangs around on street corners."[18] In another complaint written up by Kim Yusŏng, his coworker Paek Sunhŭi showed up to work, only to complain of pain. She said she was going to the hospital when in fact she headed out shopping, he charged.[19] On a more bizarre level, the column reported that a group of workers had left the Kim Ch'aek Ironworks for a holiday in Ch'ŏngjin; more than two months later, they had not returned to work—nor was there any news of what may have been the poaching of their labor by another enterprise.[20]

Many criticisms defy easy categorization, even though they spoke to the types of concerns common in advice literature. Pak Pyŏngsŏ complained about a coworker who did not treat the factory cadres with respect, swearing at them and not greeting them. "What kind of thought is that?!" he asked, before concluding that he hoped he would learn to treat people with respect.[21] Another simply complained that the showing of a drama, *Dark Shadow* (*Kŏmŭn kŭrimja*), started so much later than scheduled that workers weren't able to get home until well after midnight, making it difficult to get to work on time the next day. Given this, Comrade Rim asked, how are workers supposed to maintain "order"?[22]

If these outbursts in "My Turn to Speak" were as short as they were moralizing, letters to the editor in the same newspaper offered more lengthy examples of the growing criticism culture. Like their shorter counterparts, these letters were also filtered by the editing process, yet they, too, had a colloquial ring to them. Nevertheless, the letter writers deployed the language of advice and cultural living to frame and legitimate their criticism—or what was often little more than curmudgeonly complaining. Such was the case of an anonymous writer from the Anju coal mine, who late one night was disturbed by "singing and laughter shaking the night sky."[23] Workers from the nearby railway administration offices, including the office head, had taken over a worker cafeteria for a drinking party and were "way too drunk." They were making a racket, singing in disorderly fashion both popular songs and revolutionary tunes. When a young coworker saw this scene and advised them to respect the order of the cafeteria, they responded, "We're drinking. What does it have to do with you?" The letter writer went on to ask, "Can we say that these are people who have received a communist education? These types of violations of public order are living signs of outmoded thought. Moreover, should railway workers, who serve the people, not know better than anyone else that the morality and order of the masses must be well observed together?!" He closed his letter with a hope: that these workers might develop a communist moral character.

Both this letter writer and the many worker critics assumed a moral high ground, writing with a sense that the offender should and could be doing better, in part because they lived in a socialist society. This neatly fit the assumptions of Party-state time, which positioned ideology as lagging behind material conditions. Criticisms of coworkers, of workplace habits, of public behavior, of self-propriety—all of these shared the individuating impulse that dominated the widespread calls to raise ideological and cultural levels. It was up to the self-aware individual to get their act together, so to speak, and criticism was a means to make them realize this end.

Just as important in these criticisms was what was *not* said. Most obviously, within the parameters of comradely criticism, there was no room for gendered critique. None of the examples raised issues of gender discrimination in the workplace—despite the segregation of many workplaces and the gendered assumptions upon which it rested. The more theoretical language that was advocated for criticism by higher-level authorities also had little place in "My Turn to Speak." Newspapers and magazine editorials frequently wrote of the need to criticize such phenomena as *sogŭksŏng* (passivity), *hyŏngsikchuŭi* (formalism), and *posujuŭi* (conservatism), all of which emerged as standard categories for explaining problems in socialist construction, employed at higher political levels and promoted for use throughout the country.[24] These serious political terms were not present at this more mundane level. The Party's top-level theoretical journal continued to urge people to be on the lookout for bourgeois thought well into the 1960s, as did the newspaper that published "My Turn to Speak."[25] But in these cases, workers simply did not deploy such class categories—and the newspaper editors clearly did not expect them to do so. On the contrary, the workers structured their criticisms with the inclusive logic of the universal ability of individuals to self-improve. As intensely personal as these criticisms were—it was surely no fun to be named in "My Turn to Speak"—the personal framing of critique appeared to temper the political charges that could be leveled at coworkers. In the 1950s, the suggestion that someone was bourgeois or petit bourgeois remained a truly serious political charge—perhaps *too* serious to deploy in these situations. In the local social worlds of workers—and arguably in the broader political culture—criticism became a more tame practice due to its highly personalized form. In "My Turn to Speak," perhaps the most charged terminology invoked the violation and disruption of social order. The contemporary historical struggle came to be located inside the individual self, as an interior struggle over "outmoded" thought, rather than determined by external socioeconomic relations. The revolution was turned inside out.

DANGEROUS DORMITORIES AND MASCULINIZING IDEOLOGICAL THREATS

Advice literature and criticism were not deemed sufficient by authorities, however. The threat of slippage and the ability to read any misstep as ideologically dangerous led to various modes of surveillance, especially in worker dormitories.

Easily constructed and rapidly erected, dormitories emerged after the war as one of the most efficient temporary forms of shelter for workers. As the postwar recovery accelerated and more housing was constructed, their function gradually shifted, as they became a style of housing designed to guide young, unmarried individuals to make the transition from their natal homes into the workforce.[26] Housing dozens of workers—in some cases, up to fifteen hundred—and apportioned by workplace, dormitories steered youths (*ch'ŏngnyŏn*) in their transition to more independent living.[27]

Dormitories offered much more than just a roof over the heads of young workers. They served as a physical site that mustered various institutionalized powers to discipline and conduct surveillance of their residents. The General Federation of Trade Unions (or Workers' Federation) received the task of ensuring the quality of dormitory life—defined both materially and ideologically. Dormitories came with communal facilities designed with the goal of heightening collective consciousness, including shared bathing facilities, common cafeterias where workers were supposed to rotate cooking duties, and reading rooms, along with self-governing committees tasked with overseeing the facilities. For most urban Koreans, the days lived in dormitories offered what was likely their single most intensive experience of collective living. Living in a single room with four to eight other people, after all, would have this effect. It also provided a setting for the Workers' Federation to look out for ideological problems.

In such a didactic setting, the challenge of *how to self-reform* came to have a very different politics. Personal conduct—especially issues of hygiene— became linked to the physical conditions of the dormitory. Insufficient upkeep in this setting risked being read, more than as just a personal miscue, as disrespect for one of the most hyped socialist values, collective property.[28] Taking care of dormitory facilities became one way for residents to perform their "love of collective property" and to show in the language of advice literature that the facilities were "our things." The opposite was just as true— and dangerous. The humor of satirical cartoons did not extend into this space and these issues. Anxious to fulfill its mandate, the Workers' Federation undertook several measures to prevent dormitory residents from slipping— policies that would take on gendered dimensions.

All dormitories were segregated by gender, whether by building or within a single structure. Not surprisingly, the transitional function of preparing residents for future independent living, as became clear in publications of both the Workers' Federation and the Women's Union, imagined female residents as wives and mothers in heteronormative nuclear families. A round-table featuring several female textile workers, published in *Women of Korea*, began with its moderator opening a discussion outlining their future. Because the young women would become housewives, she bluntly began, they all had to learn how to manage the household prudently while keeping up their participation in the factory.[29] The ensuing discussion centered on how best to accomplish this balance. One participant, Kim Poksil, pointed out that this was partly a question of the wise use of time: "There are people in the dorms who spend two, three hours in idle chitchat or gossip— something that just isn't right. If you don't know how to use your own time, after you get married you'll become one of those people who won't be able to allocate your time properly to complete your many household chores."[30] For another, Kim Kyŏngse, it was about tidiness, for "if the young women in a dormitory don't know how to keep their own clothes clean, how will they be able to take care of their husbands and children?" Older women were brought into dormitories as "housemothers," expected to teach their experiences in formal classes and informal settings.[31] Motherhood schools were organized. Countless pieces of advice literature—usually published by the Women's

Union—became the subject of group study. And, of course, these activities included the promotion of "elegant character" and "feminine proprieties," including the acquisition of feminine speech.[32]

Model stories recounting the ideal life of model dormitories abounded. Yet what is interesting in these model stories is not so much the accounts of blissful collective life—how the workers of Ch'ongjin Textile Factory spent their Sundays cleaning their dorm windows and learning how to sew,[33] how one sterling factory leader chose to live in a dormitory for fifteen days to learn the needs of his workers,[34] or how the residents of one dormitory learned to save money by growing their own corn rather than buying it.[35] More interesting are the moments in these stories that critiqued existing conditions so as to muster a rationale for reform. Dormitories attracted much condemnation for their less-than-salutary conditions, in part because they were such an obvious form of collective property and collective living. One critic raised the example of a dormitory that had been ruined by smokers. A wonderful facility had been spoiled, he charged, because residents treated it as if they were guests at an inn, without ever cleaning. Cigarette butts were piled all over. "This is a house for workers," he exclaimed, "a collective family. Do we not live with order and manners?"[36] Another dormitory resident complained that he and his coworkers had little to do in their dormitories after a hard day's labor. They were bored. So they spent their off time and money, he explained, on drinking, gambling, and singing "unhealthy" songs. The result was disorder. "The discipline necessary for collective living," he remembered, "had fallen apart."[37] These were not light offenses.

Yet these critical stories and harsh language were reserved almost exclusively for male dormitories. As Party-state categories, terms like *disorderly*, *undisciplined*, and *uncultured* gave little sense of the motives for these practices, let alone what exactly people were doing. Female dormitories did get critiqued for lack of hygiene, but such disapproval rarely, if ever, escalated to their being reproached in these more politically fraught terms.[38] For the most part, the Workers' Federation assumed that problems in female dormitories could be resolved by the usual methods: mobilizing a sanitation campaign, promoting model residents, establishing a hygiene committee, or some other such measure.

This discrepancy reflected a gendered sense of political agency on the part of this mass organization, if not more broadly. In other moments, the Workers' Federation followed the Party-state's lead in celebrating the gender equality laws and extolled the advancements achieved by their female membership since the war by dint of their diligence. Yet in the specific setting of dormitories, where the issue was not so much positive engagement as fears of ideological disarray, it was as if the Workers' Federation could not quite imagine female residents having the wherewithal to pose a political threat. This presumption belied the long history during the colonial period of labor activism among women and the Party's own celebration of women's active participation in revolutionary activities and the war.[39] Nonetheless, the Workers' Federation treated similar dormitory problems—bad hygiene— distinctively by gender. It was more worried about male dormitories. It masculinized ideological dangers.

The anxieties of the Workers' Federation led officials to come up with an equally gendered solution for the dangers of male dormitories. A 1957 article published as "reference material" in its house newspaper offered strategies for local chapters to prevent dormitory problems from mushrooming into graver political threats.[40] The article began with a standard historical interpretation, blaming dormitory disarray on the colonial period and the war. These two historical moments often bore the blunt of blame for social problems, just as they were used in this case to account for the lack of opportunities for workers to heighten their "cultural levels." The article foreshadowed its conclusion by raising the role of the home in reproducing the conditions of labor—a space where workers returned home to divest themselves of the day's accumulated tiredness and restore their desire to return to work the next day. "A good home life," it declared, "is crucial for participation in production." Broken showers again served as a type of metaphor. The point was not just that showers broke down, but that once they were broken, residents made little effort to repair the faulty facilities on their own. This was precisely the combination—a lack of initiative and self-reliance in a setting of collective property—that authorities could interpret in broader political strokes.

It was no small matter. Disorder and lack of discipline in dormitories, the article fretted, might lead workers to stray politically. The article went on to use the vocabulary of Cold War division to express its security anxieties: "We cannot forget that our enemies are scheming in all sorts of ways to create harm," it warned, adding, "Capitalist and reactionary thought might be reintroduced." That dormitories were filled with the "inexperienced" and "young people with strong emotions" caused the Workers' Federation special worry. Vigilance was required. "If we do not watch over the dormitories where our workers spend most of their waking hours and if we do not engage in ideological training," it cautioned, "we will allow the sprouts of capitalist thought to arise. It will be the opportunity for reactionary thought to take hold." Unkempt living spaces, lack of discipline and order, the absence of self-initiative, and collective property—all these were interlinked and raised to the level of the Party-state's Cold War struggles. The Workers' Federation, in short, translated cultural levels into capitalist threats. It is worth noting that this was a tragedy shared with workers living in dormitories on the other side of the demilitarized zone. Whether problems were cast as reflecting "capitalist threats" or labeled "red" as they were in the South, the politicization of everyday behavior in the context of division led to a deepening of surveillance over the domestic lives of working populations. In this case, these anxieties drew the Workers' Federation even further across dormitory thresholds.

The article's first solution relied on the standard repertoire of ideological work—self-study, small-group study sessions, lectures, and the like. Yet it quickly moved on to other solutions, as though lacking confidence in these techniques. The article instead proposed to blend moral advice literature with Party-style exhortations to better organize residents. More successful organization, it averred, would offer better protection from ideological danger by keeping residents busy. In an argument precariously similar to the age-old rhetoric holding that idleness breeds discontent, the article urged local Workers' Federation units to keep workers occupied during their off-work hours. Literature groups, lectures, roundtables, movies, sports—all of these were recommended. Even dances were encouraged. The article urged special caution for Sundays, when residents would have the entire day off. "Make it so that there it isn't a day where they pass the time sleeping in their rooms or getting bored," it advised. It was a policy of distraction and preemption—keep residents busy so that they avoid falling into or causing trouble. Wider press reports showed many such events being held.[41]

The article finished by offering its ultimate solution, a proposal that, in effect, showed the Workers' Federation treating the family in terms of its depoliticizing power. Up to this point, the article did not distinguish between male and female workers, but with its turn to the family, it suddenly shifted to focus on male workers alone. In so doing, it showed how the Workers' Federation envisioned men exclusively as wage workers while it saw women as only *potential* wage workers but certainly as household managers. It urged local Workers' Federation units to "work together with workers' families, especially wives," on whom living conditions, good or bad, depended. "The life of the family," it repeated after making clear the special responsibility it believed women had for domesticity, "is linked to production." The turn to the family was in keeping with the transitional understanding of dormitory life in the life trajectory of its inhabitants. But here the transition, it was suggested, was a stabilizing one: married men in their own homes, taken care of by wives who understood the importance of adjusting home life to match the need to prioritize production, would be reliable—or otherwise rendered politically passive. While the article did not quite come out and say it directly, its ultimate solution for the ideological threat of single men gathered in dormitories was, in effect, to marry them off and get them out of dormitories and into the more settled environment of a family home. Gender was instrumentalized: one, seen as more docile, could depoliticize the other, seen as more threatening.

Imagining such a solution, of course, was easier than seeing it through. There's no evidence that the Workers' Federation tried to carry out this recommendation's final provision in any coordinated way. Of course, its vision of the family as depoliticizing, with its particular understanding of wives as household managers, was hardly met with general agreement. At the same time, the Women's Union offered a very different understanding of the family, home, and marriage. But this was not all. The construction of urban housing in 1957, it would become clear, hardly met demand. Married couples, unable immediately to arrange for themselves family accommodation, often had little choice but to prolong their stays in dormitories.[42] Given these pressures on housing, the Federation's gendered strategy was moot—a situation that would not change until the following year, when a highly politicized movement to build apartments for working families was launched.

PART TWO

The Political Economy of Apartments

HOW TO BUILD MORE EFFICIENTLY?

For an economy devasted by war, for a Party-state eager to rebuild cities in the context of labor and capital shortages, and for ordinary men and women seeking stable jobs and homes, there were few more central questions. The challenge of how to build more efficiently brought together the various scales of the economy, linking the concerns of the wage-earning population, economic planners, Party-state officials, and factory managers. Wages, factory production targets, the ability to rehouse the population, and the goal of reaching socialism through enhanced production—all these would be determined by efforts to answer this question. The result of all these concerns was an era obsessed with efficiency.

All the talk about efficiency attracted the satirical gaze of cartoonists. An illustration by Song Siyŏp from 1960 spoofed the obsession by turning to the era's preeminent symbol, the construction crane (see figure 10).[1] Depicting eleven workers clinging to a crane to form a human chain, the cartoon announced "It's Been Used!" to poke fun at the many enterprises that did not know how to use expensive equipment—or, as one contemporary report put it, at the fact that cranes were often little more than decorations.[2] The cartoonist joked that this crane, standing stock-still, had indeed been used, but only as scaffolding to support the workers while they passed bricks upward, hand to hand. Viewers of the cartoon would have immediately recognized key tropes that had emerged across the media, though in tones much less lighthearted than in the hands of this cartoonist: the messy work site, the use of small bricks that had become technically outmoded by 1960, the failure to mechanize production leaving work dependent on manual labor, and the idleness of capital-intensive machinery. Yet most readers would likely have appreciated the incongruity captured by the image: that whatever dictates

FIGURE 10. Song Siyŏp, "It's Been Used!," 1960. "At the Wŏnsan construction team's work-site, instead of enthusiastically introducing mechanized methods, they don't even make use of existing facilities and are wasting enormous labor power."

came down from the highest levels of the leadership calling for efficiency, construction sites around the country continued to waste the labor of workers and failed to use capital-intensive equipment, often in the most preposterous of fashions—even as the diligence of those same workers grew the economy and transformed cityscapes with a flood of new apartment buildings.[3]

By 1957, the question of how to build more efficiently would become deeply politicized. Any answer necessarily raised the dilemma of the relationship of ideology to economic growth. In the years immediately after the war, planners emphasized the need to deal with the capital and labor shortages by finding more efficiencies, whether at the level of the individual enterprise, by reorganizing their incentives and workplace cultures, or, at the national level, by finding ways to increase the wage-work participation of the single largest labor reserve, women at home. Even the Party-state in these years did not deem ideology the primary solution to economic growth.

By the late 1950s, however, the question of how to build more efficiently had become caught up in elite power struggles. When the construction industry failed to meet its targets, Kim Il Sung and allies seized the opportunity to redefine answers to the efficiency question, using the woes of the construction industry to eliminate rivals. The Party framed the struggle to build more efficiently as one between technical management and the primacy of ideology. This pivot toward ideology, new forms of leadership, and mass politics brought these elite politics directly into the realms of the New Living and would eventually transform work sites around the country. Eventually coalescing into the famous Ch'ŏllima movement, the effects of this pivot became most visible in a massive campaign to rebuild Pyongyang in 1958.

One witness to and participant in the era's obsession with efficiency and the pivot toward ideology was a model construction worker, Ri Myŏngwŏn. Her memoir, published in 1961, after the pivot, was one text that both recorded and promoted specific answers to the question *How to build more efficiently?* The memoir was also marked by the tensions of its author being a woman working in the male-dominated construction industry, toward which Ri aimed numerous direct and indirect critiques. When read together with the writings of economic planners, Party theorists, architects, and writers in the daily press, her memoir revealed much about the difficulties of aligning the diverse interests of planners, managers, and workers—a challenge that ultimately revealed the limits of central state institutions in managing the tensions and contradictions in the political economy. The memoir also demonstrated not only how the gendering of labor was fundamental to running the economy, but also that it was working women who often, through ad hoc organization and their unpaid labor, stepped up to resolve the bottlenecks and shortcomings of the Party-state's central plans.

———

FOUR

An Obsession with Efficiency

EFFICIENCY'S MEASURE

The struggle to improve efficiency provided Ri Myŏngwŏn's memoir with one of its overarching themes. During the war Ri served as a nurse. But following the armistice, she had a change of heart. She wanted to help rebuild the capital city, she wrote. As soon as she arrived in Pyongyang, she joined a construction team and turned her mind to the question of improving the team's practices. She immediately identified a problem. "It looks like there's some wasted labor on our work team," she told the team leader. In this way her memoir began to address the grand task of improving efficiency, about which so many economists fretted and so many editorial writers expounded, rendering it in terms of the most rudimentary of tasks: the use of buckets. "We have nine people assigned to transporting water," she noted, before proposing, "I think I can do it with just two."[1] This was her first step in a long career as a regular worker, not taking dramatic risks or making heroic sacrifices, but grappling with the most elementary challenges to help ease the national labor shortage—even if that simply meant optimizing the use of buckets.[2]

In recounting experiences like this, Ri's memoir took on the language, so prominent in advice literature, of the self-initiating, creative individual—but applied directly to labor practices in real production situations, as symbolic of Party-state policies in general. Notions of *ch'angbal*, *chabal*, and *chuindapke*—all of which reflected a sense of autonomously taking the initiative to get things done—reinforced this conception of the constantly struggling and self-improving subject. The memoir in effect acknowledged the limits of the central plan. The problems Ri is shown confronting could not possibly have been anticipated by higher authorities, who expected workers like Ri to figure out the idiosyncrasies of their individual workplaces. This was the ideal social-ist subject, able to act without specific instructions, but according to Party-state principles, to overcome unforeseen obstacles in pursuit of carrying out the policies that would accelerate the transition to socialism. Demonstrating this possibility was the main purpose of the memoir.

Ri's introduction to bucket management only presaged more complicated dilemmas, including the issue of wages. Around the socialist world, the issue of whether material incentives—especially wage differentials—should be used to motivate production was heatedly disputed.[3] But in Korea this debate made virtually no appearance. For planners and theoreticians, material incentives constituted the only path.[4] As early as March 1954, the cabinet passed regulations to raise wages for laborers with technical skills, in order to encourage others to upgrade their own skills.[5] The slogan "Socialism Does Not Mean Equalism" remained a constant throughout these years, as a reminder to both workers and managers that workers should not be paid the same amount simply for showing up to work.[6] This principle remained a mainstay of the economic system and never wavered. To this end, economic planners established a Soviet-style eight-scale wage system. Workers moved through graduated steps, each level representing a degree of skill, knowledge, and ability. At the bottom lay general laborers with few skills and education. At the top, or level 8, were the skilled technical workers. In theory, through (self-)education, experience, and hard work, a laborer could rise through this hierarchy. The better wages of the higher categories were intended to be both an incentive to make the effort and a reward for having arrived. As one economist laid out: "If we are to explain in a word the wage scale guide, it is what sets the rate of salary such that a worker with superior skills compared to a worker with inferior skills earns more money."[7]

But wages were not all. A significant portion of a worker's income came from bonuses. Every December, workers received bonuses representing a com-bination of sectoral growth, their enterprise's production, and their individual performance. In some years, such as 1955, bonuses were broadcast over the radio—all the better to publicize how well some workers were doing. Press reports showed those lucky workers picking up fat white envelopes stuffed with cash just in time for the New Year's celebrations.[8] Stay-at-home mothers emerged as a special target of such stories, as they were encouraged to imagine what a second salary might mean for their family lifestyles (a point we'll return to in part 3 of this book). Eventually bonuses would be turned into gifts from Kim Il Sung, yet initially these stories sought to tantalize by giving rewards.

The stories mobilized gaps in the material circumstances among workers to encourage more and better work. Cartoonists took up with glee the theme that socialism did not mean equal pay. Typically, they contrasted two workers. One multi-panel, two-strip cartoon contrasted the consequences of diligence and sloth. One worker, assiduously at his machine, ended the day at 150 percent of his quota; the other worker, whiling away time and smoking at his machine, ended the day astonished that his chart showed he had reached only 50 percent of his quota. The punch line arrived in the last two frames, which depicted the earnest worker heading to the movie theater with his wife and child, while the indolent worker is shown lying on the floor of his home, playing solitaire, his child crying beside him while his spouse looks on unhappily.[9] Inequities in income were thus not only acknowledged but publicized, even instrumentalized in the name of maximization of output. Moreover, gaps in quality of life were explained as the result of individual effort and laid at the feet of workers themselves. The logic of such illustrations circled back to the ways in which Ri's memoir and advice literature addressed individual self-reform and self-initiative. That the critique centered on individuals meant there was little conceptual space for workers to link cumulative wage disparities to issues of social stratification or the gendered division of labor.

Strategic and philosophical commitment to material incentives was one thing. Devising and implementing a rational system to calculate these distinctions was another matter altogether. In the variable and complex environment of a factory, office, or other workplace, figuring out who contributed how much to the end product was hardly straightforward. Moreover, divergent interests among workers, managers, local officials, and planners—to name just a few of the involved actors—created myriad challenges. And if individual workers could be blamed for their work ethic, so could managers be blamed for not figuring out and fine tuning a wage system that properly incentivized labor.

The fundamental piece of economic information underlying these challenges was denoted by the term *kijunnyang*—often translated as "quotas," though its broader implications are better captured by the phrase "labor output norms." Used to measure, quantify, and bring together an almost bewildering array of economic activities, the kijunnyang set standards for how much a unit of labor *should* produce in any given amount of time.[10] In lieu of free-floating prices, it provided the data used to try to coordinate disparate economic actors. At the macroeconomic level, the succession of national plans—from the first recovery plan of 1953 to the first Three-Year Plan (1954–

56), the Five-Year Plan (1957–61), and the subsequent Seven-Year Plan (1961–70)—depended on the aggregate sum of all the kijunnyang from the shop floors, mines, rural co-ops, offices, and other enterprises around the country. For economic sectors such as construction, this required the accumulation of information on the productivity of workers in the construction materials industry (cement and concrete block producers, for example), the transportation drivers who delivered materials to construction sites, the architects who designed plans, and all the various skilled and unskilled workers (such as Comrade Ri) involved in erecting buildings, whether they were bricklayers, cement pargers, ditch diggers, electricians, or crane operators. The aggregate of all these kijunnyang provided information about the productive capabilities of specific categories of jobs and various economic units, enabling decisions at the center and in the various ministries as to how to calibrate the future investments of capital, labor, and other inputs in their plans to maximize production. Planning all started and ended with the kijunnyang.

The kijunnyang were just as important for individual enterprises. The single-manager system, introduced from the Soviet Union, put production decisions in the hands of managers, who were judged as having the economic knowledge and experience to make their enterprises run well. Managers needed to evaluate how much to pay and charge for goods and services—key decisions that, in part, had to be factored into the wages to pay out according to the eight-scale wage system. The kijunnyang, then, also provided the basis for these factory-level calculations, including wages and plans for production. This is what managers had to get right—or as one writer put it: "When enterprises are unable to accurately set the kijunnyang, they cannot properly figure out their own capacity and they are unable to devise a production plan that suits their circumstances."[11] Such language obfuscated the implicit warning it held for managers: do not mess up the kijunnyang, for that would end up distorting central plans as well.

Any decision about the kijunnyang determined worker wages and bonuses. It is hardly surprising that workers paid keen attention to how the norms were set and adjusted. It is equally unsurprising, given the divergent interests at play, that the kijunnyang could become a source of bitter conflict. Managers were squeezed between central guidelines and workers' desires for higher wages, and at the same time were put under enormous pressure to meet, let alone exceed, production targets.

In these many ways, the kijunnyang offered a single measure to compare the work of individuals, work teams, and factories—or even complete sectors of the economy. Which was the most efficient? The kijunnyang would tell. How much should a worker be paid? The kijunnyang would tell. How had productivity changed over time? The kijunnyang would tell. From 1953 onward, the push for efficiency pressured everyone to raise the kijunnyang, whether it was by simply working harder, employing new technology to raise productivity, decreasing the costs of production materials, or organizing workers in more efficient ways—even if this meant something as simple as a better use of buckets.

The competing tensions surrounding the kijunnyang emerged as a source of conflict in Comrade Ri's memoir as well, especially as she moved up the ranks to become a leader of a team of cement pargers. Parging (*mijang*) consisted of spreading thin layers of cement over apartment interior walls—whether block or panel construction—so that the walls would be smooth and ready for painting. Once promoted to this more technical work, Ri again turned her attention to devising more efficient techniques—only now, as the leader of a team, she became embroiled in the workplace politics of wages.[12] In her quest to ramp up production, Ri turned to a specific form of labor organization, originally developed in the Soviet Union, that became widespread in Korea across the 1950s—socialist work competitions. These competitions pitted several work teams or enterprises against one another to see who could produce the most within a given amount of time. In the apartment construction industry, teams were judged by their speed in erecting buildings or by the number of rooms they could complete in a day. In theory, under these competitive conditions, workers would be inspired to come up with new techniques to enhance production, which would then be shared with everyone else during a meeting that capped off the competition. Speaking on work competition's impact on productivity, the head of one work brigade in Kangwŏn Province explained that "competition is magnificent."[13]

That planners explicitly labeled these competitions *socialist* showed their concern to distinguish them from the competition inherent in capitalism, and indeed they made every effort to deem them nonexploitative. Their reasoning in this regard relied on the final review session—when, in theory, all workers would gather and (again, in theory) cooperatively share successful strategies developed during the competition. In the ideal scenario, this sharing would then enable all workers to use the new techniques to benefit their pocketbooks while increasing overall production—a win-win, in short. Treatments of socialist competition did not discuss the distinction between wages and labor power in terms of surplus value or the extraction of capital.

Given that Ri's memoir was one of a model worker, it fit with the genre that her use of a socialist work competition succeeded. She reported that her team tripled production. Workers received impressive bonuses. Ri even acknowledged the macro context of a capital and labor shortage by emphasizing that the successes had come from the independent efforts of the workers, who had not received further capital investments or infusion of additional labor. This was the main point: they had done it on their own. For leading this exercise, Comrade Ri received her promotion to the penultimate rank in the wage system, class 7.

Yet the narrative tendencies of the model worker genre could not but erect obstacles—if only to provide the drama and didactic lessons of having the protagonists overcome them. Ri's memoir included socioeconomic challenges that—as is evident when reading it alongside other available sources on the political economy—represented widespread problems. It became clear to Ri that the relentless effort to realize what one economist called "the principle of continuously raising the labor rates of labor" did not always receive a warm welcome from her colleagues.[14] In her search for more efficient parging techniques, Ri recounted turning to one of the older members of her team. Identified only as Sŏngch'ŏl, this more experienced worker admitted that he already knew of superior techniques. When Ri, puzzled, asked him why he had not told anyone, Sŏngch'ŏl chuckled before telling her that his coworkers were not keen to change their methods. The memoir listed their concerns. Some worried the only consequence would be a rise in their kijunnyang—requiring them, in other words, to work harder without extra pay. Others suggested that a rush for more production might affect the quality of the end product—in effect deploying contemporary concerns for quality as an excuse against competitions. Still others worried that an experimental method would not work, leading to a decline in output and, consequently, a decrease in their wages. This worker unease and wariness, although ultimately resolved in Ri's memoir, also appeared in other contemporary reports, which confirmed the stresses placed on workers in the constant search for efficiencies while also suggesting they were not as easily resolved as Ri's memoir indicated.

Socialist work competitions raised questions about one of the Party's fundamental teachings—namely, that a distinguishing feature of capitalist exploitation was manipulation of work tempos to increase output.[15] Workers clearly were not fooled—and authorities knew it. As early as 1955, central economic planners had come to recognize that the types of grumblings incorporated in Comrade Ri's memoir represented a more serious problem.

A leading official in the Ministry of Construction, Pak Kyŏngdŭk, noted that some of the competitions had been plagued by "improper attitudes" among both leaders and workers.[16] This was shorthand for failed results. Without quantifying the breadth of the problems, Pak pointed out what Ri's memoir only intimated: that many competitions were driven by top-down considerations and amounted to little more than directives to work harder. Problems with maintaining consistent production levels were rife. As Kim Yŏnch'ol has pointed out, competitions would create ups and downs in produced amounts.[17] Pak admitted that competitions would often raise work to a frenetic tempo but then, once any rewards were distributed, the new tempo would be used to set new kijunnyang at the old wage rate—higher expectations without increased compensation. Production levels often plunged after a competition, since they could push work tempos to levels that were unsustainable in the long term.[18]

Pak went further. The competitions created negative incentives, he admitted, giving competing teams reason to *not* cooperate. After all, if one team had developed a comparative advantage—whether in organization of labor or in production techniques—why share their innovation with others? This is what had allowed them to win and would guarantee that their production would remain higher than that of other teams. The theory of socialist work competitions assumed goodwill in sharing, but not everyone was as generous as Ri and her team. But as much as Pak expounded on these problems, he was not about to ponder possible solutions that might question the principles themselves. Instead, as was often typical of such critiques, he reemphasized best practices—here, his solution was based on the need to conduct exhaustive, mutual reviews at the conclusion of competitions. By "exchanging the experiences reaped in the competition, criticizing and correcting shortcomings, accurately assessing the victors against those who lagged behind them," these negative tendencies could be countered.[19] The results, he argued, should be widely disseminated on factory-wall newspapers, in visual displays, and even on radio. In this way, Pak acknowledged the disgruntlement of workers, yet he ultimately laid the blame on the way socialist work competitions were implemented, suggesting that the workers, and not the principles themselves, were the problem. This would be the explanation for years to come.[20]

It did not take long for cartoonists to spoof these tensions. In an anonymous cartoon published in the magazine *Worker*, a lathe operator was depicted hiding his machine under a big, dark tarpaulin (see figure 11).[21] His upper torso also thus hidden, he said, "Share my hard-earned 'production secret' with

FIGURE 11. Anonymous, untitled, 1956. "Share my hard-earned 'production secret' with others? I have to keep my secret a secret."

others? I have to keep my secret a secret." The cartoon's humor played off the absurdity of his effort to hide under a tarp in the middle of a massive factory floor where other workers looked on—a haplessness accentuated by his rear end jutting out prominently from under the cover. Yet the cartoon's humor seemingly came with a tinge of sympathy for the worker, whom it depicted as working hard. This was the gentlest of satire—seemingly commiserating with the motivation of the worker to keep his hard-won secrets while heeding the criticism that branded such practices unacceptable. In an example that showed less sympathy, another cartoonist took aim at the workers themselves, suggesting that their complaints about the demands of kijunnyang were empty. The single panel showed a worker crouching under a bar, as if shirking his work duties, and complaining that "the kijunnyang is so high." The caption responded, "Comrade—Please Stand Up" (see figure 12).[22]

With so much at stake in the kijunnyang for central planners, enterprise managers, and workers, there was tremendous pressure to get this figure right. In a large factory with hundreds, even thousands, of workers, it was a

FIGURE 12. Anonymous,
"Comrade—Please Stand Up," 1956.
"The kijunnyang is so high."

challenge to the accounting skills of any manager to determine just who did what, in order to assign them responsibility for a certain quotient of the overall factory output. How should the kijunnyang change over time, as new technology was introduced to certain parts of the production process or as workers acquired new skills through education? How to account for bottlenecks in production, when problems in one part of the factory led to slowdowns in another?[23] Socialist work competitions in the forestry industry had so many problems that their leaders got blamed for poor-quality wood, lack of workplace discipline, and wasted materials—all leading some operations to reach as little as 16 percent of their planned output by the summer of 1954.[24] In 1955 the lumber industry again received a public drubbing, because some of its planners overestimated and others underestimated the kijunnyang of their workforce. Not able to fulfill its production expectations, the lumber industry created problems for other sectors down the production stream, leaving construction sites with idle labor in want of wood.[25] One key factory, the Ch'ŏnnaeri Cement Factory, fell behind in 1954. It reached only 18 percent of its allotted target in April and slipped further to 10.6 percent in June.[26] Without sufficient cement, construction projects slowed down. The answers to the plant's problems were many, yet according to one critic the crux lay in the fact that they wasted labor and other precious resources because they were unable to properly set the output norms for their labor force. How should those workers be compensated when their lower productivity was no fault of their own? The kijunnyang did not provide answers in these cases.

Part of the dilemma in measuring kijunnyang was related to lack of experience and knowledge on the part of factory leaders. Many enterprise managers had little education. Some had been appointed because of personal experience in the colonial period, while others had little experience. All had to receive formal training in socialist value theory and economic planning. A flood of publications emerged to assist them. Some offered the most basic of knowledge. One book, appropriately called *A Primer on Economics* (*Kyŏngje sangsik*), showed this urgency by allocating its first essay to explaining how to figure out the basic production capabilities of an enterprise.[27] At the core of this and other essays was the fact that managers had to learn, within the constraints set by the central ministries, how to figure out the value of goods when there were no free-floating prices to provide them with information. Since production was often organized through a constellation of contracts between enterprises, how much should a manager pay for the various input goods—concrete for a building-block company, for example—necessary for their enterprise? How much should they charge for the commodities they produced, and how much would this leave for the payment of wages? Enterprises were encouraged to sign contracts with one another to set these rates out.[28] These were the most basic decisions. The system of factory autonomy developed after the war gave managers considerable oversight in these realms. Yet while this system rested on the assumption that those involved directly in production were best positioned to make the necessary decisions to maximize the production of their enterprises, many planners were skeptical about the willingness of these managers to fulfill these obligations if their factory's interests diverged from the direction of central planning.

The gap between central plans and the ability of managers to carry them out was evident in the mathematical formula developed to help managers determine kijunnyang for their factories. Even though this was promoted as a "scientific method," most managers blanched at the complexity of the math and data involved. Many resorted to an alternative method. They used the previous year's output figures and rejiggered them with new statistical information about the coming year's production to come up with a figure. In the early 1950s, central authorities begrudgingly gave managers leeway to use the latter method, on the understanding that they would train themselves in the preferable, scientific method.[29] Not surprisingly, given that this method offered no systematic means of appraising one's data and risked repeating previous years' mistakes, the kijunnyang often remained wonky—as regular criticisms from central authorities attested.

As the end of the 1950s approached, the inability to rectify problems with this fundamental category of economic information came to be seen as interfering with the continued growth of the overall economy. One economist wrote, "So long as the kijunnyang are not accurately fixed, labor power cannot be rationally organized, nor can it be used judiciously. And this means that labor productivity rates cannot be raised."[30] By 1959, as the economy grew in complexity, the kijunnyang in many enterprises had become so out of line that the national cabinet ordered a general review of all kijunnyang around the country so that they could be "better rationalized" and reconfigured—a massive undertaking.[31] According to one report about the West Pyongyang Railway Company, workers in administrative positions—in other words, white-collar workers—had low kijunnyang in comparison to the blue-collar workers doing the manufacturing work of actually building railcars.[32] This meant that it was easier for administrators to exceed their quotas, often reaching 110–120 percent, whereas the blue-collar workers fell behind, reaching only 80–90 percent. Salaries followed suit, creating disincentives for those working directly on the assembly line. As a result, "production could not be normalized." It took two months of intensive review, but eventually 350 kijunnyang were identified as in need of change—a result that no doubt legitimated the original call for review, but also served to underscore just how malleable this piece of information remained.[33]

The very fact that the kijunnyang were fundamental yet elusive would eventually lead some of their underlying assumptions to be anxiously scrutinized by Party-state officials. Much of this unease centered on the autonomy of economic enterprises. The single-manager responsibility system had always rested on the assumption that the technocratic expertise of managers would allow them to make better decisions. Even if doubts existed about the degree of that expertise, it was clear that Party members had even less when it came to economic issues. In one symbolic indication of how managers could assert autonomy, they complained about the number of political meetings, arguing that they needed to be limited or held in off-work hours, since they cut into production time.[34] This complaint prioritized production over the activities of local party committees. This was one salvo in a consistent struggle on the part of managers and planners to curtail the influence of low-level Party members on production decisions. As one commentator explained, experience had shown that "when Party units interfered, it weakened the autonomous management system and resulted in tremendous losses to production."[35] Party members were supposed to stay out of production decisions—and central Party-state officials agreed, at first. The corollary of such autonomy, however, was that managers were always supposed to act within the parameters set by Party policies and in line with Party objectives.

Local Party committees were tasked with assuring this adherence.[36] Yet such a "balance," as it was called, was easier in theory than in the hurly-burly of a postwar economy, when managers were under intense pressure to maximize production and local Party members were expected to ensure a smooth functioning of economic policies. Their interests and interpretations did not always align. Nowhere was this clearer than in labor management practices. Remarkably for a self-professed proletarian country, the right to fire employees rested with managers. At a time of labor shortage, however, more problems arose from hiring than from firing. Managers frequently overrode central directives on the allocation of labor, hiring workers outside of the plan and even from the countryside, a direct violation of central labor policies, which Party committees seemed unable to stop.

These sorts of tensions abounded between managerial leaders and factory Party committees. Contemporary commentators often categorized these dual responsibilities as bringing together managerial technical expertise with local Party responsibility over long-term goals and ideology. Whenever a factory or other enterprise failed to reach its output goals, had problems with its kijunnyang, or failed to match quality expectations, the enterprise's management was sure to shoulder blame, yet the question always lingered as to what role the enterprise's Party committee had—or *should* have—played in preventing the failure. There was plenty of blame to go around. As a consequence, the Party struggled to clarify "Party leadership" over the economy at the level of the enterprise. Enterprise-level Party directors received exhortations to be sure to "guide" the enterprise's planning process and to rectify any shortcomings from the previous plan.[37] So, too, were they exhorted to make sure that their enterprises maximized the use of equipment and facilities—which, in the words of one writer, meant ensuring that facilities and technology were used efficiently.[38] Other Party units boasted about how they had been responsible for raising the quality of products.[39] That each of these cases might also fall under the supposed purview of managerial, not Party, responsibility demonstrated the vagueness of any clear boundary dividing responsibilities. The very ambiguity of the system—managerial independence so long as decisions supported Party policies and ideology—ensured an uneasy relationship. There was a lot of wiggle room. Nevertheless, no systematic critique of these tensions as inherent to the system arose. Instead, when a problem arose, individuals—whether on the managerial or the Party side—generally received the blame, their actions presented as either an overstepping of their responsibilities or an insufficient effort.[40] The shortcomings arising out of this uneasy arrangement presaged deeper conflicts that would arise as the construction sector continued to underperform and became embroiled in national-level political machinations.

GENDERED SOLUTIONS TO LABOR SHORTAGES

If all the efforts at rectifying the kijunnyang aimed to heighten productivity through efficiency gains, another strategy that likewise sought to adapt to the capital and labor shortage was to mobilize more laboring bodies—in other words, to add to the aggregate national labor pool. The difficulty, however, was that—unlike China or the Soviet Union—Korea did not have boundless supplies of potential workers, especially given the mass death of the war and the need to conscript men for military duty in the context of division.[41]

Where would extra bodies be found? At first, attention fell on private merchants, who had begrudgingly been allowed to continue trading in order to help revive the economy after the war. In 1958, when these last of the so-called petite bourgeoisie were incorporated into the national distribution system, the economic planners had to look elsewhere. Their focus turned to the single largest labor reserve—women who, unlike Ri, had yet to take up wage work. As Ri's memoir and other contemporary sources made clear, the mobilization of this labor reserve fit the logic of maximization. Yet these same sources indirectly showed that attempts to realize a more gender-inclusive working environment taxed dominant masculinist practices, even as they reinforced gender hierarchies. Along the way, they underlined the centrality of women's wage labor to the political economy.

Official mobilization policies worked themselves out against a conceptualization that juxtaposed structural obstacles against ideological commitments, as if there were no relationship between them. This binary, in turn, came to be mapped onto the differences between Party-state policies and the energies and abilities of individual women and men. As the post-1958 shift emphasizing ideology developed, this distinction became the basis for the central Party-state's devolution of many of its own responsibilities onto the shoulders of women in their local social worlds.

Comrade Ri's personal biography presented the type of transformation commonly featured in the media: that of an active wartime participant who turned into a worker committed to building socialism.[42] Soldier was transformed into worker, thus blurring the distinction between fighting and producing. This vision of the ferocious female fighter merging with the committed worker had a long staying power, becoming a standard image in the era's visual culture. Yet statistics about workforce composition revealed a less sanguine reality. Fewer women followed in Ri's footsteps than these stories suggested. In the final year of the conflict, 1953, women constituted 26.2 percent of the labor force. Three years later the figure dipped to 19.9 percent—just under one in five workers—not what the 1946 proclamation of the gender equality laws seemed to promise.[43]

Despite the emphasis they placed on mobilizing female wage labor, high-level economists and theorists devoted little energy to figuring out how to boost participation rates.[44] As much as they called for the pool of workers to be expanded, for these largely male planners the Woman Question remained largely a question for women. They looked to the leaders and members of the Korean Democratic Women's Union. Like all other mass organizations, the Women's Union was tasked with implementing and preparing the conditions for the furtherance of KWP policies. On the labor front, this meant twin priorities: creating a more inclusive work environment to meet the desires of their members for wage work, while also satisfying the Party-state goals to raise participation rates to support macroeconomic growth. Yet these seemingly consistent goals, when brought into practice in local social worlds, were often revealed not to harmonize so easily with one another.

In this authoritarian environment, in which explicit critique of Party-state policies remained unimaginable, the editors of the union's monthly *Women of Korea* faced a delicate dilemma: how could they highlight the struggles faced by their membership without their reports being seen as criticism of Party-state leaders or their policies? Writers adopted a variety of strategies. One overarching approach offered a gendered twist on the developmentalist narrative common to the era. It involved a two-step narrative. First, it acclaimed the progress achieved since the Party-state had come to power or since the end of the war. Usually told in an upbeat, appreciative tone and buoyed by statistics or case studies, this approach also often framed the dilemma in a before-and-after mode—favorably comparing the present with the past—or argued how much better it was in the North than in the South. Second, it moved to a discussion of what still needed to be done now and in the future, and how readers could help. Usually, the developmentalist approach rationalized a sense of collective delayed gratification: we have come a long way and, it seemed to promise, together we will get there. The proviso, of course, was that followers needed to heed the advice of the author.

What remained clearly off the table as a form of critique was for writers to use the gender equality laws as a standard against which to measure current practices and point out unfulfilled promises.

Writers employed this development narrative with a great variety in tone while mixing in a wide range of advice. Some authors clearly lingered longer over obstacles, elaborating and analyzing contemporary problems with only the briefest contrast with the past or nod to the future. They emphasized the challenges and what was necessary to meet them, more than their overcoming. This lent a more critical, if still careful, tone to the articles. Others hinted at deeper critiques without actually articulating them, as if they sought to stimulate readers into thinking through implications. The selection of issues to cover was also telling. Certain issues or policies received only the most cursory of treatment by editors, in comparison to others that received robust and fulsome treatment. Some Party-state policies or slogans were taken up, explored, and pushed in directions unimagined when first proposed by higher authorities, while others were quietly dropped. Open critiques tended to rest explicitly within the framework of Party-state policies—as with Ri on labor practices—yet at times expanded beyond them, if only implicitly. These varieties in coverage, however nuanced, showed editorial preferences and suggested a more varied writing culture.

Despite these nuances, writers hesitated to challenge explicitly the era's dominant masculinist sensibilities, whether in the Party-state itself or more broadly. In a time of criticism culture, when people were often called out by name, generally only the blandest, almost slogan-like expressions appeared. An "uncooperative" husband or a "benighted" man—these expressions gestured at deeper forms of discrimination, yet again deployed a common rhetorical device, reflecting the era's individuating impulse. In this way, even as writers focused on current problems, they did not delve into the structural sources of the problem, let alone invoke the gender equality laws to criticize current practices or planning strategies. A worker could be publicly called out by name for lack of discipline, and factory leadership could be named in criticisms of their own failures, but it was rare to find anyone publicly named for their discriminatory practices against women at work or at home. All this showed how the Women's Union, while working to promote the varied interests of its membership, could only acknowledge that the Party-state had silently de-prioritized what the 1946 legislation had so tantalizingly offered— even if the Party-state's own rhetoric loudly proclaimed its commitment to the overarching goal of equality, however redefined.

The parameters of critique were visible in Comrade Ri's memoir as she explored the two main causal reasons—structural obstacles and individual ideology—widely used to explain the lagging wage-labor participation rates of women. This binary structured many contemporary discussions of political economy, becoming especially powerful after 1958. On the issue of the wage-labor force, its use displayed a deeply gendered dynamic. Ri's memoir confronted one structural obstacle—the gendered segregation of labor—when she decided to form a brigade of exclusively women workers.[45] She recounted the source of her inspiration as a pair of female ditch diggers. When she was walking on the street, she saw this pair of workers keeping pace with their male colleagues. Stopping to talk to them, she learned they had been working for two years. Ri asked them what trade skills they had learned during that time, to which they replied, "Skills, what skills?"[46] Ri recalled being dumbfounded at their response.

In Ri's telling, the meeting with two ditch diggers who had not been trained during two years of labor for any other, more advanced labor became the departure for a critique of the underutilization of women's labor potential. Too often, she complained, women received only menial job assignments and were subordinated on job sites to male workers, who received choice assignments. She turned her critical eye back toward her own work unit, noting that women handled carrying and cleaning responsibilities in assistant positions to men. Ri did not explore the reasons for this disparity. She did not mention patriarchy. Her account implied gender discrimination and segregation without naming it. She did not point out how the wage scale's privileging of skill left women with lower wages. Nor did she scale up her analysis from her construction site to a broader social critique or consider larger structural issues of the political economy. She restrained herself from criticizing any individual men, let alone leaders, in her construction team. More significantly, she was silent about the gender equality laws, refraining from showing how her team's practices violated their spirit, if not their specific provisions. All these critiques were implicit, subtly made, and available for her readers to construct from the information she provided.

Despite these implications, her explicit critique remained framed within the Party's principle of maximizing the labor potential of every single worker—here brought in to address the lack of opportunities for women to do higher-value wage labor. This was about wasting the potential labor power of women and what that meant for the macroeconomy. Moreover, as her memoir went on to show, the remedy rested not with social or gendered critiques of the obstacles, however defined, but again with the individuals themselves. The key to Ri's story was that she did something about it. If workers like the two ditch diggers did not have sufficient opportunities, Ri would create them. She soon recruited women to make a work team specializing in parging. This was tricky labor and required special training. As skilled laborers, pargers received preferential pay. Moreover, the occupation was virtually a male preserve in an industry already dominated by men. Ri's efforts immediately encountered resistance and skepticism from male colleagues, who doubted her ability to carry out her plans. Other men complained that women were not needed in this line of work. "They'll give up after a few days," one anonymous observer was reported to have said.[47] As much as she registered this resistance, Ri did not explore it. She quickly brushed it aside and proved it wrong by getting on with the task at hand.

Ri's effort to launch an all-women's work team was set against a backdrop of two Party-state policies that had sought to mobilize the reserve of women wage laborers. The first initiative, begun in 1956, was intended to stem the unregulated flow of male job seekers from countryside to city. After the war, young rural men moved from the countryside, where life had been upended by collectivization, in search of work in higher-paying urban industries. However much central institutions tried to block the migration, the migrants still came—just one of the many limits of central Party-state power. The issue came to a head in 1955, when overall agricultural production fell short and the northern regions of the country were hit by a famine. There were many reasons for the famine, but one explanation the Party-state took up was that migration had left too few people in the countryside to produce food. Further crackdowns on unregulated population movement followed but remained ineffective.

By 1956, central authorities tried a gendered solution. They turned to "dependent family members" (*puyang kajok*)—an expression for adult members of a household, generally assumed to be wives/mothers who were not employed in wage labor and, thus, were dependent on the income of the husband/father—for a solution. The policy was, in effect, a substitution strategy: fill city jobs by bringing more women into wage labor, so that demand would be satisfied and there would be no empty positions tempting rural men to the cities.[48] The policy was a further admission of serious economic challenges in the countryside.[49]

As was conventional for major policy initiatives, the press followed the policy announcement with endless accounts of dependent family members following suit, partly to show the success of the policy and partly to inspire and/or pressure others. Stories abounded—sixty-one women joined the Third Pyongyang Construction Team,[50] for example, while another production team was formed by nothing but dependent family members.[51] Stories highlighted individuals—such as Yi Poksil, who found a job in the same tobacco processing plant as her husband[52]—or the large numbers of women finding wage work, like the fifteen hundred married women who were hired in four months to meet the expansion needs of a textile factory.[53] No aggregate figures appeared for the overall effect of the policy, yet it was sufficiently high-profile that some newspaper readers took it upon themselves to complain, in letters to the editor, that neither women nor officials in their part of the country did much to carry out the policy.[54]

The reportage emphasized the barriers to women's wage employment. As captured in a national newspaper headline, "How Are the Work Conditions for Dependent Family Members Being Guaranteed?," the onus rested primarily with the local factory and Party authorities. They were blamed for not preparing the type of facilities, especially day care, needed to support women. So, too, were they criticized for believing that dependent family members' "abilities just weren't good enough." Their thinking would have to change and conditions improved, the article argued, especially if mothers were to come out and put in regular workdays.[55] Others reported factories resisting the policy, with managers complaining that "older women or women with children will just be an obstacle to production." Eventually the factory turned the situation around, offering day care, kindergarten, cafeterias, and laundry facilities—this was the ideal. Some factories went so far as to deliberately employ couples in the same enterprise so as to make transport and child care more seamless, according to reports.[56]

If the efforts of employers and existing conditions provided one avenue of critique, another focused on the willingness of women to take up wage-work opportunities. "Cultural levels"—the same usage as in the advice literature—did the explanatory work.[57] Such reports celebrated the enlightenment of the dependent family member, in a form of narrative that increasingly held women individually accountable for their work status and tended to chart their path to rejection of dependence. Accordingly, *puyang kajok* took on a derogatory tone, suggesting someone who did not have self-awareness of the need to contribute their labor.

A new icon began to emerge, juxtaposed in contrast to the dependent family member: the mother-worker (*mosŏng rodongja*).[58] As Pak Yŏngja has shown, the idea of the mother-worker adapted Soviet models to Korean conditions, creating what she has called the "reformist worker, revolutionary mother."[59] Similarly, Suzy Kim has written about how, between 1945 and 1950, it was common to present "revolutionary mothers" as "ideal selfless public servants" for everyone to emulate.[60] The icon of the mother-worker—its priority tellingly indicated by the order of the two words (i.e., not "working mother")—played the type of hortative role both Pak and Kim suggest. Yet their visible presence in the media came with what might be called an "even" qualification: it was precisely because their wage labor participation *as* housewives and *as* mothers required extra effort and had conventionally been considered rare that their participation was all the more impressive. If "even" housewife-mothers could take up wage labor, the logic of these enjoinments went, then no one else had any excuses. Even as the expression extolled, it reproduced gender hierarchies. By the mid-1960s, poems were penned in praise of mother-workers.[61]

A second Party-state initiative, launched in 1958, began to formalize the instrumentalization of gender as policy by categorizing work positions as feminine or masculine. Statistics for that year revealed that despite a gradually rising participation rate, the full employment of women still fell short of goals: 34.9 percent, or a little over a third of the labor force, were women wage laborers.[62] This second policy was launched in that context. Every enterprise across the country received instructions to scour their workplaces for positions that were deemed suitable for women but currently held by men. Once identified as ostensibly "feminine," these positions would be emptied of male occupants, who would be transferred to jobs deemed inappropriate for women but fine for men—"masculine" jobs. The seriousness of this policy became clear when the prestigious Bank of Chosŏn emerged as the target of an unusually harsh critique for its hiring practices in the main national newspaper.[63] Entitled "Banks Are a Work Sector Extremely Suitable for Women," the article began by showing how even though enterprises had been actively encouraged to hire women, the percentage of female employees at the bank had declined. From roughly half, who worked "gloriously" during the war, the number had fallen to 38 percent in 1955, only to keep declining annually: 27.1 percent the following year, then 24.1 percent in 1957, and 24.0 percent in the first half of 1958—below the national average.

Statistics aside, what clearly irritated the author, Pak Chongha, were the bank's excuses. To the bank's claims that after the war women had withdrawn from work for the home and that now there were not enough willing female wage laborers in Pyongyang, Pak huffed a curt "Completely unacceptable excuse." Pak went on to undermine their second excuse—"the number of positions that women can carry out has declined"—by visiting bank branches around the country. Pak noted that in seventeen city and rural branches, there was not one woman at the level of director or above. In the Sunchŏn county branch, for example, there was only one female employee among a total of seventeen. More pointedly, Pak described observing young men sitting at the reception windows, stamping statements. Even though a couple of the employees told superiors that their jobs taking care of receipts and disbursements were suitable for women, the head of the branch—and here, Pak took the rare step of giving his name, Hwang Pongsu—ignored their suggestion. The author went on to call on the bank authorities to abandon their mistaken reasoning that bank work was "special" as an excuse not to hire women. Finally, the article urged the bank to understand the importance of Party-state policies for resolving the overall labor problem. To be called out in the national paper for not attending to central policies was no light offense and likely ensured a shake-up at the bank. No follow-up stories appeared in the newspaper to judge the impact of the criticism, however. Yet already, in the very year of its announcement, some economists expressed doubt about the initiative's efficacy.[64]

Nevertheless, the logic of the policy built on long-standing gendered assumptions that women and men had natural affinities disposing them to certain types of work and not others. At times, the Women's Union uncritically reproduced these gendered assumptions. At other times—much as Comrade Ri was to do—it turned them around to its short-term advantage. When Ri started organizing her all-female work team, she encountered precisely these naturalized assumptions about gendered work. Her memoir depicted a male worker grumbling, "There are jobs for women and there are jobs for men"—a not-so-subtle suggestion that her team should stay out of the male-dominated parging line of work and find something more suitable for women. To be sure, Ri presented this unnamed worker in a negative light and as a type of stock male character who did not appreciate the shifting gender norms on which socialism would be built. However, quoting her colleague's expression of these sentiments within a context that underlined their absurdity was as far as Ri could go in her critique. The enormity of directly challenging this gendered norm revealed itself when the most powerful man in the country, Kim Il Sung, repeatedly reproduced the same logic in his speeches. The leader, in speaking about women's wage work, encouraged them to go to the light industries "where jobs are suitable to their physique and ability" or, as he put it on other occasions, where jobs are suitable to "weaker" bodies.[65] Needless to say, Kim's comments went unaddressed in

Women of Korea or any other venue and made any general critique of these naturalizing assumptions all the more challenging.

For all the attention given to women's wage labor as holding the solution for the labor shortage, central Party-state policies did not draw distinctions about the *kind* of work, but only about whether one worked or not. It was not unusual for individual women who did not find suitable employment to be blamed for being too picky, without consideration of access.[66] Generally, however, since the end of the war, more women had eagerly entered a wider array of wage employment than had ever been open to them before. The covers of *Women of Korea* revealed women photographed in virtually every line of work, from truck assembly line workers to bricklayers, from machine gun–toting soldiers to researchers at a chemical institute, from welders to tractor drivers.[67] The import of their initiatives—for the overall political economy, family life, gender relations, and income levels, to name a few—cannot be overestimated. Nevertheless between the magazine covers and in other media, photographs revealed another stratum of women's labor, for which the Party-state did not release data, revealing that the upsurge in employment remained concentrated in segregated lines of work, often light industries (see figure 13). Photographs show food production facilities in Pyongyang, Kaesŏng, Sinŭiju, and Sunch'on populated exclusively by women.[68] Department store clerks were seen in the photographic record as exclusively female.[69] Women workers might dominate a specific job site, such as the Pyongyang Porcelain Factory or the Ch'ŏngjin Textile Factory, even if the record across the larger industry was more mixed.[70] The photographic evidence suggests that it was extremely rare to find a man sitting behind a sewing machine among dozens, if not hundreds, of female workers. Such photographs appeared without comment, often used as evidence for how the changing times led to women finding more wage work. Other photographs, of course, showed workplaces consisting solely of men—published, of course, without any remark on segregation.[71] Occasionally, sources revealed a single point of data, as was the case when authorities reported that female laborers occupied 60 percent of the consumer industries—a statistic presented as showing progress.[72] It was unaccompanied by any mention of the lower wages and inferior work conditions of light industry. Participation in wage labor itself, not the terms of that participation, was what mattered. Gendered segregation of labor, with women in lower-paid positions, was not deemed a problem by authorities.

Yet Comrade Ri used segregation as a strategy in order to create a unit that would afford greater opportunities in a skilled métier—together with the

청진 방적 공장 연사 직장의 일부

FIGURE 13. Anonymous, "Some Workers from the Chŏngjin Textile Factory," 1961.

higher wages that came with it. While the gendered circumstances surrounding her initiative did not receive a fulsome critique, the implications were clear. And nothing confirmed them better than the fact that her team grew quickly, learning new skills and earning more money.

The team's work did not go smoothly, however. The memoir again turned to efficiency. To Ri's chagrin, many new workers came late, left early, or did not show up at all. The memoir presented Ri, young and unmarried, as puzzled by workers who did not share her all-out sense of enthusiasm. She set out to search for reasons. Soon enough, Ri encountered what she called her colleagues' "everyday life problems" (*saenghwalsang munje*). Most of them were mother-workers, she realized, whose responsibilities as housewives and mothers interfered with their abilities to put in unencumbered workdays. These types of life problems became all the more evident to Ri when she got a peek at the lunch of a coworker. The food was "terrible."[73]

With this example, Ri raised one of the biggest economic challenges of the late 1950s—the provision of foodstuffs beyond the National Distribution

System. By 1958, the Party-state announced that the "food problem" had been "basically" resolved. Yet *resolved* simply meant that the rationing system had succeeded in putting the type of 1955 famine behind them and provided families a varying degree of grain and protein depending on the age, gender, and occupation of their members. What it did not provide were any type of supplementary foods—side dishes (*p'anch'an*), let alone treats—and many basic cooking ingredients. Families had to buy these on their own, which, after the 1958 elimination of private merchants, meant an exclusive reliance on various levels of central and local state-run stores. Access was uneven, as was distribution. Reports abounded of certain foodstuffs being stranded in rural areas with no transportation to get them to the cities.[74] Distribution of such basic commodities as salt was uneven.[75] Especially significant for working families, the promised industrialization of foodstuffs—*kimch'i, kkaktugi*, and the like—lagged, as did the creation of public cafeterias and restaurants. However much the media celebrated with developmentalist-style stories the opening of new restaurants and promised more to come, public eating establishments remained too few.[76] The promises that more cafeterias and industrially produced foods were imminent offered small consolation for Ri's colleague with the terrible food. The example was raised in the memoir, of course, in order to show Ri and her colleague resolving this food challenge.

Yet in providing a resolution that depended on the ingenuity of the two women—their self-responsibility and initiative—the account deflected attention away from the very real structural obstacles shaping the lives of working women. The same capital and labor shortages that shaped the center's call for introducing more female labor into the economy also led to inadequate investment in the services that would ease their entrance into the labor force. Yet, in a type of unresolved circularity, the very decision to prioritize investments in heavy industry was creating the economic growth that, by the mid- to late 1950s, was hindered by the shortage of labor that the reserve of women laborers was supposed to resolve. The political economy behind the "terrible food" of Ri's colleague did not feature in her memoir, of course. Instead, the power to resolve this immediate dilemma increasingly rested on the shoulders of individual workers. With structural solutions not coming, solutions were centered on the ideological commitment and "cultural levels" of individual women workers themselves—and the suggestion of Ri's memoir was that they should get on with it.

Nowhere was this tension between the structural challenges of the political economy and the ideological commitment of the individual more apparent than in arguably the single largest impediment to women's wage work: day care. As early as 1954, the state cabinet recognized day care's significance, calling for its expansion.[77] Its provision led to impressive growth: a twenty-seven-fold increase in available spots in 1957 compared to 1949, even if this was calculated from a low base number.[78] Nevertheless, demand far outstripped supply. The regular openings of new day care facilities enabled optimistic reports on the upward trend—precisely the type of developmentalist arguments that highlighted progress while asking readers to be patient with the immediate shortcomings.[79]

Not only did day care come to be linked to giving women the opportunity to join the paid workforce, but reports also connected child care specifically to production. Such was the case with two units in the 13th Construction Team, which had not been meeting their production goals. When the reasons for these deficiencies were investigated, according to one account, it was determined that many mother-workers regularly missed work due to the need to care for children. A ninety-spot day care, created from the unit's own resources, solved the problem, enabling "women workers with children to be at ease and restore their fervor for work."[80] And it was not unusual for these positive stories to give credit to the Party-state, typically through the voice of workers, as in the case of Kim Yongha, who, after her first few days of work while her daughter went to day care, was quoted expressing her appreciation: "This is the first time I've been able to work in a factory."[81]

Central authorities sufficiently appreciated the centrality of day care to the labor shortage that they seem to have given the green light to the media to allow criticism of day care's uneven provision. Many day care facilities, reports began to point out, were too far from worksites or too far from home. Provincial towns lagged behind urban centers, they complained, and even within a single city, some workers gained access while their neighbors did not.[82] One solution aimed to have day care administered not by state ministries but by the work enterprises themselves. Conveniently for central state organs, transferring this responsibility also relieved them of the financial burden. As factories and offices hired more women, the enterprises came under pressure to establish—with their own funds, of course—day care spots for the children of their workers. The assumption was always that the day care spots accommodated mother-workers, not father-workers.[83]

Yet factory-funded day care presented a special problem: quality. At the same time that the media celebrated the opening of new facilities, a quieter series of reports—without endearing photos of happy children quietly napping or playing—began to include complaints about the facilities.[84] Such was the case with a factory in Namp'o, which, according to one report, did not even have its own building. Instead, two people supervised thirty children in a single room in an offsite temporary worker's house—exactly the type of ramshackle housing out of which so many across the country were trying to move. The room did not have proper furniture, and what few toys it contained were of no interest to the children. Such facilities, this complaint asserted, did not help mothers relax and make progress in their paid work.[85] Another critique simply reported that many day care facilities did not even have balls for the children to play with.[86] The shifting of responsibility downward onto enterprises may have relieved the Party-state of a financial burden, but it did not resolve the problem. Enterprise managers, themselves under pressure to increase output at a time when they, too, were underfinanced, likely calculated that the returns from investing in child care facilities paled in comparison to funding production. Ball bearings over balls, in short.

This devolution also enabled a particular politics of criticism: central state authorities complained about facilities in such a way that enterprises took the blame without reflecting back on Party-state policies and decisions. It was the factory's fault, these articles suggested, and it was their shortcomings that interfered with achievement of central goals and policies. Moreover, allowing the users of day care to express their concerns in stories and letters to the editor enabled a type of bottom-up censure, putting extra pressure on enterprises. In this context, the voices of women workers—or, most powerfully, those of women *wanting* to work but unwilling to do so because they remained anxious about entrusting their offspring to what they described as ramshackle outfits—emerged as powerful reproaches of the conditions of day care facilities. "Worry-free" (*ansim*) day care emerged as a stock phrase to emphasize the urgent need for high-quality services.

Within this context of underfunding and shifting responsibility, day care became one more social realm in which the primary burden ultimately came to be shouldered by working women. In January 1956, *Women of Korea* proclaimed a new way of providing child care, one in which, in the words of the article's author, Chŏng Chŏnghyŏp, a mother of three, women took care of the problem "on their own" (*chabal*). Women in the Sŏhŭng neighborhood of western Pyongyang had access to only distant day care, Chŏng explained. The inconvenience led many mother-workers to miss work and many others not to take up wage labor at all. With the encouragement of the Pyongyang Reconstruction Bureau, women in the neighborhood decided to take matters into their own hands: they self-organized a day care service, agreeing that each mother would finance it with a small monthly donation. The neighborhood committee provided a house with a coal stove for winter, and some of the fathers did repair work. In a demonstration of the pent-up demand, seventy-five children showed up. A couple of local women with experience in teaching took up the responsibility of overseeing the day care. Children who had played on their own, causing much anxiety for their mothers, slowly became accustomed to "life with rules," Chŏng pointed out, as they benefited from the discipline. All the mothers were happy, she reported, and the number of women who placed their children in the day care and went out to work for the first time "increased every day." Soon mothers in nearby neighborhoods followed their example, the article continued, setting up their own child care facilities.[87]

From the central state, down to enterprises, down to mother-workers— the organizing, staffing, housing, and financing responsibilities all shifted downward until it was up to individual mother-workers to organize and finance neighborhood child care in order to pursue their personal desires for wage work.[88] This ad hoc organization and devolution of responsibilities without financing onto women in their local social worlds would become a regular strategy for officials to off-load their own administrative challenges.

APARTMENTS AS A REVOLUTIONARY MASTER NARRATIVE

Despite all the problems generated by the capital and labor shortages—from determining the accuracy of kijunnyang to the challenge of creating local conditions to enable more gender-inclusive work environments—apartment buildings still got built. Never in the history of the peninsula, in the North or the South, had there been such a wave of housing construction. Contemporary media coverage may, at times, have gotten caught up in its own breathless rhetoric, yet there is no denying the material makeover of urban life beginning in 1954.[89] This physical transformation from the rubble of war to soaring new-style architecture became a powerful means for the young Party-state to match its rhetoric of being at the forefront of history. It was ostensibly taking care of, protecting, and leading the people toward that promised transition—this was revolution through apartments, complete with electricity and running water.

The sprawling narrative of apartment construction was not just one for the history books. It was a material and, most importantly, a participatory narrative. It was visible, inclusive, and experienced—visible in the materiality of the blocks and mortar of buildings, inclusive in that it involved the labor of countless construction teams and all the subsidiary industries that made their work possible, and experienced insofar as people walking among and living inside buildings saw new homes as a reward for all their past and current struggles. Moreover, in a divided country, when North and South each competed to present itself as the sole legitimate government, the growing verticality of the North's cityscapes offered one of the most powerful arguments in its favor: the North's collective present was emerging out of the same past as that of the South, but the photographs hinted at a comparatively more promising future. Part of the power of this narrative was that it depended on pre-collective-era notions of time and progress that exceeded the grasp of the Party-state. It had a longer history than revolutionary time and did not need to be invented anew like the emerging histories of Kim Il Sung's anti-Japanese partisan movement. As a result, the media worked hard to bend the narrative and insert the Party-state into these accounts, crediting it with responsibility for the changes.

Photographs amplified the experience of walking the changing streets, especially for those not able to make it to urban centers. The building of worker apartments constituted a disproportionate share of media coverage. One of the first multistory worker apartments opened its doors in 1954. The image of its five-story facade appeared everywhere, becoming a prominent symbol of urban transformation and of all that seemed possible in the cities.[90] Located on the Taedong River and constructed in what was termed a "modern style," the apartment featured an elevated tower on the corner and balconies with ornate ironwork on the top floors. One commentator gushed that it was "beautiful and rich with national sentiment."[91] Yet it would soon be overshadowed by the sheer quantity of photographed edifices. Often shooting from street level, looking upward, photographers used the distorted perspective of wide-angle lenses to accentuate the looming presence of the facades. They looked like monuments—quite literally concrete testaments to the successes of reconstruction. Just as frequently, an apartment building— or even an entire neighborhood—was photographed in the middle of construction, the bustle of workers and cranes showing construction in action, a promise of future residences for more workers.[92]

Changes were also quantified, as batteries of statistics rendered development into numbers intended less to inform than to amaze. Greater productivity, more rapid speed, decreased costs, saved efficiencies—a steady stream of figures testified to all of these. Many weeks in 1958, the *Rodong sinmun* (*Worker Daily*) posted summaries of construction output for Pyongyang.[93] One team was up by 160 percent.[94] Another was up by 170 percent.[95] In 1955, there was a total of 1,399,000 square meters of new housing; the next year, 1,138,000 square meters. These figures never got broken down into numbers of residential units. Mass quantities and speed were their point. Statistics extended to the provincial cities as well, with articles regularly detailing the "changing face" of midsize cities such as Haeju, Sinŭiju, Kaesŏng, Kanggye, Ch'ŏngjin, Sariwŏn, Wŏnsan, Hyesan, and Hamhŭng.[96] Statistics became so widely used that newspapers began to be criticized by the central media watchdog for overusing numbers instead of focusing on person-centered stories.[97]

All these photographs and statistics gained meaning in the context of the peninsula's division. South Korea was experiencing its own housing crisis.[98] Historians have long emphasized competition over consumption in the Cold War, as best captured in what has come to be known as the "kitchen debate." In 1959 the secretary general of the Soviet Union, Nikita Khrushchev, argued with U.S. vice president Richard Nixon in Moscow over which country produced the superior consumer products for the homes of their citizens.[99] A meeting like this between leaders of North and South was impossible in those years—just one indication of how much more severe tensions were on the peninsula than between Washington and Moscow. Yet rivalry over quality-of-life issues was familiar to all Koreans, since each regime sought to represent itself as the best protector of popular interests.[100] In the peninsula, though, this was not a competition over kitchen appliances, which were a problem of more wealthy nations. As in much of the postcolonial world, the Cold War between the two Koreas rested more on who had a roof over their head, not what went into a dwelling.[101] On this front, already by 1957, North Korean urban residents appeared better off than their Seoul working-class counterparts—a gap that the North was not shy about trumpeting through regular and insistent coverage of the South's housing crisis.[102]

Controversies in Seoul over low-quality housing made the North's propaganda efforts easier. One of the grand ironies of the inter-Korean rivalry was that many of the domestic critiques offered by conservative groups—those most insistent on red-baiting—provided fodder for northern propaganda. Southern newspapers, government reports, and statistical yearbooks were regularly cited by the North's media.[103] Even so, what was a complicated amalgam of social and policy problems about unlawful housing inhabited by roughly one-third of Seoul's population was reframed into simplistic

가리울 수 없는 현실

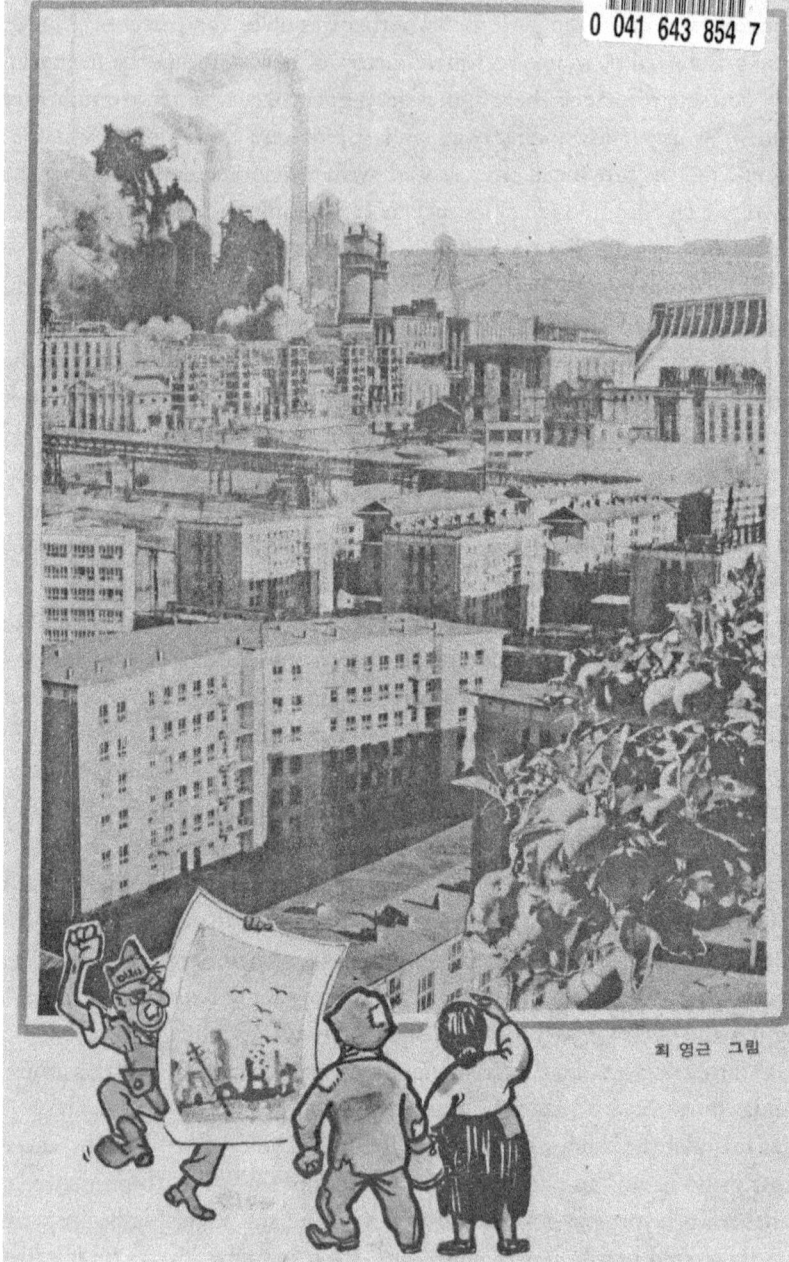

최 영근 그림

FIGURE 14. Ch'oe Yŏnggŭn, "Unconcealable Realities," 1963.

North-to-South, compare-and-contrast arguments to reinforce the refrain about the superiority of socialism.[104] Articles contrasting the two capital cities became standard fare—usually with a title like "Paradise and Hell" and featuring photographs that juxtaposed a happy Pyongyang family, ensconced in a comfortable apartment, with a homeless parent and child on the streets of Seoul.[105] Reports regularly associated homelessness with unemployment.[106] These stories were endless—and cartoonists did not miss out on this opportunity for fun. One long-running comic strip recounted the travails of a homeless mother and a shoeshine boy trying to survive on the streets of Seoul, a story line in which three men living in a discarded sewer pipe made an occasional appearance.[107]

That the South also engaged in representing the North in a reciprocal fashion did not go unrecognized by the northern media. One magazine offered a reflection on this propaganda war with a photograph-cum-cartoon that poked fun at mutually incriminating inter-Korean representation (see figure 14). In the background was a photograph of new apartments and factories built in the North. In the cartoon's foreground stood an American soldier, who was trying to block a South Korean couple's view of the background North Korean scene. Depicted as poor with their patch-covered clothing, the South Korean couple avoided the American's efforts at propaganda. He held a distorted image of the North as barren and unrecovered from the war, titled "This Is North Korea." But the American soldier was not happy and stomped petulantly on the ground in anger because the couple looked not at his propaganda but behind him at the supposedly real image of North Korea. The illustrator of the cartoon, Ch'oe Yŏnggŭn, titled this competitive representation "Unconcealable Realities."[108] Such images, together with stories about southern homelessness and poverty, were always a corollary to the images of successful construction, particularly of apartment accommodations. Their presence ensured that even images that did not directly reference the South (such as the one seen on this book's cover) would likely be read contrastively. Division culture was never far away.

And if apartment buildings, like even the most intimate features of the New Living, were always framed by the politics of division, they would also turn out to be one of the realms where contemporary high-level Party machinations would make their presence felt.

The Perils of Material Incentives?

A cartoon published in a monthly magazine, *Worker*, in 1955 offered an unusual interpretation of the relation between ideology and economic growth. The cartoon, originally published in the Chinese newspaper *Workers' Daily* (*Gongren ilbo*), was one more instance of the transnational circulation of socialist culture. Read from bottom to top and right to left, the comic juxtaposed two lathe operators on the shop floor. The perspiration of the first worker showed that he was laboring with effort while dreaming of the thick wad of money he would earn as a bonus for his troubles. The second worker, by contrast, labored while dreaming not of his earnings but of how he was contributing to the future goal of building socialism. And the panels on the left compared the economic effects of the two states of mind. The caption was blunt: "Perspectives Are Different and So Are Results."

These two visions of incentives for workers—the first material and the other ideological—touched upon a fundamental issue in Marxism that would lead to much rancor within the socialist bloc. One of Marx's most fundamental—and brilliant—economic theories was his explanation of the surplus value of labor. Wages for a day's work, Marx explained, were deceptive because at a surface level they claimed to pay workers in exchange for one day's labor. In fact, wages underpaid workers, since a worker's labor power for one day actu-

FIGURE A. Anonymous, "Perspectives Are Different and So Are Results," 1955.

ally produced greater value than the worker received in wages. This margin between the value produced and the wages received was what Marx called surplus value. That workers did not receive the full value of their labor was the exploitation Marx condemned. This analysis provided one key principle for how capitalism was organized in order to extract the maximum amount of profit from workers' labor power.

For revolutionary states proclaiming themselves socialist, Marx's analysis of capital extraction presented a quandary. How should they organize the economy so as to avoid this kind of exploitation, with its inevitable social inequities? Was increasing wages as an incentive fundamentally contrary to socialist principles because it reproduced the extractive principles of surplus value? Or should workers, as the theoretical owners of the means of production, labor solely on behalf of socialist ideals? Acrimonious debates over this question divided the socialist world. Most famously, Maoist commitments to ideological solutions pitted China against the Soviet Union, which had frequently turned to material incentives. By the 1960s, China had labeled the Soviet Union revisionist due to these differences.

As vitriolic as this debate would become on the international stage, it had little effect on North Korean policy. Economic and theoretical journals hardly mentioned it. This was because Korean central planners had, from the get-go, put material incentives at the heart of their economic growth strategies. Workers received their wages on an eight-level scale that rewarded more highly skilled and productive work. Annual bonuses were distributed according to unit and sectoral output. Socialist productivity competitions rewarded teams who finished with superior results. In the campaigns to bring more women into the wage-labor force, commentators regularly brandished the prospects of a "second wage" for the family. Even the Party-state's post-1958 emphasis on ideology did not remove material incentives from economic planning and implementation. Frequently, in workplaces around the country, there were tensions over the level of wage payouts, yet no one questioned the system itself—at least not openly.

The cartoon in *Worker* suggested otherwise. While there was nothing controversial about showing how one worker, inspired by his vision of socialism, enhanced his level of productivity, the cartoonist depicted the other worker's dream of high wages as causing harm to his output. The cartoon's correlation of material incentives with failure ran against the fundamental principle chosen by the Party-state for reaching socialism. Was this anonymous cartoonist using a Chinese cartoon to pick up on international debates that otherwise had little presence within North Korea? Was the cartoonist suggesting that the country was on the wrong, even a revisionist, path? However much the critique hinted at more radical possibilities, such potential alternatives never gained any traction with a Party-state that, whatever importance it placed on ideology, never budged from its use of material incentives for workers.

FIVE

The Ideological Pivot

DAILY READERS OF THE PRESS in 1957 must have been puzzled by a shift in the otherwise relentlessly upbeat narrative that had been so prominent in reports of apartment construction. Suddenly, problems in urban reconstruction were being reported. Celebration turned to critique. Writers noted that the scars of wartime destruction could still be seen all around Pyongyang. Rather than boast of successful building, they reported that demand for housing remained acute and that many urban dwellers remained housed in temporary wartime shelters. These observations, however true, were politically unimaginable just a short time before when supply, not lack, was emphasized. The shift provided a sense that previous coverage had been skewed. It now also hinted that there was a deeper politics at play and that coverage would shift in a different direction.[1]

What had changed?

By 1957, apartment construction had become publicly embroiled in intra-Party disputes that ultimately coalesced into the Ch'ŏllima movement. The expression "Ch'ŏllima"—derived from the legend of a horse (*ma*) that could quickly travel thousands of miles (*ch'ŏlli*)—did not appear in the media until the middle of 1958. Yet the constitutive elements of the movement—a leadership struggle, changes in technical know-how in construction building, a reassertion of Party control over economic matters, a valorization of the primacy of ideology, and an emphasis on a mass line—had emerged gradually over the previous two years. The mass line sought to get bureaucrats out of their offices and away from their documents to experience what the Party believed was the innate enthusiasm and capacity for change among ordinary women and men in their work and domestic lives. By 1957, tensions from leadership struggles ensnared the construction sector and gradually came out into the open. This was not mere naked power politics among Party elites but reflected the ways in which ideological differences over the central economic question of the day—*how to build efficiently?*—became entwined with the actual construction processes. Over the next year, the conduct of construction and the day-to-day work style of many women and men were radically altered as a result.

These politics worked themselves out in terms of what appeared to be little more than the introduction of prefabricated modular construction, which had emerged around the world as the most advanced technique for building in quantity. For media followers, the pivot became obvious: prefabricated modular construction. National newspapers began to take issue with nameless forces—"some" (*ilbu*) ministerial officials—who had allowed waste and who had not pursued the new building technique effectively.[2] The anonymity did not last, as individual names soon appeared. The minister of construction, Kim Sünghwa, came out at the top of the list, paired with the head of the Ministry of Construction Materials, Ri P'ilgyu.[3] When public reports linked the two to the already much-pilloried Pak Changok, any doubts were erased: this dispute over construction efficiencies was the extension of Kim Il Sung's 1956 rise to power, which had led to high-level purges in the Party. Now, as the turn against his opponents was working itself through the state bureaucracies, the construction sector became a primary target. Criticism soon rolled down to the provinces. The ideological charges that had been used at the highest levels of the Party now came to be directed downward, extending beyond individuals who had sought to limit Kim Il Sung's power to lower-level officials caught up in the ideological shifts that were sweeping through the construction sectors. An October 1957 plenum of the Central Party Committee verified the shift.[4] The Party's national newspaper put the challenge bluntly, stating that "the possibility and conditions for prefab construction have long ago been prepared," but why had the new technique been restricted to a measly 10.5 percent of all construction? It went on to blame the construction officials for not establishing a link between ideology and the materiality of construction, citing the industry's meek ideological struggle against remnants of outmoded ideology as the reason for its inability to achieve a turnaround in production through advanced construction techniques.[5] The plenum called for all construction to adopt prefab. Over the next two years, both high- and low-level officials became entangled with a shift in politics and ideology that—in public, at least—came to be articulated through the politicization of prefab.[6] The percentage of construction completed by prefab techniques came to be seen less as an engineering and logistical problem and more as a reflection of ideological commitments and rectitude. Annual tallies captured the pivot—only 18.1 percent of all buildings in 1957 used prefab techniques, a figure that by 1962 rose to 53.8 percent.[7]

By 1961, when Comrade Ri published her memoir, the pivot had been completed. The memoir showed how high-level politics shaped mundane issues when those issues came under the gaze of the Party-state. In her otherwise personal account, she broke the memoir's positive tone to incorporate this political drama. In one passage, she adopted the Party's line and rhetoric, labeling people like Kim Sŭnghwa as "anti-Party divisionists." She added a personal touch, though, in showing how the conflict had impacted her labor, noting that "we were unable to build more houses, more quickly and with better quality.... We construction workers wasted our labor and toiled through adversities."[8] The inefficiencies forced on workers, Ri recounted, were tantamount to a personal affront. The charge was damning. They had been inefficient. Their obstruction of prefab was framed as an obstacle to the transition to socialism and to progress itself. There were few more serious charges.

By 1957, the history of prefab construction in Korea was not long but had always been transnational. Housing shortages, after all, were a long-standing global problem since at least the early twentieth century. This housing crisis spurred designers and architects to come up with forms of housing more suitable to mass production. Prefab construction soon tantalized them, seemingly offering a solution to the contradictory ends of building ideal living spaces for residents while keeping costs within low budgets. Standardization of designs enabled the industrial production of regularized components, and mechanization began to replace localized construction by skilled craftsmen using local materials. This offered a path toward mass production and construction by large numbers of unskilled workers. In certain parts of the world, prefab eventually came to be derided as cheap, lowbrow housing, while in other places, builders of elite, luxurious housing continued to use prefab for decades.[9] But in the years after World War II, as more states became involved in building housing to help settle populations as part of new welfare policies, prefab emerged as a dominant mode of construction. Prefab, in short, became the much-vaunted solution for the series of design, production, and construction dilemmas underlying what had come to be understood in many settings around the world as a shared housing "problem."[10]

FIGURE 15. Prefabricated housing construction. "A Pyongyang construction site of a multistory apartment, where innovations are continuously accomplished in order to build ever more, even faster, and even better." Yu Hyŏngmok, untitled, 1961.

Korea participated in these global trends (see figure 15). Exchanges with other socialist countries, where such buildings were arising on a massive scale, supported this turn. Traveling displays of the reconstruction of other postwar socialist cities were held in Pyongyang.[11] Architects took part in socialist bloc conferences, where advanced prefab techniques and experiences were shared.[12] Prefab construction had quickly been seen as a type of panacea for the pressures facing the construction industry. By lowering costs, more could be built, more quickly and less expensively. Highly skilled and specialized labor became less crucial, which meant that more people could take part, whether as regular or irregular labor. Prefab was the answer to the question of how to build more efficiently.

Yet experience would show this to be easier in theory than in practice. Coordinating all the diverse stages, from the design studio to the factory to the construction site, proved a logistical challenge, however rational the central plan was deemed to be. Architects bore the brunt of criticism for their inability to produce uniform plans that could be built around the country or to decrease overall costs of construction with better designs.[13] The ambition to design and build an ideal, standardized dwelling remained elusive for years after the war. Calls from leadership, as well as from workers on construction sites, upped the pressure on architects, but to no avail.[14] Cartoonists mocked architects for being unable to produce timely designs—one cartoon showed an architect arriving so late at a building site with his plans that construction was already nearly finished.[15] A report from 1955 noted that several different sizes and designs were used in twenty-nine newly completed buildings across three Pyongyang neighborhoods.[16] The following year, one frustrated architect complained that standardization could not even be achieved in Pyongyang, let alone in the provinces, where everybody seemed to be up to their own thing.[17] In 1957 other architects were still calling for standardized designs, their irritation palpable.[18] While the shortages of key construction materials and skilled personnel accounted for some coordination difficulties, disagreements about housing features divided designers. In matching residents' desires with efficiencies, how large should an apartment be? In the early multiunit apartments, sizes tended to be around sixty square meters[19]—but with the many calls to reduce resources, that shrunk first to forty-six and then to thirty-four square meters, a 56 percent decrease in living space.[20]

Differences existed on such seemingly trivial matters as the best height for ceilings. Lower ceiling height translated into less use of resources and quicker building. The power of such arguments in an era obsessed with efficiency can be seen in the fact that even Kim Il Sung participated, confirming in one bit of on-the-spot guidance that lowerering ceilings by an extra ten centimeters would save resources.[21] Three months later, while visiting a new apartment, he revisited the issue, remarking how the lower ceilings were just as good and the home design was "elegant."[22] Others were less convinced. A decision made at the cabinet level that summer—another sign of how such mundane matters had become politicized at the highest level—raised ceiling heights slightly, perhaps in response to complaints.[23] There was no acknowledgment that the decision, in effect, reversed Kim Il Sung's recommendation.

The question of which traditional architectural features should be preserved and which abandoned also divided architects.[24] The 1954 workers' apartment building that had caused such a sensation was the first and last of its kind. Its architectural accents were dropped in subsequent buildings, victims to the drive to save building costs. Some called for more beautiful buildings, but in the end the one feature that *did* get standardized was minimal ornamentation.[25] For a few years, it appeared that the traditional Korean heating system, the *ondol*, would be abandoned in favor of radiators, due to the difficulty of making it through prefab techniques. Radiators were championed as a modern alternative. Ultimately, when a new style of prefab block that could accommodate in-floor heating was created, the *ondol* came to be seen as a convenient standard, celebrated as an updated version of a national tradition.[26] Other divisive questions extended to the setting of individual plans in neighborhoods. Should common cafeterias be built into each building or strategically located in each neighborhood? How could a building be designed to lessen the use of steel?[27] Without standardized designs, the desire to use prefab buildings to resolve housing pressures remained just that—a desire, realized with only limited success.

These many unresolved dilemmas of design stymied the mass production of standardized parts. How could standardized doors be produced if there was no uniform plan providing standardized door sizes? These problems led the construction sector to fall short again, producing only 89 percent of its target for the first half of 1957, according to one report. It was one of the few sectors not to meet its goals, with some provinces producing as little as 67 percent of the plan in the same period.[28] Falling short opened the construction sector to external scrutiny at a moment when the higher levels of the Party roiled with political intrigue. The timing could not have been worse for its officials. This pivot in the construction industry—from trumpeted successes to lost opportunities—was not just simultaneous to Kim Il Sung's ascension to power, but emerged as a realm where the ideological and cultural politics of his rise were worked out at multiple levels for all to experience.

Arguably, construction authorities received a forewarning—even if they did not appreciate the perils. Kim Il Sung had always had an interest in architecture, which he first displayed in a March 1954 address to a meeting of architects and construction specialists. There was nothing particularly original about the speech, and it was not published in the media at the time. It reflected his personal take on ideas circulating in the architectural world, particularly that prefab triumvirate of standardization, industrialization, and mechanization. Two years later, in a second speech on architecture, he prefaced a much deeper treatment of the prefab triumvirate with a warning: "I want to remind you again of what I told you about this problem at the March 26, 1954, meeting of builders."[29] He noted that some officials had listened to what he had urged and changed their ways, while others had not. That several journals followed the national party newspaper in reproducing the 1956 speech for everyone to read showed the changing priorities and power dynamics—and hinted at how ignoring Kim's exhortations about construction might have repercussions.[30]

The change in the media's tone began to capture the rollout of the campaign. For the next twenty-four months, criticism became extensive. For the error of not promoting prefab sufficiently, virtually every term in the political lexicon was leveled against construction-sector officials, from the most common—*conservatism, bureaucratism, formalism, parochialism*[31]—to phrases that were less routine and, thus, more troubling: "anti-national poisonous behavior," "anti-Party factionalists who have betrayed the revolution." The list of mistakes, shortcomings—and, eventually, "crimes"—became increasingly lengthy and detailed.[32] Architects, who had long been the subject of dissatisfaction, again bore the brunt of intense criticism. Some were so wrapped up in their own "glory and fame" (*kongmyŏngjuŭi*) that their self-proclaimed "creativity" and "architectural art," according to one critic, took precedence over deadlines, costs, and conditions. To ensure the connection between the material and the ideological, he added, "these ideological shortcomings need to be urgently purged and overcome and the standardization of architectural plans and the regularization of construction parts must be realized."[33] By 1958, media outlets could be criticized themselves for using "weak phrases" and not being bold enough in their criticism of Kim Sŭnghwa and other officials.[34] In this environment, everyone piled on.

These were not empty accusations. Criticisms turned into purges. And purges often meant jailing and torture. Reports from European allies mentioned that ministry officials were being thrown in jail and undergoing interrogation. There were repeated reports of officials committing suicide under intense pressure.[35] The scale of these purges remains unclear, though they paled in scope and numbers when compared to those in Russia and China. The campaign refrained from unleashing popular energies against a particular social category or class, remaining more tightly focused and within the control of the Party. Even architects, who could easily have been labeled bourgeois, were not labeled as a whole and experienced a less-than-complete purge of their ranks. Instead, the purge focused on the somewhat blurry boundaries between Kim's rivals, many of whom had ties with the Soviet Union, and construction-sector officials who fell on the wrong side of the now politicized line on construction. There was, of course, much overlap between these two groups. In the observation of one Polish diplomat, these internal Party-state politics did not spill over to create any broader problems, and "the internal situation in the DPRK is stabilizing increasingly."[36]

As was often the case with political purges, the attacks reflected less about what its victims had done and more about their accusers' objectives. At the top of those goals stood a pivot toward the primacy of ideology. The mistakes committed by the construction industry's leaders, according to their accusers, lay with their prioritization of technical issues over ideological ones. That previously it had been Party-state policy to promote economic expertise to the point of keeping cadres out of local-level economic decisions was conveniently forgotten. The new line was read backwards in time—and anyone who had not foreseen the shift remained vulnerable. This was not so much a voluntarist mindset, in the sense of believing that ideology could unilaterally transform the world. Rather, only a correct ideological position, it was believed, would allow one to have the appropriate perspective on economic needs, which would then shape one's acquisition and use of the necessary technical knowledge. In this sense, it was not a Korean case of red versus expert. Cultural revolution was always twinned with calls for technical revolution, itself rooted in materialism.

The head of the industry bureau in Pyongyang, Pak Wŏngŭn, brought this logic to bear on the very nature of economic thinking. Pak explained that some leaders tended to view production problems in purely technical terms without considering their ideological roots. "If you don't properly conjoin the economic and political projects," he wrote, "then it becomes difficult to inspire people in the directions demanded for the economy."[37] Soon, virtually every explanation of what one leader called the "new environment" invoked this expression—"conjoining the political and economic" (*ch'ŏngch'i saŏp kwa kyŏngje saŏp ŭi miljŏphan kyŏlhap*).[38] But this was not all. The newfound emphasis on ideology over the technical created a new rationale for the Party—always the ultimate arbiter of ideology—to reassert its primacy in the economy. Pak explained that this had become especially crucial in production problems that rose above the level of single enterprises. For Pak, it was ludicrous that some sites were ready to start construction but lacked cranes or excavators, while other sites where work was not being done had them. For another example, in some places there were not enough skilled pargers, delaying the opening of new housing, while at other places skilled pargers dug ditches because their specific skills were not yet needed. His point was that the local Party units had to engage more with economic enterprises to provide a coordinating function. "The shortcoming of the lower levels of the Party is that they do not clearly recognize the fundamental nature of Party rule over economic enterprises," he contended, pointing out that there was a tendency to bureaucratize Party activities.[39] In place of the experience and expert status of managers, Pak was bringing the Party back in as coordinator of the economy, a position legitimated by its function as the steward of ideology.[40]

Another contemporary commentator, Mun Ch'isu, brought this point down to the level of work, arguing that laborers were the "most decisive" element in production. "This is because however magnificent your machines and facilities may be, only people can create, and it is only people who can use them in production."[41] In previous times, some leaders had "one-sidedly considered machines and labor" when it came to increasing production, while paying scant attention to raising workers' consciousness and technical skill levels or improving their working conditions. Despite the many types of work that had been done on raising ideological consciousness to this date—speeches on class consciousness, guidebooks on how to be a good socialist, the development of new political language, the earlier emphasis on criticism and political study, the promotion of Party history lessons—all were waved away, deemed insufficient. Ideology now became the primary realm through which economic success and failure were to be explained.

The power of the revolutionary narrative of apartment building came to be turned against its very authors, who had so assiduously promoted it for their own purposes up through 1957. Now it was in the hands of their critics, who underplayed their ideological commitment, overplayed their emphasis on technical prowess, failed to acknowledge their achievements, and dismissed them as the obstacles to progress. "Conservatism" became another accusation added to the litany of supposed anti-Party behavior. How this would be worked out in the economy and what it meant for the day-to-day work lives of the population would become evident in a campaign launched in 1958 to rebuild Pyongyang.

By the beginning of February, the pressure to translate the new ideological line into practice—actual construction results—led to an ambitious goal. It was announced that the previous central planning objective to erect seven thousand new apartment residences in Pyongyang would be scaled up to seventeen thousand for 1958—a 143 percent increase. Apartments stood at the center of this campaign's goal to remake the city, but initiatives ranged widely: beautification with more trees and flowers, better public sanitation and hygiene, better administration, and more cultural facilities such as children's playgrounds and small parks—all these were promised.[42] Whatever the high-level, intra-Party machinations, the pivot nevertheless returned to that most pressing of contemporary questions: *How to build more efficiently?* Construction officials in this heated environment gave assurances that the goals could be accomplished with virtually no extra financial investments from the central state budget and without extra labor input. The apartments would be built by saving capital, labor, and materials already allocated to existing projects and reinvesting those savings in expanded construction.[43] That a 143 percent increase might conceivably be achieved on the basis of the original budget for seven thousand units was audacious, at best, yet construction enterprises of all types rushed to pledge their part. A feverish tone resulted. Workers in individual work teams made public declarations, such as the Number Two Pyongyang Construction Team's promise to build 318 extra housing units on its own.[44] Architects of the much-maligned Pyongyang Urban Design Research Institute made amends with designs vowing to reduce the per meter cost of construction by 46 percent.[45] Throughout the campaign, enterprises touted their goals, trumpeted their achievements, and celebrated their reduced costs—all done publicly to garner ideological credence for themselves and used by authorities to further spur the campaign along.[46] Yet, in keeping with the spirit of constantly pushing for ever greater results, as soon as this first goal was complete, enterprises announced more ambitious goals.[47] It was announced that already the initial quantitative goals of the campaign had been reached—as more than 17,800 units were currently under construction. The new goal pushed even further—twenty thousand to be completed by Liberation Day of that year.[48]

Efficiency became speed—or rather, as one title put it, "How Do We Raise the Speed of Construction?"[49] Later, it would become clear that speed came at the expense of quality. Many units categorized as "completed" for the purpose of the campaign were barely ready for residents.[50] Yet the fact that some apartments did not have their electricity completed—or that ill-sized blocks had been forced into place, leaving wonky walls—was beside the point. Instead, work teams continued to boast about their speed, increasing the time of completion by five times, in one case, due to prefab.[51] Other teams competed to decrease the average time for erecting an individual residential unit within a complex. What had taken two hours in the winter of 1957 had been reduced to thirty minutes by April, and two months later it could be completed as quickly as every sixteen minutes, in what came to be known as "Pyongyang speed."[52] Another team, building on the outskirts of Pyongyang, developed a method for erecting wall panels in two minutes and three seconds, which became the basis of a "three minute" campaign.[53] One worker, Chŏng Ch'oru, told a national press reporter after setting a record that "we can't be satisfied with this. We're already not far from setting another record and again taking off."[54] The emphasis on speed even led the cabinet to go beyond what had so long been promoted as a key feature of socialism: collective ownership of homes. They issued an ordinance to all factories to sell construction materials to individuals, who could use savings to build their own homes, presumably in rural areas.[55] More speedy, more beautiful, more magnificent, more heroic, more cultural—the adjectives flowed, always qualified by the adverb *more*.

Prefab construction was an ideal technology to help the Party-state put into practice its mass line by enfolding the residents of Pyongyang into the campaign. In the same year that the economy had been completely socialized according to Party-state assessments, the campaign served as an instrument to push forward lagging ideological levels in what was deemed the revolutionary heart of the country. The "victory already achieved by the socialist economic form," explained one national editorial on the campaign, demanded of every individual the "socialist renovation of ideological consciousness and socialist cultural revolution." Brought down to the everyday, "we cannot say that when we compare our lifestyles [*saenghwal*] to our socialist construction, that we have culturally organized it to a correspondingly high level." Thus, the building campaign was not just about resolving the housing shortage. It sought to push the goal of "conjoining the political and economic" by means of a campaign that would heighten the ideological and cultural levels of the population that the Party believed necessary to usher in the transition to socialism.[56] In many ways, it served as a public demonstration with tangible results of the new Party-state direction.

Key to this higher goal was the way Party officials used the campaign to articulate the emerging mass line. Criticism of Kim Sŭnghwa and other construction officials not only continued, but expanded in novel directions. It was not just that Kim and other "Party splittists" had supposedly overrelied on technical solutions, the story went, but in so doing they had stifled the spontaneous energies of their workers. That construction officials had argued that workers were not yet ready to adopt advanced prefab techniques, it was said, showed just how out-of-touch they were with their own workers' enthusiasm—one more reason used to get them out of positions of power. This critique of out-of-touch officials and bureaucrats was soon separated from any direct connection to Kim Sŭnghwa and other officials. A more generalized critique of Party and state officials arose. At its center stood the stock figure of cadres or bureaucrats who stayed in their offices, dealing with paperwork and holding meetings, without venturing to the spaces where production happened. The local leader locked to his desk—too busy with meetings, sitting behind a pile of papers that obscured his vision, making decisions from the office without ever going on site—became a stock image in the era's visual culture, twisted and turned in endless permutations by cartoonists. As one cartoonist put it, using the image of a bureaucrat driving a tractor from his desk, officials should not be leading from a distance (see figure 16).[57] As consequential as this critique was for the individuals caught up in its wave, it came with a certain restraint. This was not a Maoist turn against the Party itself, and many critiques went so far as to specify that the problem lay with lower-level (habu) bureaucrats, as if to ensure that the changing dynamics at the top of the Party did not get enmeshed in any backlash.[58]

What this critique presumed was popular enthusiasm for the campaign. The purge supposedly removed restraints created by officials with the wrong orientation—much in the way Comrade Ri's memoir would later explain. In theory, now everyone could participate—or, more accurately, everyone was expected to participate. In the early days of the campaign, the press showed the mass line at work in a story about the residents of southern Pyongyang neighborhoods coming out to the Taedong River.[59] Twenty-five hundred residents labored to dig four hundred cubic meters of sand and gravel in a single day for use in the manufacture of basic concrete. They planned, it reported, to excavate over thirteen thousand more square meters in the next four days. The mass line as worked out in the Pyongyang campaign mobilized not just regular wage earners, but also non-routinized laborers; temporary workers, mobilized for a specific purpose, reflected the priority of ideological

FIGURE 16. Hong Chongho, "A Behind-the-Desk Driver," 1959.

commitment over material incentive. Non-routinized labor was largely done by students, but also by housewives who, unlike Comrade Ri, had not taken up wage work for whatever reason.[60]

In this way, the mass line's overt emphasis on ideology still implicitly circled back to maximization of the national labor potential and the full mobilization of female labor. To be sure, mother-workers in regular wage-paying positions—crane operators and bricklayers, to cite two examples[61]—took part. Yet, as one call put it, the campaign's goals needed more than just routinized labor alone and had to mobilize all the people in a grand movement.[62] This meant an alternative vision of labor, separate from efforts to use material incentives to induce "dependent family members" into the paid wage-labor force or to move men out of positions deemed suitable for women. Obstacles to access were not part of the press coverage now, as mothers who had not taken up wage work came out to participate in the campaign. Photographs such as those showing the housewives of the eighth team of Ryŏnhwa neighborhood, still dressed in their traditional style of attire, called *chosŏnot*, while using hoes and shovels on the streets, became prominent.[63] In another account, a male reporter approached a shock worker, asking whether she was a worker. The unnamed woman responded, "No, I'm a housewife [*kajŏng puin*]." He said, "Then you don't have any children?" To which she replied, "My little darlings are sleeping right now. I've come out to help with construction while they're sleeping."[64]

This dialogue reintroduced the challenge of day care in the very different context of the non-routinized nature of the campaign. Again, would-be mother-workers had little choice but to depend on their own self-organization during the campaign. Some organized temporary child care services to allow them to participate. In the Ryonghŭng neighborhood on the outskirts of the capital, mothers went so far as to erect with their own hands a day care facility for their children. They even made bricks out of mud because all the blocks and panels had been taken up by the campaign.[65] If the mass line meant everyone should contribute, then housewife-mothers became examples of how, with the proper host-like attitude, one could overcome the exigencies of daily life to help build Pyongyang and further the country's transition to socialism. Yet, just as importantly, they showed one more non-routinized method by which the labor reserve of women in their domestic spaces could be mobilized toward Party-state goals.

Doing so, however, created a whole range of challenges for domestic life. And as more apartments opened their doors to families, authorities began to ask questions about how the New Living inside these new architectural spaces could be harmonized to their priorities. The answers were not always clear-cut or satisfactory to them.

PART THREE

Making Happy Family Homes

HOW TO MAKE A HAPPY HOME?

In the 1950s, such a question was neither new to Korea nor unique to the peninsula. Yet the fact that the theme of "happy homes" became so prominent in the daily media showed that the heteronormative family—and more specifically, its domestic living space—had emerged as one of the premier symbols of peace after seventeen years of nearly continuous conflict (1937–53). Behind the gloss of domestic bliss, familial homes emerged as spaces where women and men worked out the challenges presented to their families and their relationships by the tensions developing within the political economy and Party-state ideologies. The New Living's postwar turn to family—as a locus for the reform of gender relations, as a solution to the demographic crisis, as a source of labor, and as the primary locus for the ideological cultivation of the next generation—ensured that the management of domestic spaces would make diverse and uneven demands on men and women.

But coming out of the colonial era, a fundamental challenge remained: it was not quite clear what precisely constituted the normative form of the family. The ravages of war, decades of socioeconomic change, and debates that since the last years of the nineteenth century had called for family reform— all these had made the basic constitution of the family, let alone relations within that unit, a contentious issue, full of questions about gender and sexual relations inside and outside the family, and about their connections to wider political and economic demands. After 1953, as the doors of apartment buildings opened to tens of thousands of new residents for the first time in the peninsula's history, many of these same questions arose among urban dwellers in the new material and ideological environment of socialism in a divided peninsula.

FIGURE 17. Anonymous, "Cultivation Room: Let's Nicely Organize Our Living," 1958.

A tiny black-and-white illustration, published in a 1958 edition of the magazine *Rodongja (Worker)*, showed the direction these pre-collective-era debates had taken. Coarsely drawn by an unnamed illustrator, the image anthropomorphized a cute pair of bees as a conjugal couple sitting happily in their living room (see figure 17).[1] The illustration served as little more than a space filler at the end of the magazine, remarkable only for its very ordinariness. It did not bother to offer either an argument about the family or any revolutionary claims on the family's behalf. Its accompanying article, "Cultivation Room: Let's Nicely Organize Our Living," invoked a classic question of household management. This vision—of the conjugal couple as the basis of the heteronormative nuclear family—had previously been promoted by nationalist and colonialist forces alike but rested uneasily within a long history of socialist ideals that challenged the bounds of the family. In an era when the mass death and dislocation of war made it physically impossible for many women and men to attain this form of family, such images of domesticity nevertheless worked within a broader discursive environment to naturalize the nuclear family as a long-standing national tradition—only now also taking on the added burden of being called the "socialist family." The heteronormative nuclear family became the subject of much ideological, material, juridical, and moral investment.

The centrality of the family to the establishment of Party-state power became evident in its prominence in postwar memory politics. Even before stabilizing its own history, the Party-state presented itself as the historical savior and protector of the family. This masculinist narrative of rescue simplified the complex genealogy of the modern family and its deep integration with the global politics of colonialism. Party-state authorities celebrated how their design of apartment units and a new family law had rescued the family, yet that very celebration masked how these investments—together with memory politics—had structured the very form of family it presented as natural.

The macroeconomic pressures on the aggregate labor supply, the unprecedented numbers of women heading into wage work, and the completion of many worker apartment buildings reinvigorated questions about women's domestic labor. It became not uncommon for writers to represent the interiors of apartments, which were otherwise so widely celebrated for their construction, as unproductive, feminine spaces that risked hindering the transition to socialism. This dismissive critique, leveled from the highest echelons, built on and further reinforced the postwar development of the gendered segregation of labor.

Many writers in *Women of Korea* pushed back, however. It was no easy matter in the authoritarian environment to challenge the masculinist norms through which the Party-state's own power was interwoven. Yet some writers countered this current by voicing, however carefully, their disapproval of divorce law changes. Other writers expanded the use of official conceptual vocabulary and narrative strategies to emphasize the centrality of their domestic labor to the goal of socialist transition. Still others countered by highlighting the productive nature of the array of activities pursued in their homes or neighborhoods, such as ideological self-cultivation and spy-catching. What became clear, by 1965, was that many of the women pilloried for not taking up formal wage labor took upon themselves, and had placed onto their shoulders, tasks that the Party-state could not resolve without the very labor of the women it disparaged, however ad hoc and informal their organization.

Yet in taking up this struggle to show the centrality of the home to Party-state goals by emphasizing the raising of cultural levels to carry out these arrays of responsibilities, writers in *Women of Korea* built on the general ideological shift and emphasis on culture that had emptied gender and class of their potential for radical critique. Their pushback against specific policies and tendencies worked within parameters that vested impetus for the transition to socialism in individual effort, which in turn downplayed structural explanations for remaining inequities and, ultimately, turned their critiques back on themselves.

SIX

———

Supporting the Nuclear Family

THE MATERIAL CONDITIONS OF APARTMENT UNITS

Apartment buildings were more than just monuments to socialist construction. They were, after all, lived spaces. After the famine, disease, and dislocation of war, apartments provided a safe location where, quite literally, the nurturing and reproduction of life and labor took place. Domesticity, with its representation of the home space as one of happiness and laughter, emerged as a premier symbol of the end of fighting—a space where families could, ideally, reunite after being scattered by wartime forces and work out how they would engage with the possibilities and limits of the New Living. Happy families and New Living became deeply entwined.[1]

The domestic spaces where all this happiness was supposed to transpire were the apartments transforming cityscapes in the late 1950s. If, as discussed earlier, disputes divided architects on how best to build these structures, those same architects faced a related challenge: how to design apartment interiors in ways that would best suit residents while not overburdening resources. This was a global problem rooted in the mass housing crisis of the twentieth century.[2] One solution pursued on both sides of the Cold War divide—if sometimes more in rhetoric than in fact—was the ideal small home. In Korea, this idea of the "smallest apartment" focused attention on the individual dwelling within the multiunit building.[3] As architects struggled to reconcile these contradictory demands, one key assumption underlay virtually every design for the units.

Whatever the differences in overall design of the buildings, individual dwellings were largely designed for the use of a family, specifically a nuclear family led by a conjugal couple. Most published floor plans, whether actually built or just a flight of architectural fancy, consisted of a self-enclosed one-room or, more commonly, two-room unit with separate hallway access, and a door that could close off the flat from other residents. Usually it included a kitchen, running water, heating, and its own closet space.[4] Bathrooms were the most frequently shared facility, though most buildings incorporated them into individual units. The only single-room units were used as dormitories for workers or couples and were patterned on East German designs.[5] Later, some units with three rooms began to be built to accommodate larger families. Nevertheless, the considerable diversity in unit designs—a variety that, as discussed in chapter 5, stymied early efforts to standardize construction—shared the same presumption about an apartment unit's residents and purpose, namely that these houses would provide the material conditions for the reproduction of nuclear families, their labor potential, and the next generation.

To design housing for the benefit of nuclear families ran counter to a long history of socialist architectural theory. Extending from Friedrich Engels's proposition that the family posed a barrier to the development of a broader collective consciousness,[6] this design tradition sought to use the layout of domestic spaces to weaken familial bonds and succor communal sensibilities. Collectively designed living spaces, it was believed, had the potential to reconfigure gender relations. Theoretically, the transformed living spaces would also make the sharing and socialization of domestic labor easier, thus contributing to evening out relations between women and men. In short, the space of the home had the power to lead its residents to the desired gender and class consciousness.[7]

At various times, this understanding of the relation of domestic space to gender and class relations shaped architecture in the Soviet Union and China. In the postrevolutionary Soviet Union, architects proposed many utopian designs, most of which would never get built.[8] But eventually, homes with facilities shared among several families—the famous *kommunulka*—emerged out of these efforts to reimagine personal and familial space. After the 1930s, architects largely abandoned these endeavors. By the 1950s, Khrushchev pushed a massive modular-apartment building campaign to satisfy pent-up demand for housing designed to accommodate families.[9] And following the 1949 revolution, Chinese architects envisioned redesigned domestic spaces as a means of overcoming what they criticized as the Confucian legacy of family relations. Many urban dwellings—and, during the Great Leap Forward, many rural areas—were rendered communal, with shared kitchens, dining facilities, showers, toilets, and living spaces.[10] While these initiatives in both the Soviet Union and China rested on long-standing critiques of family relations, they were also driven by a practical consideration: a housing shortage. Dividing up the already existing housing stock, especially the larger homes of wealthy families deemed of questionable revolutionary pedigree, served as a quick means for a more equitable distribution of that limited housing stock. Owners of prerevolutionary housing soon had portions of their houses divided off, with new families moving in—an experience that became rich fare for storytelling.[11] Such practical considerations had little relevance to postwar Korea, where American aerial bombing had left little urban housing to be divided up and shared. For the most part, urban housing development started from scratch—or, as a contemporary phrase frequently put it, was rebuilt from the "ashes of war."

Yet, unlike their Soviet and Chinese counterparts, Korean architects never experimented extensively with communal designs for familial apartment housing. Nothing in the main architectural journal, *Architecture and Construction* (*Kŏnch'ukkwa kŏnsŏl*), touched on this history of socialist design, whether to hint at its possibilities or to critique its unacceptability for local conditions. The idea of using spatial design to weaken family bonds as part of either a gendered or a class critique was nowhere to be found. Arguably, the most collective living space that some individuals would experience was worker dormitory buildings—yet, as seen earlier, even they were used with the assumption that individuals living there would, upon marriage, leave them for apartments where, presumably, they would pursue their conjugal lives in what the Workers' Federation hoped would be a depoliticized setting.

There does not appear to have been any single cabinet edict or leadership speech that announced the decision to center apartment-unit designs on nuclear families. Nor was there any sign of a debate or a process by which anyone rejected the possibility of communal design for worker housing. As Kim Il Sung increasingly turned to on-the-spot guidance sessions in the construction sector, he never specifically addressed the relationship between living space and the family, other than to speak about convenience as part of the design. The possibility that architectural spaces might challenge rather than reinforce the prevalent vision of the family never appeared in any of the era's specialty magazines or other print media. Rather, as the floor plans from the earliest moments of imagining the rebuilding process tended to show, family-oriented design had been assumed from the get-go and celebrated precisely because it offered the physical conditions for what, from the perspective of the

Party-state, was the reproduction of working-class nuclear families on a mass scale for the first time in the history of the peninsula—or what, as likely seen from the perspective of individuals, was a space that would enable their efforts to create happy homes.

RESCUE NARRATIVES AND THE HISTORICAL FAMILY

This default presumption showed how many of the ideas that shaped the New Living emerged from the preceding half-century of social change, from the debates interwoven with those social changes, and from official memory politics about the colonial past. No brief encapsulation does justice to the complexities of the more than five decades of reforms and debates. Yet it was clear by the 1890s that the norms of family life and domesticity would be a subject of much contention for the coming twentieth century. In those waning years of the nineteenth century, the royal dynasty banned childhood marriages, altered adoption laws, and granted widows the right to remarry,[12] as only the latest steps in a centuries-long history of the Chosŏn dynasty using its juridical power to shape family formation.[13] After annexation into the Japanese empire in 1910, the peninsula's continued integration into the global economy and the colonial state's implementation of administrative and legal changes ensured that the economic and regulatory conditions that gave the family shape underwent profound changes. In an indication of just how important the family would be for colonial rule, a new household registration system (hojok) that aimed to reorder the Korean family in the direction of patrilineal nuclear families was instituted in 1909—one year before formal rule had even started.[14] As Sungyun Lim has shown, many male colonial subjects were quick to avail themselves of colonial family law, since it codified the heteropatriarchal privileges that heretofore had only been customary.[15] So, too, did women take advantage of the legal system, contesting in the courts issues as various as inheritance rights and adoption—each case offering a venue in which colonial categories of family were mediated and given further local context by Korean litigants. Cumulatively, these cases moved legal definitions of the family further away from the type of lineage-based families that had dominated the last years of the Chosŏn dynasty. As Lim shows, by the early 1940s, the emerging formulation of the family as nuclear was accepted by colonial courts as representative of Korean traditional practice in their decisions concerning civil matters.[16]

Debates about the family, gender relations, and the future of the nation accompanied these top-down state reforms. Reformers of virtually every political stripe called for a new type of family. What was proposed as "new" often came to be defined against what had emerged as the dominant upper-crust *yangban* family in the last centuries of the Chosŏn dynasty—the patri-archal clan with its patrilineal principles of organization and inheritance. That the "traditional family" hardly fit a uniform mold, had sociopolitical roots that could not be reduced to Confucianism, and had changed funda-mentally over the course of the five-hundred-year dynasty was irrelevant in the eyes of these reformers. In their rush for change, reformers sought to mobilize their version of tradition, however much they oversimplified and caricatured earlier forms of family and gender relations.[17] At first, as pro-moted largely by male intellectuals, the drive for change rested with the novel politics of nationalism and its accompanying vision of a mobilized popula-tion: *everyone* needed to partake. In this reckoning, the extended family was deemed a restraint on women in limiting them from the education necessary for strengthening the nation—even if the critique revealed its gendered bias by envisioning their participation as mothers and wives.[18]

Globally circulating forms of knowledge shaped these debates and changes. The very term *home* had to be invented for the East Asian context by Japanese reformers, as Jordan Sand has shown.[19] Japanese conceptions later became entangled in the interstices between Japan's colonial project and the national-ist movements around Asia that resisted it. Just as they had carried it with them around the world, American missionaries, as Hyaeweol Choi has shown, brought their reformist zeal for matters of the home to Korea.[20] Korean women and men keenly used these forms of knowledge for their own purposes, whether bringing back knowledge of other forms of domesticity through their foreign travels, reading Ibsen at home, or developing home economics programs. They adapted an array of foreign intellectual sources, developing multilayered, not always consistent, and at times mutually hostile series of ideas about the nature of love, sexuality, economic independence, and divorce.[21] The notion of "wise mother good wife" became so prevalent, as Choi argues, that its very recent origins were forgotten as it was read back into the Chosŏn dynasty. Koreans, female and male, were engaging with globally circulating feminist thought, handbooks on mothering practices, and con-sumerist products and representations.[22] And by the late 1920s, socialist ideals on gender and marriage had sparked interest, particularly through the writ-ings of Alexandra Kollontai, leading to an over-sensationalizing of "Red

Love" that, as Ruth Barraclough has shown, glossed over the challenges socialist feminists raised in linking class and gender critiques.[23] By the 1930s, radical visions commingled with liberal and even conservative approaches to family reform.[24]

It was as part of these debates that neologisms such as *new living*, *cultural home*, and *cultural living* first came to be explored. The media may have seized on women's fashion and cigarette smoking to sensationalize calls for free love and self-realization, but as the writings of leading intellectuals like Kim Wŏnju, Na Hyesok, and Hŏ Chungsuk showed, these debates were less about setting a singular definition of the New Woman and more about exploring, in essays and in their personal lives, a wide array of possible reconfigurations of family and gender.[25] No consensus emerged, yet as Choi rightly points out, their powerful critiques of the extended family often came with a reconfir-mation of the primacy of the domestic roles of women within the family, even if the definition of that family had been reimagined as nuclear.[26] Dominant visions of family relations headed in fits and starts toward privi-leging the heteronormative nuclear family, itself the subject of continued debate about the gender and sexual relations within and without it. Yet the bourgeois nature of many of these claims and projects became apparent. Many of these ideals about gender and family were promoted by members of elite families and were thus envisioned along class lines, often reflecting bour-geois conditions. This became only clearer as the young women entering urban factory life quickly surpassed the New Women in numbers, yet their presence in urban public spaces did not stir up nearly the same sensation.[27] The creation of nuclear family ideals, despite their class basis, was presented as pan-national and class free.

Although most nationalist and colonial initiatives promoted nuclear fam-ily ideals, they remained largely aspirational and difficult to translate into local social worlds. Neither had the sway needed to transform family forma-tion along the lines of their visions. In one study of available demographic data for the late colonial period, Mun Sojŏng demonstrated that even in Seoul, the location that was at the core of these debates and reforms, patterns of family structure and size differed enormously.[28] Citing evidence that fam-ily size varied with income—not surprisingly, wealthy families had larger households—Mun argues that disparate sizes led to a variety of family forma-tions that moved well beyond the ideal of "small nuclear families." Due to a wide range of socioeconomic patterns, including women's employment and marriage patterns, families ranged from those organized as patrilineages to various types of nuclear families, often patterned on those norms but consisting of a wider array of members. In this biggest of urban settings, at least, familial changes were underway, but no set pattern dominated.

Coming out of the colonial period, the heteronormative nuclear family had emerged as an assortment of ideals with many proponents and had become part of the social and gender reform agendas of competing political projects, including early socialism. The precise ways in which these possibilities would work themselves out across a changing political, gender, and class landscape became one of the central struggles of the last half of the twentieth century—and remains so to this day. In the North after 1945, ordinary women and men, as well as the Party-state, became the heirs of these unresolved debates and continuing social changes, the latter of which only accelerated during the war. More than this, many of the conceptual categories from the colonial era shaped the struggles to define a specifically socialist family life and gender relations, even if this inheritance was not acknowledged. By the time the Party came into power, it accepted the nuclear family as not just an ideal but also the repository of national traditions.

In the early postwar years, the earlier debates over the form of family were converted to a new use by Party authorities. In the interest of rebuilding state institutions that would be autonomous and free from social pressures, much criticism was leveled at what was called familialism (*kajokchuui*). This was a refraction of earlier debates about extended family lineages, centered not on their gendered consequences, but on their social influence. Nepotism, local power in villages, influence on official attitudes, non-prioritization of the Party—all these attributes of powerful families became the target.[29] With their smaller size, nuclear families were presumed not to carry this influence. In this way, as Pak Yŏngja has argued, family formation also linked up to state-building concerns at local levels.[30] Nuclear families meant a stronger state, whose local institutions were not swayed by powerful families.

Much could be forgotten in the name of revolution. The family became a site for a powerful memory politics. The first step was for the Party-state to disavow the complex genealogy of the conceptual categories and ideals that it used to frame its own understanding of family and gender. This was the power of revolutionary time and the "new" in New Living. And "new" came with a particular narrative, one that emerged prior to the official histories of the Party. In place of recognizing the many-sided dialogues that had converged on the nuclear family in the first half of the century, the Party-state substituted a simple, unilinear story of the family's emergence. Coming out of the Chosŏn dynasty's feudal relations, according to this account, the family was confronted by a colonialism intent on destroying it. Colonialism was not to be remembered for unleashing the forces that coalesced into nuclear family ideals or providing the socioeconomic challenges undermining extended lineages. The family served in this story as one of the few sites of resistance, a locus where notorious colonial policies like the name-change and intermarriage policies had failed due to the resistance of the very subjects they sought to eliminate. This memory politics shared much with how Partha Chatterjee describes the family in India under British rule.[31] This was one more version, seen around the world in the twentieth century, of the family as an inviolate realm and, when merged with the nation, a bastion of tradition signed as popular.

So, too, did the Party-state turn to savior narratives by seizing on the disparity between familial ideals and the actual social lives of the population. The economics of having the country stolen led to the immiseration of the Party's purported mainstay: peasants and workers. Only under socialism, the argument went, could the conditions for the realization of ideal families finally be met after centuries of feudalism and decades of colonialism. The family, in short, had been rescued from the tumult of its own history. This teleological narrative segued with national history—the liberation of the nation opened possibilities for the families that had maintained national traditions during foreign occupation. In the 1950s, these two narratives—national and familial—coalesced in the apartment-building campaign.

Accordingly, the force of these narratives culminated in what became a prominent style of story: the day families moved into their new apartments. One story, featuring Ri Sunhak, who moved residence in the summer of 1956, showed how these narratives and tropes came together. Ri expressed his happiness in historical terms on this special day. As with so much in the New Living, where popular aspirations overlapped with Party-state goals, Ri's personal story merged easily with the official memory politics.[32] He started his story in the colonial period—"before liberation"—describing how he lived with many people in a room "as small as a crab shell." All he owned had gone up in flames during the Korean War, but now he was living in a large and convenient space with his wife, daughter, and son. "How is it possible," he asked incredulously, "that we have been able to enjoy in such a short time this kind of stable livelihood?" The article made a special point of his background. "For our type of working family," he pointed out, "living in this type of amazing house was nothing but a dream." Such personal stories did not need to be fabricated wholesale. The power of Ri's story lay not in its novelty or uniqueness but in how it brought together, in the story of one working family, an array of experiences that many readers would recognize from their own or their neighbors' lives. That working people's stories, detailing their suffering-turned-to-happiness, were now in the newspaper was the point. Such stories showed how many families developed stakes in the New Living and the success of the Party-state in the mass building of apartments for family living.

Ri's story fused personal, familial, national, and modern histories into a single moment: moving-in day. It erased the relationship of the nuclear family to its most avid colonial-era supporters, bourgeois intellectuals. The story's focus on Ri as the head of the household, with little attention to his wife, suggested that the long history of critiquing the family as the social foundation for many masculinist practices was quietly forgotten in this celebration. That the nuclear family, however idealized and unevenly institutionalized, had been foundational to colonial state power remained outside the ken of this sense of the family. Affirmation of the national and individual meanings of the nuclear family trumped any class or gendered critiques of its emergence in any earlier age. No effort was launched by the Party-state to investigate the actual social lives of working families in order to imagine possible alternative ideals based on the way workers lived. It showed how there would be no attempt, as part of the purging of colonial legacies, to target these practices in the name of the socialist family, defined as anticolonial.[33]

All this meant that when Korea emerged from colonialism and then war, the family was deemed in need of saving, not elimination. Socialist visions of architecture designed to heighten communal sensibilities at the expense of family relations had little popular appeal, whether inside or outside the Party-state. Quite the opposite: the family—specifically the nuclear family—was deemed in need of support and succor. Because of this, the socialist claim for housing rested, in these early years, not with architectural design but with the idea of the *mass* production, construction, and distribution of housing. Later, in the early 1960s, the issue of the socialist content of the design of individual apartment units arose. Even then, however, socialist living in this specific context came to be seen in terms of the convenience of daily familial life rather than collective living arrangements. The nuclear family continued to be presumed. It was a roof over nuclear families' heads, understood to provide the material conditions for various forms of reproduction—biological, ideological, and that of labor power—that carried postcolonial and postwar meanings both for the apartments' residents and for the Party-state.

While these memory politics revived pre-collective-era nuclear family ideals, it might have been otherwise. Many families emerged from the war having lost members, whether killed in the war or gone missing. The more than 12 percent dip in population captures the scale of this demographic crisis, but not the sense of loss experienced by the nearly 35 percent of families that experienced a casualty or by the localities where, in some cases, villages lost virtually an entire generation of working-age men.[34] If there had ever been a moment when the physical plight of many families might have enabled a rethinking, a challenging, or an outright abandoning of received ideals in favor of the more varied lived experiences of actual working families, this was it. Yet proponents of the New Living never sought to pattern its ideals on the lived experiences of working people. Indeed, no one called for a turn away from the nuclear family and toward a more open definition of the family that would incorporate within its norms the many fragmented families that, as a result, were largely represented as incomplete. On the contrary, the fragmentation of families captured in widespread representations of widows and orphans emerged as a prominent way to remember the horrors of war that reaffirmed the nuclear family ideal.

Stories about orphans and widows played prominently in memories of the war's traumas. Usually they were presented as having sacrificed the wholeness of their families. Tens of thousands of orphans had been sent abroad during the war for safety, far away from American bombing campaigns, much in the way that British children had been sent from London to North America during the Blitz. While some Korean children were adopted by host families, the majority lived in specially appointed orphanages, which catered to their care with lessons about Korean culture and preparation of Korean food. This adoptive care in Chinese, Soviet, and Eastern European settings—from Dresden to Beijing—came to be framed in ways that expanded the usual rhetoric extolling transnational socialist solidarity.[35] Family metaphors filled these accounts, moving beyond the standard "socialist brothers." When one Korean adoptee in East Germany visited the personal home of President Wilhelm Pieck, the caption to a photo in the national press had her thanking the German people for raising and loving her fellow orphans "as if they were their own children."[36] Top officials including Kim Il Sung, Ch'oe Yonggŏn, Kim Il, and Pak Kŭmch'ŏl all got involved, whether by greeting Eastern European teachers on their visit to Pyongyang or checking in on orphan groups during their foreign state visits.[37] Despite being in distant lands, orphans such as the ones in Budapest were shown as "always having the ancestral land in their hearts."[38] By 1957, when the more than twenty thousand orphans who had been taken in by China "as if they were family" and who had been treated with "brotherly love" began to return, welcome celebrations were held around the country.[39] Their return home four, five, or more years after the conclusion of the armistice symbolized an ending to what, for so many Koreans, had been the primary experience of the war: physical displacement.

The repatriation of wartime orphans also became intertwined with reports about orphans in South Korea, usually shown to be living on the streets of Seoul. This was the classic style of comparative propaganda: orphans generously taken care of by families in the North versus orphans left to find their own way in the South. By 1958, the Women's Union began a movement appealing to mothers in the South to send homeless children to the North, where they promised to take care of them "as mothers." One neighborhood in Pyongyang promised to take in four hundred orphans while other work units promised them clothes and shoes in what was rolled out as a centrally orchestrated national movement.[40] Workers of the Pyongan Pukto Tool Factory, inspired by a colleague and former resident of the downtown Seoul neighborhood of Chunggu, swore an oath to use their savings to open an orphanage on the day of reunification.[41] As the repatriation of wartime orphans faded from the news, the focus on southern orphans continued. By 1965, factories campaigned to collect subscriptions to buy orphans clothes.[42] Concern for southern orphans emerged as another way to envision incomplete families. These offers and campaigns never made news in the South's media, of course. Yet the campaigns continued, in part because they served domestic political purposes. Later, when the South became known for its international adoptions, this style of critique led to even more critiques.

While orphans offered a familial prism through which to lament loss, it took a few years before they became twinned with widows as "families of patriotic martyrs"—the official, laudatory name for families who had sacrificed a member in the fight against either Japan or the United States. By 1956, the figure of the widow captured more systematic, nationwide attention.[43] As some officials described, in the days immediately after the war, widows were the subjects of discrimination. One account suggested that bereaved women tended to be dismissed by their neighbors as unimportant, or as people "who didn't know anything."[44] Many of them suffered, according to newspaper reports, as they struggled to raise their families without the income from working spouses.[45] Letters-to-the-editors by widows—as in the case of Ch'oe Pobu, who described the challenge of educating five children on her own—confirmed these reports.[46] Yet the turn in treatment lay with a specific reason: authorities were laying the ideological groundwork for the sŏngbun system by validating sacrifice and loyalty, which would become the criteria for the top category. Officials began to encourage neighbors to help out widows such that, in the words of an editorial in *Rodong sinmun*, they would have standards of living higher than the average in their work unit—just compensation for their sacrifices, it was argued.[47] On this rationale, widows began to receive preferential treatment in rationing, allocation of housing, job placements, and access to education for their children. In effect this was a benefits program, but it contained something more. The sacrifices of widows and orphans, it was believed, translated into a deeper loyalty based on their fuller appreciation of the Party's enemies. Already, by 1957, some officials identified them as a "core" or "heart" (*haeksim*) of the Party.[48]

Among the many personal stories recounting the travails of widows and orphans, the most powerful merged the two. One such case was that of Yun Ponggu, whose story in the national media reflected how war loss, memory, loyalty, and the provision of benefits came to be institutionalized.[49] Barely twenty-six years old, Yun lost her husband, parents-in-law, and brothers in the war when their village in Pyŏksŏng county was occupied by "enemy forces." She managed to escape, but on return to her village she discovered six orphans, whom she took in as her own children—one way, she was recorded as saying, of repaying her enemies for the crimes against her family. In the type of overachievement typical of model stories, her adoption of six children did not stop her from returning to farming, where she was depicted as managing on her own, a dedication for which she was awarded Party membership. Yet the absence of Yun's husband haunted the account. The account underlined a lack of wholeness. "As a Party member, I will take up the determination of my husband," she is quoted as saying, "and will raise these children with my own strength to be patriotic fighters." This, then, was the officially idealized spirit of the wartime widow, promoted through the selection of such cases for use in publicity for years thereafter. As "patriotic martyr families," widows and orphans may have lived in better conditions after 1958—and here the Party-state took a bow—yet their status remained defined by their incompleteness as families. They remained a living testament to the destruction of colonialism and war as experienced by families, a living memory whose tragic presence was defined by their fragmentation and, inversely, affirmed the current familial norms by what they were ostensibly missing.

DIVORCE AND THE POLITICS OF REPRODUCTION

If the historical fragmentation of families became part of the official memory of the war, authorities also faced the question of what to do about the separation of families through divorce. As part of the growing institutionalization of Party-state power, new family laws were promulgated.[50] To the material design of apartment dwellings and the memory politics of orphans and widows was added a third form of support: legal. The juridical support for heteronormative nuclear family ideals showed how officials prioritized the reconstitution of the postwar family as a remedy for the demographic crisis—a priority that would ultimately subordinate other, more widely proclaimed objectives.

Such was the intent of Cho Ilho, who, in his 1958 textbook for university law students, explained the legal and regulatory norms of the young regime's family law. In introducing the purpose of this textbook, Cho offered another version of the family-rescue narrative: "We have completely broken with what for so long was the basis of feudal family relations and created the basis to enable a new type of family to emerge, the socialist family."[51] Yet what he put in the past tense—"created the basis"—and suggested was a historical process actually remained a project that was very much still underway. His own writing constituted part of that endeavor. In promoting what he called the "socialist family," his textbook revealed what the media did not discuss: that the tumult of war had led to the formation of many ad hoc, formally unrecognized families. At the same time, Cho's opinions on the administrative and legal treatment of these ad hoc families showed how postwar decisions in family law hollowed out key provisions of the gender equality laws—even as the latter were celebrated for breaking with "feudal family relations." In the end, Cho presented the legal and regulatory grounds for shaping what the new apartment residences sought to provide the material conditions for: the happily married conjugal couple, ready to reproduce for the continuity of the nation and to prepare the next generation for the transition to socialism.

The context of Cho's regulatory advice was the continued weakness of official institutions after the war. While much was made in his book's preface about ending the effects of feudalism and colonialism, the body of the text dealt primarily with the postwar social disarray. Local-level administrators faced the dilemma of what to do with unions and separations that had never been recognized by any institutionalized authority. During the war, many couples had not registered their marriages because there had been no local Party-state presence with which to follow any mandated procedure. Women and men, in short, had lived together, had children together, and formed families together, but these key moments in their personal lives remained invisible to the state. This was not a mere idle question of registration. In a centralized economy, a wide swath of state policies—the distribution of rations, the implementation of the sŏngbun system, centrally planned labor allocation, and the allocation of housing, to name a few—depended on registration of the population.

In this sense, Cho offered another glimpse into the unruliness of social life after the war. That he devoted so much attention to explaining the challenges of the postwar family revealed that five years after the armistice, one of the most fundamental tasks of governance—the various types of population registration—remained elusive. His book reflected the limits of central state power while constituting one part of the effort to overcome those limits by ensuring a state presence in the nodal points of family life: marriage, divorce, and child custody. Making them visible and sorting out anomalies became a biopolitical enterprise that bolstered Party-state presence and power in local social worlds. While getting the family "right" offered opportunities to reconstitute the power of Party-state institutions, it also meant trying to harmonize actual families with the ideals represented by Cho's invocation of the "socialist family." Such state interventions were neither unilateral nor merely top-down, of course, since individuals often solicited the Party-state's adjudication of conflicts in pursuit of their personal interests. Cho's treatment of what he saw as the nonnormative unions arising out of the wartime upheaval presented local courts as the ultimate arbiter of the social. It was, after all, in his interest to present the state as the sole neutral actor able to adjudicate disputes—and, in doing so, he could guide the direction of what he called the family's "emergence."

Cho saw unregistered marriages as the biggest challenge, if only because they were the most common legal dispute. These cases held a special poignancy for the regime. In cases where a husband was killed during fighting, should a nonregistered spouse be recognized? What proof of marriage did a bereaved partner need to show if her husband had died or disappeared? Given the growing celebration and preferential treatment of war widows, the answers to such question had important implications not only for posthumous social recognition, but also for bereavement benefits. Cho wanted to recognize these unsanctioned relationships. Yet, as was so often the case when imposing uniform classifications on a varied social population, complications arose.

Cho detailed a case that he saw as typical of those challenging local officials at the time. Eliding the names of the litigants, Cho wrote of a Mr. A who had retired from the military in 1956 and then married a Ms. C.[52] When Mr. A followed proper procedure and registered the marriage, he met with an objection—and soon a court case—from a Ms. B, who claimed that Mr. A had married her six years earlier, before he had entered the military. The problem, of course, was that their wartime alliance had not been registered. Cho did not point out, let alone explain, why the couple had not sought to register the union after the war. Was social recognition of their union sufficient in their eyes? Was registration too expensive? Too bureaucratic? Did local officials in their unnamed region not enforce marriage registration? Cho offered no indication, a silence that itself is telling. Whatever the complexities of the unregistered union, it was not until her partner sought to take advantage of the very existence of the marriage laws that Ms. B turned to those same laws to press her grievance. That Cho provided no insight into her decision to pursue the case was consistent with his general lack of interest in the plaintiff's side of cases. Yet it is important to recognize that Ms. B. initiated the legal challenge. In so doing—like the plaintiffs in thousands of similar cases—she was seeking to protect her rights. But her actions also had the effect of inviting the state back into local social worlds as the legitimate arbitrator of disputes—even though its own designs were not neutral.

And Ms. B had a good case. She explained to the court that during the years of Mr. A's absence, she had raised their daughter under the roof of Mr. A's parental home and helped tend the family farm. When the case came before the court, Mr. A tried to take clever advantage of family law, which of course required marriage registration for recognition of a union: even though he had held a wedding ceremony with Ms. B, he argued that the marriage had never been registered. Not registered, he averred, meant not official. And, being unofficial, his previous relationship with Ms. B should not prevent him from marrying now, ostensibly for the very first time.

The court would have none of Mr. A's reasoning. Even though his claims technically followed the registration regulations, Cho explained how the court necessarily took into consideration the exigencies of war. In its reasoning for affirming the legality of Mr. A's unofficial but "in-fact" marriage to

Ms. B, the court cited the fact that Ms. B had raised their daughter and, at one point, even received spousal benefits from the military. The court's decision thus circumvented an overly legalistic reading of the very laws that, as the rest of Cho's treatise showed, the state was struggling to implement. The norms of the conjugal couple trumped the absence of registration. That Mr. A's association with Ms. B had fulfilled all expectations of the conjugal couple gave the court the grounds it needed to void what it saw as a second, illegal marriage. In explaining this decision, Cho made a rather astounding admission about the continued ineffectiveness of local administration, pointing out that many people still did not understand the procedures and significance of the marriage and registration laws. Or, in cases when they did understand, they had not always been able to undertake the proper bureaucratic procedures. Writing in 1958, Cho concluded that the still very real limits of basic state procedures had to be considered a mitigating circumstance. Cho made no overtly moralizing statements, yet his view of the court decision affirmed that the commitment to the conjugal couple was not just a social but also a moral one.

Cho's focus in this case study thus remained entirely on the relationship between marriage and the family, and at no point did he frame the decision in favor of Ms. B in terms of gender rights. Now legally recognized as Mr. A's wife, Ms. B had also gained the right to divorce him—officially, of course. By 1958, though, what this now official couple may have learned was that getting a divorce was becoming more difficult.

THE CHALLENGES OF GENDERED CRITICISM

If Cho's concern was to affirm proper conjugal relations as the basis of the new family law, this priority also shaped his treatment of divorce. The 1946 gender equality laws had ensured freedom of divorce, guaranteeing women the same rights as men in dissolving a marriage and, in cases of mutual consent, offering few barriers to its dissolution. The law's language was blunt: "When it becomes difficult to continue the married relationship, women have the same rights as men to freely divorce."[53] This was a right for which progressive women had fought since the colonial era. In 1946, no other East Asian country had promulgated an equivalent law.

This historic set of laws was announced when the country remained under Soviet occupation. As Suzy Kim has revealed, Korean authorities knew that similar laws in the Soviet Union in the 1930s had led to high divorce rates.[54] Easy divorce had also often disadvantaged women and children, as husbands and fathers absconded from their financial responsibilities to spouses and offspring.[55] Fearing social instability and less eager to undermine male privilege, Korean authorities moved quickly to blunt the power of the divorce laws. They increased the burden for divorce, adding fees requiring couples to go to court, even in mutual consent cases.[56]

A major change took place in 1956, when mutual-consent divorce was terminated. The cabinet announced this decision on March 8, International Women's Day—a timing that sought to give cover to changes that were in no way aligned with international progressive models. Cho explained the key distinction for the termination as a temporal one, determined by whether a marriage had been concluded pre- or post-liberation. According to Cho's account, there had been a flurry of divorces immediately after 1945, instigated by women eager to escape their colonial-era marriages. Colonial laws, in his accounting, allowed women to be forced by their families to wed, and many had married for economic reasons because they had no independent means of livelihood. These suits for divorce, in Cho's estimation, represented precisely what the gender equality laws had sought to remedy. They offered personal liberation from their unjust, colonial-era marriages. Colonial conditions, Cho explained, necessitated easier divorce laws. Yet this same historical argument justified their termination.

Yun Miryang has argued that the Party-state's commitment to gender equality laws was, in fact, part of its attempt to fulfill its postcolonial goal of purging remaining colonial vestiges—a social and political reasoning not committed to equality.[57] Yun's argument rings true in Cho's case, as he went on to argue that because colonial conditions no longer existed, the historical basis of divorce laws accordingly needed reinterpretation. He conflated the liberation narrative of nation and family with that of gender, arguing that after liberation in 1945 the conditions for marriage had improved to the extent that the same reasons for divorce no longer applied. All marriages after 1945, he implausibly argued, had been formed on the basis of the new equality created by the Party-state. Given the new conditions for marriage, he proposed, there needed to be a new basis for divorce. This logic provided the opening for him to argue that divorce was an impediment to the socialist family.

The dilemma for Cho, however—though he did not explicitly acknowledge it as such—was that divorces had continued even among couples married after 1945. Statistics on divorce rates were not published—a fact that itself was a sign of official disapproval—yet numbers were high enough for Cho to see them as a social problem. He shifted to explaining his rationale for divorce. From seeing the need for divorce as being socially and politically derived during the colonial era, he turned to a reasoning focused on individuals. Personal desires, in his estimation, had become misaligned with societal needs, as evidenced by these marriage disunions. "The nation's law must regulate the divorce problem while taking into account both the interests of the individual and interests of society."[58] This fusing of interests was an old strategy, subordinating the individual, usually the female spouse, to unspecified communal interests, usually aligned with those of the male spouse—exactly what the original divorce laws sought to overcome. Accordingly, for Cho, only in the rarest of cases would there be the need for divorce—what he called "true" divorce.[59] "The freedom of divorce," he went on to explain with an all-important qualification, must include the demand "to stabilize the family against hasty divorces of little basis, which run against the interests of society."[60] As in so many other areas, stability trumped revolutionary concerns.

Cho listed three conditions defining "true divorce." All three reflected a state paternalism, which removed the decision from the hands of the couple and ran contrary to the spirit of the gender equality laws. First, for Cho, divorce should not stem from a sense of ennui, antagonism, or discord. Such "momentary emotions," he averred, constituted insufficient reason. Second, a plaintiff needed to show that the continuation of the marriage did not violate the "various principles of socialist morality"—an expression that, as we have seen, became as common as it was ill-defined, though the context here gave Cho's usage a connotation of sexual impropriety. Third, in what would emerge as the most oft-repeated claim for years to come, Cho warned that the relationship of the spouses should not be considered in isolation but must emphasize the interests of children.[61] Nowhere did this definition affirm a specific right of women to initiate divorce, and, as defined by Cho, that would be virtually impermissible after women bore children. If the early gender equality laws looked back to the specifically gendered injustices of the pre-socialist era, the new regulations dispensed with a historical and gendered approach, substituting instead a forward-looking vision that subsumed issues of equality into the reformation of the family as a means for solving specific problems—social stability, a demographic crisis, and male anxieties among them—on the path to building socialism.[62] Cho's notion of "true divorce" abandoned a key right for which women in the peninsula had struggled since the 1920s. The juridical right to divorce, announced with fanfare in 1946, came to be undermined by subsequent administrative and legal procedures that privileged the masculinist nuclear family—even as gender equality continued to be trumpeted in the media as one of the historic achievements and ongoing projects of the Party-state.

This incongruity—narrowing access to divorce under the guise of a socialist family based on gender equality—became evident in the annual commemorations of the gender equality laws. Virtually every year on July 30, the day in 1946 of the new laws' promulgation, media outlets regaled their readers with explanations of the historical significance wrought by these changes.[63] On the fifteenth anniversary, a two-page spread in *Women of Korea* announced how the laws represented the long-term struggle of women for their liberation from dismissive treatment, exploitation, and inability to move out of the house—all tropes that had themselves been standard for decades prior to the collective era.[64] Yet the 1961 commemorative article made no mention whatsoever of the right to divorce as one of the achievements of the original legislation.[65] This silence also characterized the coverage in *Rodong sinmun* in that year. Even in an overly optimistic speech listing the achievements of women, Pak Chŏngae, the single most powerful woman in the country and a close ally of Kim Il Sung, left divorce off her accounting of accomplishments.[66] Not even fifteen years after the gender equality laws had been announced, the right to divorce had been gutted—and, just as ominously, erased from the official memory of the historical significance of those laws.

This must have been a wrenching reversal for members of the Women's Union. Older members would have remembered colonial-era feminist struggles that had foregrounded divorce—a priority that early propaganda had acknowledged. Many must also have remembered how central the right to divorce was to the vision of the future in the 1946 gender equality laws. And many would have witnessed, if not experienced, the personal effects—in practice as well as ideology—of the changes in the right to divorce after the promulgation of the laws. Of course, given the authoritarian environment, any dismay at the reversal of the divorce laws could not be openly expressed in Party-state publications. Nevertheless, careful readers likely discerned a discretely expressed sense of disgruntlement in the pages of *Women of Korea*. For one, the editors did not even announce the legal changes in its pages. For a publication whose mandate was to assist in creating the conditions for the implementation of Party-state policies, it greeted the abolition of mutual-consent divorce with a telling silence. No one could have learned about this change or its ramifications from its publication's pages.

Readers may also have gleaned a sense of the dismay among the Women's Union in the one article about divorce that *Women of Korea* published in 1956. Entitled "Why Did You Want to Divorce?," the story recounted the struggles of a couple to salvage their crumbling union.[67] Insofar as it represented the dissolution of marriage as socially unsavory, the piece certainly fulfilled the Union's task of supporting the shift in Party-state policies and fit neatly with what Cho Ilho would write two years later. Yet, seen within the broader context of the tone and content of the magazine, the article was highly unusual. The editorial stance of *Women of Korea* had, since its inception, given voice to the diverse ways in which women had been participating in socialist construction since the war. Yet in dealing with the marital challenges of one couple—wife Sim Chŏngsun and husband Kim Ilhun—this particular article remarkably took on the voice and perspective of the husband alone. "Why Did You Want to Divorce?" appeared under the byline of Kim Kyŏngsuk (a woman's name), who, like many press reporters of this era, is unknown to us today. It is certainly possible that, as has been shown to have occurred in women's magazines in other countries, the author was a male who simply used a female name—though it was common for many male authors to accurately self-identify in the magazine's pages. We know very little about the magazine's editorial-board politics, yet what is clear is that the article stands out for its explicit masculinist perspective—a rarity in this magazine.[68] It is also tempting to entertain the possibility that the outlier perspective of the article, together with its treatment of the husband's thoughts and behavior toward his wife—again, so out of line with the regular editorial position of the magazine—was a deliberate strategy to underline the discriminatory nature of the changes to the divorce law by showcasing extremely iniquitous consequences.

Whatever the case, no regular reader could have missed the extraordinariness of the story. They would have quickly realized that the story completely ignored Sim Chŏngsun's thoughts on her marriage, in favor of an extended treatment of her husband's interior monologue. The article began with Ilhun's conflicted thoughts on what to do about his precarious marriage, then framed his answer to the titular question as resting solely in his hands, going so far as to wonder why he had to live with the same woman for a whole lifetime. This remarkable moment of male self-pity in a women's magazine was cut short, however, when Ilhun suddenly realized that a divorce was unthinkable for the sake of their children. Ilhun is next shown hypothetically pondering, "If we didn't have children, would it *then* be OK to get an immediate divorce?" He answered negatively, taking up the logic that underpinned the changes in the divorce law: "If men and women live together and then get divorced, what will happen to social order?" Here Ilhun adopts, in effect, the voice of the Party-state, invoking reasons transcendent to himself, which were now being offered as reasons to put up with less-than-ideal marriages. In the words that Cho Ilho would later spell out, Ilhun realized he did not have the conditions for a "true divorce."

With his conviction *not* to divorce, Ilhun was next shown reflecting on the reasons for his dissatisfactory marriage—a perspective the author never gave to Chŏngsun. Instead, Ilhun listed an inventory of his wife's shortcomings, using the language of advice literature to conclude that his wife's "cultural level" did not rank sufficiently high. His critical gaze never turned to his own behavior. In Ilhun's eyes—and with little qualification by the reporter—Chŏngsun was represented as a woman without cultivation, a "wife without a spiritual life." She argued on the street, treated her husband's guests poorly, and did not teach her children properly—a "selfish, narrow" woman whose worldview, in the words of the author, "did not venture beyond herself, her husband, and her children." These qualities, Ilhun pointed out, together with Chŏngsun's inability to self-diagnose her need to improve herself, emerged as the root cause of the marital difficulties. The troubles were, in short, his wife's fault. The answer to this dilemma, as articulated by the protagonist and favorably promoted in the article's account of his thinking, fit neatly with the era's emphasis on individual self-cultivation: Chŏngsun needed to self-reform, but in this case her efforts would be possible only through what the rest of the article showed to be the gentle prodding and guidance of her husband. In an era that placed such high value on self-criticism, Ilhun never turned his evaluating gaze on himself.

The remainder of the story narrated this process of Chŏngsun's self-amelioration. While this genre of self-improvement generally linked efforts to heighten cultural levels with grander social goals, usually as a contribution to building socialism, Chŏngsun's story became a *Pygmalion*-type account of her husband's efforts to raise her cultural levels for the sake of the marriage, if not quite for her husband personally. No grander goal provided context. The article clearly positioned her as subordinate to her husband, who came across as attuned to the cultural needs of the era in comparison to his spouse. As Ilhun deprecatingly told her in phrasing that ran markedly counter to the ethos of the magazine, "I don't expect you to be especially learned. I just hope you'll have the warm humanity and propriety that an ordinary woman should have."[69] Books, movies, discussions—together the couple pursued the classic pattern of study favored by the proponents of advice literature. And, of course, the article depicted this process as successful. In an affirmation of what the author described as Ilhun's "patience" in redeeming the marriage, the final line described Ilhun's response upon hearing his wife's laughter: finally, "after a long time his cheerful heart returned." Laughter and cheerfulness, achieved without divorce, confirmed the significance of the stability of family relations. In effect, Ilhun's perspective stood in for the voice of the Party-state. This congruent and mutually reinforcing perspective, whereby it was difficult to distinguish masculinist norms from the power of the Party-state, indicated the challenges faced by feminist writers in openly opposing the changes to divorce law in this authoritarian setting.

"Why Did You Want to Divorce?" remained a stand-alone piece. No other articles of its type emerged in the pages of *Women of Korea* that year, and few other articles in the subsequent years raised the divorce issue.[70] For other issues of importance to the Party-state, the Women's Union generally devoted regular, often incessant, and impassioned coverage in the pages of the magazine. Given the significance of divorce, this absence was itself noteworthy.[71]

The evident displeasure, however restrained, was likely one reason why, when Cho Ilho published his textbook two years later, his explanation had a defensive tone. More likely than not, the dissatisfaction of the Women's Union circulated more widely than was captured in contemporary media. Because of this, Cho likely felt the need to explain that the policy changes should not be seen as a narrowing of access to divorce—a good indication that this was precisely how they were being interpreted by many. His prose reflected an awareness of this resistance or dissatisfaction, even as he disavowed it, arguing that the conditions of socialism trumped virtually every legitimate reason for divorce. It was a logic, moreover, that ultimately put the blame on individuals and the cultural work they had done—or not done—on themselves. And as "Why Did You Want to Divorce?" showed, this logic was more likely to apply to female spouses. For Cho, issues of social order, glossed as the superior conditions of socialism, took precedence—a basis he even invoked to justify the one exception he countenanced for divorce.

DEMOGRAPHIC CRISIS AND THE FAMILY

The developing legal support for the nuclear-family norm gained its urgency in the context of the mass death of war. Nowhere was this clearer than in

Cho's willingness to temper his anti-divorce stance to support the pro-natalist priorities of social planning.

Unlike in China, where Mao made much-publicized statements relating population size to national strength, neither Kim Il Sung nor any other prominent leader specifically urged more procreation. Yet the fact that Kim Il Sung addressed the All-Nation Congress of Mothers in 1961, four years before appearing at his first postwar national meeting of the Women's Union, gave a sense of his priorities.[72] Indeed, the pro-natalist leanings of the era were evident everywhere. Economists suggested that the sole long-term resolution of the labor shortage rested with procreation.[73] *Women of Korea* regularly featured advice on prenatal and postnatal care, including features on hygiene during pregnancy,[74] how to prepare for the day of delivery,[75] the prevention of miscarriages,[76] and what type of stylish clothes to wear that would keep a baby warm in winter.[77] Pediatrics emerged as one of the priority investment areas in the growing health care system.[78] And, at least in the major cities, hospitals set up counseling services for pregnant women, including home visits.[79] The establishment of motherhood schools in both cities and the countryside sought to provide a venue to formalize the advice of elder generations for young mothers, passing along knowledge about what to expect during pregnancy, birthing assistance, and nutritional advice for newborns. It is likely that in these settings, topics not discussed publicly (such as birth control) were raised.[80] Nor did writers refrain from discussing the impact of pregnancy on their bodies, one going so far as to inform the editors that she hated her post-birth body and ask how she could regain her original shape.[81] Such was the symbolic and demographic importance that national editorials wrote regularly about the happiness of children.[82]

Photographers filled the pages of magazines, especially *Women of Korea*, with images of chubby-cheeked toddlers and small children smiling as they played singly or in groups. While the trope of happy families typically featured an image of a couple with the standard two children, other stories celebrated much larger sets of offspring—"A Mother of Nine Children," extolled in a national newspaper headline, or a mother with seven soldier children.[83] Photos of babies were everywhere, often shown with their mothers, and titled with some version of "happiness" (see figure 18).[84]

There was, in short, no need for grandiose pro-natalist statements from leadership. Indeed, it would be no exaggeration to suggest that the first cult in Korea was not Kim Il Sung's but one centered on motherhood. Moreover—as in the United States, where Americans responded to the onset of peace with a

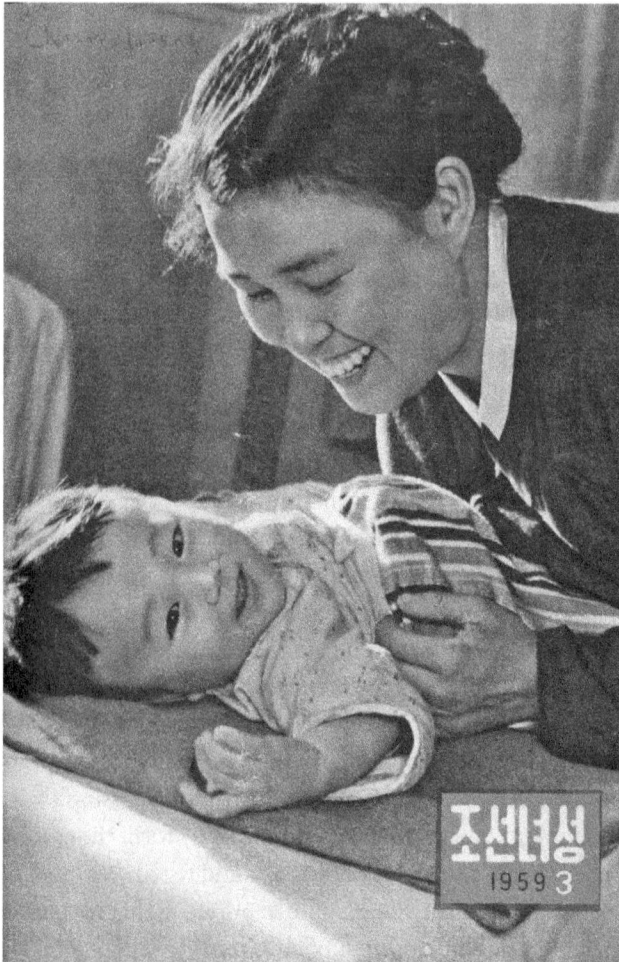

FIGURE 18. A *Women of Korea* cover showing a mother and baby. Anonymous, untitled, 1959.

famous "baby boom"—Koreans after more than seventeen years of warfare also procreated in unprecedented numbers. Yet the American boom paled in comparison to the Korean birth rate.[85] As Nicholas Eberstadt and Judith Banister have shown, when the fighting stopped in 1953, the total population of North Korea was some 8,491,000. The figure had climbed to 10,789,000 by 1960 and continued to increase, reaching 12,408,000 by 1965. The first dozen years of postwar living represented a nearly 50 percent growth in total population.[86] Meanwhile, below the DMZ, the South Korean population (over 20 million in 1953) grew at a fast, yet comparatively slower, rate of 38.9 percent over the same period.

It was in line with this pro-natalist trend that Cho raised the issue of divorce in cases of couples unable to have children. Since the war, courts had been unsympathetic to such divorces, choosing to maintain the integrity of the family, regardless of a couple's inability to procreate. Cho objected. Even in cases where there had been medical verification proving the infeasibility of a couple's having children, Cho complained, the court had rejected requests for divorce. He insisted the courts had been too rigid. If a strong desire for children impaired the marriage to the point that "spousal relations cannot be recovered," Cho thought that the request for divorce should be treated as legitimate.[87] Qualifying this slightly, while revealing the underlying gendered assumption, he recommended that so long as there was no ulterior motive, such as "intimate relations with another woman," the divorce should go ahead. His view reproduced a patrilineal assumption about divorce that could be traced back to the Chosŏn dynasty: that not bearing children provided sufficient grounds for divorce. Although Cho did not say so, the implication was that this right remained a male privilege. Cho made no connection, in this case, with what was otherwise one of his overriding concerns: social order. Nor did he invoke the language of "true divorce." Implicit to this exception to "solidifying the family" is that a primary purpose for the postwar recuperation of the family was its biological function in rebuilding the national population. The sole issue that had the power to shake his confidence in the stability of his socialist family was the absence of offspring.

But Cho did not get his way. His objection, along with the views on divorce of the Women's Union, revealed much about how writers and thinkers advanced their ideas in an authoritarian environment, when notions of "revolutionary optimism" and ideological harmony corralled open debate. Cho's direct objection, however much buried in a university textbook, contrasted with the more muted, yet more public, unease and telling silences expressed by the editors of *Women of Korea*. Yet both show how certain fundamental issues, having themselves evolved out of a longer history, could remain undetermined and reflect multiple voices speaking to one another without openly acknowledging it. But the issue did not end there.

That these divergent voices quietly coexisted, with only the barest indication of conflict in the print media, was best attested three years later, when none other than Kim Il Sung took up the issue at the 1961 All-Nation Congress of Mothers. Kim spoke not as someone who was raising the issue for the first time, but as someone using the opportunity to present himself as the arbiter on the dispute. "Some people say they are going to get divorced because their wives cannot have a son," he pointed out, revealing openly the bias for male progeny that Cho did not directly acknowledge. Kim went on to criticize this belief, seemingly addressing his comments to husbands even though he was in a room full of mothers. "Not being able to have a son is certainly sad, but how is this such a big issue for communists? Once one marries and lives with one's wife, it's not proper to abandon her for this reason."[88] Ever siding with stability, he concurred with the already established direction of the courts, affirming that the unity of the conjugal couple trumped pro-natalist concerns—no doubt much to the consternation of those who, like Cho, sought to change the laws.

By the time of Kim's speech, considerable support had been extended to families recovering from colonialism and war. Apartments designed for families repopulating the cities constituted the main form of housing. Historical narratives that privileged the family as a subject of national history merged with Party histories, the latter taking credit for rescuing the former from the tumult of the past. And new marriage laws gave primacy to the nuclear family, even at the expense of the Party's earlier support for equal access to divorce and in the face of the opposition of the Women's Union. These three realms of support made clear what the Party-state envisioned as the familial norms for the New Living. Yet as the doors of the new apartments opened to their residents, concerns quickly turned from the form that families would take to anxieties about what families were actually doing inside these new spaces.

SEVEN

The Politics of Unhappy Housewives

THE IDEOLOGICAL THREATS OF HOUSEHOLD INTERIORS

Soon enough, there emerged a contrapuntal theme to all the claims of domestic happiness: unhappiness. More specifically, in an emerging series of disapproving—though at times sympathetic—representations of a stock figure, the unhappy housewife rose to prominence, ironically, as soon as the new apartments began to open in large numbers.

New spaces generated new anxieties. Numerous authorities, ranging from the highest echelons of the Party-state to writers in the daily media, expressed alarm at the potential consequences of the very apartments they celebrated. But defining proper apartment living and how to bring it about was not straightforward. Along the way, received questions—about the definition and hierarchy of labor, the discursive juxtaposition of the home's interior and exterior, the (im)balance of wage work with domestic duties, the use of modern global ideas of scientific household management in the Korean context, and the transferral of responsibilities (domestic and otherwise) to women—reemerged, with new contextual twists, in pursuit of the "socialist family."

The irony was that the anxieties about apartment interiors arose from the successes of reconstruction. Apartments, it was feared, might be *too* comfortable and *too* enjoyable. By contrast, in the contemporary Soviet Union, which was also experiencing a boom in apartment construction, the de-Stalinization movement had, by the late 1950s, entered the home with a post-Stalin design aesthetic that emphasized domestic coziness, as Susan Reid has shown.[1] In Korea, the concern of authorities lay less with interior design itself and more with how apartments might offer a disincentive for women to head out of their homes for wage work at a time when, as every economist continually warned, the demand for their labor remained acute. Additionally, Party ideologues worried that cozy apartments might also dissuade housewifemothers from engaging in the local-level political work deemed necessary for the biopolitical and security responsibilities of local governance. Thus, even as the home was celebrated as the space of biological reproduction and the reproduction of labor, interiors came to be ideologically framed in opposition to exteriors. Eschewing the language of private versus public, the Party framed interiors as unproductive, largely feminine spaces that were subordinate to the exterior, where the ideological and cultural efforts deemed vital for the transition to socialism took place.

At the core of this discursive juxtaposition of inside and outside, and its implications for a spatial definition of productivity, lay a presumption about the nature of labor. Few issues were as central to a self-proclaimed proletarian country, yet there was very little theorization about the distinction between the official category of labor—usually indicated by the venerable term *rodong*—and what was seen as a subordinate category of unpaid domestic work done largely by women. *Rodong* as a category remained the reserve of paid participation by women and men in the economic means of production. This distinction left more pedestrian and less valued terms for women's work inside apartments, usually *kajong il* (household work) or *kasa* (domestic matters). When writers extolled "dependent family members" (*puyang kajok*) for taking up paid labor, explaining that this was the only way for them to achieve true equality with men, the corollary was that domestic work was not the equal of wage work. Over the following years, much effort went into exploring the relationship of interior and exterior through discussions of women's unpaid labor in and around the home.

Distinctions about the spatial hierarchy of work became evident in a flurry of stories about unhappy housewives featured in media of the late 1950s and early 1960s. This continued the earlier treatment of "dependent family members" yet expanded it in diverse directions. In 1960, Kim Yŏngsuk described in *Women of Korea* her domestic life, reproducing the era's dominant presumption that equated wage labor with happiness—the latter presented as impossible without the former. As Kim explained, "After I got married, all I did was isolate myself in my home, not even reading a single book and always complaining to my husband."[2] Devoting all her time to family affairs, including the raising of children, she recounted becoming so concerned with domestic matters that she even turned down the possibility of becoming a neighborhood hygiene inspector—generally considered a plum position that exemplified one's political commitments. Her story, as she put it, was one of self-indulgence. She explained that she did not even realize the joys she was missing by refusing to participate in social activities, let alone in the paid labor force. It was, as she described it, a "colorless existence." She was unhappy.

Kim Yŏngsuk's reasoning in explaining her unhappiness reflected Party-state time, specifically its post-1958 ideological line. Like people in other social settings, she was working out how this general line would be relevant to the specifics of her own domestic life. Fitting the renewed emphasis on an individual's ideological commitments, her account turned on her own responsibility, becoming tantamount to an exercise in self-blame. It was not that she had no opportunities to earn a wage, she explained, but that she had been too selfish and narrow-minded. The solution she offered also rested in her own hands: once she became aware of her situation, she simply "made up her mind" (*kyŏlshim*) to "correct her lifestyle and raise her level of culture."[3] The story ended when Kim headed out to find a paid position—and, in the logic of this genre, became happy.

Kim's account was significant not just in presenting her turn to paid labor, but also in the way she framed this as a matter of individual decision. She glossed over the pressures on women to find wage work and expressed no concern over structural obstacles to the participation of women. As she put it, "[I] made up my mind." She did not use the more overtly ideological language of self-initiation (*ch'angbal*) or "being host" of the matter (*chuindapke*), yet her sensibility fit neatly with notions about the ideological laggardness of the population. The story was also neatly timed in following a March 1958 conference that had emphasized the centrality of women's paid labor to the goals of the Five-Year Plan.[4]

A year before Kim Yŏngsuk's story was published, Pak Chŏngae addressed the issue of women's paid labor during an All-Nation Women Socialist Builders Meeting. Pak began by acknowledging the contributions of women to such postwar achievements as the socialization of the means of production, the universalization of middle school, and the rise in wages. Yet no one, she cautioned, in what was a typical turn of phrase in the era, should be satisfied with the results.[5] More was needed. Pak did not mince words in naming her target: women who had "entered the home" and now "sit comfortably and, to the benefit of their husbands, peacefully take care of living." Pak had the authority to make the rare public admission that social welfare facilities—day care, cafeterias, laundromats, and the like—remained too few, unable to fulfill demand. The situation, she admitted, left many unable to go to work "worry free." But Pak was not there to give her audience of seventeen hundred excuses by suggesting that central authorities alone would remedy this lack. Instead, she turned her admission about the lack of facilities back on the audience, exhorting them to "raise their quality," work with local authorities, and appreciate that, at root, this was an issue of "ideological struggle" (*sasang t'ujaeng*). She pinned the solution on her audience's ability to self-reform, educate themselves, and push themselves. In other words, just as Kim Yŏngsuk would figure out what was necessary for herself, so should they. Together these two accounts worked at different levels to offer a specifically gendered translation of the general Party-state goals into the local social worlds of family life and domestic relations. By the late 1950s, it had become standard in the pages of *Women of Korea* to dismiss women who did not take up wage labor. This emerged as one of the few behaviors that the magazine occasionally stooped to call bourgeois.[6]

Stories like Kim Yŏngsuk's were certainly significant for the ways they illustrated the contradictions and pressures on individual women in specific social situations. They also showed how writers carried out their responsibilities to amplify Party-state commitments by using the idiosyncrasies of their personal experiences to highlight individual responsibility. Across the media, the usual profiles of successful women in wage-labor positions were augmented with accounts of individuals who expressed an initial worry about, or resistance to, taking on wage work, or who had their fears about hard work allayed once they started.[7] An array of tropes emerged. Female college graduates admitted to wasting state investment in their education by staying at home and denying the skill-starved economy the benefits of their training.[8] Other authors wrote about how they were only willing to take up wage work close to their home, believed they did not have the strength for certain type of "tough" jobs, or—as one older worker put it—were only willing to accept "rice cakes that suited their taste."[9] Stories frequently mentioned the material awards to be reaped—the extra cash in their pockets to improve their family lives. Cartoonists lambasted women who quit their jobs upon marriage—"an excuse for hating work," wrote one.[10] Whatever strategy an individual author pursued, the sympathy that had infused accounts about "dependent family members" just a few years earlier was dissipated in these stories. Now the greater urgency of the labor shortage translated into a newfound impatience, one indicative of the growing pressure on housewife-mothers to ensure their own participation—and that of their friends and neighbors—in wage work.

These pressures led to the proliferation of expressions dismissive of women's domestic work. In an era when the media typically refrained from using contemptuous terms for any social group other than class enemies, the emergence of such derogatory expressions was remarkable. That this was possible demonstrated the power of how interiors had been framed as unproductive and feminine. In less generous hands, Kim Yŏngsuk's gentle self-reproach, with its inward-looking reflexivity, or Pak Chŏngae's unwillingness to allow for excuses, could become disparaging jabs. Most often, the expression "people playing and eating" (*nolgo mongnŭn saram*) emerged as a publicly acceptable form of ridicule and as a synonym for "dependent family members." Such phrases did not emerge from official Party-state statements, of course, but came from the ways in which writers amplified, expanded, and adapted them. This could be seen in a letter to the editor submitted to a national newspaper by Ra Chaeguk, a son in a working family who clearly perceived that there was cultural capital to be gained by boasting about one's family "happiness." Reporting proudly that everyone in his family was either gainfully employed or studying at school, he pointed out that there was not a single member of his family who was merely "playing and eating."[11] Despite Ra's ostensibly gender-neutral use of the expression, it came to be used primarily for housewife-mothers. By 1965, the spread of these demeaning terms can be seen in Kim Il Sung's speech in front of the Women's Union, in which he used the most pejorative sense of the expression.[12] His use of the term in such a prominent venue only legitimated its further circulation.

Variations arose. Nor did the editors of *Women of Korea* refrain from joining in. In a story about TaeAn Electric Factory, the director of the factory-level Women's Union, Kim Osŏp, was shown explaining how her members did not want to become "housewives who only made and ate rice."[13] Or, as one cartoonist had a character ask, "In this Ch'ŏllima era, how can one just be buried away at home?"[14] Some husbands, *Women of Korea* reported without protest, made less-than-generous references to their spouses as their home's "rice bucket" (*papt'ong*).[15] In these types of phrases, blame for what was seen as selfish idleness fell entirely on the shoulders of women, with little attention to the socioeconomic reasons for their isolation. They were seen as "hiding," of their own volition and due to their backward thinking, in their ostensibly unproductive apartments. The emphasis on the individual never went so far as to openly legitimize the choice of *not* going out for paid wage work. The underlying message was evident: a lifestyle that contributed to socialist construction meant escaping the very apartment spaces that were simultaneously celebrated as a grand achievement of the young regime.[16]

These terms of disparagement became a shorthand available to any writer—male or female—who wished to decry or criticize what they imagined going on inside apartments or exhort the inhabitants to do better. It became a strand of argumentation that established the priority of paid labor (*rodong*), highlighted the urgency of mother-workers, and rendered apartment interiors as both unproductive and feminine. Given how expressions such as "playing and eating" resonated with such powerful Party-state priorities and received the imprimatur of top leaders, it was not easy to argue against their use—and few did, at least directly. Yet at the same time that this dismissive rhetoric circulated, many writers in *Women of Korea* did push back. As much as they reproduced the hierarchy of paid labor's superiority over domestic labor, they nevertheless adopted strategies that sought to underline the significance of domestic labor to the national economy and the transition to socialism.

COOPERATIVE HUSBANDS?

In the years after the war, there was a surfeit of romantic homage to the figure named not just mother, but specifically *Korean* mother (*Chosŏn ŏmŏni*). Motherhood was more often featured in poems penned to "Chosŏn ŏmŏni" than in serious discussions of domesticity in these years.[17] Most national-level discussions of the "Women Question," such as editorials in the national newspaper *Rodong sinmun*, were focused on labor, education, and technical training. A typical editorial, published on International Women's Day in 1955, detailed everything from women's participation in central and local state organizations to how much better off they were than their South Korean counterparts.[18] There was but one mention of mothers, almost an afterthought, citing them as the beneficiaries of the Party's munificence near the end of the article. This early silence about motherhood in analyses of the challenges and advancement of women reflected contemporary top-level economic priorities.

Nevertheless, even that minimal recognition of mothers was enough for the Women's Union to push, within its broader agenda, awareness of the unaddressed challenges their membership faced on the home front. Due to their efforts, together with the high-profile opening of more apartments and the need to mediate the Party's renewal of ideological priorities, a surge of attention soon followed. The publicity surrounding the participation of the Women's Union delegation to the 1955 World Congress of Mothers in Lausanne, Switzerland, helped push this effort along.[19] By 1961, when Kim Il Sung addressed motherhood at the first All-Nation Congress of Mothers, he was playing catch-up to what had already become a surge of discussions.[20] As the ideal of the mother-worker rose to increasing prominence, *Women of Korea*—and, later, the general-interest magazine *Ch'ŏllima* (for the meaning of the word and its associated movement, see chapter 5)—redefined and expanded Party-state conceptual categories to highlight women's domestic work in all sorts of ways that neither the early *Rodong sinmun* editorials nor Kim Il Sung in his 1961 speech imagined.

This pushback against notions of interior spaces being unproductive was evident in the photographic record in *Women of Korea*, which regularly published photos of women from all walks of life in their homes *doing* things. Housewives and mothers, in these images, engaged in the self-study required of the ideologically correct, sitting alone at home with a book in hand. So, too, were they shown assisting elderly women, whether teaching them to read as part of the literacy campaign, helping them "heighten" their cultural levels, or simply visiting their neighbors (see figure 19).[21] Significantly, these photos did not celebrate the apartments' interiors themselves. That would come later. The editors instead closely cropped the photos' borders, revealing just enough to locate the activities as occurring in a domestic space while not straying from the subject(s).[22] Camera angles avoided offering readers any sense of the home as a material environment that might be too comfortable or luxurious. This was not the space of "eating and playing," but one where important work, if not quite the official version of labor, was being done. The photos reinforced a sense of feminized interiors, but as productive and connected to broader political goals.

In the pages of *Women of Korea*, the productivity of domestic space was explored most elaborately with regard to the question of how readers should pursue wage work while also meeting expectations to manage the home and rear children—what today would be referred to as the double burden. Or, in the words of one writer, Kim Sanggi: "With a husband and four children, how do I manage work life and home life?"[23] In answering Kim Sanggi's question, many writers turned to a term promoted in factories and offices around the country: *saengsan munhwa* (production culture).

This term became widespread after the war as yet another way for culture to be invoked in promoting individual self-reform and discipline.[24] The term

FIGURE 19. Anonymous, "A People's Home Care Worker," 1957.

had a distinct biopolitical slant, as can be seen in its frequent association with dirty and disorganized workplaces or worker punctuality—both problems seen as reflecting how individual cultural levels influenced work output. "Production culture" could also be invoked in writing about using proper methods and technology.[25] Or as one headline put the main point, "Hygiene Goes Hand in Hand with Production; Let Us Establish Production Culture."[26] Virtually any practice that could be categorized as *undisciplined*, *noncultural*, or *unhealthy*—all terms employed in its name—could be accused of interfering with production culture.

The expansiveness and flexibility of this key term for workplace culture proved useful to the editors of *Women of Korea*. In effect, they brought it home. The most mundane domestic issue could be connected via this conceptual framework—whether named or not—to achieving the cultural levels that would lead to socialist transition. After all, if Kim Il Sung related personal hygiene to the construction of socialism, it was no stretch to connect the many hygiene-related issues associated with the New Living to that same grand enterprise. And if Kim Il Sung made hygiene a central concern, then *Women of Korea* could assert that hygiene started in the household. Similar connections had been made during the colonial era, only now writers twisted them in the direction of a different political-economic goal. This mode of connection had writers crossing the all-too-neat inside/outside ideological division on which ideas of "eating and playing" depended. Now, in the hands of the editors of *Women of Korea*, these connections were played up to redefine interiors as still feminine, but now spaces where the ups and downs of economic production would, in part, be determined.

In answer to Kim Sanggi's fundamental question—how to manage work life and home life?—a mountain of advice emerged. Older readers would have remembered similar advice from household information tracts of the 1930s—a genealogy that, of course, remained unacknowledged. Channels of domestic advice extending back in time were joined by sources that circulated from the larger socialist world. Soviet household handbooks and parenting guides were translated and, in some cases, became standard materials for Women's Union study groups.[27]

The unspoken context of all this advice, again, was the insufficiency of promised social welfare support from the state. The lack of investment in public cafeterias or industrialization of food, for example, meant that the magazine published a wide range of self-help articles for their readers, like the recipes for preparing nutritious meals that appeared in almost every issue.[28] Similarly, light industries were producing insufficient quantities of off-the-rack clothes, but sewing guides and patterns were regularly featured in *Women of Korea* for making items like summer blouses suitable for two-piece suits, stuffed animals, stylish one-pieces, and scarf-and-glove ensembles (see figure 20).[29] One issue even had pull-out sewing patterns in a special slip pocket.[30] And with access to night programs for adult education still limited, primers for self-study were published, including guides to household science, collections of popular health remedies, readers on family life, and manuals explaining communist morality and etiquette for women.[31] Also published were collections of model women's biographies, with titles like "Beautiful Women," "Red Women," and "Korean Mothers."[32] If the 1950s and '60s were an era of advice, the amount of gender-specific advice for women was especially prolific. In short, when the Party-state was not helping, people had to make do on their own. All this practical advice would help them out.

But who had the time to manage all these recommendations? At the core of all this advice lay an exhortation to household efficiency—a feature of household advice found around the world.[33] Significantly, writers in *Women of Korea* and *Ch'ŏllima* adopted the same terms used for central planning (*kyehoek*) or Party organizing (*kujo*) for their domestic matters—how to plan and organize in the most efficient manner all the conflicting daily demands. In a typical story, Pak Pongok recounted how everyone, when they learned she had five kids and worked at a Pyongyang middle school, asked her the same question: "With five children, how do you get all your household affairs done while working in education?" Her quick answer was "If you organize your life well, there's nothing you can't do."[34] Her longer account of how she organized her life, however, showed that it was no easy matter. She explained that her day started every morning at dawn as she began to cook until it was time to go to work. Her big problem was laundry, but as she advised her readers, it was best to do a little at a time during the morning or evening's kitchen work. She also explained the challenge in squeezing political study into her schedule, but eventually she learned the best thing was to do it at night, no matter how late she returned from work. Yet Pak had certain advantages, which she mentioned in passing. Being in Pyongyang and working in the school system, she had access to child care and public cafeterias, unlike the majority of her readers, including many in the capital city. Still, her message was unaltered: rationally organizing one's domestic life was the basis of successful, happy living. While Pak did not use the language of cultural levels, others did. And they gave advice on all manner of domestic management issues, from proper nutrition to prudent management of household budgets.[35] In this way, household management was related to production, which was seen as a result of one's cultural levels. All of these elements were combined, under the Party-state's general ideological shift, to make a series of criteria for judging an individual wife-mother's mastery of household skills, which could always be opened up to ideological and political interpretations.

The turn to cultural levels as an explanatory framework, and the lionization of the remarkable discipline and tenacity of the subset of women who managed to "do it all," certainly served the expectations of the Women's Union to support Party-state policies. This was the path, it would seem, to help remedy the labor shortage: by eliminating domestic encumbrances to becoming a mother-worker and, for individuals like Kim Sanggi and Pak Pongok, garnering the not insignificant cultural capital associated with the mother-worker ideal. Moreover, in an era when it remained possible to demean the importance of domestic labor with a cutting line or two, these discussions highlighted the centrality of what went on in apartments to the political economy and the transition to socialism—even if not everyone was predisposed to listen. There was much to be gained.

FIGURE 20. Anonymous, "How to Make Winter Gloves and
Mufflers," 1956.

Within these efforts to push back, writers nevertheless remained reluctant
to raise broader gender critiques that considered deeper structural or cultural
problems. This remained a delicate political issue. The call to emulate model
mother-workers may have highlighted the value of their unpaid domestic
labor and its connection to national goals. It also rightly celebrated the shifting gender terrain created by the large numbers of women participating in
wage labor. Yet returning to a focus on the individual and her abilities to
master the necessary household management skills reflected an acceptance
of, rather than a challenge to, the reasons for the double burden. It became a
matter of planning, organizing, and managing—without raising questions
about the uneven experiences among women, about how this fit the norms of
the supposedly new socialist family, or about why such expectations should
be accepted under socialism in the first place. In the case of Pak Pongok,
rather than being asked why she should need to wake up at dawn and stay up
late into the night, she was instead lionized for her fortitude in doing so.
Turning to cultural levels and urging individuals to judge how well they rose

to the challenge made the target of critique not the continued inter-gender inequities and the ways they remained glossed over by the loud trumpeting of the gender equality laws, but rather those individual women who, due to whatever personal circumstances, could not quite master the norms of "culturedness" or juggle the demands of the double burden. In the political climate, there was little room to remind the Party-state of its promises—let alone demand that it follow through on them in order to ease domestic burdens—or simply to ask what had happened to the slogan "Liberate Women from the Kitchen"? Instead, the onus lay in remedying one's own insufficiencies—which, if not successfully achieved, risked being labeled an ideological laggardness. This became the basis of not just inter-gender but also intra-gender hierarchies—distinctions drawn and unevenness legitimized by the nebulous criteria of cultural levels. As the title of a Women's Union publication put it, "Women, Let Us Raise Our Cultural Levels."

The reticence toward raising the subject of deeper gender problems was not merely a matter of the risk, in an authoritarian environment, of challenging the Party-state. It was also, just as importantly, about how the Party-state's rule rested on broader masculinist cultural norms with roots in the pre-collective era. The interwoven nature of Party-state and male social power was best seen in the hesitancy of the Women's Union to interrogate the responsibility of husband-fathers in the imagined happy household, except in the most cursory fashion. Sonya Ryang has noted that in Korean literary works starting in the 1970s, fathers were often not present in story lines. Ryang connects this absence to the rise of the personality cult, as writers created unrivaled discursive space for Kim Il Sung to be presented as the father of all Koreans.[36] In the postwar media, notably before the full rise of the personality cult, fathers and husbands did appear regularly as part of the turn to the family. They often appeared in photographs with their nuclear family strolling through city streets or shopping.[37] So, too, did fathers appear in many stories highlighting their relationship with their children[38] or as husbands in "happy couple" stories.[39] Fathers published poems in appreciation of their children, and children published public letters to their fathers.[40] Still, while there was no absence of fathers in the media, such representations remained far less common than the presence of mothers, and there was no equivalent romanticizing of the "Korean father"—a term that did not appear. This comparative paucity had less to do with the still-forming personality cult and more to do with the ways in which gender-specific attention to the multiple roles of wife-mothers displaced any reconsideration, let alone critique, of domestic relations that might ruffle dominant masculine norms.

This gendered slant in critique was most visible in the notion of "cooperative" happy couples that festooned the national media. Representations of the conjugal couple almost always implied a mutually cooperative relationship, which was code for how husbands, as part of the New Living, should—in theory—assist with the daily chores of managing the household and parenting. No shortage of stories attesting to the existence of cooperative couples appeared in *Rodong sinmun*—a subject that matched the genre of so many other model stories. Writers in *Women of Korea* were often more temperate. Nods were often made toward this ideal. Yet Pak Pongok's account of managing the double burden, which was not explicitly framed as a happy couple story, was more typical. Her husband appeared only briefly to help take children to school or to watch them in the morning while she cooked. Otherwise, she gave him no presence in her account—and, tellingly, made no comment about cooperation. Ideal couple stories, in short, came with alternative stories that, without directly criticizing this ideal, expressed much lower expectations.

Again, it was Kim Il Sung who would cut through the ideological niceties of the daily press's use of model stories. In his speech to the All-Nation Congress of Mothers, Kim barely pretended to pay lip service to the notion of ideal couples and mutual cooperation. He asked, "Why is the responsibility mothers bear for their children's education more important than their fathers'?" His blunt answer, which had little relation to the long history of socialist critiques of family relations, was neither philosophical nor original: "Because mothers give birth and raise the children."[41] In the face of such statements by the single most powerful official, it is not surprising that use of the hopeful expression "new type of husband" (*saehyŏngŭi namp'yŏn*) faded.[42] Upbeat treatments of the possibilities of rethinking husband-wife relations largely became the reserve of the premier youth journal, seemingly an admission that the hopes for reformed spousal relations rested with future generations.[43]

The shift away from the early postwar enthusiasm for discussing the shifting roles of husband-fathers did not go unnoticed. In 1962, a reader of *Ch'ŏllima* took up the issue in a letter complaining about the disproportionate coverage given women of the household in comparison to husband-fathers.[44] Writing from the city of Hamhŭng, Sin Kŭmok encapsulated the dilemma: "In the management of the home, it's fine that there has been a lot of discussion of the role of mothers and wives, together with the problems of their cultural cultivation and their propriety and morals; however, it's regrettable that there is almost no mention of the husband-father of the household. Today the majority of mother-wives are heading out to workplaces. They urgently need the help of husband-fathers on all fronts. What does it mean that we are not talking more about husband-fathers?"[45] The open-ended quality of Sin's "what does it mean" was unusual for the era, since it risked opening lines of questioning that might broach Party-state policies or masculinist practices, even though it was unclear whether Sin had intended to raise a broader critique of domestic gender roles. At minimum her question posed a challenge to the ways cultural cultivation and the household had been feminized in a way that excepted men. Still, her letter refrained from adopting the more provocative language of mutual criticism and self-criticism. Nor did Sin pose the problem explicitly in the language of gender equality, as much as she implied an inequity in coverage and conduct. What was her answer to her query? The curated letter raised her question, but the editors left it hanging.

Instead, they assigned Sin's query to a reporter, Kim Pong, who wove the letter into the opening of an article titled "We Must Speak about Husbands." Yet if there was any ambiguity about the critical scope opened by Sin's request, Kim Pong's story quickly shut it down. Her reply reverted to the safety of the model couple story, which in repeating the usual refrains—"true happiness for the families of the era demands a high degree of cultural morality from couples"[46]—recounted the story of a busy section chief's home life as a husband-father to an equally busy wife-mother, one daughter, and one son. Kim's story depicted the section chief as a husband-father who made the decision to learn what was needed of him so that his wife could realize her equal rights by taking on wage labor. Kim did not miss the opportunity to reiterate the refrain about women's wage work, noting that "labor was the source for the creation of happiness." She resorted to the trope of laughter, describing family members enjoying themselves with pleasant music coming from a radio, which created a warm domestic feeling. Kim's story sidelined the broader implications of Sin's query—issues of masculinity, the era's general feminization of domestic spaces, and the shortage of social welfare facilities went unmentioned, let alone the continuing challenges of structural obstacles to the reconfiguration of family life. Kim Pong did talk about husbands, but, as was common in double burden stories, did so by presenting the solution for all potential problems as lying with the ideological and cultural self-improvement of the individual, only here in a rare instance of attention to husband-fathers. Problems were not socially derived in these interpretations but rested in individuals who also held the solution in their own hands.

In this way—and consistent with the patterns of personal advice literature and workplace culture—the turn to the individual as a self-reforming cultural agent worked to displace more generalized sociopolitical and gendered critiques. The logic of these stories depoliticized the radical possibilities of gender as a category of analysis and offered culture in its place.

NEIGHBORHOOD COMMITTEES

Official mobilization of notions of happiness was not just about wage work, of course. As Kim Yŏngsuk's story showed, "unhappiness" became linked to avoidance of local-level political work. Kim Yŏngsuk specifically mentioned declining to join the neighborhood hygiene inspection committee, but this was only one among a diverse assortment of local-level organizations, whose functions often overlapped. By far the most important unit—especially for those women who, like Kim Yŏngsuk, did not participate in wage work and thus provided most of the labor—was the *inminban* (neighborhood committee). In theory, neighborhood committees consisted of all the people in a neighborhood, which in large urban settings often meant they were organized by apartment building. Among local-level organizations, the inminban did not carry as much formal authority as Party committees but often carried the most immediate sway in neighborhoods, in part because it was usually organized around leading senior women whose influence in their local social worlds overlapped and built on their inminban functions. They were often key to identifying and organizing the reserve labor of "dependent family members" for various purposes, whether inviting someone like Kim Yŏngsuk to serve on a hygiene inspection committee or persuading neighborhood mothers to volunteer for a shock work campaign, as in the rebuilding of Pyongyang.

Ideally, neighborhood committees served as the premier collective unit in urban life—the most important "social cooperative unit," according to one description.[47] The constant exhortations from high up to strengthen the role of inminban suggested they did not always fulfill the expectations of top officials, yet in urban areas inminban countered the potential of apartments to isolate and separate residents. Inminban leaders were expected to immerse themselves in the lives of the membership to achieve the type of "complete understanding" that had become an expected leadership quality as part of the Ch'ŏllima movement's mass line. Because the inminban was so deeply interwoven into local social worlds, the leader had access to the most intimate knowledge. As was often said, she had to know her members like the fingers of her hand.[48] Whether the irony was appreciated by officials or not, it was precisely such women from a group that authorities often disparaged and aimed to eliminate—women not participating in wage work—who made fundamental governing tasks possible, however quietly.

The knowledge about neighborhood families served two purposes. The first, which was most widely trumpeted in the press, was a mediating function in the provision of social welfare services: who needed what type of assistance, who needed help with what kind of ideological or cultural cultivation, who was having difficulty balancing the double burden of wage work and home. In model stories from cities like Haeju, Hamhŭng, Sinŭiju, and Pyongyang, inminban members cooperatively helped each other out with their daily living challenges.[49] In the most extreme cases, reporters recounted how some inminban shared hard-to-acquire food delicacies when one member acquired them.[50] Inminban coordinated assistance for patriotic martyr families. Sometimes inminban became the informal provider of ad hoc day care services—whether for a day at the workplace or a night out at the movies. At other times, day care facilities became institutionalized as part of an inminban.[51] They organized "motherhood schools," which mixed parenting and cooking lessons with ideological work like lectures on the anti-Japanese partisan movement. Neighborhood committees could also ensure that worker families had supplies for their homes and organize hygiene competitions.[52] The committee served the function of a cooperative without being so named.

The second purpose, much less visible in the contemporary media, was the way the inminban leader's knowing her neighbors "like fingers on her hand" translated into surveillance. The inminban worked with local Party units who, as part of their remit under the mass line, likewise needed to get to know residents. Yet Party cell leaders relied on the inminban's familiarity with their neighbors to provide the information they were expected to garner. As one document explained to local cell leaders, they "above all else should first concretely understand what non-Party members think, how they are understanding Party policy, what kind of opinions and demands they are raising, how they are participating in the task of furthering the revolution, and where lies their political ideology and cultural level."[53] The advice did not stop there. "You have to know how many spoons are in whose home, what type of personality they have, and what hobbies they share." All this, in theory, was to help the primary Party cells figure out how best to work with people, to improve their commitments and persuade them of the worthiness of Party-state policies.

The implications of such knowledge could be much bleaker, of course—though such negative purposes in building the power of the Party-state obviously never arose in the public record. Nevertheless, neighborhood committees were expected to ensure that central regulations were observed in local social worlds. At times, especially as the final step in the nationalization of private commerce was completed in 1958, the inminban were charged with the responsibility of detecting and reporting black marketeering.[54] With many young men and women in rural areas willing to violate central proscriptions against unapproved migration to the cities, it was the inminban who received the charge of ensuring the registration of all visitors to members' homes. The inminban acted as the choke point for authorities, ensuring registration so that there would be no floating population and that people would not "double up" in apartments intended for single-family use.

Surveillance for registration purposes segued into detecting security threats—spies, in short. Little is publicly known about the mutual endeavors by the two Koreas to gain intelligence and foment political dissent by sending spies—north or south—across the DMZ. Both sides accused their counterparts, even as they disavowed partaking. Moreover, both sides engaged in anti-spy campaigns, encouraging citizens to report suspicious behavior and be careful of with whom they shared secrets. Calls for vigilance were about domestic discipline as much as about fear of their counterparts—or, in the vocabulary of the North, to be "on high alert" and "unite strongly around the Party."[55] Newspapers regularly reported on captured spies, complete with photographs of their espionage paraphernalia. Public exhibitions were even held.[56] At times, anti-spy campaigns were harnessed to high-level political intrigue and the early postwar trials. The trial of former leader Pak Hŏnyŏng and literary figure Im Hwa accused them of being American spies, which had a trickle-down effect on local campaigns.[57]

More typically, the onus of spy catching lay with neighborhood committees. Their on-the-ground presence and more intimate relations within neighborhoods, it was believed, put them in the best position to identify unusual behavior or unknown people, thus flagging possible espionage activity.

Reports in *Women of Korea* sought to convince their readers that spies sent by "American imperialists and their running dog, Yi Sŭngman," were not far away but living among them, trying to "break our happy living." "All the women in charge of the important tasks of the inminban," wrote the author of one story, "should not carelessly consider impure thoughts and behavior as small matters but should right away reveal those who harm our Party-state's policies or spread baseless rumors. They must raise their everyday vigilance and never give our enemies a place to set foot."[58] Cartoonists abandoned their humor on this front, depicting nefarious characters eavesdropping outside windows, lurking around offices and cafeterias, or sifting through waste disposal bins in search of secrets.[59] It was this sense of spies "living among us" that gave the inminban the task of rooting them out, especially by enforcing "residential order and registration discipline" for anyone showing up in their neighborhoods, even if they claimed to be visiting relatives.[60] The words people used in their daily conversations were often good indicators, inminban members were told—another indication about the growing distinctiveness and expectations of speech.[61]

Whatever their effectiveness as spy catchers, it was to the unpaid and informal labor of women in the inminban that the Party-state turned in order to fulfill their local security needs.

A New Style of Husband?

Magazines in the 1950s featured cartoonists lampooning social and cultural life, including domestic gender relations. Illustrators used their humor to reinforce official targets of criticism, yet in some cases they played off the ambiguity of their humor to suggest alternative, double meanings. In one 1959 cartoon, illustrator Ch'oe Hanjin seemingly reinforced a much-publicized ideal: that men after liberation had done the necessary ideological work on themselves to now share in the household tasks they had previously disdained.[a]

Ch'oe's two-panel illustration used a before-and-after story line common to revolutionary narratives. The first panel showed a couple under the title "The Past." A stock figure of the hardworking wife was seen scrubbing the floor, sweat streaming from her brow, while her husband was depicted sitting leisurely on a chair, smoking a cigarette, lost in his own thoughts, and not even paying attention to his wife. In the second panel, titled "Now," the husband was shown joining his spouse on the floor to assist with the scrubbing. The result of doing the chore together was that now, neither of them was seen to be sweating. He had become the ideal, cooperative husband of "today."

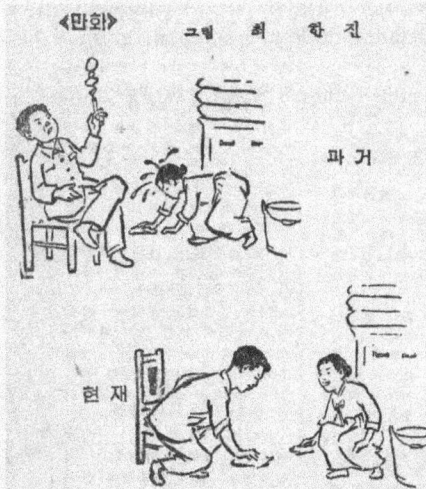

FIGURE B. Ch'oe Hanjin, "The Past and Now," 1959.

Yet the context and the specifics of the illustration raise questions about whether Ch'oe was not, in fact, parodying the official narrative and model itself. The cartoon was published in *Women of Korea*, a magazine whose treatment of the double burden faced by its female readership came with more than a little skepticism about this ideal and that had begun to turn away from discussing seriously the very idea of "a new style of husband." The illustration was also published in a section of the magazine that, by 1959, had come to be reserved for humor-filled illustrations. Indeed, Ch'oe's cartoon was one of a three-part series, the other two of which humorously targeted other aspects of domestic behavior—a mother scolding her daughter over studies, and another mother not sharing food with her child.

Was Ch'oe's illustration an anomaly for cartoonists, insofar as it offered a straightforward reproduction of official ideologies on gender without the slightest hint of satire? Or was Ch'oe mocking the very idea of "cooperative husbands," prodding his largely female audience to laugh at what they all knew was the ludicrous notion that their husbands "today" might actually get down on their knees to help them scrub a floor? No definitive answer is possible, which reveals much about the limits of the era's historical sources. Yet it is also possible to surmise that while some of the audience for this cartoon might have nodded their head in agreement with the image's straightforward claim about the desirability of changed gender relations, perhaps even more would have responded with an incredulous guffaw in appreciation of Ch'oe's subtle send-up of this model story.

a. Ch'oe Hanjin, untitled, *Chosŏn nyŏsŏng*, May 1959: 40.

PART FOUR

The Ambivalences of Consumption

HOW TO CONSUME PROPERLY?

No question revealed the tensions besetting the political economy and official ideologies more than how men and women should consume. Any answer to the question necessarily dealt with what was arguably the grandest contradiction of centrally planned economies around the world: how to reconcile the promise of improved material well-being with a developmental logic that prioritized heavy industry.[1] Answers around the socialist bloc diverged, providing the grist for much theoretical and inter-Party conflict. In Korea, the decision to lean toward heavy industry left light industries short of investment capital, and the responsibility for producing consumer goods shifted down to localities. By the late 1950s, as newspaper reports repeatedly pointed out, light-industrial production was not meeting demand.

By 1960, the media had started to pay more attention to consumption—and the goods pictured in magazines attracted many eyes and comments. A pair of photographs on the back cover of the magazine *Commerce* (*Sangŏp*) featured wooden furniture—chairs, tables, shelves, dish cabinets, and more (see figure 21).[2] Displaying a modernist, midcentury Scandinavian style, these pieces were to fill the rooms of new radiator-heated apartment buildings. Yet the photographs also reflected a shift underway. It had always been easier for authorities and writers to speak about production than about consumption, yet this photograph suggested both. By 1964, the layout of the furniture display spoke to a history of photographs seeking to impress viewers with the *mass* production coming out of factories.[3] Yet the *Commerce* magazine's furniture photograph invited viewers to consider sitting in the chairs and eating at the tables, as if now the chance to bring these objects into one's home lay not

FIGURE 21. Modernist wooden furniture. Anonymous, untitled, 1964.

just in some hazy indefinite future. The picture offered the possibility of possession.

Even as Party-state leaders remained reluctant to explicitly address the question of how to consume properly, others did so. And as the furniture photograph suggests, the movement of workers into their first-ever apartments meant that questions of consumption often became questions of interior décor. Yet advice on what room colors or window treatments to select was given while light-industrial enterprises continued to come under heavy political pressure, as both officials and, increasingly, ordinary men and women began to voice their complaints about unmet demands—even as the newspapers boasted about rising living standards. The tantalizing possibilities of personal consumption became entangled in the contradictions of light industry. The challenges of uneven access to consumer goods could not, in the authoritarian environment, be immediately raised by frustrated consumers. Yet, in making consumer goods essential to the performance of heightened cultural levels, the décor advice reflected the growing social stratification that came with economic growth. Moreover, by explaining these distinctions through cultural levels, it separated consumption and home life from any consideration of class.

Discussions about décor reinforced the feminization of domestic spaces. With class displaced, purveyors of advice foregrounded the attributes of a superior decorator as reflected in their cultural levels or "culturedness" (*munhwasŏng*). Previously, writers in *Women of Korea* had sought to present the home space as productive in the face of criticisms about its unproductivity, but now décor advocates pushed in the opposite direction. They opened the possibility—without quite saying it—that a homemaker might choose not to participate in wage work, instead occupying her daytime management of the home in a cultured fashion. That this possibility rested uneasily with Party-state policies and that it made gendered assumptions about consumption as a marker of status were connections that no writer chose to make explicitly, even though it was fundamental to this realm of advice.

EIGHT

Savings and Silences

"PRODUCE AND SAVE!"

"Produce and Save!"—in an era when many slogans had short life spans, few had as much staying power as this exhortation. Already circulating in 1953 and still commonplace in the mid-1960s, the slogan distilled the core Party-state priority about maximizing production as the path to socialist transition. Yet its secondary emphasis on frugality—save!—reflected a more ambivalent sensibility, an injunction *not* to consume even as newspaper headlines announced that ever more daily necessities were rolling off assembly lines and ever higher salaries were being paid to workers. It was as if the authors of the slogan did not quite know what to make about consumption under socialism.

Calls for frugality were hardly unique to the Pyongyang regime. In other socialist settings, similar demands were made of working populations; and on the other side of the DMZ, as Laura Nelson has shown, anti-consumption drives were a consistent feature of daily economic life for decades after the war.[1] While targeting ordinary men and women, "Produce and Save!" concerned, at a macro level, the circulation of capital. It aimed to recoup the scarce capital paid out in worker wages back into central Party-state coffers via savings. In theory, this allowed central economic planners to maximize capital use by reinvesting back into the prized heavy industries. In the words of one national editorial, the Party-state sought "to mobilize and use all domestic sources of capital."[2]

Authorities quickly focused on their preferred instrument for savings, the savings certificate. Soon after the war, they launched a nationwide campaign encouraging workers to purchase certificates—an action billed as patriotic.[3]

Anyone could buy a certificate at a bank.[4] In remote areas, where no banks existed, patrons could walk into a post office to make a purchase.[5] Post offices competed with banks, advertising in boastful tones about the special convenience of their savings services and their 4 percent rate of return, for a term of up to a year, in 1957.[6] Rates varied, as did term length, the possibilities clearly inscribed on large images of certificates published as advertisements in newspapers.[7] Indeed, images of certificates became a staple of the era's visual culture. By 1957, such images were so ubiquitous that *Rodong sinmun* could feature a savings certificate without any explanation, the editors assuming that everyone knew what it was.[8] Newspapers tracked the success of the campaign in terms of the percentage of workers who had purchased certificates. Often divided by location, economic sector, or another designation, these reports fostered a sense of competition, heightening pressure on workers by revealing their differing rates of saving.[9]

A parallel strategy for saving that reached equal levels of nationwide attention deployed not a slogan but an old proverb: "Specks of dust, collected, make large mountains" (*t'ikkŭl moa t'aesan*). The end goal—saving capital—remained the same, only this movement targeted waste.[10] Entire neighborhoods could be shown, as rendered by the hands of illustrators, picking up discarded metal and other refuse to be repurposed.[11] Less earnest illustrators poked fun at laggards: a group of friends chatting at the village tap, immersed in conversation and oblivious to the unused flow of water, or apartment residents sleeping with the lights not off.[12] Yet complaining about wasted resources could come with risks, as was the case with one unnamed worker who in a satirical cartoon was depicted listening to his Workers' Federation leader explain that he would take to heart the workers' criticism, from the day before, that too much labor was being wasted. He explained the first step in the interest of reducing labor costs: firing the worker.[13] Authorities reported on the results of all this saving, going so far as to announce that in 1956 the primary cost (*wŏnga*) of production—the rather fantastical sum of all costs in the economy—had been reduced by 8 percent.[14] Success only signaled that more calls for ever more vigilance over expenses would be coming.

The injunction to save came with a reticence, even silence, in regard to what workers should do with their higher salaries. In an era of so much advice, the regular sources of advice offered few specifics about consumption, other than the injunctions to save. A key early publication of the Women's Union—*Women, Let Us Raise Our Cultural Levels*—offered a few words on the subject, tucked into a back section about frugality.[15] Hwang Yŏngsik's

Guide to Living only barely touched on consumption, in its treatment of clothing.[16] Judging from his silence on the matter in his 1958 speech on communist morality, Kim Il Sung seemed to see no correlation between consumption and morality.[17] The Party's main theoretical journal, *Kŭlloja* (*Laborer*), was no more forthcoming. In an era of advice, virtually no authorities made recommendations on how to consume properly.

This silence extended to the question of the commodity form. In the Soviet Union, as Christina Kiaer has shown, designers in the constructivist movement imagined a "new world of things" in which capitalist commodities would yield to "active socialist things" that carried a "transformative potential of material culture of everyday life."[18] Thinkers such as Boris Arvatov aimed to eliminate not material objects themselves but our "possessive relationship to them."[19] They sought an alternative model of consumption in which materiality, not just formal ideological education, would assist in the transformation of the population into socialist subjects through the creation of a specifically socialist commodity. This was a short-lived phase in the world history of state socialisms. It did not continue in the Soviet Union, nor was it taken up in most other socialist settings such as North Korea, where no proposals challenging the commodity form were forthcoming. Essays on industrial design examined the importance of aesthetics to matching demands and needs—an attribute seen as socialist insofar as it served popular interests—but did not venture into imagining alternatives.[20]

The under-theorization of the commodity form included a silence on the relationship between class and consumption. In China, as Karl Gerth has shown, Mao Zedong's constant fears about postrevolutionary class formation ensured that consumption became immersed in debates about class.[21] Specific objects became defined in official discourse and popular imagination as bourgeois, with often dire consequences for individuals and families discovered to possess those goods. It was not just one's relationship to the means of production, but also the objects in one's lifestyle, that came to define one's class—a relationship that would animate, in spectacular fashion, interpersonal politics during the Cultural Revolution.[22] In Korea, the relationship between consumption and class attracted little theoretical attention, perhaps because, unlike Mao, Kim Il Sung did not overly concern himself with postrevolutionary class relations. Treatises on class in *Kŭlloja* did not include consumption in their ruminations. Economic treatises offered little more: one book, designed to popularize understanding of socialist economics, dealt extensively with the circulation of goods but addressed neither their consumption nor class relations—a good example of how it was always easier to talk about production than about consumption.[23] *Rodong sinmun*, in all its editorials about the production of and shortages in daily necessities, never raised the connection between products and class.

This silence about the relationship between class and consumption had much to do with the ways class came to be displaced to the South. Consumption became a lens to describe the consequences of southern bourgeois rule and what was criticized as "American-style living." Representations ranged from wildly unreliable exaggerations to quieter critiques that used South Korean newspaper sources for the author's own purposes. Yet the South always served as *the* bastion of bourgeois behavior, where reports were used to show money corrupting social and, in particular, familial relations. One critic, citing a southern women's magazine, concluded that "respecting one's parents is like returning a loan, raising a son is like making a deposit, and raising a daughter is nothing other than a charitable act."[24] He went on to report that "trial marriages," together with "contract marriages," had become common, resulting in the situation that divorce had become a "popular disease" by 1963—a neat contrast to the desired direction in the North. The South represented, in short, a vision on how *not* to spend money and consume. This propaganda translated class struggle into ensuring that the danger presented by American-style living "down there" below the DMZ did not infiltrate northward.[25] Accordingly, reunification became a question of resolving the national bourgeois question, which meant ridding the South of class relations—as had been done, it was assumed, in the North. That there might be internal factors generating new postwar formations of class in the North remained outside the ken of class theorists. The danger remained external. Such displacement ensured that class as a category of analysis for contemporary developments in the North was, in effect, rendered irrelevant.

Other critiques of consumption that moved beyond the South were hard to find in the early postwar years. When they did emerge, it was in a piecemeal fashion, and usually by way of framing negative practices in the logic of advice literature. Easily the most widely critiqued consumption practice—because of its relation to absenteeism and ill health and its likely widespread public presence—was excessive alcohol drinking. Seen as another form of waste that represented a lack of self-discipline, alcohol consumption offered a gendered moralizing critique linked to family stability. Excessive drinking was masculinized behavior. It is hard to find a single report of disruptive drinking among women. The constant coverage of this problem did not extend to the central planners, who made alcohol so readily available at a time when other goods were in short supply—or mention that the Pyongyang Beer Factory was one of the first factories to open after the war.[26] This was a rare case in which contemporary coverage gave precedence to consumption over production.

Importantly, excessive drinking was framed as deleterious for family life. A worker at the Chŏngpŏng Porcelain Factory, Ri Sugil, submitted a cartoon to a newspaper that captured the typical manner of critique. It divided male workers into those who saved and those who wasted. Ri depicted the latter as a worker tumbling into the depths of a bottle, an envelope clutched in his hands labeled "salary"—the implication being that he had wasted his salary on booze. In the next panel, he was shown drunk and gesticulating wildly on the family dining table, his wife holding their baby to the side, a big question mark hovering over her head as if to ask, "What the heck is going on?!" A second family, characterized by a worker who brings his pay home, is represented as the opposite: peaceful, prosperous, and happily sharing a good family dinner.[27] Another showed a father walking through a store, telling his son he did not have enough money to buy him a toy. The second frame showed the son with that ever-critical question mark hovering over his head as his father unfolded a wad of cash to buy a bottle of booze.[28] Not all criticisms attempted humor, however.

In a rare public story about domestic violence, a courageous head of an inminban wrote a letter of complaint to the newspaper, entitled "Can't Stand It Anymore." She protested that every month on payday her husband would get drunk, return home, and beat her.[29] She wrote that she had complained about his behavior to local authorities. No one had done anything. Yet her letter, in its very rarity, did not break through this sense that alcohol, no matter how harmful to domestic relations, had only a single remedy: better self-discipline on the part of men. That some saw domestic abuse as a deeper problem was hinted at in a cartoon by Om Byŏnghwa (see figure 22).[30] In the final panel of his triptych, Om depicted a husband pounding on the dinner table after spending his payday earnings on booze, rudely demanding, "Why is there no food?" Overhead, above the panel, the cartoonist asked, "Who's to blame?" Again, the critique made the connection between drink, lack of discipline, masculinity, and familial disruption—here with the menacing possibility of spousal violence—yet it also reiterated the point about individuals' lack of self-discipline and wasting of resources, their own earnings, as the crux of the problem. The readymade answer of self-improvement would remove the

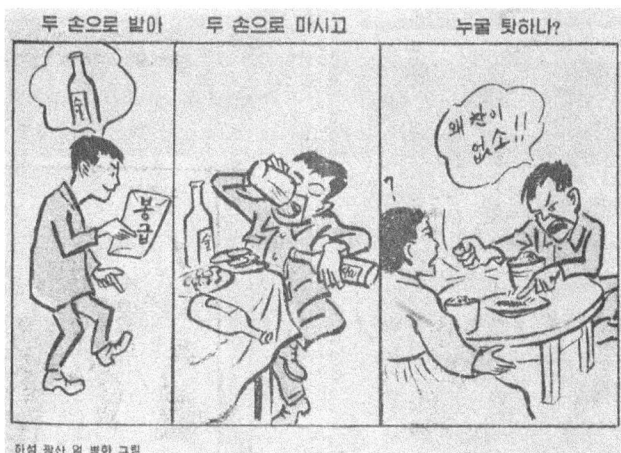

FIGURE 22. A cartoon on the ills of alcohol. First panel caption: "[Wages] received in two hands." Second panel caption: "[Booze] drunk with two hands." Third panel speech balloon: "Why is there no food!!" Third panel caption: "Who's to blame?" Om Byŏnghwa, untitled, 1960.

source of the problem and, as Ri Sugil's cartoon also suggested, a happy family would be the result.

If alcohol was a consistent source of negative coverage, the one opening for more positive coverage came every December. During the first few years after the war, workers across the country learned from the radio and workplace notice boards how much their year-end bonuses would be. Announced as a decision made by the cabinet, the advent of the year-end bonus was a heady moment for many lucky workers in enterprises that met or exceeded their quotas. The envelopes they picked up from their workplaces represented a substantial portion of their annual income, received just before the New Year's celebrations.[31] Contemporary reports did not reveal exact sums, but they never shied away from showing workers expressing their gratitude—in the stock phrase prior to Kim Il Sung's ascension—for the "endless care of the Party and government."[32] For many, the bonus constituted the single biggest payday of the year—and coverage sought to impress readers with how recipients were being rewarded for their labor.

What to do with the bonus money? The upbeat tone of these stories mixed in an undertone of wariness, suggesting a concern that the bonus might not be used for the best ends. Ultimately, the aim of these stories was to guide how bonuses would be spent. They constituted one of the rare moments of seeking to directly answer the question of *how to consume properly*. Typical stories followed a worker—almost always depicting the husband-father as the income earner—home to his family on the big day. Families were shown not spending the funds willy-nilly but making careful decisions and selecting modest purchases. Kim Namho, a worker in the Pyongyang Eighth Construction Unit, bought a white shirt, along with some pencils and erasers for his son and daughter.[33] Living-room discussions about expenditures were often featured, in conversational style. One father expressed to his spouse that the bonus should be used for his son: "Honey, what if we don't spend this extra cash and instead save it to buy a suit for Okchin?" To this the son replied, "Rather than a suit, Mom, what about a radio?"[34] These stories, in short, blended into the typical "happy family" stories. Consumption was represented as one more way of shoring up family relations.

Ultimately, these year-end bonus stories were transitory. A regular feature of December coverage in the mid-1950s, by the end of the decade they had disappeared from the media. No reasons were offered, of course, but likely they became another casualty of the post-1958 pivot toward ideology—even as the politics of consumption and light industries attracted more media coverage. By the 1970s, these bonuses were often converted into "presents" from Kim Il Sung.

THE POLITICS OF DEVOLUTION

In early 1964, *Ch'ŏllima* magazine included an advertisement for a new brand of sewing machine, called the Pyongyang model (see figure 23).[35] Historians of centrally planned economies have disagreed over the meaning of advertisements in settings where production and distribution were not determined by markets. Some have seen these advertisements as consumerist, underpinned by state capitalism.[36] Others have seen them as educational or as a media leftover from the pre-collectivist past.[37] In this specific Korean case, the sponsoring Pyongyang Precision Machine Factory used the advertisement defensively at a time of mutually recriminating politics within light industrial production. The advertisement boasted that the new style of machine spun at a rate four times that of the earlier Pigeon model and much more quietly. The Pyongyang sewing machine, it claimed, was suited to both industrial and home use. Yet the notice lacked two valuable pieces of information: neither a price nor a location for purchase was included. Clearly, driving sales was not this adver-

FIGURE 23. Advertisement, "The Pyongyang Brand: New Product," 1964.

tisement's primary goal. Instead, it reflected one idiosyncratic attempt to stave off criticism and escape the political pressures that, by the early 1960s, had accumulated around light industrial enterprises.[38]

By the time the sewing machine advertisement appeared in 1964, the political economy of consumption had changed remarkably. The dispute about economic trajectories among the leadership may have been settled in favor of heavy industry, yet the decision was not without criticism. Representatives from other socialist countries regularly voiced critiques, in their reports and in their conversations with their Korean counterparts, about the imbalances in the economy—a point made directly by Khrushchev to Kim during the latter's 1956 Moscow visit.[39] Less is known about internal discussions within economic planning circles, yet the national press increasingly took note of the unmet consumer demand for daily necessities and the growing popular expectations as the economy grew. As part of the Five-Year Plan (1957–61), the leadership—begrudgingly, if European diplomatic reports are to be trusted—tagged mention of light industries and agriculture to the still greater priority of heavy industry.

This admission came with a specific strategy: the burden of expanding light industries was shifted downward onto local state administrative units and enterprises. At first the reasoning was economic. Like savings certificates, this policy was intended to sop up whatever excess capital circulated at local levels outside of the official plan and pressure local officials to invest that capital in the production of consumer products. Heavy industrial enterprises, too, received directives to include in their output greater numbers and more varieties of daily necessities—using their own funds, of course. Every county was instructed to open at least one factory. Later, that was increased to five.[40] Local enterprises and administrative units that asked for extra resources from the center—whether technology or capital—were castigated for not being *self-sufficient*, a term that increasingly came to shape the economic terrain.[41] All enterprises received notices that they should develop a commitment to "revolutionary self-sufficiency."[42]

By the late 1950s, the devolution of responsibility and blame also became politically expedient for central authorities. The Five-Year Plan aimed to resolve the basic problem of clothing, food, and housing (*ŭisikchu munje*). By 1958, many reports showed that large swaths of the population—especially in urban areas—had already "basically" solved these problems, though qualifications on this claim were many. Increasingly, authorities openly acknowledged that in moving beyond the deprivations of colonialism and war, people longed to pursue more than just the fundamental necessities. As *Rodong sinmun* put it, "In the past, we lacked things to wear and things to eat. But today, when this problem has been basically solved, people are hoping to wear better clothes and eat better food."[43] It offered a list of their consumption hopes: better-quality shoes, pens, furniture, and higher-end goods such as radios, bicycles, and sewing machines. Two years later, *Rodong sinmun* again pointed out—with a restrained tone of frustration—that production still could not keep up with demand, which it described as "extremely high."[44] This time it listed a larger assortment of in-demand goods, including tasty and nutritious side dishes; textile goods such as suits, various styles of pants, and children's outerwear; pens and pencils; and varieties of paper, such as wrapping and wallpaper. Other goods, like cosmetics, buttons, sewing needles, and sports balls, remained in short supply, as were "beautiful and fashionable yet practical" household goods like pottery and "sturdy yet beautiful types of furniture suitable for a modern cultural home" such as chests of drawers, desks, and chairs.

It was not as if the shifting of responsibility onto local units did not lead to results. Counties such as Songch'on announced the opening of five new factories and, at a national level, one report indicated that 68.6 percent of everyday goods were being produced at the local level by 1958.[45] The devolution took on the overtone of the Ch'ŏllima movement. The secretary of the Light Industrial Committee of Pyŏngbuk province boasted how the province was meeting basic consumer demands all on its own, listing food products, textiles, pulp and paper, leather, furniture, and daily necessities. This was due, he pointed out, to the province's development of the "revolutionary spirit of self-sufficiency."[46] The assumption of his report, however much it may have been exaggerated, was that few other units had attained such levels—an admission of the continuing problems around the country. By

1964, the city of Hamhŭng emerged as a model in the production of "life necessities" for supposedly doing just that. Everyone should follow its example, they were told.[47]

Local enterprises could not, however, keep up with the growing purchasing power of many urban-based workers. Figures on salaries, cost of living, and prices were not publicly reported and are difficult to ascertain given the only partial and problematic data available.[48] To be sure, reports frequently announced substantial wage increases—for example, a 1955 report claimed that real incomes had increased by 25 percent on average—and often cast them statistically as increases compared to the low base figures of wartime.[49] Even in these reports, though, enthusiasm was tempered because the cited achievements were always qualified by memories of wartime destruction and poverty. One year later, a cabinet decision citing improvements contextualized them against the remaining scars on contemporary life from the "barbaric attacks of American imperialism." Nevertheless, they could be touted and celebrated as reflecting "the peaceful recovery out of the ashes of war."[50] This comparative strategy of accomplishment—look how far we have come!—remained a constant. As the fighting and poverty of the war became more distant, keeping its memory alive served as a political buffer for the contemporary challenges of the economy.

Meanwhile, diplomatic reports from socialist allies told a less enthusiastic story—reporting, for example, that real wages for many workers had gone down in 1956 because people had to buy certain goods beyond state-run stores from private merchants, who had yet to be collectivized. Prices outside the public distribution system were high, rendering official statistics unrealistic.[51] Some reports in these early years went so far as to suggest that propaganda about rising living standards sought to convince people of what was not actually there.[52]

More reliable than the self-serving central statistics were newspaper accounts that sought not to trumpet successes, but to report an unusual problem: many workers held more cash than they could spend.[53] One account of male dormitories explained that the excessive cash in workers' hands had become a social problem. Workers drank too much and gambled with abandon because, the author claimed, they had nothing else to do with their money.[54] The official response—buy a savings certificate—was hardly effective but confirmed these reports.[55] Additionally, there was a long history of using appeals based on the possibility of a second family wage to convince "dependent family members" to join in wage labor. Yet, according to reports by the Women's Union, this incentive was now increasingly less appealing. What use was a second wage, some of its membership asked, if there was nothing to spend it on? Soviet reports confirm this surplus of circulating cash in North Korea, at least in the countryside.[56] The disparity was glaring enough that it became a regular theme in the media. For those segments of the population lucky enough to have well-paying jobs, there was simply not enough to buy.

Given heightening popular expectations, the growth in purchasing power, and the prioritization of heavy industry, central authorities used their strategy of devolution to shift responsibility—blame, in other words—downward. The strategy sought to direct the frustrations of wannabe consumers away from the central Party-state and toward local entities. Even in this authoritarian context, with no viable challenge to their rule, central authorities concerned themselves with the politics of economic bottlenecks. This was a testament to the sensitivity of the problem and to the ironic effect of the center's own reports about escalating production and standards of living. To this end—and to further increase pressure on local enterprises—central authorities gave an outlet to the mounting frustrations by unleashing the satirical power of cartoonists. They also seem to have allowed the media to print letters from workers venting about their consumer challenges, with one important caveat: the target of their ire was always localized.

Cartoonists had a field day with both shortages and product quality problems. Perfumes that smelled so horribly, department store staff warned, "Hold your nose, and try it";[57] mirrors that made people look fat;[58] suitcases with handles that fell off as soon as you picked them up[59]—all became viable subjects for ridicule. Under the skeptical banner of "New 'Products,'" two children stood arguing over the shape of a crudely produced stuffed animal. "No, it's a puppy!" shouted one, to which the other yelled back, "No, it's a bunny!" A tag hung from the neck of the nondescript stuffy, identifying the producer—the Sariwŏn Co-op Factory (see figure 24).[60] Another illustrator, Ch'oe Hanjin, lampooned (in a rare image of queuing) the experience of shoppers in a lineup: a mother examined the socks on display, while her daughter at the back of the line drew attention to the gendered skewing of production. "Mom," she asked, "why are there so many socks for men and so few for women?" Another illustration by Ch'oe featured a customer with a puzzled expression asking a saleswoman, "Don't you have one a bit bigger?"—only to receive an equally vexed response: "Sorry, we don't have anything other than this single size."[61] His fellow cartoonist, Ri Ch'unsu, depicted a young

FIGURE 24. Ch'oe Yŏnggun, "New 'Products,'" 1960. "No, it's a puppy!" "No, it's a bunny!"

woman happily buying a stylish floral-patterned dress. Yet by the time she walked home on a beautiful day, the sun had washed out the colors from what was clearly inferior cloth and dye, turning the pretty dress into drab apparel.[62] Satirical humor had been turned on local producers.

A more direct expression of exasperation took the form of letters to the editor.[63] Letters reflected a more barbed sense of irritation than the light-hearted cartoons, as frustrated consumers recounted not the generalized complaints of cartoonists but their own personal experiences. As much as editors likely curated them, the letters still personalized the stresses and imbalances of the macropolitical economy. A letter might be as simple as a complaint about buying a raincoat that did not shed rain—asking of the workers who produced the product, "How is that possible?"[64] Light bulbs emerged as a particular sore point—many did not last for more than three days, and some did not fit sockets. Shoes whose soles fell off after a few uses, brands of ink such as "University Ink" and "Cultural Ink"—all labeled with phrases like "superior grade"—came with an assortment of defects.[65] Several letters arrived in the office of *Rodong sinmun* complaining about the matches produced by the Chonch'on Match Factory, which gave off such a weak flame that they could not start a fire. Shoes came in sizes that varied only in length and not in width. Colored pencils barely wrote a word before breaking.[66] One shopper complained about distribution and inconstant prices. For twenty days, she searched for a simple type of towel, returning repeatedly but in vain to the premier store of the capital, the Pyongyang No. 1 department store. But when she went to a daily goods store in western Pyongyang, she found an abundance of the towels, in various colors. Even more frustrating, she complained, was that a few days later, in another store, she saw the exact same towel for a cheaper price—an experience than ran against claims of even distribution and consistent pricing.[67] Product availability also featured in a letter by Ch'oe Kwanhua, a quality inspector at the Pyongyang Leather Factory, only his complaints centered on corrupt practices without actually using that expression. Ch'oe pointed out that his factory's shoes for men could not be purchased at either the No. 1 or No. 2 department stores but could be found—at a high price—from the remaining private merchants.[68] The implication was that products were being diverted from the formal distribution system. That stores ran out of goods came through in a complaint by Ch'oe Kŭmok, who pointed out that at her local store all the fresh vegtables, tofu, and bean sprouts would be snapped up by housewives before she could get off work and get to the store. As she asked, in this situation, "how can we housewives go out to work with an easy heart?" She demanded that the store procure more food products.[69]

There may have been shortages of certain goods, but there was no shortage of complaints. Yet the focus of all this satire and complaining was clear. All the ire, as can be seen in Ch'oe Kŭmok's frustration with her neighborhood store, targeted the local enterprises. Much as in the public criticisms featured in the newspaper column "My Turn to Speak" (see chapter 3), the names of offenders were listed—publicly singling out enterprises to ramp up pressure and serve notice to others. The curated direction of these cartoons and letters ensured, however, that their critiques did not move beyond individual enterprises and their local leadership. They did not address how the problems of unmet demand and poor quality were related to larger issues of political economy. None questioned, for instance, how the root causes of local failures were structured by the investment priorities of central planning. None questioned the devolution strategy or the politics of blame that came with it. It is difficult to know whether consumers actually excused the central state, as the crafters of this strategy hoped. Scholars of Eastern European socialist consumption have pointed out that the central planning system, Party-state ownership of retail establishments, and state interest in regulating consumption led consumers, from their vantage point, to see the multifarious parts of the state as a united, monolithic whole that was unresponsive to their priorities as consumers.[70] As a result, public ire over problems in consumption in those countries was directed at the central state. In North Korea, the political strategy of devolution was used to disaggregate, from the perspective of consumers, the parts of the economic system in an attempt to divert blame and shift responsibility.

It was in this context that the sewing machine advertisement from the Pyongyang Precision Machine Factory, discussed above, found its way into the press. Even enterprises in the capital felt squeezed between the downward pressure exerted by the central state, with its calls to meet consumer demand self-sufficiently, and the upward pressure from consumers eager to translate their hard-earned cash into goods. The advertisement publicly announced, in both directions, that this enterprise was in fact doing exactly what was expected of it: producing new products of the highest quality with the best technology. The advertisement was thus part of a defensive strategy to stave off critiques of a vulnerable enterprise.

The Namp'o Glass Factory found itself in a similar situation. Its opening had been key in the timely production of the windows necessary for early apartment construction, and it had even developed an export trade, which garnered praise for earning foreign currency. But as focus began to shift to light industries, the factory found itself singled out in a *Rodong sinmun* editorial for its "inability to produce in great quantities the bowls and other glass products that the people were demanding."[71] Such public approbation even extended to much-vaunted steel plants like the premier Songjin Steel Factory, castigated for not producing a single consumer good.[72] That was not the end of the story. A little over a year after its public dressing down, the Namp'o Glass Factory had successfully rejiggered its output. Moreover, management had worked with the same newspaper that criticized it, in order to get reports about its turnaround covered in the press. Now *Rodong sinmun* reported that the Namp'o Glass Factory produced more than twenty types of consumer goods of "high quality," including twin-colored flower vases, thermometers, and other household items.[73] The report announced the factory's plan to expand its ouput by another fifty types of goods. By July 1958, yet another story showed that even this plan had ballooned. If the reports are to be believed, the plant's production soared to over five hundred varieties.[74] The coverage cast doubt on the goods it had boasted about only a few months before, calling them "inferior goods" and stating they had been "decisively improved."

This sense of an ever-ameliorating situation was a constant in the press. Its effect was achieved not by careful use of aggregate data, but by concentrating on the specific experiences of individual units like the Namp'o Glass Factory. Stories of less-than-successful enterprises counterbalanced these success stories, as did the regular reporting on how demand remained unmet. Other stories outlined the plans of specific factories to ramp up production or reported on the oaths sworn by workers of a particular enterprise to do better in the coming year. By the mid-1960s, this seesawing coverage—the criticisms, the upticks, the problems, the promises—must have become tiresome to many readers, even if it created a teleology of eventual consumer gratification, however postponed. In November 1963, the *Ch'ŏllima* magazine wrote about the need for a "generational change" in the production of consumer goods; yet two months later it seemed to have forgotten its concerns, boasting that the number of daily consumer products had increased by over thirty thousand in the previous two or three years.[75] When, in early 1964, *Rodong sinmun* ran a front-page headline reading "Let's Bring about a Turning Point in the Production of the People's Consumer Goods" and featured a story about how it was taking only three to four minutes to assemble each new Man'gyong brand radio, many readers may have wondered how many times they had heard about such "turnarounds" and new products since the war.[76]

BRINGING THE FACTORY HOME

The problems in the light industries—undercapitalized and insufficient production combined with consumer frustration—came to be seen by authorities as entangled with the challenges of expanding the size of the aggregate labor supply by employing more women in wage work. In the latter case, women's double burden, the lack of socialized services, masculinist norms governing wage work, and continued structural obstacles ensured that the Party-state's goal of full employment would not be reached. Statistics for 1964 showed that despite gradual increases, participation rates of women in wage work still reached only 37.3 percent of the total workforce, far below expectations given the decade of policy innovations and mounting pressure.[77] The situation ensured continued efforts on the part of central planners to tap into the potential labor reserves of women.

These diverse developments led to a new form of labor organization in the light industries that, again, targeted female dependent family members: institutionalizing what was called "household factories" (*kanae kongjang*) or, in Ch'ŏllima rhetoric, "household work teams" (*kanae chagŏpban*). These expressions' focus on the household did not signify a belated recognition of the domestic work of women within the official category of labor (*rodong*). Quite the opposite. The logic of household work teams was that if laborers could not be brought to the factory, then the factory could be brought to the laborers (see figure 25). For many local officials and enterprise heads, who were under pressure to increase light industrial production, this meant reorganizing the potential labor power of housewife-mothers by making what they saw as the unproductive space of apartments into the equivalents of informal, flexible factories.[78] The initiative for "household factories" built on previously informal labor conventions that, since wartime mobilization in the colonial era, had sought to organize non-routinized labor of women at home.[79] After 1953, the promotion of "home-front" (*hubang*) production was taken up with great publicity, mobilizing women to produce foodstuffs to supplement the rations received by their working family members and neighbors. By 1960, these efforts had coalesced into "household factories," which were given the imprimatur of Kim Il Sung when he made a speech on the subject. The Women's Union took up the cause, telling its membership that all women should head out of the home for wage work. But if they could not, they were told to be part of a household factory.[80] It was a secondary form of labor, but one that offered the potential to produce consumer goods in the localities that used them.[81]

Not surprisingly, it proved easier to call for household factories than to organize them. In one high-profile account of the struggles of setting up a household factory in the small northern town of Kanggye, Kim Kyŏnghŭi described how roughly half the women she recruited had at first outright refused—even after she quoted to them Kim Il Sung's words on the subject. It was still early enough in the rise of Kim's personality cult that Kim Kyŏnghŭi, while expressing incredulity, could admit publicly that some of her interlocutors had never heard Kim Il Sung's instructions on the topic and did not care.[82] It is difficult to know whether such refusals were widespread. Other locations reported more successful participation. In Kaesŏng, local officials brought a textile factory together with more than a thousand neighboring families. Factory workers came to the neighborhoods to teach housewife-mothers how to make children's underwear, socks, and hats from factory remnants in their own homes.[83] In many localities, neighborhood

FIGURE 25. Kim Pongun, "In One Apartment," 1961.

women's groups received praise for their "creative initiative" (ch'angbalsŏng) in setting up household factories, though in some cases they were spurred on by neighborhood Party committees and the Women's Union.[84] More than 550 Pyongyang household teams were organized in 1961, involving 4,698 women, who produced more than seventy different products.[85] Sometimes the production could be significant. In eighteen neighborhoods across the city of Haeju, 137 household work teams involving more than five thousand women accounted for 10.2 percent of the city's locally produced goods in 1964—a not insignificant amount.[86] Yet official sources never combined such anecdotal statistics with aggregate data over time at a national level. It is also unclear how the more flexible wage workdays translated into employment data or what the staying power of household factories was over time—all key issues revealing the shortcomings of available data.

Yet ultimately the significance of household factories may not have been in their economic production alone. Household factories served the interests of various groups. Often organized on an ad hoc basis, household factories offered wage-work possibilities for women outside the discipline of factory and office time. For some, this was a secondary choice when other wage work remained unavailable. For others, it was a welcome, more flexible option, which they could take up on a part-time basis. For still others, like those who at first refused Kim Kyŏnghŭi, it may have been the best means to stave off the relentless pressures to join the paid labor force. And for a few women like Kim Kyŏnghŭi, such initiatives offered local political capital and, occasionally, as in her case, national attention. Whatever their motivation, the combination of greater convenience in time (shorter workdays) and space (closer to home) offered more opportunities for women to enter wage-work positions that they organized for themselves. With these results, central economic planners could relieve at least some of their concern about maximizing participation rates. Leaders at all levels, including Kim Il Sung, could be told that their instructions were being carried out. Local officials who oversaw light industries could point to household factories as one way they were creatively working to enliven the production of daily necessities in their local areas. Party ideologues could assess household factories as an indication of how rising cultural levels—specifically, in this case, those of housewife-mothers—would accelerate the transition to socialism. And leaders of the Women's Union could claim credit for it all. Diverse interests, in short, were served by household factories.

Yet all this celebration of the economic and ideological value of household factories could not hide the fact that the national political economy regularly turned to women's labor to provide the ad hoc solutions for bottlenecks in the central economic plan. Paid, routinized labor—preferably on the front line of production—remained glamorous and the best paid. The shock work of campaigns like the 1958 movement to rebuild Pyongyang had also turned to women's labor. Now, in the early 1960s, a third and even more flexible form of female labor, household factories, sought to remedy the problems created by the investment decisions underlying the central economic plan that the Party-state had not been able to resolve. In this context of capital shortage and devolution of responsibility, the initiatives taken by activists like Kim

Kyŏnghŭi proved indispensable to the workings of the political economy—even if this went unacknowledged for what it had to say about the limits of planning and the power of the Party-state. Much as they had done with the neighborhood committees, local officials turned to the labor potential of women to solve macro-level problems and the contradictions inherent in the central plan.

NINE

Home Décor, Culturedness, and the Class Politics of Style

ALL THE STRUGGLES OF THE LIGHT industries did not stop people from imagining themselves consuming new products. In an environment in which the usual authorities remained relatively silent about consumption norms and refrained from venturing into proactive statements, this imagining took place in magazines, where photographs did much of the work. As more apartments opened, official anxieties about unproductive interiors were soon accompanied by a parallel concern of the residents themselves: how to decorate these new spaces. Along with fashion, home décor emerged as a leading form of consumption through which the New Living came to be conceived as the economy continued to expand in the early 1960s.[1] Editors and writers began to use the familiar language of ideological renewal and cultural cultivation, including cultural levels and "culturedness" (*munhwasŏng*), to frame their recommendations on everything from how to choose room colors to which vases matched which season. While these efforts were far removed from the ideological assumptions of Party-state time, editors and writers appropriated and expanded its conceptual vocabulary, putting it to their own uses.

As discussed earlier, immediately after the war, photographs in the media tended to focus on the monumentality of apartment buildings' exteriors as a testament to construction. When *Women of Korea*, in order to emphasize interiors as productive spaces, published interior photos, they tended to crop them tightly, keeping the camera's focus on their female subjects who were pursuing activities, and not on the space itself. *Rodong sinmun* similarly remained reticent to move across thresholds to photograph apartments as lived spaces full of objects. Other interiors—study halls and meeting rooms, Party offices and factories, schools and theaters, to name a few—often appeared in the newspaper's pages during these early years.[2] The ratio of exterior to interior photographs skewed toward the former. A 1957 photo spread on Pyongyang's recovery "from the ashes" displayed thirteen diverse city settings, including worker apartment buildings and families enjoying the city, yet not one of these photos ventured into an apartment interior.[3] A common trope used by photographers, one that appeared widely for years, consisted of a family jauntily walking down a street, their apartment building or new department store soaring in the background. It was easier, in short, to photograph them outside than inside.[4]

Gradually, as more homes were constructed, cameras did move inside. The resulting photographs often narrowed in on the residents themselves in a genre that matched contemporary ideals of the "happy couple" or "happy family" (haengbokhan kajong).[5] Camera angles focused tightly on the inhabitants, revealing little of the apartment space itself or the objects that shared the room. Such was the case in Chu Hyŏngdo's 1956 photograph of a family that illustrated a story on ringing in the New Year (see figure 26). Closely cropped around the four family members, the photograph showed only the edge of what was apparently furniture. Other photos in the same feature likewise revealed little more of the apartment than parts of furniture, which staged the family's activities. Even the sizes of the rooms were difficult to discern.[6] The camera had certainly moved inside the apartment, yet its focus was not on the architectural interior itself or the objects within the space, but on the family. These photographs, in their simplicity and plainness, reproduced the official silence about consumption practices and, by shunting to the outside of the camera frame most material objects, seemingly reproduced the Party-state's prioritization of saving. Happiness, these photographs suggested, relied only on the family's proper conduct within the protection of their new, Party-provided home.

This reticence about interiors and their objects began to dissipate in 1958. That was the year of the big push for apartment construction that became part of the Ch'ŏllima campaign. It was also the year in which Party-state authorities were beginning to announce that the "clothing, food, and housing" problem had been basically solved for many people. Newspapers continued to proclaim, in slogan-like terms, that living standards were on their way up. It was the year of the pivot as well, when the Party-state renewed its emphasis on ideology, which gave extra impetus to notions such as "cultural living." And in the last month of 1958, Women of Korea published one of the earliest articles to explore the possibilities of how to "arrange" (kkuri) one's new urban apartment space.[7]

FIGURE 26. Chu Hyŏngdo, "Greeting the New Year," 1956. "She's more beautiful for wearing the multicolor jacket."

This anonymous article, "Let's Arrange Our Rooms Culturally," still treaded lightly, taking care to frame its suggestions within official language and policy by slipping its décor advice into typical recommendations about hygiene. Noting that the housing challenge was now a thing of the past, it sweepingly asserted, "We women are now all living in cultural and clean homes." The point, it argued, was that "arranging one's life culturally was not just about spotless cleaning." In urging readers to expand their thinking beyond previous notions of hygiene, the unnamed author still spoke largely in the idiom of scientific management of the household. Advice on hygiene and scientific management had always contained an aesthetic sensibility. Cleanliness, after all, is a constructed cultural category, one that makes claims well beyond the science, for example, of ridding germs from the kitchen.[8] The article appealed to what had long been expert opinion: a well-managed and hygienic household was necessarily also beautiful. This aesthetic sensibility was, in turn, commonly promoted as the basis for proper rearing of children and education of their emotional sensibilities—necessary, it was said, for future generations to further the revolution. It was within this conventional relationship between hygiene and aesthetics that the 1958 article expanded its consideration of home décor. The article raised, however briefly, issues that in future years would be expounded upon in much detail.

The article's broader conception of aesthetics centered on home space and tidiness—a "clean" look, so to speak. It advised readers not to place too many pictures on the wall, just one or two to avoid clutter. It explained that pleasing pictures should be chosen for a child's room to assist in their cultivation of aesthetic sensibilities.[9] For window treatments, it recommended a light, white curtain, especially for those units that had big windows, so as to prevent people from peering inside. It was important to select colors appropriately, it informed readers, though without making any specific suggestions. It may have been, for some families, an era of "cultural and clean homes," yet these short suggestions only barely began to move beyond standard treatments of household hygiene. Nevertheless, in comparison to many contemporary articles, this piece moved into new areas and pointed to issues that other writers in the coming years would render mainstream.[10]

At roughly the same time this early attempt at décor advice appeared, the reticence to photograph interiors with their objects began to dissipate. Photographs of apartment interiors became more numerous, not just in *Rodong sinmun* and *Women of Korea* but across many different print media. Dozens appeared. It was no longer rare to get a peek inside the apartment of another family. With the boom in urban building, curiosity about how others lived peaked, and magazine editors responded with an ever-increasing coverage of lifestyle possibilities. At this point, photographers took the lead, venturing beyond what was written. Snapshots of interiors addressed central Party-state claims of constantly rising living standards, suggesting ways that readers—at least some readers with the means—might put the growing varieties of consumer goods to use.

The earlier tight shots of interiors became looser. Camera angles panned outward, showing residents within their rooms living among the objects they had brought home and arranged for their own comfort. The objects of consumption themselves became visible, now presented as an essential part of the home. A two-page photo spread of the interiors of a Pyongyang apartment, featured in *Women of Korea*, showed a supposedly "unplanned" photo shoot of multiple rooms in an apartment, replete with residents living in their material surroundings (see figure 27).[11] Taken by staff writer and photographer Chu Hyŏngdo while on his way to work, this series showed walls full of mirrors, photos, and paintings. Electric cords snaked across walls, accenting the presence of lamps, clocks, and radios big and small. A child was shown reaching for a radio to turn up the volume. A large wooden clothes cabinet sat beside a chest of drawers. Purses and briefcases rested on tables and a radiator.

FIGURE 27. Chu Hyŏngdo, "An Unplanned Photo Shoot," 1959.

The ever-present potted flower stood on a desk. Cushions and tablecloths protected furniture. Each photo in Chu's series captured the residents doing something, whether writing letters, sweeping the floor, or getting ready to head out the door. Yet always their presence was defined by what—in the 1960s, during a shortage of consumer goods—must have been an eye-catching array of objects for many readers.

None of these interior photographs would have been imaginable just a few years prior. To be sure, this was partly due to the improving economic context: more was being produced in 1959 than in 1954, allowing some families to live materially more prosperous lives. Yet the shifting ideological context also created space for editors, writers, and photographers to frame "happy family" stories to include the families' homes, not just as roofs over their heads but as interiors personalized through the arrangement of objects. Chu's photo series, showing a minimal-consumption lifestyle, worked within the key official tensions—between the exhortation to save and the emphasis on increased living standards—to capture a sense of the changing material possibilities since the devastation of the war, even as it testified to the remaining poverty.

At the same time, the proliferation of photos like Chu's had the potential to raise questions about the relationship between class and consumption. This might have been used proactively to promote a style of consumption marked as specifically working-class lifestyle—a proletarian home décor, in short. Or it might also have been an opportunity to provide a class critique of this emerging consumption culture as risking the re-creation of bourgeois lifestyles. But neither of these possibilities was pursued. Despite having obvious associations with pre-collective-era bourgeois ideals, the photograph continued the memory politics of the New Living, which emphasized revolutionary breaks by denying its own history. Read as "new" in the most general sense, it shunted aside any explicit association between class and consumption, rarely even arguing on behalf of a specifically socialist lifestyle. Moreover, in its developmentalist promise that everyone could eventually attain such a lifestyle, the photograph worked to depoliticize consumption by denying any connection to postwar social stratification. As a result, writers, photographers, and experts could discuss apartment interiors with little worry that their color, furniture, or wall-hanging choices opened them to political charges.

RADIOS AND SEWING MACHINES

Across the 1950s and '60s, two objects emerged as the most sought-after consumer goods: the radio and the sewing machine. Expensive, in demand, and hard to come by, these two commodities had a long presence in the peninsula, extending back to the colonial period. Between 1933 and 1940, Koreans across the peninsula purchased 89,317 Singer sewing machines for their homes. That number increased by another 39,040 machines over the subsequent four years, for a total of 128,357 household machines.[12] One estimate puts the number of Korean purchases of radio receivers by 1940 as 126,047.[13] Tellingly, it is easier to come by statistics from the colonial period than to find comparable statistics for North Korea. In the immediate post-liberation and postwar periods, collective spaces such as dormitory common rooms, official meeting rooms, and study halls regularly featured radios for communal listening to key broadcasts.[14] Sewing machines, central to the growing textile industry, at first were seen, row after row, in photographs of the segregated spaces of factories. By the late 1950s, as production ramped up and wages rose, families began purchasing radios and sewing machines again—a phenomenon immediately visible once photographers began entering home interiors. Even in the most remote village up in the mountains, radios emerged as a marker of the New Living, the urban-rural divide seemingly erased by the presence of this single shared commodity.[15]

Contemporary photographs again attested to the growing significance of the two objects, as evident in a photograph in the magazine *New Living* of the home of a shipping worker for the Pyongyang Electric Factory, Ri Samok (see figure 28). The photo was part of an article treating Ri's family life in three successive photos: one at home, a second at the bank, and a third at a department store.[16] The first offered a wide-framed view of the main living room, giving a sense of scale—clearly Ri had been allocated an older, more expansive room. Ri and his wife (not named in the article) sat on either side of a large window, revealing a view of Pyongyang, while three daughters played on the floor below. Between them sat a sewing machine and a large radio. In the photograph's composition, the radio and sewing machine were in a central focal point, granted just as much prominence as the family members. "It's now come to be that we no longer have any worries with regard to eating, clothing, or housing," the unnamed author wrote, reproducing the language of the Five-Year Plan. Continuing, he claimed that "the only things people are thinking about in all households is how to live a more frugal life, how to create a more interesting life, and how to properly teach their sons and daughters"—in short, basic material means had been met. Yet for many readers this likely appeared to be much grander than just a "worry-free" life. The size of the room, the radio, the table and tablecloth on which it sat, the sewing machine, the children's clothing—these were unattainable by most families.

Radios and sewing machines, however, carried special meanings in the political climate of the 1950s and '60s. To be sure, they were objects of conspicuous consumption, indicative of a general rise in living standards and among the most desired major purchases after moving into an apartment. As the Ri family photo suggested, these two objects were symbols of individual and familial success while also trumpeting possibilities under the Party-state. This type of deliberate display in images throughout the print media announced that the pictured family had risen through the levels of attainment—labor training, wage scales, education, and other markers of achievement—that, by the late 1950s, had become the basis for the formation of social hierarchies about which the Party-state remained silent.[17] Photographs like the Ri family portrait show how consumption became a realm that at once constituted and reflected social distinctions. Yet any suggestion that radios were only about material acquisition could be fended off by connecting them with ideological and cultural

FIGURE 28. Anonymous, "Visiting Their Homes," 1961.

self-cultivation. Radios were about learning. Illustrations and photographs often paired them with books.[18] In a type of circular yet powerful logic, the radio's very presence related the family's success to its ideological commitments, in part by way of the radio's function in enabling the family to raise its cultural level. Consumption and self-improvement merged with the radio—and both reinforced the idea of a happy nuclear family.

Sewing machines had a similar duality, only they emphasized production. Just as conspicuous as possession of radios, possession of sewing machines countered the notion of homes as unproductive spaces. Given the gendered critique of domesticity, Ri's wife (again, not even named in the article) sat behind the sewing machine, as if she was about to start sewing at any moment. The photograph left little doubt that Ri's wife was not "playing and eating," while at the same time leaving her wage-labor status unclear. Was she one of the legions of women segregated into the lower-paying jobs of light industry? Did she instead contribute her sewing skills in a local household factory? Or was she simply making clothing for her family to compensate for the shortages in ready-to-wear clothing in the stores, perhaps using one of the designs in *Women of Korea*? Whatever the answer, the photograph did the unspoken work of naturalizing the connection between women, sewing, and labor while blurring the divide between factory and home through production. In this way, both of these premier consumer goods came with a political pedigree that shunted away questions of inequity while legitimating the choices and commitment that led to the lifestyle. No one could charge their owners with consumption for consumption's sake. This was a happy family showing how they pursued a path of self-improvement and production at home.

ADVICE FOR APARTMENT INTERIORS

However troubled by unevenness and problems in the light industrial sector, the economy continued to expand into the mid-1960s, even as its growth slowed in comparison to the first postwar decade. In urban areas, where growth and expansion were concentrated, the material transformation of cityscapes continued apace. Moreover, with the war nearly a decade past, new popular interests less shaped by memories of destruction and recovery emerged. One indication of the spread of this forward-looking sensibility was the anxiety of Party ideologues, who openly worried that as life got better, people would forget the "difficult lives of the past." The concern was especially acute given that most youths "did not even know the word *tenant*" because they had not experienced exploitation. "The happier we become," as one piece wrote, "the more we need to heighten our class consciousness."[19] Memories of colonialism and the wartime served their purposes.

Party ideologues were right to be worried. Many people were eager to move on from the dominance of wartime memories. Writers began to ask questions unimaginable in the early 1950s. "How long can a person live?" pondered one, or as another asked, "How much should one eat?" Wartime fears of survival and starvation were slowly being displaced by concerns of longevity and health.[20] Such shifts reflected the improved security and economic conditions, providing the rationale for a more fulsome exploration of how the New Living might incorporate a greater role for consumption. Writers made an explicit connection between the economy and opportunities to explore new possibilities for daily life—an exploration that manifested across a wide range of areas, including food culture, fashion, exotic holidays, and interior décor.

The shift appeared in journals as varied as *Ch'ŏllima*, *Women of Korea*, and *Worker*. In the early to mid-1960s, they all published extensively about home interiors. If, in earlier years, photographers had taken the lead in imagining the possibilities of interior décor and consumption, writers were now foremost in addressing the same questions, and they began to push the boundaries of Party-state rhetoric in articles that explored consumption and décor decisions. Hygiene, now presumed as a given and still part of official movements, faded as a framing device for household décor articles.[21] Writers created a separate discursive space. Décor advice remained in support of "happy families," but the photographs and other illustrations took on a new form. Rather than focusing on smiling children, foregrounding residents and their activities, or remaining locked in discussions of household management, these articles presented domestic interiors purely as spaces to decorate.

The result was an aesthetics of interior design—promoted by experts ranging from lecturers at art institutes, to officials in the Ministry of Light Industries, to unnamed staff writers—that centered on discriminating tastes, or culturedness. This approach to domestic décor again displaced questions of class in its discussions of "harmony" and beauty, implicitly reviving themes about décor that had first arisen in the colonial era but were now being loosely—and somewhat awkwardly—tied to revolutionary advocacy, while quietly adding to the repertoire of ways of writing about femininities. It remained easier to write about gender distinctions than class differences, even if discourses on home décor further depoliticized both categories.

To the photos of "happy families" were added new types of images: standalone interior photographs and illustrations showing the arrangement of a room, its furniture and wall hangings given prominence, yet without a single person present.[22] Such images used objects and their relationship to each another as the primary subject, unmediated by the presence of inhabitants. One highly stylized line illustration of a living room, published in mid-1964, showed the decorative sensibility of these images in its spartan yet careful distribution of key objects: a wall cabinet and drawers, a table, a lamp, a painting, curtains, a clock, and a few personal objects.[23] Drawn from a slightly elevated perspective in three dimensions and showing the entire room, the image put the viewer in the position of a potential decorator/consumer surveying the scene, as though critically considering the décor decisions that went into this design (see figure 29). Significantly, no radio, with its suggestion of ideological self-cultivation, or sewing machine associated with production, sullied the pristineness of the image. Similar styles of photographs appeared, again showing uninhabited rooms and highlighting an array of desirable furniture (see figure 30).[24]

Parallel to these roomscapes, images of blueprint-like layouts of rooms became common, showing preferences for the arrangement of various types

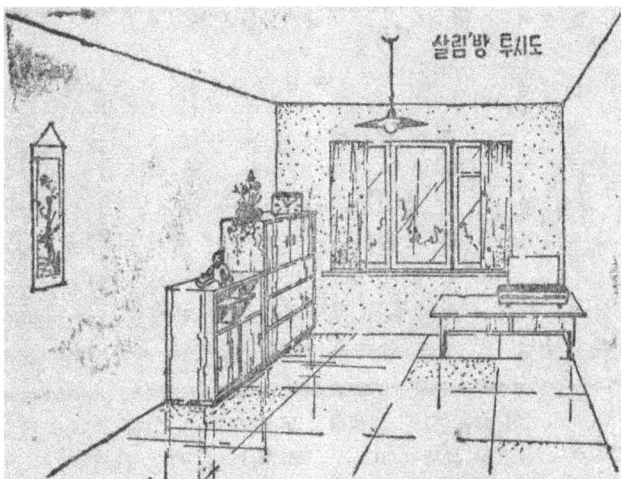

FIGURE 29. Anonymous, "A Three-Dimensional Plan for Living Rooms," 1964.

of furniture, whether in an urban or rural setting.[25] One such diagram for the "arrangement of furniture in a two-room home"—the standard design for most family apartment units—used a rough-sketch format that allowed readers to imagine moving the individual pieces of furniture around the rooms.[26] What to do with one's furniture? These plans had answers (see figure 31). Although the explicit subject of both images was the furniture itself, the unspoken subject was the unseen yet crucial figure of the viewer, understood at once as the reader of the magazine who was consuming these images and as a potential designer of a similar room. As repeated references to "we women" and other such phrases demonstrated, the viewer/designer was, without exception, assumed to be the woman of the household—one more in a long line of ways that these apartment interiors became feminized.

By 1965, writers were making it clear that their readers should distinguish between two types of rooms in their décor decisions, one centering on the traditionally inspired heated floor, or *ondol*, and the other on rooms heated by radiators. When prefab technology had first been introduced in the early years after the war, the challenge of creating blocks that could stream hot water to heat floors in multistory, multiunit buildings had bedeviled engineers and architects (as discussed in chapter 5). At first, builders installed central boilers with radiators, celebrated as the most "modern" of technologies. By the end of the 1950s, engineers had resolved the *ondol* design problem, and an increasing number of floor-heated buildings were erected. Thus, when writers began to

FIGURE 30. Anonymous, "Finding Apartments," 1962.

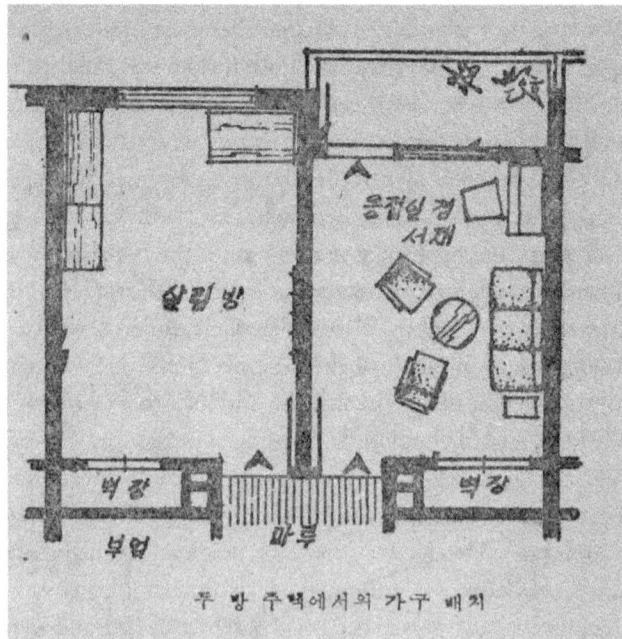

FIGURE 31. Anonymous, "The Arrangement of Furniture in a Two-Room Home," 1965.

create a detailed aesthetic for apartment living, the first question to ask concerned the type of apartment in which a resident lived: one heated by *ondols* or by radiators? This was not a choice that residents made—people moved into apartments assigned to them by their workplaces or state organs. Yet, as experts opined, it was necessary to distinguish the different styles of furniture designed to be suitable for the different heating technologies. In theory, if the *ondol* meant much sitting on the heated floor, while radiators meant sitting on chairs, the way the furniture should be arranged would be dramatically different.

Furniture styles varied according to this distinction. The low tables and dressers suitable for *ondol* floors tended to adopt and adapt received traditions, often with inlaid patterns reminiscent of aristocratic, Chosŏn-dynasty designs. Articles extolling the beauty of Chosŏn furniture made this connection with contemporary styles, as did pieces that described the artisanal handicrafts of the last dynasty.[27] Even the Chosŏn-dynasty scholar Sin Chaehyo could be quoted in appreciation of the national character of furniture design.[28] By contrast, alternative styles of furniture came in a slightly heavier midcentury Scandinavian design. Featuring lightly colored wood, this transnational socialist-cum-modernist aesthetic received a boost with the 1957 opening of a Soviet-built wood furniture factory.[29] As contemporary photographs also show, this same lightly colored wood could also be used innovatively for reformed traditional furniture, downplaying the contrast between the two styles.[30] Furniture became one of the many objects— notably including paintings—for which notions of "inheriting and developing" (*kyesŭng paljŏn*) traditions would be worked out in the materiality of everyday life. For purveyors of design advice, a sense of proportion, reflecting these two modes of construction, was the first priority. The worst possible scenario, readers were warned, was to mix, in a single space, pieces of furniture designed for these two divergent modes of living.[31]

Such a contrast and framing of styles enshrined the distinction of modern versus traditional in the design of furnishings. At no point did designers debate, let alone produce, any objects aimed at being distinctively socialist. Instead, socialist design came to be glossed as "modern," seen as one part of the modern-national dyad. The possibilities of proletarian-specific design remained unexplored, as slightly modified elite traditions often came to stand in for a national aesthetic. Rather than concern themselves with imagining a possible socialist design, writers transcended this modern-traditional framing with a shared sense that the premier principle unifying all interior design should be harmony (*chohwa*) and stylishness (*maepsi*). This sensibility, in turn, needed to be defined to match the tenor of "our era."[32] What exactly constituted the definition of the era varied by expert—some wrote of a style befitting "the tastes and emotions of Ch'ŏllima-era people," while others wrote simply of a "new era," implying an indistinct recent time of material prosperity.[33] All agreed that certain unspecified past styles, however defined, were inappropriate for the age. What was necessary, in the words of one, was a "contemporary beauty" (hyŏndaemi).[34] This was a type of minimalism that abided by notions of frugality and practicality without becoming an anti-materialist ascetism.[35] Indeed, as in the Soviet Union under Khrushchev, the emphasis began to turn on comfort and coziness.[36] Yet the few interior photographs of Soviet home interiors published in the Korean print media suggested that this newly promoted Korean sensibility was a comparatively more minimal style of living, perhaps because people owned comparatively fewer objects. The imperatives of frugality, given the still widespread poverty, were mediated as a minimalist modernism. This translated as a clean and uncluttered look, yet by the mid-1960s it had evolved into a much more highly articulated consideration of a far wider array of factors—a careful consideration of the emotional effects of color and the positioning of objects with one another in a living space, to name just two—while not forgetting the practical uses of these objects, as well as their connection to the interests of the family.

The myriad factors that constituted this "contemporary beauty" needed to be harmonized, designers agreed. Yet as much as "harmony" lent a unifying thread in this décor advice, designers also acknowledged that this ideal neither fit a set pattern nor constituted a single, fixed standard. Their advice offered directions, but within flexible parameters that were expected to be interpreted by the creativity of individuals—a task that once again reflected idiosyncratic "cultural levels." Advice articles regularly spoke about the immense spectrum of décor possibilities. "If you ask how to decorate and adorn a room, the answer will differ depending on the interests and feelings, the ages and occupations, as well as the local customs of the family members."[37] Others pointed to increasing varieties of goods as an indication of not just improved living standards, but the opening of more possibilities for how to adorn one's living spaces. A specialist in wood paint at the Fine Arts University, Pang Ch'iwŏn, made this point in a treatise on the aesthetics of furniture. Marveling at the boom in quality and types of furniture, Pang wrote about the curved and straight lines in furniture design, the different sizes and uses, and the variety of tones for wood furniture. This variety, he argued, put the onus on users, who needed to select what he called "balanced" furniture that reflected their own emotions, interests, ages, and genders.[38] Variety in furniture, in short, both enabled and required greater self-expression—and, accordingly, was more challenging. What, for Pang, was true for furniture applied equally, for others, to flower vases, wall colors, cupboards, and the like.[39]

That most urban dwellers lived in virtually the same style of standardized apartments motivated the individuating possibilities of décor—as was the case with the plain, standardized flats being built simultaneously in cities around the world.[40] Despite some small differences in style, height, and size, the average apartments built in the late 1950s and early 1960s were otherwise monotonously similar. The drive to lower costs and standardize led to uniformity—all the more reason to emphasize the variety of possible interiors as a way of distinguishing apartments from one another and countering the sameness of architectural space. In the eyes of one writer, this impulse extended to the exteriors of the buildings by way of window treatments. This writer hoped that residents would take the time to decorate their own units' windows, so that buildings would not look too boring from the streets. This was a form of self-expression, explained the author, insofar as windows "reveal the type of lives lived by the people within,"[41] similarly to how human eyes allow one to see into a person's heart. Clean glass, nice curtains, and a tasteful vase of flowers—choices like these would highlight the tastes of the family, advertising them to people on the streets, and make buildings look more lively.[42] This individuating impulse among the sea of monotony was not risk free, however. Expression of one's family character could come precariously close to "individualism"—a substitute for the rarely uttered charge of "bourgeois." Yet it also captured what historians of socialism in other settings have long argued: in these repetitive spaces, consumption enabled the creation of lifestyles that were differentiated and hardly uniform.[43]

Much décor advice became a series of don'ts. Few refrained from expressing strong opinions: don't put a complicated picture on a wall opposite a desk, since that will interfere with concentrating on studies; don't position your sewing machine in relation to the window such that it casts a shadow over the work; don't use dark paints—reds and greens—for wall color; don't use glass cupboard doors that will reveal the mess within; and don't hang your laundry in the windows.[44] More serious were the warnings against an overly "showy" or "flowery" décor—using a term, *hwaryŏ*, sometimes used to describe the excessive consumption of the bourgeoisie in South Korea.[45]

Despite all the options and all the instructions, designers nevertheless admitted that there was a certain ineffable quality to what made one room beautiful and another room not. Kim Chinsŏng explained this mystery: "Even if the orientation and structure of homes are the same and the furniture and decorations inside the rooms are similar, some feel soft and cozy and others do not." For Kim, the determining factors rested with paint color. Others, such as Kim Unbong, had more general concerns. When entering some homes, she pointed out, one immediately had a strong sense that the rooms had been made cozy. How so? She admitted: "In truth, it is not so straightforward to explain in a few words from where the harmonious beauty and cultural taste of a room comes."[46] Like others, Kim Unbong went on to offer more than a few words in her attempt to describe what she readily admitted remained indescribable. These solutions, after all, were the very purpose for which purveyors of design advice did what they did. At the same time, the scope of possibilities and indescribable qualities encompassed precisely the conditions necessary if they were to muster for themselves the mantle of experts bearing solutions. Yet in framing the aesthetics of rooms in terms of culturedness, these designers put the onus back on individual residents to make the appropriate decisions that suited both the age and their family's specific temperaments and interests. They needed to raise their cultural levels through self-cultivation. Whether someone "arranged a room culturally" reflected, in the eyes of these critics, the cultural level of the family. "Just like how you can guess a person's interests, character, and cultural levels from the way they dress, you can tell everything about a family's life from the way they arrange their decorative items in the living room."[47] Of course, not everyone was as adept or as interested as these critics hoped. Photographs from these years that were published in stories unrelated to interior design showed rooms decidedly not up to standards promoted by specialists. Some residents jammed furniture into the small rooms—hardly the uncluttered look to which so many writers aspired. Others allowed their rooms to become overgrown with plants stretching in all directions—not quite the single, tastefully placed flower vase.[48]

Nevertheless, discussions of décor served both to entrench the widespread use and applicability of cultural levels and to expand their meanings and use further into new realms. What, in the years after the war, had largely been about ideological cultivation and propriety had—while still inclusive of these meanings—proliferated by the 1960s to include notions of taste and culturedness as realized through consumption and décor. The strong political connections of this language in the mid-1950s had, a decade later, become much more attenuated. Still, these discussions of interior décor rested within the conceptional frame of Party-state time, even as writers stretched its inclusiveness into realms not originally imagined.

To the list of the responsibilities of all mother-workers—which already included scientific management of the household, serving as primary caregiver of children, and meeting the demands of the workplace—was added the responsibility for décor. The discourse on décor, with all of its attention to aesthetics and cultural levels, became one more realm where writers produced and propagated representations of contemporary ideals of femininity. Mastery of furniture and of paint colors, the correct positioning of mirrors, the skillful selection of paintings—all these elements combining, in theory, to form a harmonious whole—brought "cultural levels" together with consumption in ways that would not have been possible just a few years earlier. But unlike how linguists linked ideals of feminine speech to cultural levels through self-reform, experts on décor sensibilities promoted ideals that depended on the acquisition of possessions. This connection, in turn, would bring gender into play with the very social unevenness that apartment interiors both displayed and constituted.

MATERIAL CIRCULATION, CLASS, AND THE RETURN HOME

The magazines in which writers explored their interior décor ideals were the same magazines in which other writers complained about light industry. The former tended to be tucked in the back pages, whereas the latter, given the subject's connection to central economic planning and production, tended to find a place in the more prominent sections of the magazine. Writers on décor paid little heed to this obvious contradiction—if light industrial production was lagging in quanitity and quality, how could readers follow their advice? The upbeat tone of advice literature seemed oblivious to the conundrums of its audience. One could write breezily that readers should rotate vases or paintings between seasons. Yet readers were simultaneously reading articles reporting that even though the six porcelain factories in Pyongyang were producing more than ever, their output still was insufficient.[49]

This meant that for most readers, décor advice was more a fantasy than a how-to guide. It was the photographs, more than the objects, that these audiences consumed. Given that monthly magazines circulated in the tens of thousands—*Women of Korea* reached 120,000 issues by 1960[50]—the numbers of magazines outnumbered the pieces of furniture annually produced by the new Soviet-donated wood furniture factory. Photo layouts seem to have been set by editors to appeal to the seeing desires of readers. Brand names were displayed prominently, letting readers ogle the differences between Ch'ŏllima radios and the Seagull brand.[51] Photographs allowed them to wonder about the merits of rival sewing machines: which of the models—Rich Harvest, Twin Horses, Pyongyang, or Kŭmgang—was best?[52] Photographs titillated the would-be consumers. Yet even as they might imagine future possibilities, magazine editors never combined the light-industry and consumption stories to discuss how limits in available consumer goods meant that many would be unable to perform the "culturedness" they were told to cherish as a contemporary ideal. Nor did any writer consider these problems in lieu of the many other articles telling readers to raise their class consciousness. These different segments of discourse remained separate.

By 1964, this separation, as part of the depoliticization of class and gender, enabled writers to edge away from the pillar of the Party-state's gender policies—namely, women's participation in wage labor as a means of realizing gender equality. A 1964 article in *Women of Korea* validated the nonparticipation in wage labor by some women, while dismissing any consideration of the class implications of that validation.[53] Writer Chang Chŏngin described her visit to the home of Ri Sangsuk, a Pyongyang resident. Upon entering Ri's home, the author immediately sensed from the surroundings—the mirrors, the vases—that Ri was "no ordinary woman." Adopting the style more usually employed for model worker stories, Chang continued to describe in detail the adornments of the apartment in near-breathless prose, telling readers that her whole body was thankful for the sense the apartment gave her of basking in the scent of a sunny spring day.[54] As the two sat for a chat, Chang kept asking herself how Ri managed to be frugal like this, yet still carry a sense of elegance. Each piece of furniture, she observed, was neatly put in its own place, and each piece of décor was stylishly arranged. Rather than have too many colors in her room—a major faux pas, according to many critics[55]—Ri had chosen yellow, using varying tones of the same base color on different surfaces, to create a "delicate yet noble" atmosphere. The décor of the child's room impressed Chang the most: in it she sensed Ri's motherly love and self-cultivation.

Yet Chang hesitated. She realized that her unstinting praise might rest uneasily with some of her readers. She knew that people would be extremely curious as to how Ri organized her life to manage all that the article had described. After all, following the Party-state's measures to open the opportunities for wage labor to women, a policy that had been expanded in 1958 to help enhance production levels, magazines such as the one in which Chang was writing had devoted much attention to helping women manage the challenges of the double burden. How did Ri juggle these demands on her time? "Perhaps there will be some," Chang ventured, "who think that Ri only has this kind of time because she doesn't head out of the house to participate in wage work." Therein lay the crux. It was an astonishing admission. Chang was telling her readers that such an accomplished room took time and was possible only because Ri stayed at home without engaging in wage work. Yet Chang deliberately raised this question only to dismiss it. Her answer appealed defensively to notions of scientific motherhood and efficient household management to legitimize Ri's perfecting of her household interior. Remarkably, Chang argued that the proper running of the home in all its facets, including consumption, was in itself good enough without requiring wage work. She specifically noted that Ri worked no less than those who headed out of the home for wage work. Chang did not go quite so far as to use the privileged term for participation in the means of production, *rodong* (labor), instead settling for the more colloquial *il* (work) to describe Ri's activities. But she did highlight how Ri lived a disciplined and highly planned life. The rest of the piece defended this resolutely domestic life by recounting Ri's busy day, from taking care of the kids in the morning and getting them to school, to doing sewing work at home, to her single hour of lunchtime, followed by shopping for family needs and other "effective uses of her time," including self-study and various chores until 11 p.m. "In this way, she's able to manage today's type of neat and wonderful home." The article suggested that the tranquility of the home helped ease the day's exhaustion of family members when they returned in the evening.

What was most noteworthy about Chang's piece was how she abandoned a wide array of themes that, for the past decade, had framed the gendered relationships entangling home and work. The division of interior and exterior that had enabled a critique that represented the home as unproductive was here rejected by both Chang and Ri. The article distanced itself from notions of "people who play and eat"—even though Ri's lifestyle would have matched the conditions of people who deployed the logic of this derogatory expression. Nor does the article reflect on how Kim Yŏngsuk, only a few years earlier in the same pages (see chapter 7), had described her own life at home as "colorless," one that left her conflicted and unhappy until she found wage work. Ri exhibited no such dissatisfaction and was praised by Chang as content. The article had nothing to say directly about Party-state policies such as the 1956 policy on dependent family members or the 1958 substitution policy. Chang felt no compunction to show Ri participating in neighborhood work, whether through an inminban, hygiene inspection, or part-time work in a household production team. Only Chang's defensive tone about Ri's nonparticipation in wage work ("perhaps there will be some who will think . . .") alluded to this more complex history and what she knew would be the sensitivities of readers who did not have Ri's luxury of time.

Chang tried to overcome her defensive tone on this point by writing excitedly of Ri's mastery of domestic time management. This explicit focus on time reproduced the silences featured in décor writing. Chang, too, glossed over the challenges readers faced in accessing the very consumer goods her story prescribed as necessary to become a Ri-like "no ordinary woman." This was not an era when it was easy to challenge Party-state definitions about what constituted labor. Yet Chang did so. Her story affirmed the value of Ri's domestic work as—what we can call, even if Chang did not—labor. Nevertheless, Chang's willingness to push back against the Party-state's priorities came at the expense of considering how her own defense of Ri's domesticity relied on a specific relation between gender, consumption, and class that by the 1960s, following the growth of the economy, was becoming increasingly complicated. That Ri did not need the double income of wage work, and yet could use multiple shades of yellow to paint her curtained rooms, which were filled with top-of-the-line home furnishings, did not disrupt the universalist tone with which Chang offered Ri up for emulation by her female audience. Ten years earlier, it would have been difficult to publish such a story in *Women of Korea*. Ri must have appreciated the significance of this changing environment. Her willingness to publicly reveal her "cultural living" through Chang's reporting showed that she had no worry that her lifestyle might be labeled bourgeois or that she might be critiqued for "hiding" at home.

Chang's story was both a record of the past decade's changes and a legitimation of them. It was in the formation of such gendered socioeconomic hierarchies—which, in stories like Chang's, were at once rationalized and depoliticized—that Party-state rule came to be consolidated. Neither Chang nor Ri once mentioned Kim Il Sung, but the story hinted at the developments and tensions within the New Living that Kim, at first, used to assert his own power and, later, abandoned for an alternative strategy that sought to separate his personal rule from these socioeconomic and cultural dilemmas.

Fetishizing Purses?

By the 1960s, magazines increasingly began to tempt their readers with elaborate pictures and illustrations of the rising number of consumer goods available. Personal style and fashion captured more attention, with articles and photographs describing what clothes to wear for what season, how to match clothing to body types, and what makeup was best to wear. One two-page photo spread in the *New Living* magazine featured recent lines of handbags.[a] On the left side of the collage, a woman was smartly dressed in a *choson'ot* and protected herself from the sun with a parasol. She carried the prized object of the photo spread, a fashionable purse. On the opposite side, a mannequin stood wearing a stylish spring raincoat. At the top and bottom, the spread displayed a bountiful array of purses, suitcases, and even shoes, as if boasting about the plenitude and variety being produced for consumers. Yet in the middle rested a picture of the female workers producing these items—a nod to the value of labor in a self-proclaimed proletarian country. Published in 1961, the collage seemed to fit with that year's emphasis on increasing the production of high-quality light-industrial goods—"more and better!"

Or did it?

FIGURE C. A collage of consumer goods. Anonymous, untitled, 1961.

This type of consumer-goods image was common in the era. Less common, however, was the way the centering of the photograph of workers had the effect of pushing the consumer products to the margins. Emphasizing production had always been easier than emphasizing consumption, but here the spread seemed to be a reminder: with all the recent attention in magazines to consumer goods, readers should not forget that they still depended on shop floors full of workers who made the snazzy purses.

The collage's insistence on centering labor and not being bedazzled by the end products is reminiscent of Marx's critique of the commodity fetish. Marx believed that the true value of a commodity arose out of the relationships of the people who produced the commodity—in other words, the investment of labor in the good. He lamented that this value was mystified and overlooked by consumers who saw their purchases as having an intrinsic value all their own, divorced from the people who made the objects. There was, of course, no room in 1961 Korea for a commodity-fetish-style critique. In a country that had socialized all property and claimed to have ended exploitation, no economic or theoretical journal dared raise the possibility. Yet this photo spread seemed to query the proper place of the commodity under socialism. At minimum, it reflected a degree of discomfort with the growing frequency of media images that worked to extol consumer goods while glossing over their inherent labor value, as well as depersonalizing the social relations underlying their existence. The spread reminded readers that purses, however stylish, were just another widget that had no value other than that produced by people. People not goods at the center, it insisted.

With no explanatory text, the meaning of the collage remained open-ended—a display of photographs merely celebrating light-industrial production, or one raising questions about the implications of those celebrations in a self-proclaimed workers' state?

a. Anonymous, untitled, *Sinsaenghwal*, June 1961.

Conclusion

LOOKING UP AT COMRADE KIM

THIS BOOK'S COVER PHOTOGRAPH of a family on their apartment balcony was taken in 1959, six years after the war. It was published as one image among an immense variety of texts, photographs, cartoons, monographs, and other print media that imagined the possibilities of the New Living under socialism. This family faced the same questions that shaped the lives of most North Korean urbanites in the postwar years: How to self-improve? How to build efficiently? How to make a happy family home? How to consume properly? Six years later, by 1965, many of the New Living's basic directions had been set, even though people would continue to search for definitive answers in the decades to come. The pursuit of these questions led urban women and men to engage in a variety of processes that were deeply interwoven with, and mutually constitutive of, the rebuilding of the Party-state. This combination helped set the foundations for a regime that has now outlasted the life span of the Soviet Union.

As much as the family portrait sought to present the New Living as smooth and easy, I have tried in the preceding pages to show how unruly and uneven was the quest. Many urban dwellers likely agreed that the family on the balcony represented a worthy ideal, but most also understood by 1965 that the photograph glossed over the struggles and tensions that marked their efforts to make their way into their own homes and onto their own balconies. To be sure, there was no end to the Party-state's exhortations and policy prescriptions that sought to harmonize people's pursuit of their personal and family goals with its own objective of reaching socialism. Yet even the Party-sanctioned media could not but reveal that many women and men had their own ideas about how to go about this, even if they needed to act within set parameters. Across the twelve years covered in this book, media commentators working in the context of the peninsula's long twentieth century can be seen reviving subjects and challenges that had a pre-collective-era history and fitting them to the new meanings and usages of old terms, such as *New Living* itself. Experts and advice purveyors of all types followed the shifts of the political economy to expand on received themes, using rhetoric in tune with the political culture to push them in new directions—to the point that, by 1965, they had begun to explore areas that had only the most tenuous connection to Party priorities and even ran counter to them, even if no one said that out loud.

The struggles and tensions shaping this pursuit were due in part to the power of the Party-state. Its coercive clout was immense. Stories throughout this book have shown how this was a regular feature of the New Living: people lost lives in the Pyongyang building campaign, were forced into formal loyalty categories by the sŏngbun system, and were regularly subjected to both direct and indirect surveillance. The supremacy of the Party-state has arguably been the premier theme of most historical work on North Korea. Yet, in the preceding pages, I have sought to counter this tendency by writing about the limits of that rule. This is partly a historical argument. The power of every state waxes and wanes. In 1953, the Party-state was weak and had to rebuild. Yet even as it reestablished and expanded its prewar powers, limits to its capacity remained. To borrow Mary Fulbrook's description of East Germany, North Korea "was not only a dictatorship."[1] There was much more afoot. The New Living revealed these dynamics.

The population's struggles were shaped just as much by these limits. The two main macroeconomic problems that the Party-state could not resolve— the capital and labor shortages—deeply impinged on every city dweller's daily life. Whether it was the pressure to save, the lack of investment in social welfare facilities, the gendered organization of irregular labor, or the differing investments in and wage structuring of heavy versus light industries—all these and many more features of the New Living were conditioned by the inabilities of the Party-state to resolve the capital and labor challenges. The constant call to get things "right"—the kijunnyang, wage scales, discipline of planning cycles, marriage laws, circulation of consumer goods—was an indirect admission of official frustration in translating plans and goals into the local social worlds of the population. Moreover, the theoretical assessments about the stages of revolution, which led to what I have called Party-state time, also took on a pragmatic bent insofar as they, too, responded to the two grand shortages. In effect, by turning to individual ideological levels as an explanation for the remaining socioeconomic ills and as the way to transition to socialism, the Party-state placed the onus outside of its institutions and programs and on the individualized masses of the people. Self-improvement as a solution to national challenges was a well-trodden path among anticolonial nationalists in the pre-collective era. It also gained impetus from Soviet and socialist precedents. Whatever its varied origins, this shift amounted to an announcement of the Party-state's dependency on the determination of individuals to become modern socialist subjects—even as it sought to control, cajole, and exhort what the proper actions might be. Yet, as I have shown in this book, as extensive as the endeavors of the Party-state to guide this process were, there was much wiggle room for women and men to participate in this project in ways that did not strictly follow injunctions and guidelines. Or they could do so in the most superficial fashion, using Party rhetoric to achieve their own goals. Party officials knew it, hence the endless cycles of exhortations. In this situation, a classic dynamic of modern subject formation, glossed as becoming a good proletarian, came into play: becoming an individual subject simultaneously entailed the subjugation of that individual—a dilemma that was by no means contradictory.

That the Party-state turned to practices of self-cultivation as the prioritized form of struggle for socialist transition turned critiques inward. Self-examination and self-improvement, whether achieved through advice literature or small-group criticism—always under the gaze of surveillance—involved a politics of self-responsibility that easily segued into a politics of self-blame. This took place at the same time that the growth of the economy, growth of state institutions, and other macroeconomic phenomena were leading to social stratification among city residents. Although it is not possible to describe empirically the consequences of this stratification, I have argued that these uneven social relations shaped the era's discourse. These discursive indications were not mere reflections. The New Living helped produce and legitimize these hierarchies while at the same time denying their existence—a point that can be perceived in the family balcony portrait.

Nowhere was this clearer than in gender relations. Any history of socialist revolution is incomplete without attention to gender politics. As seen throughout this book, gender was a foundational organizing principle, both materially and representationally, for virtually every feature of the political economy, social relations, and discourse. To ask about gender in the New Living is to inquire about the workings of power—not just in the local social worlds of men and women, but in the national political economy and the

Party-state itself. In areas such as language and the use of labor, domestic living arrangements and consumption, the New Living naturalized binary gendered distinctions, which in turn were used not just to rationalize hierarchies between and within genders but also as a way of forming and marking class distinctions. It should not be surprising that even if the Party-state did not theorize how its own policies became the source for the formation of new hierarchies in the postwar world, it is through an analysis of gender that these hierarchies most readily reveal themselves throughout the texts of the era. This worked, in part, because at the very moment that women across the country made use of the gender equality laws to enter the wage-labor force and challenge received gender norms, there was a simultaneous proliferation of discourse on femininities, which ultimately reconfigured and naturalized those hierarchies, rather than flattening them as it claimed. One of the grand ironies of the New Living was that, as the tensions in the political economy became more severe, it was often urban women not engaged in wage work—those often said to be "playing and eating at home"—whose various kinds of non-routinized labor filled in as stopgaps. Whether in household labor units or in neighborhood committees, it was their efforts that eased the tensions in the political economy and made things "work," so to speak, though the cruciality of this irregular labor was not recognized publicly by the Party-state.

The depoliticization of gender and class did not mean the complete erasure of criticism. Even under the authoritarian rule of the Party-state, it is possible to trace divergent opinons in the print media. My work addresses two different types. One was centered in the Women's Union, which used its institutional basis and house journal to offer a subtle critique of specific Party-state policies, like the narrowing of divorce laws, which had negative consequences for its membership. The subtlety of the Women's Union's critique was certainly necessitated by the authoritarian politics of the Party-state. But just as important was that postwar consolidation rested on the reaffirmation of the centrality of male power, both in the Party-state itself and in local social worlds. To admonish the masculine nature of power in this context was to hazard criticizing the Party-state itself and the way its very constitution rested on gendered hierarchies. Critiques more easily dealt with specific policies.

A second form of critique offered what I have called "flashes of criticism." These had no institutional basis and are marked by their ephemeral and anonymous qualities. These flashes of criticism suggested discontent with the directions taken since the war. Whether they were whimsical mentions of roads not taken, inspired by Chinese politics, or were earnest critiques in vain search of support, these flashes came from a more radical perspective. They appealed to classic Marxist tenets—the commodity fetish, surplus value, the function of class ideologies, and social contradictions—or poked fun at claims of gender equality to suggest that Korean socialism had gone astray. These flashes were part of the more complex discursive environment that, as I have shown, cannot be reduced to a single, monolithic ideology—however much the Party tried to do so for its own purposes.

That the Party aspired to a singular ideology, of course, was very different from achieving it. And if the New Living gives us a more varied history of contemporary discourse, political economy, gendered social relations, and Party-state power, these same dynamics can pry open the personality cult's aspiration to make Kim Il Sung transcendent of history.

THE 1950S CONTEXT FOR KIM'S ASCENDANCE

Histories of Kim's rise to power have dominated most histories of North Korea. The ins and outs of that ascendancy have usually been recounted as following two primary story lines. At its most basic, the story told by historians has been one of intra-Party elite conflict. After the war, Kim Il Sung famously outmaneuvered his rivals, in particular Pak Hŏnyŏng, the head of the domestic group that had stayed inside the country to fight colonialism. Blaming Pak and his supporters for setbacks in fighting during the Korean War and the failure to reunify the country, Kim had Pak tried and executed. Soon thereafter, Kim took advantage of several institutional and ideological debates to purge still other competitors. These debates were generally not exclusive to North Korea, but were debated in other socialist settings. How much emphasis should be placed on heavy industry? How widely open should Party membership be? How collective should leadership be? Though the questions did not originate with Kim Il Sung, he did use the very real differences over them to attack his opponents. Eventually all his adversaries, real and imagined, had been expelled, fled the country, were killed, or disappeared. According to an estimate by Andrei Lankov of the members of the first central committee, at least half were purged.[2] Between 1958 and 1961, these tense struggles were followed by mop-up work, which extended the purges into the rural areas and lower reaches of the state bureaucracy. These conflicts impinged on the New Living, as the construction sector reverberated with the downward effect of elite politics. The new mass line, with its emphasis on leadership, and the politicization of prefab construction techniques cost officials their lives. This shifting environment provided the everyday work styles through which women and men did their wage work. The role of ideology in their lives and the economy was redefined.

The story of intra-Party machinations intersects with a second story line, which historians have used to recount the connections between elite maneuvering and relations with socialist allies. More often than not, this story examines North Korea's struggles for autonomy.[3] Kim, the nation, and sovereignty are often conflated in these accounts, which emphasize the fluctuating influence of China and the Soviet Union. A key moment in this story is Khrushchev's de-Stalinization speech of 1956, which famously reverberated around the socialist world. Unlike in most other allied countries, Kim staved off international and domestic pressure to continue building his personality cult. Much of this story line is about how Kim managed to balance the international tensions within the socialist bloc, often to his advantage, through deft maneuvers that mustered his allies' support while keeping them at arm's length. Increasingly, historians have added further dimensions to this story by shifting focus to North Korea's relations with countries in Asia, Africa, and South America. This brings to the usual European and Chinese inter-socialist story a more global dimension that includes North Korea's shared postcoloniality in the story line.[4] This setting also provides historians with the geopolitical conditions to explain the systemization of Kim's thought, variously referred to as Kim-ism or "Juche thought." Developed in the interstices of Chinese and Soviet pressures, Juche's emphasis on autonomy also appealed to the decolonizing world. This second story line also intersected with the New Living, even if in less dramatic ways. The circulation of knowledge that followed North Korea's ties with its socialist allies cannot be underestimated. From architectural designs to air-conditioned buses, from the roles played by consulting specialists to treatises on motherhood—all these and much more shaped the New Living. Economic assistance after the war—from the opening of Soviet furniture factories to the People's Liberation Army building bridges, from the GDR's rebuilding of Hamhŭng to an Albanian delegation helping out with agricultural co-ops—enhanced material possibilities.

Histories of Kim's ascendancy vary tremendously in details and conclusions, depending on the author. Despite these differences, virtually all studies agree that by the early 1960s, Kim Il Sung had completed the consolidation of his personal power. The strength of these studies is their tracing of Kim's formal power through official institutions. In the best studies, Kim's rise is shown not as a mere grabbing of an already powerful, ready-for-his-rule Party-state, but as consolidation of a series of institutions that needed to reassert and rebuild their capacity after the war. As Sŏ Tongman and others have shown, it took the Party years after the war to establish its control over state institutions.[5] In these pages, I have built on their work to show how the Party-state continued to expand its power by working to resolve problems in policy areas such as rural-to-urban migration and the legal definition of family forms. The mature personality cult has done much—deliberately, of course—to obscure the historical processes behind Kim's rise as well as the problems faced by the Party-state.

As Kim dominated the levers of the Party-state, his challenge was to translate his monopoly over institutions into a very different form of power, the personality cult. For historians, the personality cult has been much more of a challenge to explain.[6] Gaps in information and the question of the personality cult's reception among the population—*do they really believe?*—have led many writers to turn to national culture as an explanatory device. The most common approach regards Kim's personality cult as a vestige of the Chosŏn dynasty. Confucianism is often leveraged into this analysis. Another links the personality cult to the wartime Japanese emperor system, suggesting that Korean socialism was in fact an inversion of Japanese fascism. In both approaches, Kim's personal rule is seen as a product of the feudal era—of a Korea still ruled by a dynasty (albeit a communist one) in the twenty-first century because at its inception, this logic goes, it was not thoroughly modern. This is personal power as a historical leftover, out of touch with the flow of history and due to collapse at any moment—or so it would seem. Not coincidentally, this approach works contrastively to affirm the South and its capitalism as the only properly modern—and thus legitimate—regime on the peninsula. The shadow of Cold War interpretations, which have always had difficulty admitting the modernity of socialism, lingers over this evaluation.[7] Whatever the (de)merits of these explanations, they appeal to unexplained national continuities and point to vague cultural traits that the three Kims have been able to exploit. More ironically, these cultural approaches reproduce within their own analytical framework key features of the personality cult. Their near exclusive focus on Kim—his maneuvers, his speeches, his diplomatic encounters—ultimately shares the same obsessive subject as the Pyongyang propaganda that these studies simultaneously tell us not to believe. All explanations lead to Kim Il Sung. The approaches remain pervasive to this day because the division of the peninsula continues to breathe life into conceptions of history that have been discarded for decades in the case of other socialist countries.[8]

By looking up at Kim's rise to power from the level of the New Living, a more varied story line emerges. As a growing number of scholars have been showing, it is necessary to see North Korea as part of a broader twentieth-century global modernity.[9] As reiterated throughout this book, the New Living was part of the peninsula's long twentieth century. Everything from the design of apartment houses to dormitory surveillance, from Taylorist strategies of production to patterns of consumption, were rooted in global circulations in which Korean women and men had been participating for decades before North Korea's establishment. The proliferation of attention to motherhood, while arising from local conditions and defined with the word *Chosŏn* to mark its indigeneity, came with a simultaneous immersion in global discourses of domestic management and scientific rearing. The two cannot be disentangled. But the combination of nationalist and Cold War politics meant that none of the countless articles, poems, plays, and movies about Korean motherhood would ever draw this connection.

Looking up at Kim from the perspective of the New Living also reveals the struggles to establish Kim's personal authority outside official institutions. In this perspective, at its bluntest, Kim was often ignored—a point he unhappily acknowledged in his 1956 speech on architecture. As we have seen, economists well into the 1960s bemoaned the rural migrants to the cities who did not heed his injunctions to stay put. Kim Kyŏnghŭi's account recorded that many people she approached to help her start up household work teams were not inspired by Kim's words—and worse, from her model worker perspective, some had not even heard about them. More often, however, if one of his speeches or pieces of on-the-spot guidance was to be ignored, it was done quietly and without drawing attention, as was the case with some of his architectural suggestions.

These limits contextualize the uses to which Kim's speeches have been put—both by his contemporaries and by historians today. His first volume of selected speeches, issued in 1953, was almost never referred to in the print media. The habit of citing Kim's words arose gradually and accelerated after the second edition began to be published in 1960.[10] Even then, the frequency and ways of citing his words varied substantially from publication to publication. Youth journals such as *Youth Life* (*Ch'ŏngnyon saenghwal*) tended to reflect a more enthusiastic stance, whereas the journal for folklorists and anthropologists, *Cultural Heritage* (*Munhwa yusan*), reproduced a photo of Kim at the front of each edition before getting on with their business. This unevenness among publications also held for the slowly developing practice of printing Kim's name or his words in bold or larger font. Photographic evidence from the era shows only a minority of homes hanging his portrait. And in all the advice by interior decorators on how to select and where to hang a wall painting, there was never a whisper about Kim Il Sung portraits. Yet in photographs of rooms prepared for the arrival of Koreans from Japan in the late 1950s, Kim's portrait hangs on the wall.[11] The lack of uniformity in personality-cult practices suggests they did not come about solely through top-down instructions and, in some cases, took years to establish themselves.

Historians have long recognized that each subsequent edition of Kim's selected works was edited—and distorted—according to shifting political winds. Most famously for the postwar era, any call by Kim to "Learn from the Soviets," as the mainstream slogan of the 1950s put it, was erased from his past. This post facto editing sought to align with later Juche notions of autonomy. The excising of politically sensitive portions of Kim's past was not the only political motivation for collecting Kim's speeches, however.[12] Another purpose was the deliberate separation of his speeches from the discursive environment that produced them. This canonization decontextualized his words, creating the illusion that Kim himself was outside of and transcended the era that produced him. When his speeches are read as most women and men encountered them in the print media, published among other articles, cartoons, and photographs, it becomes apparent that Kim used the same language—the same expressions, slogans, and syntax—characteristic of the era's publishing culture as he dealt with the same challenges as his contemporaries. His speeches are one more piece of proof, if any is needed, that no one lives outside of discourse—not even the Great Leader.

There was little in his speeches about issues pertaining to the New Living that was novel. Originality may never have been the point of his speeches—even if originality would be attributed to them later. His speeches on architecture, communist morality, motherhood, female labor, and work culture all picked up on themes, points, and language that had already been expounded upon by experts in these fields and had circulated in the national print media, often for years prior. What made his speeches politically significant was the act of delivering comments on already established topics. Among all the many possible topics available to Kim, to choose one over others was to ensure that wider attention would be brought to that issue. His speeches' choices of topic were often more important than their content.

There was also a distinction, important in the era but erased by the collected works, as to what speech was considered sufficiently important to be reproduced in the print media at the time. Why were some speeches immediately republished? Why were some reproduced word for word, while others received only the briefest of paraphrasing in the following day's newspaper? And why did other speeches have to wait, in some cases for decades, to find life again in his *Complete Collected Works*, published in the 1980s? This hierarchy gave each speech a different contemporary significance. Those that were not reproduced in the contemporary media came to be known only to those contemporaries attending the event. For key but not all speeches, Kim's delivery would be followed by other commentators, who would rush to write about and amplify his message. His 1958 speech on communist morality showed that Kim had no unique thoughts to offer on the topic. But his choice to raise the issue ensured that many others would follow suit.[13] Moreover, Kim's choice of vocabulary was significant. That he chose the expression "communist cultivation," which previously had been only one among several options used by others, ensured that the expression became standard though not exclusive usage. This created a type of discursive circularity and narrowing: Kim used already existing expressions, yet his choice privileged certain options, often serving to narrow future choices. That these expressions and the themes he raised were already well known to anyone familiar with the subject meant that Kim's speeches did not appear as alien or out-of-the-blue interventions to his audiences. Together, his choices both depended on contemporary discourse and sought, successfully or not, to nudge it in certain directions as opposed to others. The relationship was dynamic.

The situation was very different with Kim's 1965 speech at the opening of the national conference of the Women's Union. Kim's speech opened the event, but it was not even mentioned in the national newspapers and was not reproduced anywhere—not even in *Women of Korea*. The editors of *Women of Korea* did include a photograph of Kim cheerily greeting delegates and standing in line for an official photograph. But instead of his speech, they reproduced the much more uplifting and fiery address of the head of their organization, Kim Oksun, word for word, covering more than twenty-five pages of text.[14] Was this substitution made because the editors were offended by Kim's sexist opening, in which he admonished the Union's illustrious and accomplished audience for not keeping the streets and public venues of the country properly clean? The politics behind these editorial decisions remain opaque to us. Yet its contemporary disappearance meant that the speech had no discernible impact beyond its place of delivery. It would not otherwise be known to us but for its appearance, years later and with no historical context of its production, in Kim's *Collected Works*.[15] This gives context to Kim Kyŏnghŭi's astonishment that Kim Il Sung's words about household factories remained unknown to many of the residents of her northern town. Like his 1965 speech to the Women's Union, the speech had not been given special attention by the media. For many people, it must be remembered, Kim's speeches were often irrelevant to their local social worlds.

Indeed, Kim aimed to use already popular subjects for his speeches as a leveraging strategy to translate his institutional power into a broader personal authority. Often his speeches played catch-up. He marshaled key issues in the New Living for his own purposes. When he made his 1961 speech at the All-Nation Congress of Mothers, it was not that Kim had anything special to offer on motherhood, nor did it reflect a long-standing interest of his. But since the war, there had been an outpouring of writing on mothers, often stylized as the Korean mother (*Chosŏn ŏmŏni*), which had not been prompted by him or by the Party-state. This was part of the population's turn to the family after the war and the reestablishment of male social power. The figure of the mother had become increasingly relevant to numerous economic challenges, and the mother-worker rose to prominence in the context of the labor shortage. Kim's speech ensured that later discussions on motherhood would cite his words, even if the ideas had not originated with him. These speeches, especially when they were reproduced in contemporary publications, gained Kim entrance to a core, popular topic, placed his personal imprint on it, and rallied interest in the subject behind his personal rule. Where multiple opinions existed, as in the case of divorce among childless couples, his speech determined directions as he chose sides. It is not difficult to surmise that Kim would not have even broached the issue of childless couples if it had not arisen as an issue in the context of discussions of divorce and pro-natalist sentiment. The difference of opinions gave him the opportunity to play arbiter. In this sense, there was an upward effect on Kim's speeches that is discernible only when they are returned to their original discursive setting.

The discursive context for his speeches can also be seen at play in the rise of Juche ideology. One of the most famous dilemmas for Pyongyang watchers interested in the origins of Kim's thought is to explain why he used the term *juche* in a 1955 speech, only for the term to disappear from his speeches until he brought it to prominence years later.[16] This is a mystery only if analysis is restricted to Kim's personal history of speech giving. Looking at this single term, *juche*, within the broader context of that era's discourse, it is evident that Kim never monopolized the term. *Juche* was used in conjunction with near-synonymous, overlapping expressions—such as *chabal*, *chuindapke*, and *ch'angbal*, all of which invoked a sense of autonomy and self-action—that were used widely in the 1950s and '60s as part of the New Living. They also appeared regularly in Kim's speeches. These expressions had their own, longer genealogies, but in the 1950s they were foundational, as a group of terms, to contemporary understanding of the relation between ideology, the individual, and socialist transition. Kim and his supporters eventually centered Kim Il Sung Thought around one of these terms, *juche*. But in the early 1960s, none of his audience would likely have been struck by the novelty of the term itself, the way Kim used it, or the general sensibility it expressed. What was arguably new was that these meanings were extracted from their domestic context, where they shaped discussions of the socialist subject, and then were elevated to the international level. In the future, more layers of meanings would be foisted onto *juche*, as Kim's son sought to establish his own ideological credentials in the 1980s. The term *juche* became political ideology: Juche, now capitalized to show its rise to preeminence. In that process, the domestic context out of which Juche thought arose was erased.

Kim's speeches and his on-the-spot guidance also sought to direct the memory politics that were so central to the New Living. It has often been noted how, in the late 1950s, Kim and his supporters began pushing a version of Party history emphasizing its origins in the anti-Japanese Manchurian partisan movement. This became the core of the Party's identity.[17] Unlike the uneven promotion of his portrait for home interiors, the push for Manchuria-centered versions of history was a top-down command. Periodicals were subjected to criticism for not promoting the Manchurian story sufficiently, and day care teachers had to be told to teach it.[18] Central to domestic politics, this Manchuria-centered Party history solidified Kim's personal rule. Yet because this history was promoted from scratch among the population, it required significant investment in its invention and distribution.[19]

Its authority paled in comparison to the already long-familiar conceptions of developmentalist time. This metanarrative worked through countless specific projects in all their idiosyncratic detail to underpin the greatest modern promise and teleology of them all: a shared material prosperity. The Party's and Kim's dilemma was how to ensure that this narrative, given its pre-collective-era history and its internalization by the population, reinforced rather than worked against their power. It was an elusive form of historical thinking not entirely in their control. One way to intercede in the conduct of these projects was to insert, at first, the Party and later Kim Il Sung into these story lines. Often this intercession depended on masculinist tropes of rescue, in which Kim claimed to have provided the conditions for the particular subject in question—the nation, the working class, women, the family, or specific individuals—to realize its historical potential. Separate but intertwined histories were produced for each of these subjects, not in distinct articles or books, as was necessary to promote the Manchurian partisan story, but as a constant of socioeconomic life.

Developmentalism was everywhere in the New Living. In the first two decades, the most powerful was the sprawling participatory narrative of apartment construction. This appealed to popular aspirations and inspired their participation. It gave people stakes in the project's success, and affirmed their sense of striding toward a materially defined modernity together with their families. At the same time, the rise of apartments seemed to affirm the Party's claims to be at the forefront of history, achieving the security of working-class families and, in at least its own eyes, proving the superiority of socialism by one-upping the capitalist competition to the South.

The significance of this apartment construction as a *historical* achievement was not lost on Kim Il Sung. It is for this reason that he moved to put himself at the center of the rebuilding campaign in 1958. At least five times in that year, he made on-site visits: three times to construction sites, once to an exhibition of construction materials, and once to an architecture research center (see figure 32). In each case, he was performing the politics of the mass line as it was playing out for all to see—a leader leaving his office to come to sites where men and women labored. With his institutional power increasingly secure, he turned to these performances to present himself as a sociable, almost avuncular figure on the side of workers, showing concern, giving advice, and even hectoring and scolding at times. This was no distant monarch or emperor hidden away in the palace, who never let the people hear his voice. For the tens of thousands of women and men working on sites, producing materials or designs, and moving into houses, Kim's presence in the field of construction was as participatory as their own. This was a story about their labor and achievements as the way to the teleological end of modern prosperity, but the Party-state had to make it about Kim Il Sung. It was a defensive posture. In this way, he sought, after years of wartime dislocations, to present himself as quite literally the provider of the New Living.

북구 건설 현장을 시찰하시는 김 일성 수상.

FIGURE 32. Chang Sŏgyŏng, Pak Pyŏngch'u, and Rim Tŏkpo, "Kim Il Sung Inspecting a Reconstruction Site," 1958.

This personalization of historical metanarratives lifted Kim above the Party. The shifting ways the media addressed the relationship were telling. Immediately after the war, *Rodong sinmun* tended to leave Kim out of formulas used to refer to the Party-state—most commonly, "The Republic and Party" (*konghwagukkwa tang*). Occasionally and then increasingly, Kim's name was added to the list to make a triptych: "the Republic, the Party, and leader Kim Il Sung." Over time, editors reversed the triptych, often prefaced Kim's name with "dearest" or "beloved," and downgraded the "Republic" to "government" (*chŏngbu*): "dearest Kim Il Sung, the Party, and the government." By 1965, the term *republic/government* was dropped, and increasingly, by the early 1960s, Kim was referred to on his own or still twinned with the Party in a fashion that implied no separation. Kim was the Supreme Leader, now also called the Marshal (*wŏnsu*). This representational strategy of conflation served his supremacy.[20]

It also left him vulnerable. In the eyes of the population, any problem potentially reverberated back to him as the all-responsible leader. Yet, as discussed throughout this book, there were always strategic moments where this policy of conflation and claims of unity could be shifted to one that emphasized the multiple layers of the Party-state. The devolution of responsibility was the most obvious—and Kim avidly performed it in public. It allowed him to shift responsibilities, and the politics of blame, "downward." Amid all the consternation about unmet consumer demand, Kim emerged with his leadership team and the Soviet ambassador in 1958 at a newly opened local products store.[21] The store was the joint effort of Pyongyang and Kaesŏng rural factories and co-op production enterprises. The store opened in "adherence to the Party's guidance" to provide more and better products to urban residents. A photo at the head of the story shows Kim standing at the counter, beaming with a broad smile, holding one of the items for sale: a parasol. He is quoted, indirectly, saying that the rural enterprises had succeeded in actively mobilizing local resources and capital to produce, in great volume and better quality, goods that reflected the character of their locality. He finished by uttering the make-or-break word, in a direct quotation, saying he was "satisfied" with their efforts. That this was all happening on August 15, Liberation Day, gave his appearance there a special symbolism.

These stories of Kim showing up on location to look at goods are often ridiculed by foreign observers today.[22] In these early days, however, they were powerful political performances, critical to the extension of his personal power beyond institutions. This publicized moment aligned Kim with success—and a success that he could claim arrived for people who listened to the policies he inspired. Just as importantly, it also ensured he was not tainted by the contentious details that led to the production of the parasol. What the story, on its own, does not reveal is that accounts of his "satisfaction" were published within a steady stream of stories about consumer demand not being met, satirical cartoons of shoddy products, and letters to the editor from consumers about their frustrating experiences. Readers of the parasol story would have known this broader context, since those items appeared in the same pages of the same print media, but these moments of on-the-spot guidance extracted Kim from the messy processes that beset the economy yet made the parasol possible. Whether this strategy of turning the frustrations of consumers on local producers ultimately succeeded in relieving Kim of responsibilities in the eyes of consumers is difficult to determine. Yet the fact that he turned to this style of on-the-spot guidance to show himself as having a direct connection with workers or consumers, thus bypassing the institutions that could be blamed for the economic tensions, also revealed that Kim understood his vulnerability. He always reserved the option to dissolve the otherwise much-hailed Party-state unity to mete out blame and separate himself from responsibility. He presented himself at the teleological end of both Party-state time and developmentalist time, pushing history along in the direction it should go, always separating himself from any of the disorder or anxiety resulting from this struggle. The politics of extracting Kim from these elusive versions of history, as his personality cult expanded, turned to a related but different logic. As the 1960s unrolled, Kim and his ideologues increasingly turned to the use of direct personal connections and affect.

THE PRIMACY OF THE PERSONAL AND EMOTIONAL

An early glimpse of these novel dimensions was exemplified by Kim's bringing of his family into the cultural politics of his personality cult—a development that has been commonly referred to as the formation of the family state.[23] This advent would not have been possible without the specific routes the postwar turn to the family took as part of the New Living. The widespread attention to motherhood, which Kim was late to come around to, provided the cultural resources for his personality cult. If the postwar period had witnessed socialist-style critiques of the family as the repository of feudal or bourgeois values, it is hard to imagine how he could have included his immediate family and, subsequently, incorporated three generations, with the possibility of more to come. Even the early postwar critique of familialism faded to make room for the growing celebration of Kim's family. Representations of his mother, Kang Pansŏk, pushed in this direction.

Early on, Kang took on the presence of that figure who featured so prominently in poetry after the war, the Korean mother or *Chosŏn ŏmŏni*, as in a poem by Min Pyŏnggyun.[24] Not for this version of Kang Pansŏk were the biopolitics of careful schedules of daytime household management, the keeping of accounts, or the demands of scientific motherhood. The poem hinted instead at how the personality cult was moving in a direction that substituted affect for the heroic resolution of socioeconomic and everyday life problems. It still rested on the New Living idea of mastering of Korean maternal virtues, only here the most important were emotional sensibilities. "With love for her child," the poem read, "she gives him the true love of a mother and the true tears of a mother." Such evocative words took the more prosaic vocabulary used by writers who, for several years in the same journal, had been advising mothers on how to cultivate proper emotional sensibilities among their children and pushed it to new heights.

This move toward affect as a new form for Kim's personality cult found its way into Comrade Ri's 1961 memoir. Only now, in spelling out a personal relationship between leader and worker, the affect shifted from maternal love to a near ecstatic one, blurring parental and leadership roles. As seen earlier, Ri's memoir was a record of problems solved, whether at the workplace or at home. She was the efficient bucket carrier, the promoter of women's participation in wage labor, the creative force behind increased production, the provider of foodstuffs, the local leader who understood the mass line. Her memoir, like most model worker stories, offered a testament to her abilities in confronting and overcoming the obstacles that stood in her way to further Party-state goals in the struggle for socialist transition. Along the way, the memoir recorded aspects of her emotional life, usually in regard to her happiness at work with colleagues or her joy at successfully figuring out a problem. But the "love" of labor and the "joy" of production, which had been promoted widely as socialist values by advice literature, achieved a different quality in the memoir when Ri described a brief encounter with Kim Il Sung. This shift to a new logic for the personality cult was hardly seamless and was not integrated with the rest of the memoir, appearing in a separate section describing how Ri met Kim during a ceremony marking the completed construction of the Culture Palace on which Ri had worked.

Ri in this moment framed her labor not as building socialism, but as the fulfillment of a personal task set by Kim. As Kim showed up at the ceremony, Ri described herself calling out among cheers from her colleagues, exclaiming, "Premier! I've completed the task you gave to me, Premier!" As he stepped near her, she recounted, "at the moment that I met the Supreme Leader, my throat choked up and I couldn't say a word." All the other motivations she had detailed throughout her memoir for her many undertakings disappeared at this moment. So, too, did any of the institutions that had been so crucial to her story, such as the Party-state, local Party committees, the Women's Union, socialist work competitions, or neighborhood committees. At this moment of triumph, the troubles and problems of the modern development project and the socialist transition that provided the main narrative tension of her memoir collapsed into a celebration of her personal fulfillment of what was now little more than Kim's assignment. The very language of her self-portrait and her self-image of steady levelheadedness is transformed in this passage.

"You worked hard!" Ri described Kim calling out to the group. She recalled being overwrought and unable to say anything in response. "The Supreme Leader's deep yet tender voice rose to my ears. And suddenly the

Supreme Leader was firmly shaking my hand. In that moment, grasping the Supreme Leader's soft hand, I was so moved that tears washed down my face."

"Amazing! Wonderfully constructed!" Kim extolled. Seeing the satisfied smile he directed at their construction, Ri continued: "This happiness! This joy! How can I contain them in this small heart? I'm not sure there will ever be anyone as happy as me in the world! What is there to fear or to see as difficult? Not when the Supreme Leader teaches and guides us. . . ." If this was not enough, she went on to depict his impact on her: "It was as if a new strength surged through my body, and I could rip down mountains and dry up oceans. Whatever the job, I felt there was nothing I could not do."[25]

Such rapturous passages would only grow in frequency as an ever-growing number of publications would fall in line to reproduce anecdotes of "first meetings" as a staple of this new form of the personality cult.[26] Such stories began to offer a new and parallel logic to the mundane style of stories that shaped the New Living and that constitute the core of this book. This new logic—stripped of the messiness of social relations, shorn of institutional challenges, and extracted from the tensions of the gendered political economy, even as it claimed for itself the successes of the population's labor—asserted Kim's status through a purported direct emotional connection with each individual worker. It vacated the genre of model workers struggling to push along the transition to socialism. It abandoned developmentalist, revolutionary, or Party-state time. It no longer dealt with the ordinary problems confronting men and women in their local social worlds. It now operated from a position beyond the "tasks" (*kwaŏp*) and "problems" (*munje*) set out by so many contemporary commentators. This was no longer a mundane revolution.

Instead, this new form of personality cult took the masculinist trope of the savior to extreme heights, as Kim ostensibly rescued virtually all subjects from history itself, and reduced socialist transition to an individual, direct relationship with him. The sentiments expressed in passages such as Comrade Ri's testimony emerged as part of a personality cult that, rather than seeking a resolution of the New Living's contradictions, presented itself as at once a solution to and an escape from them. Even as the personality cult was symptomatic of these contradictions, it denied any claims on the leader himself. In his megalomania, Kim Il Sung was already showing how he would turn his back on the New Living as a mass utopian project that, however challenging, enabled Korean women and men to envision a better modern life as imagined through socialism.

APPENDIX

An Essay on North Korean
Print Media Sources

I've often been asked, "How are you studying North Korea?" Inevitably the question comes with a dose of disbelief, reflecting a skepticism about the possibilities of studying a country to which virtually no one can travel for archival research. Sometimes the question comes with a sense of amazement, however misplaced, at the presumed difficulties scholars must face in getting their hands on historical sources. As tempting as it may be to play up this drama of research as exploration, nothing could be farther from the truth.

The not-so-hidden secret of the North Korean history I have written is that it is based on sources available in some of the most reader-friendly libraries in the world. But it took me a long time to figure out this simple fact—an ignorance reflecting how much I needed to unlearn about North Korea. Increasingly over the past few years, more historians—especially in South Korea—have begun to examine these sources.[1]

My own introduction to the world of North Korean sources began late one night when I was browsing the website of the Harvard-Yenching Library. Noticing that its search function had added place of publication, I entered—on a bit of a lark and without much expectation—"Pyongyang" for the period 1953–65. I was stunned by the result: over seven hundred titles.

I quickly—and tellingly—ordered the entries by author, suspecting that most titles would fall under the name Kim Il Sung. By 1965, however, there were fewer than ten titles under Kim's name in the collection—an early sign for me that something was askew in the way I had come to understand North Korean history. I spent the rest of the night reading the titles. Each entry—for example, books on theories of aesthetics and treatises on the early nineteenth-century scholar Chong Yagyong—was surprising. This list of publications clearly did not jibe with the overdetermined, totalitarian-focused approaches to North Korea that had dominated my imagination.

A few years later, I attended a conference in Moscow as an excuse to check out its famous central research library. Its collection of North Korean materials, at the time still accessed through a paper card catalogue, is vast. As I sat in the reading room, I again realized my ignorance: I was sitting in the bibliographic epicenter of the socialist world, and—during the period I was researching, when relations with the Soviet Union had not completely soured—Pyongyang had shipped copies of many of its publications to this depository-like library. The collection included magazines from wartime whose very materiality—the crummy paper, the errors in pagination—spoke to the crisis under which they were produced, as well as local newspapers that, I would eventually learn, are unavailable anywhere else outside of North Korea.

My third stage in unlearning came at the Library of Congress in Washington, D.C. I had been told that the Asian section had extensive North Korean materials. Acquired through American Cold War commitments to "knowing thy enemy," these materials still have the postage stamps of the third-party intermediaries— Warsaw, Prague, and the like—through which they were purchased by the CIA before being transferred for public use at the library. Thousands of monographs still remain uncatalogued. Recently, online digital versions of some magazines referred to in the pages of this book have been made available through the library's website. In accessing them in the comfort of one's living room, any sense of a remote North Korea evaporates.

In these ways, the North Korean archive itself reflects Cold War politics. Nowhere is this more evident than in Seoul. South Korea practiced a different strategy of knowing thy enemy than the United States, one that sought for decades to restrict research on North Korea to a few reliable figures. No South Korean university library dared risk violating the National Security Law, which prohibited the circulation of North Korean materials. Some newspapers and magazines were made available in the National Central Library, but only in a special reading room, open to the limited number of South Koreans who passed a vetting procedure. Although the best research in the world about North Korea still takes place in Seoul, researchers have always been hampered by the infantilizing security laws—which, to this day, show that the state and its intelligence agencies do not trust their own citizens to have unmediated contact with anything North Korean. However ironically, the advent of the digital age has bypassed these controls, and digital copies now circulate privately. Materials that I previously could access only in paper form in Moscow now rest in my hard drive. This ease of availability has been transforming research on North Korea. And South Korean publishers have begun to republish these types of North Korean sources, including in a recent, massive, multivolume compilation of extracts.[2]

I hasten to point out that the materials I use in these pages are not top-secret documents about the inner workings of the North Korean government. And that, arguably, is one reason why these materials had been largely ignored for so many years. For decades, studies on North Korea emphasized security issues, the leader- ship, and decision-making processes.[3] The belief that power was concentrated solely in the Kim family and the upper echelons of an absolutist state meant that these types of materials, read by North Koreans in their everyday lives, seemed irrelevant. After all, you were not going to learn much about Kim Il Sung's private thoughts or activities from a pictorial magazine or the monthly metallurgy journal. Moreover, because these newspapers and magazines came out of Pyongyang, received the sanction of the Party, and left zero room for oppositional voices, they were dismissed solely as propaganda. They remained largely untouched, even though anyone could walk in off the street and read them.

Of course, these materials *are* propaganda. Yet as our questions about North Korea have expanded, their usefulness has become more apparent to new generations of scholars, who find in them ways of challenging many of the cartoonish understandings of North Korea that have developed over the decades and are so prominent in our media. Most obviously, as much as top-down mobilization of the state remains a constant in North Korean political and social life, these materials enable consideration of the complex ways in which that mobilization took place, the limits of central state power, and the obstacles to these processes. Reading a Kim Il Sung speech and taking for granted that it reflects what actually happened—a methodology that reproduces the assumptions of his personality cult—is no longer a viable historical methodology, given what these materials reveal. The complexities of modern power, not reducible to the formal organs of the state alone, become apparent. Coercion and fear remain part of the story, to be sure, yet so does active participation by large segments of the population for what were likely far-ranging motivations, whether enthusiasm for revolutionary politics, self-interested advancement, material profit, careerism, or pleasure—to name a few possibilities, none of which are mutually exclusive.

Although these sources open many new avenues of inquiry, like all historical documents they have their own limits. Most obviously, one cost of shifting downward in the political and social hierarchies to a more diverse assortment of historical actors is that we know very little about the individuals in these sources other than their names and, in some cases, their official positions. These are not the types of people famous enough to appear in historical dictionaries. Moreover, these media venues were not places where authors pondered their self-motivations or reflected on their self-doubts, even if they were being urged to be fully self-conscious ideologically. Their writings are, in short, part of the era's discursive record, but it often becomes difficult to make any connections to the writer beyond the text itself.

These writers were both creators of and subjected to the era's discourse. In the pages of this book, I've tried to show how the era's discourse was not completely controlled by high-level Party-state institutions. The easiest evidence for this is the way key terms—*New Living* itself being a prime example—had a prehistory in the colonial era and were in widespread use even though they were never part of a Party resolution or conceptual treatment in the Party's ideological journal. The power of the term *New Living* lay in its nebulous definition, one that fit the Party's modern developmentalist and revolutionary commitments and simultaneously allowed individual writers to explore its boundaries and develop contemporary themes on their own—again, so long as they did not violate central Party dictates.

This discursive wiggle room contains several problems for historians. These sources can certainly be used for how they discussed certain gendered socioeconomic problems that befuddled state authorities and shaped the lives of ordinary people. There was frequent discussion of problems, usually in line with the criticism culture of the era. Yet whether decrying the macroeconomic problems caused by labor shortages or condemning a miner for such bad hygienic practices that weeds sprouted from his coal-dust-covered floor, these issues are available to us only through the official categories and vocabulary that did not run afoul of the Party-state. When an article tells us, as was common after the war, that there was a serious problem with alcohol among male dormitory residents—that they were getting drunk, gambling, and singing unhealthy popular songs—one can only surmise that alcoholism was sufficiently prevalent that authorities concerned with health, hygiene, or work efficiency decided that it merited public discussion in order to combat it.

An issue like alcoholism also suggests another fundamental challenge: determining what the Party discourse actually was in many realms of social and cultural life. While it is easy to include top-level Party resolutions, Kim's speeches, and the highly vetted editorials of the Party newspapers within this category of "official ideology," as soon as one complicates the totalitarian approach and begins to look at other media lower on the scale of textual authority, the answer is not so straightforward. How does one reconcile admonitions in the journal *Hygiene Culture* about the health consequences of alcohol consumption with the continued investment, through centralized economic planning, in alcohol production? At the same time that Party propagandists produced overwhelming amounts of media coverage about the problems of alcoholism, the Pyongyang Beer Factory, one of the first factories resurrected after the war, increased the production of beer 2.3-fold, despite the calls for temperance in Party-approved journals.[4] The explanation for these tensions is likely competing bureaucratic interests. Clearly, an author's call for sobriety could not be extended to question central-planning decisions about capital expenditures on alcohol production. Instead, it was more viable and fit the increasing emphasis on ideological self-reform to blame individuals for their behavior without considering the broader political and economic conditions. For these reasons, the bureaucratic politics behind tensions and contradictions in the press remain opaque to us.

Much more is left unanswered by the plethora of articles describing an unruly social world. What precisely were these "unhealthy" songs that drunken men were singing? Why were they being sung? Did the explicit concern with alcoholism mask a deeper political problem? There are no answers in these sources. Moreover, given that alcoholism was coded as a specifically male social problem, there is little to be learned about alcoholism among women, showing how sources often make it difficult to get outside of contemporary gender biases.[5] On top of this, cartoonists made light fun of inebriated men and, in their eagerness to be humorous, appeared not always to take this male-inscribed social ill as seriously as did health and production authorities.[6] One food company published a full-page color photograph of a pretty woman sitting behind—though noticeably not drinking—several bottles of Samno brand ginseng alcohol—about as close to a commercial advertisement as was visible in the era.[7] The discussions in the media of such social challenges give us glimpses into the social textures of urban life and some of the complexities surrounding state initiatives. Yet they only reveal issues that propagandists chose to highlight because, rightly or wrongly, they deemed public exposure effective in either addressing them or warning readers. The many issues that did not fall into this category and were deemed unworthy of public discussion, whether for practical or political reasons, remain outside the ken of my research. There is thus an anecdotal character to the materials—often there are no aggregate data against which to question the representativeness of a story, and no follow-up to an exhortation available to trace how these calls fared over time.

Moreover, the use of data in these publications is often unreliable. This was not just because authorities chose to hide problems. Institutional incentives led to exaggeration—a trait shared in other state socialisms, particularly in regard to economic campaigns. One consequence was that economists did not have access to accurate data for their own planning processes—a problem they warned about as early as 1955.[8] Russian statistical experts, brought in soon after the war, noted problems but could not resolve them. The Korean media themselves warned about exaggerated claims, error-filled reports, and the challenges of measuring certain sectors of the economy.[9] The best indication that these problems continued was that by the mid-1960s, many statistical categories that had been detailed in annual yearbooks were terminated. For historians, then, these statistics offer daunting choices.[10] A few examples from this book indicate the kinds of choices I made. The drive to build more apartments led to a surge in statistics to demonstrate success and demonstrate, from the perspective of officials in charge, that they had successfully adhered to the shifting political line. Aggregate figures show the total amount of apartment living space built per year. When it was reported that 1,259,000 square meters of urban housing was built in 1957, how did this figure convert into numbers of apartments or people housed?[11] Average sizes of apartments shifted over time, making mathematical calculations unreliable. Nor is there any information on how this housing was spread across different cities, let alone to whom it was distributed, even though there are suggestions of "better" neighborhoods. Ultimately, it is difficult to judge how many families were housed in successive years, even if we know that investment in housing was a priority.

Data for labor participation rates pose a different problem. No official definition of participation was publicly offered with the statistics. Given the gendered segregation of wage labor, it remains unclear how the varieties of female labor—such as in household factories or on collectivized farms—were categorized. How many hours a week did a laborer need to work to be included in the statistics? The answers remain unclear. Given the much wider range of irregular forms of labor undertaken by women, this makes it especially problematic to quantify women's wage-labor participation. It is only possible to assume that the standards for a given category remained constant so that the relative changes could be assessed from year to year.

Little is known about the reading culture in this era. The national newspaper, *Rodong sinmun*, annually held a call for subscriptions on behalf of all the serial publications in the country.[12] Circulation figures for some magazines are listed on their last page and varied substantially. *Women of Korea* ranged from 20,000 copies of its July 1955 issue to as many as 120,000 in the year it stopped publishing its circulation data. It spun off another journal, aimed for a rural audience: *Agrarian Women*, which distributed 49,800 copies in July 1959. The main journal for propaganda workers, *Sŏndongwŏn such'ŏp*, reached some 100,000 copies in January 1957 but slipped down to the precise number of 81,207 copies in December—perhaps losing readers to the multiplication in the number of start-up journals that year. These circulation figures do not capture the extent of the readership. Reading rooms featuring magazines, newspapers, and books were common in dormitories and workplaces. Mass organizations held meetings, and workers held study groups where single articles from a magazine would be the subject of study and discussion.[13] Magazines regularly put out calls for contributions, often telling readers the subjects they were most keen to solicit.[14] Library copies of these magazines still occasionally hold slips of paper listing survey questions for their readers to fill out and send back to the editors. And readers frequently wrote letters to the editors to react to a previous article or to tell them, as did one *Women of Korea* reader, that they had adopted the magazine as a textbook for how to go about living.[15]

If these records can be used to loosen the bounds and the directions of Party discourse, they can also be used to ask questions about popular agency. Yet there is equally reason to hesitate. To the question "What *was* Party discourse?" can be added "Where was the Party?" Clearly, the media available to us show people engaging in a whole range of social, economic, and cultural activities. Yet this participation needs to be contextualized within the representational strategies used by Party officials in the media. It was, after all, in their interest to show people participating of their own accord and, ideally, out of enthusiasm to support various Party policies. This presented Party officials with conflicting desires: they wanted to show the significance, necessity, and wisdom of Party rule, yet at the same time wanted to downplay their own roles in eliciting what they sought to represent as the spontaneous self-initiative of new socialist subjects. One led to a tendency to boast about Party accomplishments and showed people thanking the Party for its guidance; the other obscured the presence of Party officials, showing individuals working on their own. For social historians or anyone interested in Party relations with the population, this dual representational strategy leads to a circularity that cannot be broken through this archive alone. As much as these media sources offer new ways to think about North Korean history, they—like any other set of sources—also present their own dilemmas that arise from their very virtues as historical sources.

NOTES

INTRODUCTION

1. Ri Ponggŭm, "Saejibi tto nŭllŏtta" [New houses increase again], *Chosŏn nyosŏng*, March 1959: back cover.

2. There were various expressions for the New Living, the most common of which were *saesallim* and *sinsaenghwal*.

3. Susan Buck-Morss, *Dreamworld and Catastrophe: The Passing of Mass Utopia in East and West* (Cambridge, MA: MIT Press, 2000).

4. I use the term *Party-state*, as in the study of other state socialisms, to capture the Party's control of state administrative units. I use *Party* to refer to the Korean Workers' Party (KWP) during a time when certain activities—such as elite rivalries, ideological debates, and membership recruitment—remained largely within its purview. Admittedly, the distinction is often a difficult one to make.

5. Robert Moeller, *Protecting Motherhood: Women and the Family in the Politics of Postwar West Germany* (Berkeley: University of California Press, 1993); Paul Betts and David Crowley, eds., "Introduction," *Journal of Contemporary History* 40.2 (2005): 213–236; Joy Parr, *Domestic Goods: The Material, the Moral and the Economic in the Postwar Years* (Toronto: University of Toronto Press, 1999); Laura L. Neitzel, *The Life We Longed For: Danchi Housing and the Middle Class Dream in Postwar Japan* (Honolulu: University of Hawaiʻi Press, 2016); Elaine Tyler May, *Homeward Bound: American Families in the Cold War Era* (New York: Basic Books, 1988).

6. I borrow the expression "long twentieth century" from Giovanni Arrighi, *The Long Twentieth Century: Money, Power, and the Origins of Our Times* (New York: Verso, 1994).

7. Pak Hyŏnsŏn long ago made a related argument that studies of North Korea need to get away from Kim Il Sung, the state, and "Juche thought" (the systemization of Kim's thought) to focus on the family as the basis of the regime's staying power. Pak Hyŏnsŏn, *Hyŏndae PukHan sahoewa kajok* [Contemporary North Korean society and family] (Seoul: Hanul akʼademi, 2003).

8. Accounts of Lenin and his family life were a constant feature, and articles about Lenin's mother supported Kim Il Sung's personality cult. See Kim Kŭmja, "Reninŭi ŏmŏni" [Lenin's mother], *Chosŏn nyŏsŏng*, December 1964: 88–90. Lenin's famous question first appeared in a 1902 political pamphlet, which has been reproduced and commented upon regularly ever since. For example, Victor Pavlovich Filatov, *Lenin's 'What Is to Be Done?'* (Moscow: Progress Publishers, 1987). Celebrations of his birthday were held in Pyongyang. Anonymous, "Renin t'ansaeng 88 chunyŏn Pyŏngyangsi kyŏngch'uk taehoe chinhaeng" [Big celebratory meetings held in Pyongyang on the 88th anniversary of Lenin's birth], *Rodong sinmun*, April 23, 1958: 1.

9. Maggie Clinton, *Revolutionary Nativism: Facism and Culture in China, 1925–1937* (Durham, NC: Duke University Press, 2017); Arif Dirlik, "The Ideological Foundations of the New Life Movement: A Study in Counter-revolution," *Journal of Asian Studies* 34.4 (1975): 945–980.

10. Sinsaenghwal undong chungang ch'ongbonhoe, *Uriŭi sinsaenghwal sŏlgyesŏ* [A planning guide for our new living] (Seoul: Chinsaenghoe, 1952). Not surprisingly, it became the subject of criticism. "NamChosŏn-esŏ Ri Sŭngman tobaedŭri ttŏdŭnŭn 'Sinsaenghwal undong'ŭi chŏngch'e" [In South Korea, Syngman Rhee and his clique clamor about the "New Living Movement"], *Rodong sinmun*, September 5, 1956: 3.

11. Harry Harootunian, *Overcome by Modernity: History, Culture, and Community in Interwar Japan* (Princeton, NJ: Princeton University Press, 2000), xix.

12. Janet Poole, *When the Future Disappears: The Modernist Imagination in Late Colonial Korea* (New York: Columbia University Press, 2014), introduction.

13. My use of *Party-state time* was inspired by Gail Hershatter's idea of "campaign time" in her *The Gender of Memory: Rural Women and China's Collective Past* (Berkeley: University of California Press, 2011).

14. The leeriness toward private merchants up to 1958 can be seen in Anonymous, "Kaein sanggongŏpchadŭrŭn inmin-ege ch'ungsilhi Pongmuhayŏya handa" [Individual merchants must sincerely serve the people], *Sŏndongwŏn such'ŏp* 22 (November 1957): 13–16.

15. Editorial, "Ch'ŏllimaŭi kisudapke munhwajŏgŭro saenghwalhaja" [Let's live culturally like a rider of the Chŏlli horse], *Rodong sinmun*, June 14, 1959: 1.

16. Kim Chaeŭng notes that this was part of the Party's class political line from 1946 onward. See Kim Chaeŭng, *PukHan ch'ejeŭi kiwŏn: inminwiŭi kyegŭp, kyegŭpwiŭi kukka* [The origins of the North Korean system: Class above people and state above class] (Kyŏnggi-do Koyang-si: Yŏksa pip'yŏngsa, 2018).

17. Kim Il Sung Thought received a big push with the publication of the second edition of his selected works in the early 1960s.

18. For one early political study-session manual, see Chosŏn nodongdang, *Chunggŭp haksŭppan ch'amgo charyo* [Reference materials for midlevel study classes] (Pyongyang: Chosŏn nodongdang ch'ulp'ansa, 1957); and for a personal account of a session, see Kim Yŏnguk, "Ŏnŭ han kundang wiwŏnhoeŭi ch'ogŭp haksŭppan chidojadŭrŭi saŏp-esŏ" [In the work of one county-level party committee's study session leader], *Kŭlloja* 133 (October 1956): 109–117.

19. By the mid-1960s, the relationship between ideological revolution and cultural revolution attracted some more considered attention. See Anonymous, "Sasang hyŏngmyŏnggwa munhwa hyŏngmyŏng" [Ideological revolution and cultural revolution], *Ch'ŏllima*, May 1964: 32.

20. An excellent introduction to North Korean biopolitics is Pak Yŏngja, "PukHanŭi 'saengch'ejŏngch'i'" [North Korean "biopolitics"], *Hyŏndae PukHan yŏn'gu* 7.3 (2005): 97–149. For one fascinating North Korean account of public health changes, see Hong Sunwŏn, *Chosŏn Pogŏnsa* (Pyongyang: Kwahak, paekkwasajŏn ch'ulp'ansa, 1981). On biopolitics, see Michel Foucault, *Society Must Be Defended: Lectures at the Collège de France*, tr. David Macey (New York: Picador, 1997), in particular 239–264; and Michel Foucault, *The History of Sexuality, vol. 1: An Introduction,* tr. Robert Hurley (New York: Vintage Books, 1978).

21. On Fordism, see David Forgacs, ed., *The Gramsci Reader: Selected Writings, 1916–1935* (New York: NYU Press, 2000), 275–299.

22. On earlier Korean masculine nationalism, see Sheila Miyoshi Jager, *Narratives of Nation-Building in Korea: A Genealogy of Patriotism* (London: Routledge, 2003).

23. James C. Scott, *Seeing Like a State: How Certain Schemes to Improve the Human Condition Have Failed* (New Haven, CT: Yale University Press, 1998).

24. Stephen Kotkin, *Magnetic Mountain: Stalinism as Civilization* (Berkeley: University of California Press, 1995); Jochen Hellbeck, *Revolution on My Mind: Writing a Diary under Stalin* (Cambridge, MA: Harvard University Press, 2006). Anna Krylova offers a cautionary rebuttal in "The Tenacious Liberal Subject in Soviet Studies," *Kritika* 1.1 (2000): 119–146.

25. See her study of autobiographies in Suzy Kim, *Everyday Life in the North Korean Revolution, 1945–1950* (Ithaca, NY: Cornell University Press, 2013), 140–173.

26. It is for this reason that most films about class struggle are put in historical and not contemporary settings.

27. For a study of the statements made by various women's delegations at international conferences, see Suzy Kim, *Among Women across Worlds: North Korea in the Global Cold War* (Ithaca, NY: Cornell University Press, 2023).

28. For a detailed analysis of class in 1945–50, see Kim Chaeŭng, *PukHan ch'ejeŭi kiwŏn: inminwiŭi kyegŭp.*

29. Yun Miryang, *PukHanŭi yŏsŏng chŏngch'aek* [North Korean policies on women] (Seoul: Hanŭl, 1991); Son Pongsuk, Yi Kyŏngsuk, Yi Onjuk, and Kim Aesil, eds., *PukHanŭi yŏsŏng saenghwal: yiron'gwa silje* [The lives of North Korean women: Theory and reality] (Seoul: Nanam, 1991); in English, see Kyung Ae Park, "Women and Revolution in North Korea," *Pacific Affairs* 65.4 (1992/1993): 527–545.

30. Anna Krylova makes this case for the Soviet Union in "Stalinist Identity from the Viewpoint of Gender: Rearing a Generation of Professionally Violent Women-Fighters in 1930s Stalinist Russia," *Gender and History* 16.3 (2004): 626–653.

31. Catherine A. MacKinnon, *Toward a Feminist Theory of the State* (Cambridge, MA: Harvard University Press, 1989), 161.

32. It should be noted that this approach to the state as inherently masculine has been widely challenged by studies that have seen the liberal democratic state as more open, transactional, variegated, and open to feminist reform. This critique of the masculinist nature of the state is less applicable to the Korean Party-state, however, and I adhere to the earlier approach. See MacKinnon, *Toward a Feminist Theory of the State*; Kathy E. Ferguson, *The Feminist Case against Bureaucracy* (Philadelphia: Temple University Press, 1984); Wendy Brown, "Finding the Man in the State," in *States of Injury: Power and Freedom in Late Modernity* (Princeton, NJ: Princeton University Press, 1995), 166–195.

33. This is a rephrasing of a question Wendy Brown asks of liberalism. See Brown, "Finding the Man in the State."

34. On the fate of the Workers' Federation, see Kim Yŏnch'ŏl, *PukHanŭi sanŏphwawa kyŏngje chŏngch'aek* [North Korea's industrialization and economic policies] (Seoul: Yŏksa pip'yŏngsa, 2001), 264–67; PukHan yŏn'gu sent'ŏ, ed., *Chosŏn rodongdangŭi oegwak tanch'e* [North Korea's extra-Party organizations] (Paju City: Hanul ak'ademi, 2004).

35. A classic analysis for the Soviet Union can be found in Tony Cliff, *State Capitalism in Russia* (London: Pluto Press, 1974). For a recent interpretation of China, see Karl Gerth, *Unending Capitalism: How Consumerism Negated China's Communist Revolution* (Cambridge: Cambridge University Press, 2020).

36. Hyun Ok Park, *The Capitalist Unconscious: From Korean Unification to Transnational Korea* (New York: Columbia University Press, 2015); Cheehyung Harrison Kim, *Heroes and Toilers: Work as Life in Postwar North Korea, 1953–1961* (New York: Columbia University Press, 2019); Owen Miller, "War, the State, and the Formation of the North Korean Industrial Working Class, 1931–1961," *Third World Quarterly* 37.10 (2016): 1901–1920; Owen Miller, ed., *State Capitalism and Development in East Asia since 1945* (Leiden, The Netherlands: Brill, forthcoming).

37. For a description of the North Korean International Documentation Project, see James F. Person, "Narrating North Korea through Socialist Bloc Archives: Opportunities and Pitfalls," *Journal of Korean Studies* 26.2 (2021): 229–249. Of course, many historians working in English access these works directly; see the various works of Andrei Lankov, Natalia Matveeva, Balàzs Szalontai, and Fyodor Tertitskiy, to name a few.

38. For similar arguments, see Gregg A. Brazinsky, "Remembering Ŏmŏni: Using Chinese Memoirs to Understand Sino-North Korean Interactions during the Korean War," *Journal of Korean Studies* 26.2 (2021): 251–270; Cheehyung Harrison Kim, *Heroes and Toilers: Work as Life in Postwar North Korea, 1953–1961* (New York: Columbia University Press, 2018), 6.

39. Lynne Viola, "Introduction," in *Contending with Stalinism: Soviet Power and Popular Resistance in the 1930s* (Ithaca, NY: Cornell University Press, 2002).

40. Ch'oe Sŏn, "Pyŏngbukto nyŏmaengdanch'edŭrŭi kangyŏn sŏnjŏn saŏp-esŏŭi myŏtkaji kyŏrham" [Several shortcomings in propaganda lectures in the Women's Union of Pyŏngbuk Province], *Chosŏn nyŏsŏng*, December 1953: 12–16.

41. On photography, see Ri Hyojŏm, "Chŏngch'isŏnggwa yesulsŏngi nop'ŭn podo sajin" [Reportage photography with high political and artistic qualities], *Chosŏn kija*, February 1959: 37–38; Hyŏn P'ilhun, "Sahoejuŭi kŏnsŏrŭi kojowa ch'ulp'an bodo ilgundŭrŭi kwaŏp" [The task of publishing workers at the high tide of socialist construction], *Chosŏn kija*, December 1958: 10–17; Kim Ch'angsuk, "Hyŏngmyŏng chŏnt'ong kyoyang-esŏ ŏdŭm myŏtkaji kyŏnghom" [Several experiences gained in cultivating the revolutionary tradition], *Chosŏn kija*, July 1959: 11–13; Kim Hich'ŏl, "Sasangi tamajin sajinŭl" [Photographs full of ideology], *Chosŏn kija*, March 1959: 43–44. On statistics, see Kim Taeŭl, "Chungyohan kŏsŭn su'jaga anira saramida" [People are what's important, not numbers], *Chosŏn kija*, September 1959: 31–33.

42. Ŏ Hongt'aek, "To ilbodŭl-esŏ namChosŏn munjerŭl soholhi ch'uigŭphal su ŏpta" [The South Korean question cannot be treated with neglect in provincial newspapers], *Chosŏn kija*, April 1959: 44–46.

43. A version of this can be seen in my lecture at the Library of Congress entitled "Is a North Korean History without Kim Il Sung Possible?," available at https://www.youtube.com/watch?v=CgdPeXAhlVc.

CHAPTER ONE

1. Cement figures for 1953–57: Kukka kyehoek wiwŏnhoe chungang t'onggyeguk, ed., *1946–1957 Chosŏn minjujuŭi inmin konghwaguk inmin kyŏngje mit munhwa paljŏn t'onggyejip* [1946–1957: The Democratic People's Republic of Korea's statistics collection on the national economy and cultural developments] (Pyongyang: Kungnip ch'ulp'ansa, 1958), 12; sock figures: *Chosŏn chungang nyŏngam, 1961* [The Korean national yearbook, 1961] (Pyongyang: Chosŏn chungang t'ongsinsa, 1962), 235.

2. Yun Haedong, *Singminji kŭndaeŭi p'aerŏdoksŭ* [The paradox of colonial modernity] (Seoul: Hyumŏnisŭt'ŭ, 2007), 43–44.

3. Kim Pyŏngno, "Han'guk chŏnjaengŭi injŏk kŭ sonsilgwa PukHan kyegŭpchŏngch'aegŭi pyŏnhwa" [Human losses in the Korean War and changes in North Korean class policy], *T'ongil chŏngch'aek yŏn'gu* 9.1 (2000): 230–231.

4. *Chosŏn chungang nyŏn'gam, 1963* [The Korean national yearbook, 1963] (Pyongyang: Chosŏn chungang t'ongsinsa, 1964), 316.

5. *Chosŏn chungang nyŏn'gam, 1961*, 321.

6. Ch'oe Pongnam, "Yugajokkwa hamkke" [Together with bereaved families], *Chosŏn nyŏsŏng*, July 1957: 18–19.

7. On the land survey, see Pae Yŏngsun, *Hanmal Ilche ch'ogiŭi t'oji chosawa chise kaejŏng* [Land surveys and tax reform in the Hanmal and early Japanese colonial period] (Taegu: Yŏngnam taehakkyo ch'ulp'anbu, 2002). On comfort women, the literature is long. For an early, key contribution, see Yoshimi Yoshiaki, *Comfort Women: Sexual Slavery in the Japanese Military during World War II* (translated by Suzanne O'Brien) (New York: Columbia University Press, 2000); Ken

C. Kawashima, *The Proletarian Gamble: Korean Workers in Interwar Japan* (Durham, NC: Duke University Press, 2009). Of course, there were even earlier moments of out-migration. See Alyssa M. Park, *Sovereignty Experiments: Korean Migrants and the Building of Borders in Northeast Asia, 1860–1945* (Ithaca, NY: Cornell University Press, 2019); Hyun Ok Park, *Two Dreams in One Bed: Empire, Social Life, and the Origins of the North Korean Revolution in Manchuria* (Durham, NC: Duke University Press, 2005).

8. There is a wide range for this figure. For one treatment, see Pak Kyŏngsuk, "Singminji sigi (1910–1945) Chosŏnŭi in'gu tongt'aewa kujo" [Colonial (1910–1945) Korea's population movement and arrangement], *Han'guk in'guhak* 32.2 (2009): 29–58; Bruce Cumings posited a figure of 11.6 percent for the population outside the country in *The Origins of the Korean War, vol. 1: Liberation and the Emergence of Separate Regimes, 1945–1947* (Princeton, NJ: Princeton University Press, 1981), 54.

9. Lori Watt, *When Empire Comes Home: Repatriation and Reintegration in Postwar Japan* (Cambridge, MA: Harvard University Asia Center, 2009).

10. The advisor to the Bureau of Statistics, Theodore Pritzker, noted in the preface to the census that an estimated 350,000 people had repatriated in just over one month after liberation and before records were kept. He noted that people continued to enter through unregistered ships. Department of Public Health and Welfare, Bureau of Vital Statistics, *Population of South Korea, by Geographical Divisions and Sex* (Seoul: U.S. Army Military Government in Korea, 1946), preface. The 22 percent figure represents the growth in population as measured against the 1944 Japanese colonial census. Ibid., 2–3.

11. Kang Chŏnggu, "Haebanghu wŏllaminŭi wŏllam tonggiwa kyegŭpsŏng-e kwanhan yŏn'gu" [Research on the motivations and class character of people who crossed south after liberation], in Han'guk Sahoe Hakhoe, ed., *Han'guk chŏnjaenggwa Han'guk sahoe pyŏndong* (Seoul: Pulp'it, 1992), 93–131. See also Cho Hyŏng and Pak Myŏngsŏn, "PukHan ch'ulsin wŏlnaminŭi chŏngch'akkwajŏngŭl t'onghae pon NamBukHan sahoegujoŭi pyŏnhwa" [Changes in North and South Korean society as seen through the settlement process of refugees from North Korea], in *Pundan sidaewa Han'guksahoe* [The division period and Korean society] (Seoul: Kkach'i, 1985).

12. For a discussion of population in the interwar period as well as during the war, see Kim Tongch'un, *The Unending Korean War: A Social History* (Larkspur, CA: Tamil Vista, 2008).

13. Kim Il Sung makes this comparison in "Kongsanjuŭi kyoyang-e taehayŏ" [On the communist cultivation], *Rodong sinmun*, December 9, 1958: 2–3.

14. Janice Kim, "Living in Flight: Civilian Displacement, Suffering, and Relief during the Korean War, 1945–53," *Sahak yŏn'gu* 100 (2011): 285–329.

15. Anonymous, "Naemusŏng-esŏ chungang chuso annaesorŭl sŏlch'i" [The establishment in the Interior Ministry of a Central Information Center for Addresses], *Rodong sinmun* August 2, 1957: 3.

16. I take the figure of 1.2 million from Yi Yonggi, "Yisangajok yŏn'gu ŏdikkaji wanna?" [How has the state of research on separated families developed?], *Yŏksa*

pip'yŏng 44 (1998): 258. The figure of 350,000 comes from Tai-Whan Kwon, *Demography of Korea* (Seoul: Seoul National University Press, 1977), 190.

17. Kim Sŏngun, "Sŏul-e kyesinŭn abŏjigge" [To my father in Seoul], *Sae sedae*, September 1958: 10; see three letters with a Pyongyang postage mark in "Ponaeji mot'han p'yŏnji" [Unsendable letters], *Ch'ŏllima*, April 1964: 18–20; Lee Soo-Jung, "Making and Unmaking the Korean National Division: Separated Families in the Cold War and Post–Cold War Eras," PhD dissertation, University of Illinois at Urbana-Champaign, 2006.

18. Bruce Cumings interpreted this population dislocation as a major factor in the outbreak of the Korean War in *The Origins of the Korean War, vol. 1: Liberation and the Emergence of Separate Regimes, 1945–1947* (Princeton, NJ: Princeton University Press, 1981).

19. "Report No. 5 of the Embassy of the People's Republic of Poland in the Democratic Republic of Korea for the Period of 1 August 1953 to 30 September 1953," Polish Foreign Ministry Archive, obtained for NKIDP by Jakub Poprocki and translated for NKIDP by Maya Latynski, https://digitalarchive.wilsoncenter.org/document/114958.

20. Heonik Kwon, *After the Korean War: An Intimate History* (Cambridge: Cambridge University Press, 2020), ch. 4.

21. Suzy Kim, *Everyday Life in the North Korean Revolution, 1945–1950* (Ithaca, NY: Cornell University Press, 2013), ch. 5; Kim Chaeung, *PukHan ch'ejeŭi kiwŏn: inminwiŭi kyegŭp, kyegŭpwiŭi kukka* [The origins of the North Korean system: Class above people and state above class] (Kyŏnggi-do Koyang-si: Yŏksa pip'yŏngsa, 2018), 319–326.

22. Kim Chaeung, *PukHan ch'ejeŭi kiwŏn: inminwiŭi kyegŭp, kyegŭpwiŭi kukka*, 406–430.

23. Ibid., esp. 295–430.

24. Kim Namsik, "PukHan kongsanhwa kwajŏnggwa kyegŭpnosŏn" [The process of North Korea's communization and the class line], in *PukHan kongsanhwa kwajŏng yŏn'gu* [Studies on the communization process of North Korea] (Seoul: Tonga ch'ulp'ansa, 1972), 91–216.

25. "Memo from I. Byakov to the Charge d'Affaires of the Soviet Embassy in the DPRK," December 20, 1954, History and Public Policy Program Digital Archive, AVPRF F. 0102, Op. 11, P. 65, Delo 45, translated for NKIDP by Gary Goldberg, https://digitalarchive.wilsoncenter.org/document/115703.

26. Paek Sangbŏm, "Ne nammaeŭi ŏmŏniin aeguk yŏlsaŭi anhae" [The wife of a patriotic martyr and mother of four children], *Rodong sinmun*, May 25, 1957: 3; Kim Yŏnggŏl, "Ŏnjena ap'chang-e sŏsŏ" [Always standing at the vanguard], *Rodong sinmun*, June 6, 1957: 3. See this first-person letter: Ch'oe Pobu, "5 nammaerŭl k'iumyŏnsŏ" [While raising five children], *Rodong sinmun*, March 8, 1957: 3. For an editorial condemning the way war widows were treated, see Editorial, "Aeguk yŏlsa kajoktŭl-e taehan wŏnho saŏbŭl chon inminjŏk undongŭro" [Toward making the task of supporting patriotic martyr families a nationwide movement], *Rodong sinmun*, April 27, 1957: 1.

27. Anonymous, "Uridŭrŭn yŏngyeguninŭl chongyŏnghamyŏ saranghaja" [Let's love and respect our glorious retired soldiers], *Wisaeng munhwa*, November 1959: 4–5. On their educational privileges and problems, see "Sasol: yujanyŏ, ch'odŭng hakwŏn mit aegukwŏn saŏbŭl kailchŭng kaesŏn kanghwa haja" [Editorial: Let us strengthen and improve our orphanages, early education, and patriotic units], *Rodong sinmun*, May 25, 1958: 1.

28. Kim Il Sung often made this point: "Aeguk ryŏlsayugajok, inmingundae hubang kajoktŭrŭn modŭn humun-esŏ haeksimjŏk yŏkharŭl hayŏya handa" [The families of patriotic martyrs and homefront families supporting the People's Army must play a central role in all sectors], in Chosŏn rodongdang, ed., *Kim Ilsŏng chŏnjip* [The collected works of Kim Il Sung] (Pyongyang: Rodongdang ch'ulp'ansa, 1995; hereafter cited as *Collected Works*), vol. 20 (April 13, 1957): 199–208. This speech was not reprinted in *Rodong sinmun*, and only his meeting with these families was mentioned (*Rodong sinmun*, April 14: 1). On complacency: Anonymous, "Kongjang tang tanch'edŭrŭi saŏp-e taehan myŏt kaji munje" [Problems in the work of factory Party units], *Tangganbudŭl-ege chunŭn ch'amgo charyo*, July 1960: 7–13.

29. Anonymous, "Panhyŏngmyŏng kanch'ŏp punjadŭlgwaŭi t'ujaengŭl tŏuk kanghwahaja" [Let's further strengthen the struggle against antirevolutionary spy elements], *Choguk powirŭl wihayŏ*, August 1958: 56–57.

30. Kim Namsik, "PukHan kongsanhwa kwajŏnggwa kyegŭpnosŏn," 209–214.

31. Early publications from the 1960s provide the basis of current understanding but were published without source citations. Word-of-mouth accounts suggest that key scholars were invited by South Korean security services to consult confidential intelligence sources on which to base these sources. Subsequent studies cited these early publications, ensuring an unconfirmed recycling. I repeat this recirculation. However, I have omitted the numbers that have been countlessly repeated that quantify the percentages of the population in each category, given that there is no public data for these years.

32. This was in a speech not reprinted in the *Rodong sinmun*. Kim Il Sung, "Sahoejuŭi kyŏngje kŏnsŏl-esŏ nasŏnŭn tangmyŏnhan myŏt kaji kwaŏptŭl-e taehayŏ," *Collected Works*, vol. 24 (December 4, 1959): 393–462.

33. An Chaebok, "Rodong haengjŏng saŏp chido-esŏ chegidoenŭn myŏt kaji munje" [Several problems in the leadership of the administration of labor], *Kyŏngje chisik* 9 (1962): 19–23.

34. Sŏ Tongman, *PukChosŏn sahoejuŭi ch'eje sŏngnipsa, 1945–1961* [The history of the establishment of the North Korean socialist system, 1945–1961] (Seoul: Sonin, 2005), 603–610.

35. Kim Yŏnch'ŏl, *PukHanŭi sanŏphwawa kyŏngje chŏngch'aek* [North Korea's industrialization and economic policies] (Seoul: Yŏksa pip'yŏngsa, 2001), 89.

36. Balàzs Szalontai, *Kim Il Sung in the Khrushchev Era: Soviet-DPRK Relations and the Roots of North Korean Despotism, 1953–1964* (Stanford, CA: Stanford University Press, 2005), 45–46.

37. Rüdiger Frank, "Lessons from the Past: The First Wave of Developmental Assistance to North Korea and the German Reconstruction of Hamhŭng," *Pacific Focus* 23.1 (2008): 46–74.

38. Kim Yŏnch'ŏl, *PukHanŭi sanŏphwawa kyŏngje chŏngch'aek*, 202. One Soviet memo reports a figure as high as 31.6 percent for 1954: "Memo about the Situation in the DPRK," January 17, 1955, History and Public Policy Program Digital Archive, AVPRF F. 0102 Op. 11 P. 65 D. 45, translated for NKIDP by Gary Goldberg, https:// digitalarchive.wilsoncenter.org/document/115798.

39. Anonymous, "Pyongyang mokchae kagu kongjang choŏp" [The Pyongyang Wood Furniture Factory starts operations], *Rodong sinmun*, October 23, 1957: 1.

40. Rim Tŏkpo, "Kŏnsŏljangŭi chiwŏn'gun" [The assistance army at a construction site] *Rodong Sinmun*, June 30, 1955: 2. Anonymous, "Ttŏnagi chŏn-e hankaji irirado tŏ towa chuja" [Before I leave let me help you with one more thing], *Rodong sinmun*, April 23, 1958: 4; Anonymous, "Hyŏngjejŏk pangjomit-e" [With brotherly assistance], *Minju Chosŏn*, November 5, 1955: 3.

41. "Political Report No. 8 of the Embassy of the People's Republic of Poland in the Democratic People's Republic of Korea for the Period of 1 December to 31 December 1953," December 31, 1953, History and Public Policy Program Digital Archive, Polish Foreign Ministry Archive, obtained for NKIDP by Jakub Poprocki, translated for NKIDP by Maya Latynski, https://digitalarchive.wilsoncenter.org /document/114962.

42. Anonymous, with photographs by Chu Hyŏngdo, "Ssoryŏn inminŭi wŏnjoro" [The assistance of the Soviet people], *Chosŏn nyŏsŏng*, August 1957: 6–7.

43. See An Kwangchŭp's two essays," Che 1 ch'a 5 kaenyŏn kyehoek silhaenggwa chagŭm munje" [The implementation of the first five-year plan and the capital problem], *Rodong sinmun*, April 5, 1957: 2; and "Che 1 ch'a 5 kaenyŏn kyehoek-e issŏsŏŭi ch'ukchŏkkwa sobi" [Savings and consumption in the first five-year plan], *Rodong sinmun*, April 26, 1958: 2.

44. For studies of two famous reformers, see Hong Tŏkki, *Tasan Chŏng Yaggyongŭi t'oji kaehyŏk sasang* [The land reform thought of Tasan Chŏng Yagyong] (Kwangju: Chŏnnam taehakkyo ch'ulp'anbu, 2001); James Palais, *Confucian Statecraft and Korean Institutions: Yu Hyŏngwŏn and the Late Chosŏn Dynasty* (Seattle: University of Washington Press, 1996).

45. Yi Chuch'ŏl, *Chosŏn rodongdang tangwŏn chojik yŏn'gu* [Studies of the Korean Workers' Party's membership and organization, 1945–1960] (Seoul: Sŏnin, 2008), 409–417.

46. Kim Sŏngbo [Seong Bo], *NambukHan kyŏngjegujoŭi kiwŏn'gwa chŏn'gae: PukHan nongŏpch'ejeŭi hyŏngsŏngŭl chungsimŭro* [The origins and development of the North Korean economic structure: With a focus on the formation of North Korea's agricultural system] (Seoul: Yŏksa pip'yŏngsa, 2000), 173–186.

47. "Record of a Conversation with Editor of the Journal 'Novaya Koreya' Song Jin-hwa," April 4, 1955, History and Public Policy Program Digital Archive, RGANI Fond 5, Opis 28, Delo 314, translated for NKIDP by Gary Goldberg, https:// digitalarchive.wilsoncenter.org/document/116314.

48. For one study of how the New Village movement in South Korea, like collectivization in the North, used this unevenness, see Sungjo Kim, "The Countryside and the City: A Spatial Economy of the New Village Movement in 1970s South Korea," PhD dissertation, University of Toronto, 2015.

49. Sŏ Tongman, *PukChosŏn sahoejuŭi ch'eje sŏngnipsa, 1945–1961*, 604.

50. Anonymous, "Maegae kun-e hangae isangŭi kongjangŭl wihayŏ" [Toward the construction of one or more factories in each county], *Rodong sinmun*, August 23, 1958: 2; Sin Pŏmjun, "5 kae ŭi kongjangŭl saero kŏnsŏl" [Five newly opened factories], *Rodong sinmun*, August 27, 1958: 3; P'i Ch'angnin, "Maegaegun-e p'yŏnggyun 4-5gae isang kongjangŭl kŏnsŏlhayŏttda" [Each county has built on average at least four or five factories], *Sŏndongwŏn such'ŏp* 21 (November 1958): 14–15.

51. Anonymous, "Kŏnsŏljang-esŏ ŏmgyŏkhan chedowa chilsŏrŭl hwangniphaja" [Let us establish stricter systems and order at construction sites], *Sŏndongwŏn such'ŏp* 22 (November 1957): 6–8.

52. Sŏ Rimsŏp, "Kŏnsŏl pumun-esŏ chedowa kyuryurŭl hwangniphaja" [Let's establish order and discipline in the construction sector], *Kyŏngje kŏnsŏl*, June 1957: 22–23.

53. Hong Chongho, "Naemilgi choahanŭn saram" [People who like stretching out], *Hwasal* 120 (February 1960): 4.

54. I first learned of this report from Owen Miller. CIA Intelligence Memorandum, *North and South Korea: Separate Paths of Economic Development*, General CIA records, May 1, 1972, https://www.cia.gov/readingroom/document /cia-rdp85t00875r001700030082-7. For a critique of such reports, see Natalia Matveeva, "Building a New World: The Economic Development Strategies of the Two Koreas in the Cold War, 1957–66," PhD dissertation, School of Oriental and African Studies, London, 2021, 18.

55. Report from the USSR Ministry of Foreign Affairs to A. A. Okhotin, "Some Issues of the Domestic Political Situation in the DPRK," April 14, 1956, History and Public Policy Program Digital Archive, RGANI Fond 5, Opis 28, Delo 412, translated by Gary Goldberg, https://digitalarchive.wilsoncenter.org/document /120798.

56. Matveeva, *Building a New World*, 31–36.

57. "Notes from a Conversation between the 1st Secretary of the PRL Embassy in the DPRK with Comrade Pimenov, 1st Secretary of the Embassy of the USSR, on 15.X.1957," October 16, 1957, History and Public Policy Program Digital Archive, Polish Foreign Ministry Archive, obtained by Jakub Poprocki and translated by Maya Latynski, https://digitalarchive.wilsoncenter.org/document/111722.

58. "Journal of Soviet Ambassador to the DPRK A.M. Puzanov for 8–11 October 1957," October 8, 1957, History and Public Policy Program Digital Archive, AVPRF F. 0102, Op. 13, Delo 5, Listy 257–307, translated for NKIDP by Gary Goldberg, https://digitalarchive.wilsoncenter.org/document/115936.

59. Kim Ŭnggi, "Roryŏk munje haegyŏrrŭl wihan kinjŏlhan che kwaŏp" [Several challenges in resolving the labor shortage], *Kyŏngje kŏnsŏl*, March 1958: 30.

60. Kim Chongil, "Hyŏnsigi roryŏk munje haegyŏl-esŏ roryŏk puwŏnŭi hamnijŏk paech'i" [How to rationally organize supplemental labor to resolve the current labor problem], *Kyŏngje yŏn'gu*, February 1965: 3–9.

61. "Notification from the Ministry of Interior on Opinions Relating to Marriages between Chinese People and Korean Women," October 18, 1958, History and Public Policy Program Digital Archive, Hubei Provincial Archives, SZ67–01–0540, 6–7, obtained by Shen Zhihua and translated by Jeffrey Wang and Charles Kraus, https://digitalarchive.wilsoncenter.org/document/115320.

62. Kim Ryak, "Nyŏsŏng roryŏk inip-esŏ irryŏnŭi p'yŏnhyangdŭrŭl sigŭphi sijŏnghaja" [Let's rapidly improve the many biases in recruiting women's labor power], *Kyŏngje kŏnsŏl*, November 1958: 64–65.

63. Robert Collins, *Marked for Life: Songbun, North Korea's Social Classification System* (Washington, DC: Committee for Human Rights in North Korea, 2012).

64. Pak Chŏngae, "Sahoejuŭi kŏnsŏl-esŏ nyŏsŏngdŭrŭi yŏkharŭl nop'igi wihan sasang saŏbŭl kanghwa halde taehayŏ" [On strengthening ideological work for heightening the role of women in socialist construction], *Rodong sinmun*, April 12, 1957: 2. For a recent English biographical treatment of Pak, see Suzy Kim, *Among Women across Worlds: North Korea in the Global Cold War* (Ithaca, NY: Cornell University Press, 2023).

65. For an article explaining this to officials, see Kim Ingŏl, "Ch'ogŭp tangdanch'edŭr-esŏ pidangwŏndŭrŭi saŏbŭl ŏttŏge hal kŏsinga" [How do local Party units carry out work among non-Party members], *Tangganbudŭl-ege chunŭn ch'amgo charyo*, October 1960: 20–25.

66. This figure was likely on the low side, since Kim addressed only workers in industrial and transport enterprises, and his count did not include accompanying family members. Kim Unjong, "Hyŏn sigi roryŏk munjeŭi ollŭn haegyŏrŭl wihayŏ" [To solve the contemporary labor problem], *Kyŏngje kŏnsŏl*, November 1959: 29.

67. Pak Myŏngnim, *Han'guk 1950 Chŏnjaenggwa pyŏnghwa* [1950 Korea: War and peace] (Seoul: Nanam, 2002); Han Sŏnghun, *Chŏnjaenggwa inmin: PukHan sahoejuŭi ch'ejeŭi sŏngnipkwa inminŭi tansaeng* [War and people: The establishment of the North Korean socialist system and the birth of the people] (Tolbegae: Kyŏnggi-do P'aju-si, 2012); Kim Kwangun, *PukHan chŏngch'isa yŏn'gu: kŏndang, kŏn'guk, kŏn'gunŭi yŏksa* [North Korean political history: A history of the construction of the Party, the state, and the military] (Seoul: Sŏnin, 2003); Wada Haruki, *The Korean War: An International History* (Lanham, MD: Rowman and Littlefield, 2018).

68. Ch'oe Sŏn, "Pyŏngbukto nyŏmaengdanch'edŭrŭi kangyŏnsŏnjŏn saŏp-esŏŭi myŏtkaji kyŏrham" [Several shortcomings in propaganda lectures in the Women's Union of Pyŏngbuk province], *Chosŏn nyŏsŏng*, December 1953: 12–16.

69. Yi Chuch'ŏl, *Chosŏn rodongdang tangwŏnchojik yŏn'gu, 1945–1960*, 66–70, 419–423.

70. Ibid., 421. Scalapino and Lee give a different figure for total members in 1961 of 1,311,563 applicants. Robert Scalapino and Chong-sik Lee, *Communism in Korea: Part II, The Society* (Berkeley: University of California Press, 1972), 712.

71. Yi Chuch'ŏl, *Chosŏn rodongdang tangwŏnchojik yŏn'gu, 1945–1960*, 69, 420–421.

72. For Party-state leadership rosters, see Dae-sook Suh, *Korean Communism, 1945–1980: A Reference Guide to the Political System* (Honolulu: University of Hawai'i Press, 1981).

73. For one example, see Kim Kyesun, "Tongmaeng saŏp-esŏ hyŏngmyŏngjŏk kip'ungŭl suriphaja" [Let us establish a revolutionary spirit in union work], *Chosŏn nyŏsŏng*, February 1960: 2–3.

74. Andre Schmid, "Comrade Min, Women's Paid Labor, and the Centralizing Party-State: Postwar Reconstruction in North Korea." In Alf Lüdtke, ed., *Everyday Life in Mass Dictatorship: Evasion and Collusion* (London: Palgrave Macmillan, 2015), 184–201.

75. Ch'oe Sŏn, "Pyŏngbukto nyŏmaengdanch'edŭrŭi kangyŏnsŏnjŏn saŏp-esŏŭi myŏtkaji kyŏrham" [Several shortcomings in propaganda lectures in the Women's Union of Pyŏngbuk province], *Chosŏn nyŏsŏng*, December 1953: 12–16.

76. Pak Kŭmch'ŏl, *Tangŭi t'ongilgwa tangyŏrul tŏuk kanghwahalde taehayŏ* [On strengthening the unity and solidarity of the Party] (Pyongyang: Chosŏn rodong-dang ch'ulp'ansa, 1958), 7.

77. Sŏ Tongman, *PukChosŏn sahoejuŭi ch'eje sŏngnipsa, 1945–1961*, 590–600. Kim Yonghyŏn nevertheless argues that the economy was also militarized; see Kim Yonghyŏn, "1950–6onyŏndae PukHan kyŏngjeŭi kunsahwa" [The militarization of the North Korean economy in the 1950s and 1960s], *Saehoe kwahak yŏn'gu* 9.1 (2003): 164–183.

78. On mass organizations, see PukHan yŏn'gu sent'ŏ, ed., *Chosŏn nodongdangŭi oegwak tanch'e* [North Korea's extra-Party organizations] (Paju City: Hanul ak'ademi, 2004).

PART ONE

1. This cartoon is part of an article by Chŏn Sŏnggŭn, "Ch'ŏngnyŏngwa yejŏl" [Youth and propriety], *Ch'ŏngnyŏn saenghwal*, July 1956: 9.

2. For a direct link between norms and order, see Editorial, "Sahoe chilsŏwa kongjung todŏk" [Social order and public morality], *Rodong sinmun*, May 28, 1955: 1. For one study of how war memories were invoked for construction, see Sanghun Cho, "Memory as Propaganda: The Molding of Official Memory of the Korean War and Its Employment in the DPRK from 1953 to 1958," MA thesis, University of Toronto, 2007.

CHAPTER TWO

1. Hwang Yŏngsik, *Saenghwarŭi kŏul* [A guide to living] (Pyongyang: Chosŏn sahoejuŭi rodong ch'ŏngnyŏn tongmaeng, 1965), 10.

2. Ibid., 45–46, 61–66, 81, and 67–74, respectively.

3. Ibid., 28–29, 77–78.

4. Ibid., 93–94.

5. Anonymous, "Irŏnjomŭn koch'ipsida" [Let's correct these tendencies], *Chosŏn nyŏsŏng*, February 1956: 17; Anonymous, "Igŏsŭn rodong kyegŭptaun haeng-dongi anida" [This is not working-class-like behavior], *Rodongja*, November 1958: 40. On gossip, see "Uridŭrŭi sasang saenghwal" [Our ideological lives], *Ch'ŏngnyŏn saenghwal*, June 1956: 10.

6. Ri Sam, "Irŏn saramdo ittda" [Yes, there are people like this], *Rodongja sinmun*, February 13, 1959: 4.

7. Hŏ Il, untitled comic, *Rodongja*, January 1957: 13.

8. Anonymous, "Pukkŭrŏun chuldo morŭgo" [Without embarrassment], *Wisaeng munhwa*, November 1959: 22.

9. Anonymous, "Irŏn hyŏnsangŭl ŏpsaeja" [Let's get rid of these phenomena], *Sŏndongwŏn such'ŏp* 13 (July 1958): 12.

10. For one example in another socialist setting, see Catriona Kelly, *Refining Russia: Advice Literature, Polite Culture, and Gender from Catherine to Yeltsin* (Oxford: Oxford University Press, 2001).

11. See the two anonymous cartoons, "Ch'ŏngnyŏndŭrŭn sahoejuŭijŏk todok p'umsŏngŭl katch'uja" [Youth—let's be sure to have a character with socialist moral-ity] and "Nuga pongsahaeya hanŭnga?" [Whom should one serve?], *Ch'ŏngnyŏn saenghwal*, July 1958: 40 and 37, respectively.

12. Yinghong Cheng, *Creating the "New Man": From Enlightenment Ideals to Socialist Realities* (Honolulu: University of Hawai'i Press, 2008).

13. For one example, see Ko Myŏngjin, "Kŭnŭn saesarami toeyŏttda" [He became a New Man], *Rodongja sinmun*, February 13, 1959: 3.

14. Vadim Volkov, "The Concept of *Kul'turnost'*: Notes on the Stalinist Civiliz-ing Process," in Sheila Fitzpatrick, ed., *Stalinism: New Directions* (New York: Taylor & Francis, 2000), 210–230; Jochen Hellbeck, *Revolution on My Mind: Writing a Diary under Stalin* (Cambridge, MA: Harvard University Press, 2006).

15. Kelly, *Refining Russia*.

16. Chŏn Sŏnggŭn, "Ch'ŏngnyŏndŭrŭi kongsanjuŭi todŏk kyoyanggwa Mŭ.I. Kkallinin" [The Communist morality of youth and M.I. Kalinin], *Ch'ŏngnyŏn saenghwal*, August 1953: 45–52.

17. Kim Obok, "Nyŏmaeng tokbopan-esŏ" [In a book reading club of the Women's Union], *Chosŏn nyŏsŏng*, February 1957: 18. For a book review, see Cho Kwiun, "'Kajŏng kyoyang-e kwanhayŏrŭl ilgo" ["On reading: 'About family cultiva-tion'"], *Chosŏn nyŏsŏng*, April 1956: 36–37; A.Essŭ.Makkarenkko [A.S. Makarenko], "Pumorŭl wihan ch'aek" [A book for parents], *Chosŏn nyŏsŏng*, November 1958: 40.

18. Pŭ.Nŭ.Kkolbnopŭssŭkki [Viktor Nikolaevich Kolbanovsky], "Sahoejuŭi sahoe-esŏui sarang, kyŏrhon, kajok" [Love, marriage, and family in socialist soci-ety], *Ch'ŏngnyŏn saenghwal*, December 1955: 56–61.

19. For example, an extract from the *Liaoning People's Press*: "Saranggwa kajŏng" [Love and family], *Chosŏn nyŏsŏng*, December 1958: 34–36.

20. Travis Workman, *Imperial Genus: The Formation and Limits of the Human in Modern Korea and Japan* (Oakland: University of California Press, 2015).

21. Harry Harootunian, *Overcome by Modernity: History, Culture, and Community in Interwar Japan* (Princeton, NJ: Princeton University Press, 2000), 14.

22. Mark A. Jones, *Children as Treasures: Childhood and the Middle Class in Early Twentieth-Century Japan* (Cambridge, MA: Harvard University Asia Center, 2010). For its earlier history, see Jordan Sand, *House and Home in Modern Japan: Architecture, Domestic Space, and Bourgeois Culture, 1880–1930* (Cambridge, MA: Harvard University Asia Center, 2004).

23. For late colonial-era nutritional studies, see Sunho Ko, "Food for Empire: Wartime Food Politics on the Korean Homefront 1937–1945," PhD dissertation, University of Toronto, 2018.

24. See Todd A. Henry, *Assimilating Seoul: Japanese Rule and the Politics of Public Space in Colonial Korea, 1910–1945* (Berkeley: University of California Press, 2014); Ruth Rogaski, *Hygienic Modernity: Meanings of Health and Disease in Treaty-Port China* (Berkeley: University of California Press, 2004).

25. Takashi Fujitani, *Race for Empire: Koreans as Japanese and Japanese as Americans during World War II* (Berkeley: University of California Press, 2013). See also Theodore Jun Yoo, *The Politics of Gender in Colonial Korea: Education, Labor, and Health, 1910–1945* (Berkeley: University of California Press, 2008).

26. For a North Korean study, see Hong Sunwŏn, *Chosŏn pogŏnsa* [A history of Korean public health] (Hambuk: Kwahak paekkwasajŏn ch'ulp'ansa, 1981).

27. This comic was submitted to *Chosŏn nyŏsŏng* by middle school teacher Pak Yŏngsik. See "Uri ŏmaga kŭraessŏyo" [My mother said this], *Chosŏn nyŏsŏng*, October 1960: 40.

28. Anonymous, "Yŏrŭmch'ŏl wisaeng" [Summer hygiene], *Ch'ŏllima*, April 1965: 144–146; Pak Changhwan, "Tisŭt'oma chunggan sukchurŭl ch'ŏljŏhi pangmyŏrhaja" [Let's thoroughly eradicate distoma's intermediary hosts], *Wisaeng munhwa*, April 1959: 4–5.

29. Michel Foucault, *Society Must Be Defended: Lectures at the Collège de France, 1975–76*, tr. David Macey (New York: Picador, 2003), 241.

30. We do not, for example, have the type of diaries that have enabled Soviet historians to examine this question more closely even if answers are always hard to come by. See Hellbeck, *Revolution on My Mind*.

31. Alf Lüdtke, ed., "Introduction," in *The History of Everyday Life: Reconstructing Historical Experiences and Ways of Life* (Princeton, NJ: Princeton University Press, 1995), 8.

32. Jie-Hyun Lim has spearheaded the mass dictatorship project. Among his publications, see Jie-Hyun Lim and Karen Petrone, eds., *Gender Politics and Mass Dictatorship: Global Perspectives* (London: Palgrave Macmillan, 2010); Paul Corner and Jie-Hyun Lim, eds., *The Palgrave Handbook of the History of Mass Dictatorship* (London: Palgrave Macmillan, 2016). On the challenges for historians in determining the legitimacy of regimes, see Stephen Kotkin, *Magnetic Mountain: Stalinism as Civilization* (Berkeley: University of California Press, 1995).

33. Michel Foucault, *Society Must Be Defended*, 261.

34. For example, the journals *Hygiene Culture* (*Wisaeng munhwa*) and *Popular Public Sanitation* (*Inmin pogŏn*).

35. Hwang Yŏngsik, *Saenghwarŭi kŏul*, 83.

36. Ibid., 86.

37. Ch'oe Pyŏngch'un, "Tongdang tanch'e saŏp-esŏ chegidoenŭn myŏt kaji munje" [Several problems in the tasks of neighborhood party units], *Tangganbudŭlege chunŭn ch'amgo charyo*, November 1960: 20–24.

38. For bourgeois aesthetics in the film industry, see Anonymous, "Yŏnghwa saŏbŭl kailch'ŭng paljŏnsik'ija" [For the further development of the movie industry], *Chosŏn yŏnghwa*, April 1958: 3–7. For the politics of the literary world, see Brian Myers, *Han Sŏrya and North Korean Literature: The Failure of Socialist Realism in DPRK* (Ithaca, NY: East Asia Program, Cornell University, 1994); Tatiana Gabroussenko, *Soldiers on the Cultural Front: Developments in the Early History of North Korean Literature and Literary Policy* (Honolulu: University of Hawai'i Press, 2010).

39. Chŏn Changsŏk, *Miguksik saenghwal yangsikkwa namChosŏn-e mich'in kŭ hugwa* [American-style living and its effect on South Korea] (Pyongyang: Chosŏn rodongdang ch'ulp'ansa, 1965).

40. For one wartime treatment of this concept, see Anonymous, "Nalgŭn sasanggwa t'ujaenghaja" [Let's struggle with outmoded thought], *Sŏndongwŏn such'ŏp*, May 1952: 30–39.

41. For examples of "acting like a host" [*chuin*], see Ri Tonggŭn, "Il'gundŭrŭi chuindaun t'aedowa orhŭn saŏp chakp'ungi toenda" [Workers' host-like attitude and upright style is demanded], *Rodong sinmun*, October 22, 1957: 2; Ri Kyuhyŏng, "Chuin toen simjŏngŭro" [With the heart of a host], *Rodongja sinmun*, June 16, 1962: 3. For "standing up on one's own" [*charip*], see Kim Sanghak, "Uri naranŭn charipchŏk kongŏp-nongŏp kukkaro chŏnbyŏnhago ittda" [Our country is changing into a self-dependent industrial and agricultural nation], *Rodong sinmun*, April 10, 1958: 2. For *ch'angbal*, see Ryu Ch'ikyŏng, "Rodong taejungŭi yŏnggungsŏnggwa ch'angbalsŏngŭl yonggwangno kŏnsŏl-e chojik dongwon" [The working masses' heroism and creative initiative were mobilized by the furnace], *Rodong sinmun*, November 18, 1958: 2.

42. Anonymous, "Nalgŭn saenghwal p'ungsŭbŭl pŏrigo saeroun saenghwal kipungŭl suriphapsida" [Let's abandon outmoded life practices and establish the spirit of new living], *Sŏndongwŏn such'ŏp*, January 1957: 24.

43. On the urban-rural labor imbalance, see Editorial, "Kŭllojadŭrŭi puyangkajogŭl chikchang-e kwangbŏmhi iniphaja" [Let's bring the dependent family members of workers into the workplace], *Rodong sinmun*, January 7, 1956: 1. On the postwar labor shortage in general, see Sŏ Tongman, *PukChosŏn sahoejuŭi ch'eje sŏngnipsa, 1945–1961* [The history of the establishment of the North Korean socialist system, 1945–1961] (Seoul: Sonin, 2005), 627–631. On mobility, see Andre Schmid, "Historicizing North Korea: State Socialism, Population Mobility, and Cold War Historiography," *The American Historical Review* 123.2 (2018): 439–462.

44. Chang Sehun, "Han'guk chŏnjaenggwa nambukHanŭi tosihwa: Sŏulgwa P'yŏngyangŭi chŏnhu pokku kwajŏngŭl chungsimŭro" [The Korean War and the

urbanization of North and South Korea: With a focus on the postwar recovery process of Seoul and Pyongyang], *Sahoewa yŏksa* 67 (2005): 237–238.

45. For one such story of a worker, having just moved into their home, writing a letter back to their parents, see Pak Chaehwan, "Saejip-e tŭnŭn nal" [Moving-in day], *Rodong sinmun*, December 13, 1955: 3. This point of analysis was first proposed to me by Sungjo Kim.

46. The journal *Commerce (Sangŏp)* was full of stories describing the difficulties of getting goods to the countryside, including a case study for South Hwanghae province: O Sŏn, "Chinanhae saŏbi wae rakhudoeyonnŭn'ga" [Why did last year's enterprise fall behind?], *Sangŏp*, March 1956: 42–47. On problems in circulation of consumer goods between city and countryside, see Editorial, "Taejung sobip'um saengsan mit gonggŭp saŏbŭi kaesŏn kanghwarŭl wihayŏ" [For the improvement and strengthening of the task of producing and supplying mass consumer goods], *Rodong sinmun*, December 6, 1956: 2.

47. For treatments of the imbalances, see Ri Sŏksim, "Uri nara kyŏngje paljŏnŭi nopŭn soktowa kyunhyŏng munje" [The high speed of our country's economic development and the balance problem], *Kŭlloja* 192 (November 1961): 46–52; Ri Myŏngsŏ, "Tosiwa nongch'on kanŭi ch'ai chonjaeŭi sahoe kyŏngjejŏk kŭnwŏn" [The socioeconomic roots of the existence of a gap between cities and agricultural villages], *Kyŏngje yŏn'gu*, March 1965: 15; Ch'oe Kŭnhwan, "Nongch'on-esŏŭi sangp'um ryut'ong" [Commodity circulation in agricultural villages], *Rodong sinmun*, May 29, 1955: 2.

48. For example, Anonymous, "San'gan maurŭi chillryoso" [A mountain village's medical clinic], *Rodong sinmun*, August 30, 1957: 3.

49. There were exceptions, of course. See Anonymous, "Irŏn sangt'aega kyesokdoeyŏnŭn andoenda" [It's not OK for this situation to continue], *Wisaeng munhwa*, July 1959: 29. For contemporary southern usage of these terms, see Sungjo Kim, "The Countryside and the City: A Spatial Economy of the New Village Movement in 1970s South Korea" (PhD dissertation, University of Toronto, 2015).

50. Editorial, "Charangsŭrŏun minju sudo—Pyŏngyang" [The proud democratic capital—Pyongyang], *Rodong sinmun*, October 15, 1957: 1. See the report "Pyŏngyang ch'anggŏn 1530 chunyŏn kinyŏm Pyŏngyangsi kyŏngch'uk pogohui-esŏ han Hong Myŏnghŭi pususangŭi pogo" [The report of Vice Minister Hong Myŏnghŭi at the Pyongyang celebration report meeting for the commemoration of the 1,530th anniversary of the founding of Pyongyang], *Rodong sinmun*, October 15, 1957: 2.

51. This issue had several stories on Pyongyang. Yang Sŏngnyŏp, "Pyŏngyangsirŭl tŏuk arŭmdapko ŭngchanghan tosiro" [Toward an even more beautiful and majestic Pyongyang], *Rodong sinmun*, August 15, 1964: 2.

52. Yang Sŏngnyŏp, "Pyŏngyangsirŭl tŏuk arŭmdapko ungchanghan tosiro" [Toward an even more beautiful and majestic Pyongyang], *Rodong sinmun*, August 15, 1964: 2.

53. Anonymous, "Ssoryŏn-esŏ ponae on ryŏgaek ppŏsŭ" [A passenger bus sent from the Soviet Union], *Chosŏn nyŏsŏng*, December 1953: 43.

54. See Han Sŏnggyŏl, "Tongmuwŏn-esŏ" [At the zoo], *Ch'ŏllima*, May 1964: back cover. A 1959 cabinet decision established the zoo with a botanical garden, as recorded in *Rodong sinmun*, June 11, 1959: 2.

55. Anonymous, "Nyŏsŏng kwan'gwangdan" [A women's tour group], *Chosŏn nyŏsŏng*, November 1957: 36.

56. Anonymous, "Pyŏngyangsi-esŏ irryoil yuram ppŏsŭ unhaengŭl kaesi" [Sunday tour buses begin in Pyongyang], *Rodong sinmun*, August 6, 1957: 3.

57. For reports of other groups organized to tour Pyongyang, see Anonymous, "Kakto kwan'gwangdan P'yŏngyangsi kŏnsŏl chŏnghyŏngŭl kyŏnhak" [Tour groups inspect the current state of Pyongyang construction], *Rodong sinmun*, November 21, 1955: 1. For tour groups that specifically mention workers' housing, see Anonymous, "Kakchi kwan'gwangdan ilhaeng minju sudoŭi pokku kŏnsŏl mosŭbŭl ch'amgwan" [Groups from across the nation observe the recovering face of the democratic capital], *Rodong sinmun*, August 12, 1955: 1.

58. Pak Chaehwan, "Pyongyang-e osin sanch'on halmŏni" [A grandmother comes to Pyongyang from the mountain village], *Rodong sinmun*, May 1, 1957: 3.

59. For an exception, see Anonymous, "Pat' kiri anida" [Fields are not roads], *Ch'ŏngnyŏn saenghwal*, November 1958: 65.

60. Anonymous, "Tu ch'angmunga-esŏ" [Two windows], *Ch'ŏngnyŏn saenghwal*, August 1958: final page; Kim Yŏnghwan, "Arŭmdapchi mothan otch'arim" [An outfit that cannot be beautiful], *Ch'ŏngnyŏn saenghwal*, August 1958: 58; Anonymous, "Pamjamŭl morŭnŭn 'kasu'" [A 'singer' who doesn't understand night sleep], *Ch'ŏngnyŏn saenghwal*, December 1958: 45.

61. Hwang Yŏngsik, *Saenghwarŭi kŏul*, 75–81.

62. Ibid., 76.

63. For a critique of the masculinization thesis, see Zheng Wang, *Finding Women in the State: A Socialist Feminist Revolution in the People's Republic of China, 1949–1964* (Oakland: University of California Press, 2017).

64. Janet Poole, *When the Future Disappears: The Modernist Imagination in Late Colonial Korea* (New York: Columbia University Press, 2014).

65. For a treatment of dialects aimed at a non-linguist audience, see Pang Sukkyŏng, "P'yojunmalgwa sat'uri" [Standard language and dialects], *Chosŏn nyŏsŏng*, June 1964: 62.

66. For example, the journal *Speech and Writing* (*Malgwa kŭl*).

67. Ch'oe Wanho, "Nyŏsŏnggwa ŏnŏ munhwa" [Women and language culture], *Chosŏn nyŏsŏng*, May 1957: 36–37.

68. Han Chŏngjik, "Ch'ŏngnyŏngwa mal" [Youth and speech], *Ch'ŏngnyŏn saenghwal*, September 1957: 27.

69. My admittedly not-so-clever attempt to use the Old English term *geostran* to capture the contrast made by Hwang between *chagil* and *ŏje*. Hwang Yŏngsik, *Saenghwarŭi kŏul*, 18.

70. Kang Kiyŏp "'Hwajŏnmin' iran yet'mal ida" ["Hwajŏnmin" is an old word], *Rodong sinmun*, December 21, 1957: 2.

71. Anonymous, "Han salggajiŭi kyoyang" [Education until the first year], *Chosŏn nyŏsŏng*, January 1957: 31.

72. Hwang Yŏngsik, *Saenghwarŭi kŏul*, 15–16.

73. Pak Sunsŏ, ed., *Taejung chŏngch'i yongŏ sajŏn* [Popular dictionary of political terms] (Pyongyang: Chosŏn rodongdang ch'ulp'ansa, 1964).

74. Anonymous, "Murŭmgwa taedap" [Questions and answers], *Rodongja*, July 1954: 55.

75. For a non-socialist critique of shortages and prices, see János Kornai, *Economics of Shortage* (Amsterdam: Elsevier North-Holland, 1980). For the use of price incentives in the Soviet Union, Cuba, and China, see Cheng, *Creating the "New Man."*

76. These three forms in Korean are "Nan mollayo," "Morŭgessŭmnida," and "Chŏnŭn morŭgessŭmnida. Chega tarŭn saram-ege murŏ tŭrijiyo." Hwang Yŏngsik, *Saenghwarŭi kŏul*, 16.

77. Ibid., 19–24.

78. Chosŏn minju nyŏsŏng tongmaeng chungang wiwŏnhoe, *Nyŏsŏngdŭrŭn munhwa sujunŭl nop'ija* [Women, let us raise our cultural levels] (Pyongyang: Chosŏn nyŏsŏngsa, 1956), 25.

79. Ch'oe Wanho, "Nyŏsŏnggwa ŏnŏ munhwa" [Women and the speech culture], *Chosŏn nyŏsŏng*, May 1957: 36.

80. Pak Yongsun, "Ryejŏl innŭn marrŭl ssŭpsida" [Let's use decorous words], *Chosŏn nyŏsŏng*, February 1964: 78–79.

81. Ch'oe Wanho, "Nyŏsŏnggwa ŏnŏ munhwa," 37.

82. Pak Yongsun, "Ryejŏl innŭn marrŭl ssŭpsida," 78.

83. Chŏn Sŏnggŭn, "Nyŏsŏnggwa ryejŏl" [Women and manners], *Chosŏn nyŏsŏng*, July 1957: 32.

84. Anonymous, "Kyŏmsonhan momkajim" [Modest deportment], *Chosŏn nyŏsŏng*, December 1959: 39.

85. For example, feminine language became a prominent theme in the journal *Speech and Writing* (*Malgwa kŭl*), and new publications by the Women's Union included proper speech as de rigueur. See Chŏn Sŏnggŭn, *Nyŏsŏngdŭrŭi kongsanjuŭijŏk ryeŭi todok* [The communist etiquette and morality of women] (Pyongyang: Chosŏn nyŏsŏngsa, 1963), 13–15.

86. Hwang Yŏngsik, *Saenghwarŭi kŏul*, 15.

CHAPTER THREE

1. For an example of a self-criticism about the fear of slipping, see Kim Hanp'il, "Naega kwayŏn ch'amdaun rodongjayŏttdŏnga?" [Am I actually a true worker?], *Rodongja*, November 1955: 54–56.

2. Andre Schmid, "'My Turn to Speak': Criticism Culture and the Multiple Uses of Class in Postwar North Korea," *International Journal of Korean Studies* 21.2 (2016): 121–153.

3. Ri Hongjong, "Pip'angwa chagi pip'anŭn tongmaeng saŏp paljonŭi kangryŏkhan sudan" [Criticism and self-criticism are a powerful means for advancing the task of solidarity], *Ch'ŏngnyŏn saenghwal*, July 1953: 22–32.

4. For one example of the invective, published in a children's magazine, see Chang Hyŏngjun, "Ri T'aejunŭi chakp'umdŭrŭi pandongsŏng" [The reactionary nature of Ri T'aejun's literary works], *Sae sedae*, April 1958: 53–56.

5. Kim Ŭngsŏn, "Pip'angwa chagi pip'an" [Criticism and self-criticism], *Rodongja*, June 1955: 19–22.

6. Ri Sun'gil, "Minch'ŏng mit sonyŏndan yŏlsŏngja tongmudŭl-ege" [To the enthusiastic comrades of the Youth League and Children's Corps], *Sae sedae*, August 1955: 16–18.

7. For a cartoon mocking two types of workers, see An Kyŏngnyong, "Naega pon tu chingmaeng ilggun" [Two Federation workers I have seen], *Rodongja sinmun*, July 8, 1959: 2.

8. Anonymous, "Muŏsi mit'ŭroput'ŏŭi pip'anŭl ŏkche hanŭnga?" [What is repressing bottom-up criticism?], *Ch'ŏngnyŏn saenghwal*, September 1954: 53.

9. For one reader's submission on this issue, see the unfortunately named Pak Chŏnghŭi, "Sŏlbokkwa kyoyangŭl ap'seuja" [Prioritizing persuasion and cultivation], *Rodongja sinmun*, July 29, 1959: 2. See also Pak Chongt'aek, "Sŏlbogŭi him" [The power of persuasion], *Rodong sinmun*, September 15, 1959: 3.

10. Han Chŏngjik, "Ch'ŏngnyŏn'gwa mal" [Youth and speech], *Ch'ŏngnyŏn saenghwal*, September 1957: 26–27.

11. Sŏ Yŏngbŏm, "Nado han madi" [My turn to speak], *Rodongja sinmun*, June 7, 1959: 3.

12. Ri Sŏk, "Nado han madi" [My turn to speak], *Rodongja sinmun*, April 17, 1959: 3.

13. Ch'oe Tŏkkil, "Nado han madi" [My turn to speak], *Rodongja sinmun*, May 13, 1959: 3.

14. Ko Myŏngjin, "Nado han madi" [My turn to speak], *Rodongja sinmun*, June 7, 1959: 3.

15. Hong Ŭngun, "Kim Sunhŭi tongmu-ege chŏnhago sip'ŭn mal" [Some words I would say to Comrade Kim Sunhŭi], *Rodongja sinmun*, April 19, 1959: 3. The original story: Chang Pyŏnghyŏn, "Nado han madi" [My turn to speak], March 18, 1959: 3.

16. Ri Hwanju, "Nado han madi" [My turn to speak], *Rodongja sinmun*, May 6, 1959: 3.

17. [Indistinguishable name], "Nado han madi" [My turn to speak], *Rodongja sinmun*, May 10, 1959: 3.

18. Kang Ch'ŏlju, "Nado han madi" [My turn to speak], *Rodongja sinmun*, April 17, 1959: 3.

19. Kim Yusŏng, "Nado han madi" [My turn to speak], *Rodongja sinmun*, July 8, 1959: 3.

20. O Taeguk, "Nado han madi" [My turn to speak], *Rodongja sinmun*, June 7, 1959: 3.

21. Pak Pyŏngsŏ "Nado han madi" [My turn to speak], *Rodongja sinmun*, May 31, 1959: 3.

22. [Indistinguishable name], "Nado han madi" [My turn to speak], *Rodongja sinmun*, July 31, 1959: 3.

23. Anonymous, "Kunjung todŏgŭl wibanhanŭn sillyŏk ilgundŭl" [Workers who violate public morality], *Rodongja sinmun*, May 20, 1959. For another story of drunken behavior, see Pak Yong, "Kŭŭi pigyegŭpjŏk haengdongŭl rodongjadŭrŭn kkŭnnae mukkwahaji anattda" [In the end workers could not be silent about his non-class behavior], *Rodongja sinmun*, February 15, 1959: 3

24. O Kyut'ae, "Sogŭksŏnggwa posujuŭirŭl kŭkpokhago tŏ ppalli naagagi wihayŏ" [In order to get out more quickly and overcome passivity and conservatism], *Rodong sinmun*, October 12, 1958: 2; Ri Yangsŏp, "Wisaeng saŏp-e taehan hyŏngsikchŏgin chidorŭl sijŏnghaja" [Let's straighten out formalist leadership in hygiene affairs], *Rodong sinmun*, January 24, 1959: 5; Anonymous, "Hyŏndae sujŏngchuŭinŭn pip'an toeyŏya handa" [We must criticize contemporary revisionism], *Sŏndongwŏn such'op* 12 (June 1958): 4–5.

25. Anonymous, "Purŭjyoa sasang kwaŭi t'ujaengŭl tŏuk kanghwa haja" [Let's strengthen the struggle against bourgeois thought], *Kŭlloja* 209 (October 1962): 21–28; Anonymous, "Kyegŭp kyoyangŭi kanghwanŭn hyŏngmyŏng chŏnjirŭl konggohwahanŭn chungyo tambo" [The strengthening of class cultivation is an important matter in securing the revolutionary base], *Kŭlloja* 222 (April 1963): 31–38.

26. There was a great deal of attention paid to this moment of transition in becoming a laborer. See "Sinip rodongjadŭrŭl sahoejuŭi kŏnsŏrŭi t'usaro kyoyang-haja" [Let's cultivate newly enrolled workers as warriors of socialist construction], *Rodongja sinmun*, May 29, 1959: 1.

27. The figure of fifteen hundred comes from Ri Hyŏngju, "Kkaekkŭthan hap-suk, chŭlgŏun saehwal" [Clean dormitories, enjoyable lives], *Rodongja sinmun*, September 16, 1960: 3. Housing pressures likely made such a transition less than seamless, and eventually dormitories for couples appeared; see Ri Ch'angho, "Rodong pubudŭrŭl wihan hapsuk" [Common living for working couples], *Rodongja sinmun*, January 6, 1960: 3.

28. Anonymous, "Sat'aegŭn chejibi aninga?" [Isn't the house my home?], *Rodongja sinmun*, June 23, 1957: 2.

29. Anonymous, "Chikchanggwa kajŏng saenghwal" [Work and home life], *Chosŏn nyŏsŏng*, January 1958: 9.

30. Ibid., 12.

31. For a story of an older woman being brought in to teach feminine propriety to a dormitory of five hundred women, see Kim Sundŏk, "Uri hapsuk sagamjang" [Our dormitory's housemother], *Chosŏn nyŏsŏng*, August 1957: 16–17. See also Son Susŏng, "Hapsugwŏndŭrŭi ŏmŏni" [A dormitory residents' mother], *Rodongja sinmun*, October 18, 1960: 3; Sin Tongu, "Rodongjaŭi ŏmŏni" [Workers' mother], *Rodongja sinmun*, March 30, 1961: 3.

32. See Chosŏn minju nyŏsŏng tongmaeng chungang wiwŏnhoe, *Nyŏsŏngdŭlŭn munhwa sujunŭl nop'ija* [Women, let us raise our cultural levels] (Pyongyang: Chosŏn nyŏsŏngsa, 1956).

33. Ri Ponggŭm, "Hapsuk saenghwal" [Dormitory life], *Chosŏn nyŏsŏng*, May 1957: 32–33.

34. Anonymous, "Hapsuk, siktangŭl kkaekkŭt'age kkurinda" [Let's make our dormitories and cafeterias clean], *Rodong sinmun*, July 17, 1960: 4.

35. Kim Chŏngnak, "Hapsuk-e yŏngyangga nop'ŭn kŭpsigŭl wihae" [To raise the nutritional quality of dormitory food], *Rodongja sinmun*, July 3, 1957: 3.

36. Anonymous, "Hapsugŭn nagŭneŭi ryŏinsugi anida" [Dormitories are not inns for drifters], *Rodongja sinmun*, June 23, 1957: 2.

37. Ri Kŭnsam, "Haksŭpto hago hapsugwŏn chasindŭri hwadan to kakkunŭn chŭlgŏun saenghwarŭl ch'angjo" [Studying themselves and making their own flowerbeds, dormitory residents create their own enjoyable lives], *Rodongja sinmun*, August 21, 1957: 3.

38. Anonymous, "Sŏro towa kkaekkŭthan hapsugŭro" [Toward a mutually cooperative and clean dormitory], *Rodongja*, October 1960: 33.

39. For labor activities during the colonial period, see Janice C. H. Kim, *To Live to Work: Factory Women in Colonial Korea, 1910–1945* (Stanford, CA: Stanford University Press, 2009).

40. Anonymous, "Kŭllojadŭrŭi hapsuk mit chut'aek saenghwarŭl munhwajŏgŭro chojikhaja" [Let's culturally organize the lives of worker dormitories and houses], *Rodongja sinmun*, September 4, 1957: 2.

41. Dances emerged as a favorite theme of photographers. See No Chaeryong, "Pyongyangŭi haru" [A day in Pyongyang], *Chosŏn*, July 1958: 4–5. For one account of a highly self-organized dormitory, see Anonymous, "Hapsuk saenghwarŭl munhwa wisaengjŏgŭro" [Toward a cultural and hygienic dormitory life], *Rodongja sinmun*, November 13, 1962: 3.

42. One of the most prestigious factories, the Hwanghae Steel Works, expressly designed single-room dormitories for couples. Ri Ch'angho, "Rodong pubudŭrŭl wihan hapsuk" [Dormitories for working couples], *Rodongja sinmun*, January 6, 1960: 3.

PART TWO

1. Song Siyŏp, "Riyong toeŏttda!" [It's been used!], *Hwasal* 129 (July 1960): 5.

2. Kim Yongrak, "Kijungginŭn kŏnsŏljangŭi changsingmuri anida" [Cranes are not decorations for construction sites], *Kyŏngje kŏnsŏl*, March 1958: 61. For another example in a Pyongyang factory, see Paek Yŏngch'ol, "Riyongdoeji anŭn sŏlbi" [Unused equipment], *Rodong sinmun*, November 8, 1958: 2.

3. Kim Chungsam, "Sŏlbi riyongnyul chegowa roryŏk chŏryagŭl wihan t'ujaengesŏŭi tang tanch'edŭrŭi yŏkhal" [The role of party units in the struggle to raise the usage rate of equipment and save labor], *Kŭlloja* 128 (July 1956): 73–85.

CHAPTER FOUR

1. Ri Myŏngwŏn, *Kŏnsŏl chagŏppanjangŭi sugi* [A construction brigade leader's memoir] (Pyongyang: Minch'ŏng ch'ulp'ansa, 1961), 34. For other media references to Ri, see Anonymous, "Nyŏsŏng kŏnsŏljadŭl: Mijanggong Ri Myŏngwŏn" [Women builders: parger Ri Myŏngwŏn], *Chosŏn nyŏsŏng*, January 1959: 18–19; Paek Sangbŏm, "Nyŏsŏng mijanggongdŭl" [Women pargers], *Rodong sinmun*, December 19, 1958: 3.

2. For a treatment of more heroic figures, especially in fiction, see Cheehyung Harrison Kim, *Heroes and Toilers: Work as Life in Postwar North Korea, 1953–1961* (New York: Columbia University Press, 2018).

3. Yinghong Cheng, *Creating the "New Man": From Enlightenment Ideals to Socialist Realities* (Honolulu: University of Hawai'i Press, 2008).

4. For a typical piece, see Kim Insŏn, "Togŭpcherŭl chal silsihamyŏn rodong saengsan nŭngnyuri nop'ajinda" [If wage scales are properly implemented, the productivity rate of labor rises], *Kyŏngje chisik*, June 1960: 29–31.

5. March 1954 cabinet decision no. 32, as cited in Kim Chiok, "Rodong imgŭmjeŭi chŏnghwakhan silsirŭl wihayŏ" [For the accurate implementation of the labor wage system], *Rodong*, June 1954: 60–64.

6. Pak Kibok and Pak Ch'anyang, "Ch'aejomjerŭl silsihayŏ roim punbae-esŏ p'yŏngyunjuŭirŭl ŏpsaetda" [Equalism was stricken from the implementation of the marking system and wage distribution], *Kŏnsŏlja*, Feburary 1960: 30; Ri Kyuch'ŏl, "Togŭpche silsi-esŏ nat'anan myŏt kaji kyŏrhamdŭl" [Several problems in the implementation of the wage system], *Rodongja*, December 1955: 21–23; Kim Wŏnbong, "Roryŏk munjeŭi orhŭn haegyŏrŭn kŭmhu kyŏngje kŏnsŏl-esŏ kajang chungyohan munjeŭi hanaida" [One of the most important problems in today's economy is the proper resolution of the labor problem], *Kyŏngje kŏnsŏl*, March 1956: 39–49; Kim Unjong, "Hyŏnsigi roryŏkmunjeŭi orhŭn haegyŏrŭl wihayŏ" [Toward the proper resolution of the contemporary labor problem], *Kyŏngje kŏnsŏl*, November 1959: 29–32.

7. Anonymous, "Imgŭn tŭnggŭpp'yo" [Wage scale charts], *Kyŏngje chisik,* April 1960: 10.

8. For a story written by a worker, see Ko Sunhŭi, "Nyŏnmal sanggŭmŭl padŭn kippŭm" [The happiness of receiving a year-end bonus], *Chosŏn nyŏsŏng*, January 1955: 20–21. See also Anonymous, "Kajŏng mada p'iyŏnanŭn sanggŭm t'an kippŭm" [The happiness of receiving bonuses in every home], *Rodong sinmun*, December 28, 1955: 3; Anonymous, "Nyŏnmal sanggŭmŭl padŭn kippŭm" [The happiness of receiving a year-end bonus], *Rodong sinmun*, December 28, 1954: 3.

9. Anonymous, untitled cartoon, *Ch'ŏngnyŏn saenghwal*, February 1957: 28–29.

10. Or, conversely, it was sometimes measured as the amount of time required to produce a certain commodity. For a basic explanation, see "Rodong kijunnyang" [Labor output norms], *Kyŏngje chisik*, August 1956: 116–117.

11. Ch'oe Kŭksu, "Rodong kijunnyangŭn ŏttŏge chejŏnghanŭnga?" [How is the kijunnyang set?], *Kyŏngje chisik*, May 1960: 26.

12. Ri Myŏngwŏn, *Kŏnsŏl chagŏppanjangŭi sugi*, 36–38.

13. Pong P'iryun, "Kyŏurŭl ap'dun chut'aek kŏnsŏljang" [At a construction site with winter approaching], *Rodong sinmun*, November 2, 1956: 2.

14. See the opening two pages of Anonymous, "Rodong saengsan nŭngnyurŭi pudanhan changsŏngŭi pŏpch'ik" [The principle of continuously raising the productivity rates of labor], *Kyŏngje kŏnsŏl* 2 (1956): 126–132.

15. Ibid., 127.

16. Pak Kyŏngdŭk, "Kŏnsŏl kiŏpsodŭl-esŏ chŭngsan kyŏngjaeng undongŭi kwangbŏmhan chŏn'gaerŭl wihayŏ" [Widely promoting production increase competitions among construction enterprises], *Kyŏngje kŏnsŏl* 6 (1955): 60–69.

17. Kim Yŏnch'ol, *PukHanŭi sanŏphwawa kyŏngje chŏngch'aek*: chapter 3. See also Rim Hakchun, "Chŭngsan kyŏngjaeng undongŭl poda nop'ŭn sujun-ero" [Toward higher levels of production competitions], *Rodongja*, January 1955: 12–15. For a Kim Il Sung speech on this point, see "Modŭn munje haegyŏl-esŏ chungsim korirŭl t'ŭnt'ŭnhi t'ŭrŏ chapko kŏgi-e ryŏngnyangŭl chipchunghaja" [Let us focus our strength on firmly grasping the key point to solve all problems], *Collected Works*, vol. 24 (1959): 193–222.

18. Pak Kyŏngdŭk, "Kŏnsŏl kiŏpsodŭl-esŏ chŭngsan kyŏngjaeng undongŭi kwangbŏmhan chŏn'gaerŭl wihayŏ."

19. Ibid., 68.

20. Ri Kisŏk, "Sahoejuŭi kyŏngjaeng-e taehan ch'onghwa p'yŏngga saŏbŭl ŏttoge halgŏsinga" [How should we do review assessments in socialist competitions?], *Rodongja*, November 1965: 44–45.

21. Anonymous, untitled cartoon, *Rodongja*, July 1955: 57.

22. Anonymous, untitled cartoon, *Ch'ŏngnyŏn saenghwal*, June 1956, collection of Russian State Library.

23. For an open letter with this complaint, see Yanghwa susan saŏpso, "Tangsindŭrŭi kyehoek midalsŏngŭn uridŭl-ege ŏttŏn yŏnghyangŭl chugo innŭnga?" ["What type of impact does your inability to fulfill your plan have on us?"], *Rodongja*, December 1954: 46–47.

24. Ri Myŏngryong, "Rimŏp pumun chŭngsan kyŏngjaeng undong-esŏ nat'anan myŏt kaji kyŏrham-e taehayŏ" [Several shortcomings that have arisen in the production competition movement in the forestry industry], *Rodongja*, October 1955: 20–23.

25. Ri Ponghak, "Kiŏpsodŭl-esŏŭi kyehoek chaksŏng-e taehan tangjŏk chido" [Party leadership of enterprise-level planning], *Kŭlloja* 133 (September 1956): 112.

26. Chŏng Sunjŏng, "Ch'ŏnnaeri Ssement'ŭ kongjangŭn oe rakhuhayŏnnŭnga?" [Why has the Chonnaeri Cement Factory fallen behind?], *Kyŏngje kŏnsŏl* 9 (1954): 109.

27. Chosŏn rodongdang, *Kyŏngje sangsik: kongŏp, nongŏp, sangŏp* [A primer on economics: Industry, agriculture, and commerce] (Pyongyang: Chosŏn rodongdang ch'ulp'ansa, 1960), 3–9.

28. For contracts, see Ch'oe Taesik, "Kyeyak kyuyul wiban hyŏnsang sigŭphi t'oech'ihara" [Let's urgently end the phenomenon of violating contracts], *Kyŏngje kŏnsŏl*, June 1958: 66; Anonymous, "Sahoejuŭi ha-esŏŭi kach'i pŏpch'ik" [The

principles of value under socialism], *Kyŏngje kŏnsŏl*, January 1956: 112–114; Ri Sŏngnin, "Uri nara-e issŏsŏŭi kukchŏng kakyŏk ch'egyeŭi kaep'yŏngwa kŭŭi kibon naeyong" [The reorganization and basic nature of the state pricing system in our country], *Kyŏngje kŏnsŏl*, February 1957: 33–44.

29. Anonymous, "Rodong kijunnyangŭl ŏnŭ kŏtput'ŏ ŏttŏn pangbŏpŭro chaesajŏnghal kŏsinga?" [From what and how can the labor output norm be reconfigured?], *Kyŏngje chisik*, January 1960: 45–46. See also Kim Kiok, "Roryŏk kijunnyangŭi chŏnghwakhan sajŏngŭl wihan myŏt kaji munje" [Problems in setting an accurate labor output norm], *Rodongja*, January 1955: 40–42.

30. Ch'oe Kŭksu, "Rodong kijunryangŭn ŏttŏke chechŏnghanŭnga?" [How are labor norms established?], *Kyŏngje chisik*, May 1960: 26.

31. Anonymous, "Rodong kijunnyangŭl ŏnŭ kŏtput'ŏ ŏttŏn pangbŏpŭro chaesajŏnghal kŏsinga?," 45.

32. Yun Changsŏp, "Saeroun rodong kijunnyangŭl ch'angjohayŏ rodong saengsan nŭngryurŭl nop'yŏtta" [Creating new labor output norms and raising the productive capacity of labor], *Kyŏngje chisik*, February 1960: 30–32.

33. This review did not resolve the challenge of ascertaining this fundamental piece of information for planners. See Ra Chinch'an, "Kongŏp kiŏpso-esŏ rodong saengsan nŭngryul kyehoegŭl ŏttŏkye sewŏya hanŭnga?," *Kyŏngje chisik*, February 1960: 18–22.

34. Kim Unjong, "Hyŏnsigi roryŏkmunjeŭi orhŭn haegyŏrŭl wihayŏ," 12.

35. Ri Ilgyŏng, "Kyŏngje saŏp-esŏŭi yuil kwallijewa tangjŏk t'ongjeŭi kanghwarŭl wihayŏ" [For the strengthening of party control and single-person management in economic enterprises], *Kŭlloja* 118 (September 1955): 53–64, 59.

36. Ibid., 53–64.

37. Ri Ponghak, "Kiŏpsodŭl-esŏŭi kyehoek chaksŏng-e taehan tangjŏk chido," 110–119.

38. Kim Chungsam, "Sŏlbi riyongnyul chegowa roryŏk chŏlyagŭl wihan t'ujaeng-esŏŭi tang tanch'edŭrŭi yŏkhal" [The role of party organizations in the struggle to raise the usage rate of equipment and the saving of labor], *Kŭlloja* 128 (July 1956): 73–85.

39. Kim Kwansŏp, "Chep'umŭi chil chegorŭl wihan Chagangdo tang tanch'eŭi saŏp kyŏnghŏm" [The experience of party organizations in Chagang province in raising the quality of products], *Tangganbudŭl-ege chunŭn ch'amgo jaryo*, April 1959: 37–45.

40. Ri Ilgyŏng, "Kyŏngje saŏp-esŏŭi yuil kwallijewa tangjŏk t'ongjeŭi kanghwarŭl wihayŏ," 53–64.

41. For a general treatment of women's labor beyond 1965, see Kim Aesil, "Yŏsŏngŭi kyŏngje hwaldong," in Son Pongsuk, Yi Kyŏngsuk, Yi Onjuk, and Kim Aesil, eds., *PukHanŭi yŏsŏng saenghwal: yirongwa silje* [The lives of North Korean women: Theory and reality] (Seoul: Nanam, 1991), 173–220.

42. This approach is already featured before the armistice is a month old. See O Ikkŭn, "Kongjangŭl pokkuhanŭn nyŏsŏngdŭl" [The women resurrecting factories], *Chosŏn nyŏsŏng*, September 1953: 29–34.

43. Chosŏn chungang t'ongsinsa, *Chosŏn chungang nyŏn'gam, 1961* [The Korean national yearbook, 1961] (Pyongyang: Chosŏn chungang t'ongsinsa, 1962), 341.

44. Kim Ryak, "Nyŏsŏng roryŏk inip-esŏ irryŏnŭi p'yŏnhyangdŭrŭl sigŭphi sijŏnghaja" [Let's rapidly improve the many biases in recruiting women's labor power], *Kyŏngje kŏnsŏl*, November 1958: 64–65.

45. Ri Myŏngwŏn, *Kŏnsŏl chagŏppanjangŭi sugi*, 55–66.

46. Ibid., 56.

47. Ibid., 58.

48. Kim Pyŏngnin, "Kŭllojadŭrŭi puyang kajogŭl chikchang-e kwangbŏmhi iniphaja" [Let's broadly bring workers' dependent family members into the workplace], *Rodong sinmun*, January 7, 1956: 1; Anonymous, "Roryŏk munjeŭi olhŭn haegyŏrŭl wihayŏ" [For the proper resolution of the labor problem], *Rodong sinmun*, January 16, 1956: 2. More piecemeal efforts existed prior to 1956. Paek Chongchŏn, "Puyang kajoktŭri ilhanda" [Dependent family members are at work], *Rodong sinmun*, December 13, 1955: 3.

49. Kim Pyŏngnin, "Kŭllojadŭrŭi puyang kajogŭl chikchang-e iniphaja."

50. Kim Ŭnnyŏn, "Kŏnsŏljang-e nasŏn puyang kajoktŭl" [Dependent family members coming out to construction sites], *Rodong sinmun*, January 23, 1956: 3.

51. Pak Yongno, "Puyang kajoktŭllo kusŏngdoen saengsan chohap" [A production co-op formed by dependent family members], *Rodong sinmun*, January 31, 1957: 2; Kim Chŏnghye, "Saenghwarŭi sae kyosil" [Life's new classroom], *Choson nyŏsŏng*, March 1956: 12–14; Anonymous, "Puyang kajoktŭri chikchang-e anch'aktoego ittda" [Dependent family members are settling in to work], *Rodong sinmun*, February 12, 1956: 1.

52. Anonymous, "Puyang kajoktŭri ilhanda" [Dependent family members are working], *Rodong sinmun*, December 13, 1955: 3.

53. An Sangnok, "Puyang kajogŭl saengsan-e iniphagikkaji" [Until dependent families enter production], *Rodong sinmun*, February 3, 1959: 2.

54. Kim Kyeryong, "Puyang kajok nyŏsŏng roryŏgŭl hyŏptong chohap-e iniphaja" [Let's get dependent families' female labor into cooperatives], *Rodong sinmun*, May 30, 1957: 2.

55. Kim Pyŏngnin and Han Myŏngnok, "Puyang kajoktŭl-ege chagŏp chogŏnŭl ŏttŏke pojanghayŏ chugo innŭnga?" [How are the work conditions for dependent family members being guaranteed?], *Rodong sinmun*, March 18, 1956: 3.

56. An Sangnok, "Puyang kajogŭl saengsan-e iniphagikkaji."

57. Paek Sangbŏm, "Puyang kajoktŭri ilhanda: rodongŭn haengbokhada" [Dependent family members are working: Labor brings happiness], *Rodong sinmun*, January 7, 1956: 3.

58. On motherhood discourse, Yi Migyŏng, "PukHanŭi mosŏngideollogi: 'Chosŏn nyŏsŏng' naeyong punsŏgŭl chungsimŭro'" [North Korea's motherhood ideology: "A study of the content of *Women of Korea*"], *Han'guk chŏngch'i woegyosa nonch'ong* 26.1 (2004): 391–422.

59. Pak Yŏngja, "PukHanŭi yŏsŏng chŏngch'i: 'hyŏksinjŏk nodongja—hyŏngmyŏngjŏk ŏmŏni' roŭi chaegusŏng'" [North Korea's women politics:

"Reformed workers—remaking reformed workers into revolutionary mothers"], *Sahoe kwahak yŏngu* 13.1 (2005): 356–389.

60. Suzy Kim, *Everyday Life in the North Korean Revolution, 1945–1950* (Ithaca, NY: Cornell University Press, 2013), 196; Suzy Kim, "Revolutionary Mothers: Women in the North Korean Revolution, 1945–1950," *Comparative Studies in Society and History* 52.4 (2010): 742–767.

61. Kim Ch'ŏrung, "Rodong ilgaŭi ŏmŏni" [A working family's mother], *Chosŏn nyŏsŏng*, February 1965: 117.

62. Central Statistical Board under the State Planning Commission of the DPRK, *Statistical Returns of National Economy of the Democratic People's Republic of Korea, 1946–1960* (Pyongyang: Foreign Languages Publishing House, 1961), 123.

63. Pak Chongha, "Ŭnhaengŭn nyŏsŏngdŭr-ege maeu chŏkhaphan saŏp pumun ida" [Banks are a work sector extremely suitable for women], *Rodong sinmun*, August 14, 1958: 4.

64. Kim Wŏnsuk, "Sahoejuŭi kŏnsŏrŭi piyakchŏk paljŏngwa roryŏk munje" [The remarkable development of socialist construction and the labor problem], *Kŭlloja* 156 (November 1958): 31–35.

65. "Everything for the Postwar Rehablition and Development of the National Economy," *Kim Il Sung: Works* (Pyongyang: Foreign Languages Publishing House, 1981), vol. 8 (August 5, 1953): 9–54, 39. "Weak people": see "Nyomaeng chojiktŭrap'-e nasŏnŭn myŏtkaji kwaŏp-e taehayŏ" [On several tasks facing the Women's Union organizations], *Collected Works*, vol. 35 (September 2, 1965): 415–426; "Sahoejuŭi kŏnsŏrŭi saeroun anyangŭl wihayŏ nasŏnŭn myŏtkajimunje" [Several problems that have arisen in newly promoting socialist construction], *Collected Works*, vol. 22 (September 25, 1958): 362; and "Nongch'on-e taehan roryŏkchiwŏnsaŏbŭl chŏninminjŏk undongŭro pŏrrimyŏ kŏnsŏl-e taehan chido ch'egyerŭl koch'ilde taehayŏ" [On launching the labor support for villages into a national movement and correcting the leadership system of construction], *Collected Works*, vol. 30 (January 7, 1963): 185–209, 195. None of these was reprinted in *Rodong sinmun*.

66. Anonymous, "Ŏnje kkaji chikchangŭl korŭlgŏsinga?" [When will you choose to work?], *Chosŏn nyŏsŏng*, October 1958: 8; "Kajŏng-e p'amut'innŭn nyŏsŏng" [Women buried at home], *Rodong sinmun*, April 6, 1955: 3. See also Kim Ryak, "Nyŏsŏng roryŏk inip-esŏ irryŏnŭi p'yŏnhyangdŭrŭl sigŭphi sijŏnghaja."

67. See the covers of the following issues of *Chosŏn nyŏsŏng*: truck factory, December 1960; bricklaying, July 1955; soldier, February 1963; chemical institute, March 1957; welder, April 1961; tractor drivers, January 1964.

68. These photos include, for Pyongyang: Han Sihwan, "P'yŏngyang changyu kongjang-esŏ saengsan toen kakchong singnyo kagongp'umdŭl" [Various types of processed food goods from the Pyongyang Food Factory], *Rodong sinmun*, July 8, 1958: 2; for Sinŭiju: Hong Sŏkp'yo, "Tajong tayanghan singnyo kagongp'umŭl saengsan" [The production of various processed food products], *Rodong sinmun*, July 11, 1958: 1; Chu Hyŏngdo, untitled photograph, August 6, 1958: 2; for Kaesŏng: Hong Sŏkp'yo, untitled photograph, *Rodong sinmun*, November 12, 1958: 3; for Sunch'on:

Anonymous, "Kagong panwŏndŭrŭi yungnyu kagong changmyŏn" [A scene of a worker processing meat], *Rodong sinmun*, March 19, 1959: 5.

69. Kim Chich'ang, "Saero ipha toen sangp'umŭl chŏngnihago innŭn kugyŏng sŏp'yŏngyang paekhwajŏm ilkkundŭl" [Workers at the west Pyongyang department store arranging newly arrived goods], *Rodong sinmun*, October 5, 1954: 3; Anonymous, "Chŏnhu ne pŏntchaeŭi mulga inha!" [The fourth time since the end of the war that goods have been reduced!], *Rodong sinmun*, August 2, 1955: 5; Han Sihwan, "Inha toen kagyŏgŭro munbanggurŭl sanda" [Buying the stationery goods that have been reduced in price], *Rodong sinmun*, April 16, 1956: 1.

70. For Pyongyang Porcelain Factory, see Ri Taeyŏng and Hong Sŏkp'yo, "Tayanghago chil chohŭn tojagirŭl tŏ manhi saengsanhagi wihayŏ" [To produce more and better porcelain], *Rodong sinmun*, November 27, 1959: 3. For a nonsegregated porcelain factory, see Anonymous, "Yesulsŏng nop'ŭn kongyep'um saengsanŭl hwaktae" [Increasing the production of highly artistic artisanal goods], *Rodong sinmun*, May 7, 1958: 3.

71. Han Sŏnggŏl, untitled photograph, *Ch'ŏllima*, November 1962: 66–67.

72. This figure is widely repeated with slightly different definitions. See Kim Oksun, "Kajŏng puindŭrŭn kanae chagŏp-e chŏkkŭk ch'amgahaja" [Let housewives enthusiastically participate in household labor], *Chosŏn nyŏsŏng*, April 1960: 12–13; and Anonymous, "Kajŏng puindŭri saengsannodong-e ch'amgahanŭn kŏsŭn chasingwa nararŭl wihayŏ choŭn irida" [The participation of housewives in productive labor is good for them and the country], *Rodongja sinmun*, March 23, 1960: 2.

73. Ri Myŏngwŏn, *Kŏnsŏl chagŏppanjangŭi sugi*, 65.

74. These reports began early, such as Editorial, "Taejung sobip'um saengsan mit konggŭp saŏbŭi kaesŏn kanghwarŭl wihayŏ" [To improve and strengthen the production and supply of mass consumer goods], *Rodong sinmun*, December 6, 1956: 2.

75. Ibid.

76. Anonymous, "Hyangsang toenŭn uri saenghwal" [Our rising living standards], *Chosŏn nyŏsŏng*, August 1957: 34–35; Kim In'gon, "Kkaekkŭt'ago kapssan ŭmsigŭro irŭm nan siktang" [A clean cafeteria with cheap food], *Rodong sinmun*, January 9, 1957: 3.

77. Cabinet Decision no. 122 in 1954 recognized the centrality of day care for women's labor conditions and called for a reorganization of its administration. "Yuch'iwŏn saŏbŭl kaesŏn kanghwa hal te taehan naegak chisi palp'yo" [The release of the cabinet decision regarding the improvement and strengthening of day care], *Rodong sinmun*, October 4, 1954: 1.

78. The figure of a twenty-seven-fold increase comes from Chungang t'onggyeguk, ed., *Chosŏn minju inmin konghwaguk inmin kyŏngje mit munhwa paljŏn, t'onggyejip, 1946–57* [The DPRK statistical report on economic and cultural development] (Pyongyang: Kungnip ch'up'ansa, 1958), graph 28: 12. Even in the early 1960s, the position and allocation of day care spots was an issue in the call for reforms in the way neighborhoods were designed. See Ri Sungŏn, *Chut'aek soguyŏk kyehoek* [Residential neighborhood planning] (Pyongyang: Kungnip kŏnsŏl ch'ulp'ansa, 1963), 71–72, 89–91.

79. Anonymous, "T'agaso sisŏl hwakchang" [Expanding day care facilities], *Rodong sinmun*, April 30, 1955: 1; "Kŭmnyŏn-e kukka yuch'iwŏni changnyŏn 9wŏl siljŏk poda 6 paero nŭrŏ kanda" [The September results for national day care facilities increased by six times over last year], *Rodong sinmun*, June 6, 1959: 5; Anonymous, "Chinan 5 nyŏn tongan-e t'agaso sunŭn 32.5pae, yuch'iwŏn sunŭn 29.6paero!" [In the past five years, day care 32.5 times more and nurseries, 29.6 times], *Rodongja sinmun*, August 3, 1962: 3.

80. Kim Sangchŏl, "T'ŭresŭt'ŭwa yuch'iwŏn" [Work teams and day care], *Rodong sinmun*, February 18, 1957: 3.

81. Chŏn Yŏng, "Mosŏng rodongjawa t'agaso" [Mother-workers and day care], *Rodong sinmun*, March 19, 1956: 3.

82. For a discussion of some of these problems, see Hyŏn T'aesŏp, "T'agaso, yuch'iwon kwalli saŏp-e sahoejŏk kwansimŭl nop'ija" [Let's raise the social awareness of the task of running nurseries and day care facilities], *Rodong sinmun*, December 7, 1959: 3.

83. For an early example at the Hŭngnam Fertilizer Factory, with a photograph by Chang Hyeja, see "Mosŏng rodongjadŭl-e taehan paeryŏ" [The care toward mother-workers], *Rodong sinnmun*, October 19, 1954: 3. The cooperativization of agriculture created a very different day care dynamic; for one example, see Cho Kŭnwŏn, "Sikhyŏn nongop hyŏptong chohabŭi t'agaso" [The Sikhyŏn agricultural cooperative's nursery], *Rodong sinmun*, November 28, 1955: 3.

84. For a photo spread of an ideal day care, see Chu Hyŏngdo, "Pon'gung hwahak kongjang tagaso" [The Pon'gung Chemical Factory's day care], *Chosŏn nyŏsŏng*, March 1956: 24–25. For an account of one day in a day care, see "T'agasoŭi haru" [One day in a day care], *Rodong sinmun*, May 27, 1955: 3. Other stories of "ideal" day care include the following: in Pyongyang Textile Factory, Pak Chaehwan, "Ttattŭthan p'ŭmsok" [A warm embrace], *Rodong sinmun*, June 1, 1956: 3; in Pyongyang Rubber Factory, Anonymous, "Hwalbarhi unyŏngdoenŭn t'agasowa yuch'iwŏn" [Lively-run day care and nurseries], *Rodong sinmun*, November 25, 1959: 3; and for what came to be known as Ch'ŏllima day care, Ri T'aeyŏng, "Ch'ŏllima t'agaso" [Ch'ŏllima day care], *Rodongja sinmun*, February 2, 1962: 3.

85. Hyŏn Am, "Tu chikchang t'agasoŭi siljŏng" [The situation of two workplace day care facilities], *Rodong sinmun*, July 15, 1956: 5.

86. Hyŏn T'aesŏp, "T'agaso, yuch'iwon kwalli saŏp-e sahoejŏk kwansimŭl nop'ija."

87. Chŏng Chŏnghyŏp,"Ŏmŏnidŭri chojikhan yuch'iwŏn" [A day care organized by mothers], *Chosŏn nyŏsŏng*, January 1956: 13. Similarly, women within work units were reported to launch new day care facilities on their own initiative, freeing up labor. For one construction unit's experience, see Kim Sangch'ŏl, "T'ŭ resŭt'ŭ wa yuch'iwŏn" [Trusts and nurseries], *Rodong sinmun*, February 18, 1957: 3. Economists appreciated the financial effects of self-responsible day care.

88. For an extended ideal day care story, see Ri Kŭmok, "Mobŏm t'agaso" [Model day care], *Chosŏn nyŏsŏng*, May 1964: 39–42.

89. Even poets penned odes to construction. See Pak Munsŏ, "P'yŏngyang kŏnsŏl sich'o" [The start of Pyongyang construction], *Rodong sinmun*, May 8, 1955: 3.

90. Anonymous, "Sin Kyesŭng kajŏnggwa kŭŭi ap'at'ŭ" [Sin Kyesŭng's family and apartment], *Chosŏn nyŏsŏng*, December 1956: 19.

91. Anonymous, "Chun'gong toen rodongja appat'ŭ" [A completed workers' apartment], *Rodong sinmun*, December 29, 1954: 1.

92. For an elevated perspective, see Yu Hyŏngmok's photograph of a worker's dormitory, "Saero kŏnsŏl toen hwanghae chech'ŏlsso rodongjadŭrŭi hapsuk" [The newly built dormitory of the Hwanghae steel workers], *Rodong sinmun*, November 21, 1959: 2. For an elevated perspective of Moranbong neighborhood under construction, see Anonymous, "Moranbong kuyŏk kirimdong-e kŏnsŏldoenŭn t'ap'yŏng tach'ŭng chut'aek kŏnsŏljang" [The construction site of large-size mass housing being built in the Kirim neighborhood of Moranbong], *Rodong sinmun*, October 19, 1960: 2. For a completed Stalin Street, see Hong Sŏkpy'o, "Sŭttallin kŏriŭi ilbuin Sach'angdong negŏri-esŏ" [At the Stalin Street intersection of Sach'andong], *Rodong sinmun*, November 2, 1958: 2.

93. Anonymous, "Pyongyangsi pokku kŏnsŏl sokpo" [Pyongyang reconstruction updates], *Rodong sinmun*, March 30, 1955: 1.

94. Ch'ŏn Kich'ŏl, "Chut'aek kŏnsol soktorŭl chego" [Raising the construction speed of housing], *Rodong sinmun*, October 17, 1955: 2.

95. Anonymous, "Chut'aek kŏnsol soktorŭl chego" [Raising the construction speed of housing], *Rodong sinmun*, November 14, 1955: 1.

96. Haeju: Anonymous, "Haejusiŭi saeroun myŏnmo" [The new face of Haeju], *Rodong sinmun*, November 21, 1954: 3; Sinŭiju: Anonymous, "Chibang tosidŭrŭi sae myŏnmo" [The new face of provincial cities], *Rodong sinmun*, December 11, 1954: 3; Anonymous, "Pokku kŏnsŏl toenŭn Sinŭijusi" [Reconstructing Sinŭiju], *Rodong sinmun*, October 5, 1955: 1; Kaesŏng: Anonymous, "Chibang tosidŭrŭi sae myŏnmo" [The new faces of provincial towns], *Rodong sinmun*, December 11, 1954: 3; Anonymous, "Onŭrŭi Kaesŏngsi" [Today's Kaesŏng], *Rodong sinmun*, June 11, 1955: 1; Kanggye: Anonymous, "Chaegŏn toenŭn Kanggyesi" [Reconstructing Kanggye], *Rodong sinmun*, December 21, 1954: 3; Ch'ŏngjin: Anonymous, "Pokku kŏnsŏl toenŭn Ch'ŏngjinsi" [Ch'ŏngjin under reconstruction], *Rodong sinmun*, May 19, 1955: 1; Sariwŏn: Anonymous, "Sariwŏnsi-e irŏsŏnŭn sae kŏnmuldŭl" [New buildings arising in Sariwŏn], *Rodong sinmun*, May 28, 1955: 1; Wŏnsan: Anonymous, "Hanggu tosi—Wŏnsansi-e irŏsŏnŭn sae kŏnmuldŭl" [Port city—new buildings arising in Wonsan], *Rodong sinmun*, June 8, 1955: 1; Hyesan: Anonymous, "Hyesansi-esŏ konggong kŏnmul mit chut'aek kŏnsŏl kongsa hwalbal" [Public building and housing construction thriving in Hyesan city], *Rodong sinmun*, September 29, 1955: 1; Hamhŭng: Anonymous, "Arŭmdaun Hamhŭngsirŭl kŏnsŏl" [The construction of beautiful Hamhŭng], *Rodong sinmun*, April 29, 1955: 3.

97. Kim Taeŭl, "Chungyohan kŏsŭn sujaga anira saram ida" [The important thing is not numbers but people], *Chosŏn kija*, September 1959: 31–33. For a specific example of critique, see Hyŏn P'ilhun, "Sahoejuŭi kŏnsŏrŭi kojowa ch'ulp'an podo

ilgundŭrŭi kwaŏp" [The high tide of constructing socialism and the task of workers in the publishing sector], *Chosŏn kija*, December 1958: 10–17.

98. For a history of housing in the south, see Chŏn Namil, *Han'guk chugŏŭi sahoesa* [A social history of South Korean housing] (P'aju: Tol Pegae, 2008).

99. Greg Castillo, *Cold War on the Home Front: The Soft Power of Midcentury Design* (Minneapolis: Minnesota University Press, 2009); Susan E. Reid, "The Khrushchev Kitchen: Domesticating the Scientific-Technological Revolution," *Journal of Contemporary History* 40.2 (2005): 289–316; Susan E. Reid, "Cold War in the Kitchen: Gender and the De-Stalinization of Consumer Taste in the Soviet Union under Khrushchev," *Slavic Review* 61.2 (2002): 211–252.

100. Roy Richard Grinker, *Korea and Its Futures: Unification and the Unfinished War* (New York: St. Martin's Press, 2000).

101. Nancy Kwak shows how this became a working assumption of American foreign aid work in Asia but that forms of finance were just as central. See Nancy Kwak, *A World of Homeowners: American Power and the Politics of Housing Aid* (Chicago: University of Chicago Press, 2015).

102. For a study of the interactions between North and South Korean texts, see Jonathon Kief, "Reading Seoul in Pyongyang: Cross-border Mediascapes in Early Cold War North Korea," *Journal of Korean Studies* 26.2 (2021): 325–348.

103. Even photographs of South Korean newspaper front pages were reproduced. See "Tong-a ilbo-esŏ" [In the Tong-a daily], *Rodong sinmun*, April 5, 1958: 3.

104. Chŏn Namil, *Han'guk chugŏŭi sahoesa*.

105. Anonymous, "Ragwŏngwa chiok" [Heaven and Hell], *Rodongja sinmun*, April 29, 1959: 4.

106. Pak Ch'angsu, "Ŏnŭ han sirŏpchaŭi iyagi" [The story of one unemployed], *Rodongja* (January 1957): 30–33.

107. Ri Ch'unsu, "Sudori ŏmma" [Sudol's mother], *Chosŏn nyŏsŏng*, January 1962: 38–39.

108. Ch'oe Yŏnggŭn, "Kariul su omnŭn hyŏnsil" [Unconcealable realities], *Hwasal*, September 1963: back cover.

CHAPTER FIVE

1. Kim Yŏnch'ol, *PukHanŭi sanŏphwa kyŏngje chŏngch'aek*, 245–320. Kim Ŭisun, "Minju sudo chut'aek kŏnsŏl-esŏŭi ildae hyŏksin" [For a complete renovation of the democratic capital's house construction], *Kŭlloja* 148 (March 1958): 76.

2. Editorial, "Sŏlgye-esŏ yebi t'amgunŭn kŏnsŏl wŏn'ga chŏhaŭi chungyo kori" [Searching for savings in design is an important key to lowering overall construction costs], *Rodong sinmun*, June 4, 1957: 1.

3. In the intra-elite jockeying of 1956, Kim Sŭnghwa and Ri P'ilgyu had been critical of Kim's personality cult. See James F. Person, "'We Need Help from Outside': The North Korean Opposition Movement of 1956," *Cold War International History Project Working Paper 52* (August 2006): 28–35; Balàzs Szalontai, *Kim Il*

Sung in the Khrushchev Era: Soviet-DPRK Relations and the Roots of North Korean Despotism, 1953–1964 (Stanford, CA: Stanford University Press, 2005): 94–96; Andrei Lankov, *From Stalin to Kim Il Sung: The Formation of North Korea, 1945–1960* (New Brunswick, NJ: Rutgers University Press, 2002): 156–160. For a summary of 1950s politics, see Sŏ Tongman, "1950 nyŏndae PukHanŭi chŏngch'i kaldŭnggwa ideollogi sanghwang" [The situation of political conflict and ideology in 1950s North Korea], in *PukChosŏn yŏn'gu* [Research on North Korea] (Seoul: Ch'angbi, 2010): 122–168.

4. See Pak Kŭmch'ŏl, "Kibon kŏnsŏl saŏbŭl kaesŏnhal de taehayŏ" [On the improvement of basic construction], *Rodong sinmun*, October 19, 1957: 2–3.

5. Editorial, "Kibon kŏnsŏl saŏp-esŏ hyŏngmyŏngjŏk chŏnhwanŭl irŭk'ira" [Initiate a revolutionary turnaround in basic construction enterprises], *Rodong sinmun*, October 22, 1957: 1.

6. Anonymous, "Kibon kŏnsŏl pumun-esŏ hyŏksini yogu toenda" [Reform is demanded in the basic construction sectors], *Rodong sinmun*, September 14, 1957: 2.

7. *Chosŏn chungang nyŏn'gam, 1963* [The Korean national yearbook, 1963] (Pyongyang: Chosŏn chungang t'ongsinsa, 1964), 343.

8. Ri Myŏngwŏn, *Kŏnsŏl chagŏppanjangŭi sugi*, 44.

9. Florian Urban, *Tower and Slab: Histories of Global Mass Housing* (London: Routledge, 2012).

10. For a sense of the globality of prefab, see *Journal of Housing* 9.4 ("Housing around the World," April 1952), in articles as varied as "Prefabrication System Used in Le Havre Cuts Costs 20 Per cent" (130–131) and "Newfoundland Builds Low Rental Project" (127–128), as well as stories on workers' housing in Yugoslavia (125) and the use of prefab construction in Austria (117); see also Phyllis M. Kelly and Caroline Shillaber, *International Bibliography of Prefabricated Housing* (Cambridge, MA: MIT Press, 1954).

11. For photos of Stalingrad in a domestic exhibition, see Anonymous, "Kŏnch'uk chŏllamhoe sŏnghwang" [A successful architecture exhibition], *Minju Chosŏn*, August 27, 1955: 2. On Germans rebuilding Hamhŭng, see Rüdiger Frank, "Lessons from the Past: The First Wave of Developmental Assistance to North Korea and the German Reconstruction of Hamhŭng," *Pacific Focus* 23.1 (2008): 46–74.

12. Han Chesŏn, "P'yojun sŏlgye-e kwanhan sahoejuŭi kukkadŭl kanŭi hoeŭi-e ch'amga hago" [Participating in the conference of socialist countries on standardized design], *Kŏnch'ukkwa kŏnsŏl*, April 1957: 30. See also a report on an architecture conference in Moscow: Hwang Ŭigŭn, "Ssoryŏn kŏnsŏlja taehoe sosik" [Report on the Soviet architects conference], *Kŏnch'ukkwa kŏnsŏl*, January 1955: 46–49.

13. Editorial, "Sŏlgye ilgundŭl-ege tŏuk nop'un ch'aegimsŏngi yoguŏdoenda" [Greater responsibility is demanded of design workers], *Minju Chosŏn*, October 10, 1955; Editorial, "Sŏlgye-esŏ yebi t'amgunŭn kŏnsŏl wŏn'ga chŏhaŭi chungyo kori."

14. Kim Il Sung, "Ch'ŏn'guk kŏn'ch'ukka mit kŏnsŏlja hoeŭi-esŏ hasin Kim Il Sŏng Wŏnsuŭi yŏnsŏl" [Speech given by Marshal Kim Il Sung at the National Architects and Builders Conference], *Rodong sinmun*, February 4, 1956: 1–3.

15. Song Siyŏm, untitled, *Hwasal* 128 (June 1960): 7.

16. Han Ch'angjin, "Tach'ŭng chut'aek-esŏŭi sae sallim" [The New Living in multistory housing], *Minju Chosŏn*, September 29, 1955: 2.

17. Kim Ungha, "Chut'aek p'yojun sŏlgye saŏp-e chegidoenŭn myŏtkaji munje" [Several problems in the task of standard house designs], *Kŏnch'ukkwa kŏnsŏl*, April 1956: 6–8.

18. Kim Chŏlsu, "Chut'aek kŏnsŏrŭi 10 nyŏn—minju sudo Pyŏngyangŭl chungsimŭro" [Ten years of home construction—focusing on the democratic capital, Pyongyang], *Kŏnch'ukkwa kŏnsŏl*, September 1958: 17. For an overview of types of dwellings, see Ri Sungŏn, *Chut'aek soguyŏk kyehoek* [Residential neighborhood planning] (Pyongyang: Kungnip kŏnsŏl ch'ulp'ansa, 1963): 60–68.

19. As reported in Han Ch'angjin, "Tach'ŭng chut'aek-esŏŭi sae sallim." Sixty-six-square-meter apartments were reported in Han Ch'angjin, "Saenghwal-e dŏuk chŏkhamnan kujoro" [Toward a better living design], *Minju Chosŏn*, August 30, 1956: 2.

20. Kim Ŭngsang, "P'yŏngyangsi kŏnsŏl ilgun yŏlssŏngja hoeŭi-esŏ han kukka kŏnsŏl wiwŏnhoe Kim Ŭngsang wiwŏnjangŭi pogo" [Committee report of national construction committee member Kim Ŭngsang at the conference of Pyongyang construction worker enthusiasts], *Rodong sinmun*, February 13, 1958: 2.

21. Anonymous, "Kim Ilsŏng susang kŏnsŏl pumunŭl chikchŏp chido 18 il-enŭn P'yŏngyangsi sŏlgye ilgundŭlgwa tamhwa" [Premier Kim Il Sung directly guides the construction sector], *Rodong sinmun*, January 19, 1958: 1.

22. Anonymous, "Kim Ilsŏng susang P'yŏngyangsi kŏnsŏljangŭl sich'alhago kŏnsŏl saŏbŭl chido" [Premier Kim Il Sung's inspection of Pyongyang construction sites and his guidance of construction enterprises], *Rodong sinmun*, April 6, 1958: 1.

23. Anonymous, "Tach'ŭng munhwa chut'aek" [Multistoried cultural homes], *Rodong sinmun*, July 13, 1958: 4.

24. This was a wider debate, as can be seen in a publication by a Soviet contributor, whose name is indistinguishable in my copy of the newspaper: "Ssopet'ŭ kŏnch'uk yangsigŭi minjokchŏk t'ŭksŏng" [The national characteristics of Soviet architectural style], *Minju Chosŏn*, July 30, 1955: 4. See also Ri Yŏsŏng, "Uri nara kŏnch'uk-e minjokchŏk yangsigŭl toiphanŭn munje-e kwanhayŏ" [On the problem of introducing national style in our country's architecture], *Munhwa yusan*, January 1957: 13–24; Kim Yongjun, "Uri kŏnch'ugŭi t'uksaegŭl ŏttŏgye sallil kŏsinga?" [How will we save the special features of our architecture?], *Munhwa yusan*, January 1958: 35–36.

25. Yun Ch'angsik, a self-identified artist, wrote a letter to the editor requesting more beautiful buildings that later generations would be proud of; see *Kŏnch'ukkwa kŏnsŏl*, January 1957: 28–29.

26. Early construction did have *ondol*, due to the use of semi-conventional, non-prefab building techniques. Han Ch'angjin, "Saenghwal-e tŏuk chŏkhamhan kujoro" [Toward a structure more appropriate for living], *Minju Chosŏn*, August 30, 1956: 3. Pang Tŏkkŭn noted that they caused coordination difficulties for new-style buildings, in "Haebanghu Chosŏn chut'aek kŏnsŏrŭi kyŏnghom" [Experiences in postwar Korean house building], *Kŏnch'ukkwa kŏnsŏl*, January 1955: 26–31. Kim

Ungha reported that some designers advocated abandoning *ondol* due to these difficulties, in "Chut'aek p'yojun sölgye saŏp-e chegidoenŭn myŏtkaji munje." The technique was introduced at the end of 1958 according to Yang Ryungsung, "Taeyong choripsik ondol pŭllok'urŭl doip" [Prefab *ondol* blocks are widely introduced], *Rodong sinmun*, November 30, 1958: 4. On the early emphasis on radiators and a competition to produce them, see Anonymous, untitled photograph, *Rodong sinmun*, November 9, 1955: 3; Anonymous, "Chagije rajiaedarŭl taeryang saengsan" [Mass production of self-regulating radiators], *Rodong sinnmu*, August 2, 1959: 1.

27. Kim Ungha, "Chut'aek p'yojun sölgye saŏp-e chegidoenŭn myŏtkaji munje"; Sin Sungyŏng, "Chut'aek kŏnsŏrŭi choriphwa-esŏ ŏdŭn sŏnggwawa kyŏnghŏm" [Results and experiences from the prefabricated construction of housing], *Kŏnch'ukkwa kŏnsŏl*, February 1958: 6–8.

28. Anonymous, "Kŏnsŏljang-esŏ ŏmgyŏkhan chedowa chilsŏrŭl hwangniphaja" [Let us establish stricter systems and order in construction sites], *Sŏndongwŏn such'ŏp*, 22 (November 1957): 6–8. For Chagang province, see O Songhak, "Chut'aek kŏnsŏl soktorŭl nop'ija" [Let's raise the speed of building houses], *Rodong sinmun*, October 31, 1957: 2. The Soviet ambassador reported figures for the provinces in 1957 at 67 percent; see "Journal of Soviet Ambassador to the DPRK A. M. Puzanov for 24 October 1957," October 24, 1957, AVPRF F. 0102, Op. 13, Delo 5, Listy 257–307, translated for NKIDP by Gary Goldberg, https://digitalarchive .wilsoncenter.org/document/115945.

29. Kim Il Sung, "Ch'ŏn'guk kŏn'ch'ukka mit kŏnsŏlja hoeŭi-esŏ hasin Kim Il Sŏng Wŏnsuŭi yŏnsŏl."

30. The speech was reproduced in *Kyŏngje kŏnsŏl*, March 1956: 5–22; and in *Kŭlloja* 123 (February 1956): 3–23.

31. Perhaps the most talented at the fine art of using multiple synonyms for criticism would be Kim Ŭisun. See Kim Ŭisun, "Minju sudo chut'aek kŏnsŏl-esŏŭi ildae hyŏksin." See also Kim Sangin, "Kŏnsŏl-esŏ choriphwa sujunŭi chegorŭl wihan che pangdo" [Several methods for raising the levels of prefabrication in construction], *Kyŏngje kŏnsŏl*, December 1957: 13–19.

32. One 1958 article castigated them for shipping in sand from the Ch'ongch'on River instead of mobilizing people to use the city's Taedong River; see Ch'oe Chaeha, "Tosi kŏnsŏl saŏbŭi kailch'ŭngŭi ch'okchinŭl wihayŏ" [Toward advancing one more stage the construction of cities], *Kyŏngje kŏnsŏl*, May 1958: 27.

33. Kim Sangin, "Kŏnsŏl-esŏ choriphwa sujunŭi chegorŭl wihan che pangdo," 14. See also Ri Honggu, "Sŏlge kigwan saŏp kaesŏngwa p'yojun sŏlgye saŏp ch'okchinŭl wihan myŏt kaji munje" [Several problems in promoting the standardization of plans among design institutions], *Kyŏngje kŏnsŏl*, October 1956: 40–49.

34. Kim Tongch'ŏn, "Tangŭi kŏnsŏl chŏngch'aek kwanch'ŏrŭl wihan chŏkkŭkchŏgin komu ch'udongjaga toeja" [Let's become enthusiastic promoters for the implementation of the Party's construction policies], *Rodong sinmun*, February 7, 1958: 4.

35. "Journal of Soviet Ambassador to the DPRK A. M. Puzanov for 29 September 1957," September 29, 1957, History and Public Policy Program Digital Archive,

AVPRF F. 0102, Op. 13, P. 72, Delo 5, Listy 275–300, translated for NKIDP by Gary Goldberg, https://digitalarchive.wilsoncenter.org/document/115661; "Notes from a Conversation between the 1st Secretary of the PRL Embassy in the DPRK with Comrade Pimenov, 1st Secretary of the Embassy of the USSR, on 15.X.1957," October 16, 1957, History and Public Policy Program Digital Archive, Polish Foreign Ministry Archive, obtained for NKIDP by Jakub Poprocki and translated for NKIDP by Maya Latynski, https://digitalarchive.wilsoncenter.org/document/111722.

36. "A Note from Sluczanski to Several Comrades in Warsaw concerning the 'August Group' and the Political Situation in the DPRK," December 9, 1957, History and Public Policy Program Digital Archive, Polish Foreign Ministry Archive, obtained for NKIDP by Jakub Poprocki and translated for NKIDP by Maya Latynski, https://digitalarchive.wilsoncenter.org/document/111730.

37. Pak Wŏngŭn, "Kyŏngje saŏp-e taehan tangjŏk chidoŭi myŏt kaji munje" [Several problems in the Party leadership of economic enterprises], *Kŭlloja* 152 (July 1958): 31–37, 32.

38. For one article titled with this common phrase, see Kim Ch'osŏk, "Ch'ŏngch'i saŏp kwa kyŏngje saŏp ŭi miljŏphan kyŏlhabŭl wihayŏ" [For the conjoining of the political task with the economic task], *Kŭlloja* 163 (June 1959): 15–20.

39. Pak Wŏngŭn, "Kyŏngje saŏp-e taehan tangjŏk chidoŭi myŏt kaji munje," 36.

40. In regard to light industry, see Rim K'yech'ŏl, "Kyŏnggongŏp chep'umŭi chirŭl kyŏljŏngjŏguro kaesŏnhagi wihan tangjŏk chidorŭl kanghwahaja" [Let's strengthen Party leadership to improve decisively the quality of light industrial products], *Tangganbudŭl-ege chunŭn ch'amgo charyo*, April 1959: 30–37.

41. Mun Ch'isu, "Rodong saengsan nŭngnyurŭi chegonŭn sahoejuŭi kŏnsŏl ch'okchinŭi kyŏljŏngjŏk yoin" [Raising the labor productivity rate is the decisive factor in promoting socialist construction], *Kŭlloja*, December 1959: 61–62.

42. Editorial, "Uriŭi minju sudorŭl tŏ arŭmdapko munhwajŏguro kŏnsŏl haja" [Let us build our democratic capital more beautifully and more culturally], *Rodong sinmun*, March 22, 1958: 1.

43. O Ikkŭn, "Chŏryakhan chagŭmŭro 1manyŏ sedaeŭi chut'aegŭl tŏ chiŭl yebirŭl t'am'gu" [Prepping to build ten thousand more housing units with saved capital], *Rodong sinmun*, February 4, 1958: 1.

44. Anonymous, "Chŏryaktoen chagŭmŭrossŏ 318 sedaeŭi chut'aegŭl tŏ chinnŭnda" [Building 318 extra housing units with saved capital], *Rodong sinmun*, February 5, 1958: 2.

45. Anonymous, "Sŏlgye-esŏ p'yŏngbangdang wongarŭl 46% chŏha" [Plans reducing the per pyŏng cost by 46%], *Rodong sinmun*, February 5, 1958: 2.

46. Chang Ikchae, "5 wŏl han tal dongan-e 2,313 sedaeŭi chut'aegŭl choŏp kaesi" [In the single month of May, the task of building 2,313 residences began], *Rodong sinmun*, June 5, 1958: 3.

47. O Ikkŭn, "1man4ch'ŏnyŏ sedaeŭi chut'aegŭl kŏnsŏlhal gŏsŭl kyŏrŭi" [Pledging to build fourteen thousand more housing units], *Rodong sinmun*, June 8, 1958: 1. Plans for longer-term development of Pyongyang were featured in Anonymous, "Tŏuk ungjanghago hwaryŏhage kŏnsŏldoel minju sudo—P'yŏngyangŭi

chŏnmang" [Building the democratic capital more gloriously and more spectacularly—Pyongyang's prospects], *Rodong sinmun*, July 13: 4.

48. Editorial, "Minju sudo P'yŏngyangsi kŏnsŏljadŭlŭi widaehan palgi" [The great iniative of the construction workers of the people's capital, Pyongyang], *Rodong sinmun*, June 6, 1958: 1.

49. Pak Seguk, "Ottŏgye kŏnsŏl soktorŭl nop'yŏnnŭnga?" [How do we raise the speed of construction?], *Rodong sinmun*, August 10, 1958: 5.

50. For one example of finished prefab buildings not being ready for residents due to various problems, see Anonymous, "Wae sarami mottŭlgo innŭnga?" [Why aren't people moving in?], *Rodong sinmun*, September 26, 1958: 2.

51. Anonymous, "Chorip soktorŭl 5 paero" [Five times faster prefab], *Rodong sinmun*, June 5, 1958: 3.

52. Anonymous, "16 pun!" [Sixteen minutes!], *Rodong sinmun*, June 5, 1958: 3.

53. Anonymous, "3 pun'gan chorip undong" [The three-minute prefab movement], *Rodong sinmun*, June 13, 1958: 2.

54. Paek Sangbŏm, "Ilddŏsŏnŭn Chosŏnŭi kisang" [The spirit of Chosŏn springing up], *Rodong sinmun*, September 4, 1958: 5

55. Anonymous, "Konghwaguk naegak-esŏ rodongja, samuwŏn mit tosi chumindŭri chach'ero chut'aegŭl kŏnsŏlhal su ittorok kŭŭi chogŏnŭl pojanghayŏ chul te kwanhan taech'aegŭl kanggu" [The cabinet assures a solution to ensure conditions so each worker, office worker, and urban resident can on their own build a house], *Rodong sinmun*, August 5, 1958: 2.

56. Editorial, "Uriŭi minju sudorŭl tŏ arŭmdapko munhwajŏgŭro kŏnsŏl haja."

57. Hong Chongho, "Ch'aeksang unjŏnsu" [A-behind-the-desk driver], *Hwasal* 115 (December 1959): 3.

58. Kim Ch'ŏnil, "Habu chido-esŏ chojik chŏngch'ijŏk sujunŭl nop'igi wihayŏ" [To raise the organizational and political levels of lower-level officials], *Rodongja sinmun*, July 31, 1959: 1.

59. Anonymous, "Chagal ch'upki-e nagal simindŭl" [City residents come out to dig gravel], *Rodong sinmun*, March 25, 1958: 2.

60. For students, see Anonymous, "Minju sudo kŏnsŏljang-e nasŏn haksaengdŭl" [Students coming out to the democratic capital's construction sites], *Rodong sinmun*, March 6, 1958: 1.

61. Anonymous, "Sudo kŏnsŏrŭi kŭngji" [The pride of the capital's construction], *Chosŏn nyŏsŏng*, September 1958: 32–33.

62. Editorial, "Uriŭi minju sudorŭl tŏ arŭmdapko munhwajŏgŭro kŏnsŏl haja."

63. Anonymous, "Hwadanŭl mandŭlmyŏ kŏrirŭl ch'ŏngso hanŭn Ryŏnhwa-dong 8 dan kajong puindŭl" [Housewives of the eighth group of Ryŏnhwa neighborhood making flower beds and cleaning the street], *Rodong sinmun*, March 22, 1958: 3. See also a photograph of housewives cleaning streets: Anonymous, "Minjok sudo Pyŏngyangŭl dŏuk arŭmdapke" [Making the people's capital, Pyongyang, more beautiful], *Chosŏn* 22 (May 1958): 18–19.

64. Paek Sangbŏm, "Ilddŏsŏnŭn Chosŏnŭi kisang."

65. Kim Ch'unhŭi, "Chut'aek kŏnsŏl-e nasŏn ŏmŏnidŭl" [The mothers coming out to construction sites], *Chosŏn nyŏsŏng*, April 1958: 10–11.

PART THREE

1. Anonymous, "Kyoyangsil: sallimŭl chal chojik haja" [Cultivation room: Let's nicely organize our living], *Rodongja*, March 1958: 40.

CHAPTER SIX

1. The expression "happy family" (*haengbokhan kajŏng*) was a constant. See Anonymous, "Haengbokhan kajŏng" [Happy family], *Chosŏn nyŏsŏng*, January 1959: 30–32. It came in many other variations as well; see, for example, Anonymous, "Rodongja pubuŭi haengbok" [The happiness of a working couple], *Rodong sinmun*, October 28, 1954: 3; Ri Inguk, "Kajonggwa haengbok" [Home and happiness], *Chosŏn nyŏsŏng*, June 1959: 29–31.

2. Florian Urban, *Tower and Slab: Histories of Global Mass Housing* (London: Routledge, 2012).

3. Ri Honggu, "Ch'oesohan sedaeŭi chut'aek p'yojun sŏlgye-e taehan myŏtkaji munje" [Several problems concerning the standardized design for the smallest housing unit], *Kŏnch'ukkwa kŏnsŏl*, April 1956: 17–20.

4. Rural cultural homes (*munhwa chut'aek*) commonly consisted of a single room. Kim Hyŏngsik, "Chŏninminjŏgŭro chŏn'gaedoenŭn danch'ŭng munhwa chut'aek kŏnsŏl-e taehayŏ" [On turning the construction of one-story cultural homes into a national movement], *Kŏnch'ukkwa kŏnsŏl*, February 1958: 13–15.

5. Gunsoo Shin and Inha Jung, "Appropriating the Socialist Way of Life: The Emergence of Mass Housing in Post-war North Korea," *The Journal of Architecture* 21.2 (2016): 159–180, 163.

6. Friedrich Engels, *The Origin of the Family, Private Property and the State* (New York: International Publishers, 1893).

7. Susan E. Reid and David Crowley, eds., *Socialist Spaces: Sites of Everyday Liife in the Eastern Bloc* (New York: Berg, 2002), 1–22.

8. Richard Stites, *Revolutionary Dreams: Utopian Vision and Experimental Life in the Russian Revolution* (New York: Oxford University Press, 1989), 190–204.

9. Steven E. Harris, *Communism on Tomorrow Street: Mass Housing and Everyday Life after Stalin* (Baltimore: Johns Hopkins University Press, 2013).

10. Jie Li, *Shanghai Homes: Palimpsests of Private Life* (New York: Columbia University Press, 2014).

11. Ibid.

12. Yu Yŏngik, *Kabo kyŏngjang yŏn'gu* [Studies on the Kabo reforms] (Seoul: Ilchogak, 1990).

13. In English-language studies, this has long provided one of the main areas of research in Chosŏn history. See Martina Deuchler, *The Confucian Transformation of Korea: A Study of Society and Ideology* (Cambridge, MA: Harvard University Press, 1992); John Duncan, *The Origins of the Chosŏn Dynasty* (Seattle: University of Washington Press, 2000).

14. Michael Kim, "Sub-nationality in the Japanese Empire: A Social History of the Koseki in Colonial Korea, 1910–45," in David Chapman and Karl Jakob Krogness, eds., *Japan's Household Registration System and Citizenship: Koseki, Identification and Documentation* (New York: Routledge, 2014): 111–126; Hong Yanghŭi, "Singminji sigi hojŏk chedowa kajok chedo ŭi pyŏnyong" [Colonial-era changes in the family registration and family systems], *Sahak yŏn'gu* 79 (2005): 167–205.

15. Sungyun Lim, *Rules of the House: Family Law and Domestic Disputes in Colonial Korea* (Oakland: University of California Press, 2019), 1–16.

16. Ibid., 95–118.

17. For a classic treatment of the complexity of the Chosŏn dynasty family, see Kim Tuhŏn, *Han'guk kajok chedo yŏn'gu* [Studies of the Korean family system] (Seoul: Sŏul Taehakkyo ch'ulpanbu, 1968).

18. Vipan Chandra, *Imperialism, Resistance, and Reform in Late Nineteenth-Century Korea* (Berkeley: Institute of East Asian Studies, University of California, 1988), 173–210.

19. Jordan Sand, *House and Home in Modern Japan: Architecture, Domestic Space, and Bourgeois Culture, 1880–1930* (Cambridge, MA: Harvard University Asia Center, 2004).

20. Hyaeweol Choi, "Transpacific Aspiration toward Modern Domesticity in Japanese Colonial-Era Korea," *Journal of Women's History* 30.4 (Winter 2018): 60–83; Kristin Hoganson, "Cosmopolitan Domesticity: Importing the American Dream, 1865–1920," *The American Historical Review* 107.1 (2002): 55–83.

21. Hyaeweol Choi, *New Women in Colonial Korea: A Sourcebook* (New York: Routledge, 2013), 94–139.

22. For another interpretation, see Hong Yang-hee, "Debates about 'A Good Wife and Wise Mother' and Tradition in Colonial Korea," *The Review of Korean Studies* 11.4 (2008): 41–60.

23. Ruth Barraclough, "Red Love and Betrayal in the Making of North Korea: Comrade Hŏ Jŏng-suk," *History Workshop Journal* 77 (Spring 2014): 86–102.

24. Kim Keong-il, "Alternative Forms of Marriage and Family in Colonial Korea," *The Review of Korean Studies* 11.4 (2008): 61–82.

25. Kim Hyegyŏng and Chŏng Chinsŏng, "Haekkajok nonŭiwa singminjijŏk kŭndaesŏng: singminji sigi saeroun kajokkaenyŏmŭi toipkwa pyŏnhyŏng" [Debates on the nuclear family and colonial modernity: The introduction and transformation of new concepts of the family in the colonial era], *Han'guk saehoehak* 35.4 (2001): 213–244.

26. Hyaeweol Choi, *Gender and Mission Encounters in Korea: New Women, Old Ways* (Berkeley: University of California Press, 2009).

27. Kim, Janice C. H., *To Live to Work: Factory Women in Colonial Korea, 1910–1945* (Stanford, CA: Stanford University Press, 2009); Theodore Jun Yoo, *The Politics of Gender in Colonial Korea: Education, Labor, and Health, 1910–1945* (Berkeley: University of California Press, 2008), 95–160.

28. Mun Sojŏng, "Singminji sigi tosigajokkwa yŏsŏng-ŭi hyŏnsil-e kwanhan yŏn'gu" [Studies on the situation of urban families and women in the colonial period], *Hyangt'o Sŏul* 70 (2007): 5–49.

29. This was a concern in the military as well. See Han Haksŏn, "Chibangjuŭi kajokchuŭinŭn chongp'aŭi onsangida" [Localism and famialism are the breeding grounds of factions], *Choguk powirŭl wihaeyŏ*, July 1958: 42–44; Ri Simsuk, "Kajokchuŭi kyŏnghyangŭl yonghŏhaji malmyŏ tang kanbudŭrŭi Tang saenghwarŭl kanghwahaja" [Let us strengthen the Party life of Party members by not allowing familialism], *Rodong sinmun*, April 26, 1958: 2.

30. Pak Yŏngja argues that the Party deliberately promoted the nuclear family for ease of rule, in "PukHanŭi namnyŏ p'yŏngdŭng chŏngch'aegŭi hyŏngsŏnggwa kuljŏl" [The formation and shifts in North Korea's gender equality policy], *Asia yŏsŏng yŏn'gu* 43.2 (2004): 305–307.

31. Partha Chatterjee, *Nationalist Thought and the Colonial World: A Derivative Discourse* (Minneapolis: University of Minnesota Press, 1993).

32. Pak Kŭmsun, "Haengbokhan saesallim" [A happy new life], *Minju Chosŏn*, August 30, 1956: 2; for other examples, see Paek Sangbŏm, "Saejibŭi chuindŭl" [The hosts of new homes], *Rodong sinmun*, July 27, 1957: 3; Sŏk Yŏng, "Saejip" [New home], *Minju Chosŏn*, November 22, 1956: 3; Pak Chaehwan, "Saejip-e tŭnŭn nal" [Moving-in day], *Rodong sinmun*, December 13, 1955: 3. For a photo spread of moving-in day, see Hong Ch'un'gŭn and Pak Sŭngha, "Saejiptŭri" [New homes], *Chosŏn*, January 1958: 12–13.

33. Some attention was paid to rural patterns of living by folklorists and anthropologists, primarily in the context of collectivization, in the journal *Cultural Heritage (Munhwa yusan)*. Ri Chongmok, "Uri nara nongch'on chut'aegŭi ryuhyŏnggwa kŭ hyŏngt'ae: 19 segi chungyŏp—20 segi ch'oyŏp" [Types and forms of our country's rural village houses: From the mid-nineteenth century to the early twentieth century], *Munhwa yusan*, May 1960: 1–22.

34. For one account of such a village, see Ch'oe Pongam, "Yugajokkwa hamkke" [Together with bereaved families], *Chosŏn nyŏsŏng*, July 1957: 18–19. See also Kim Pyŏngno, "Han'guk chŏnjaengŭi injŏk kŭ sonsilkwa PukHan kyegŭpchŏngch'aegŭi pyŏnhwa" [Human losses in the Korean War and changes in North Korean class policy], *T'ongil chŏngch'aek yŏn'gu* 9.1 (2000): 230–231.

35. For one treatment of Polish orphans based on letters, see Intaek Hong, "North Korea's War Orphans: Transnational Education and Post-war Society," *Sources and Methods: A Blog of the History and Public Policy Program*, June 18, 2020, https://www.wilsoncenter.org/blog-post/north-koreas-war-orphans-transnational-education-and-postwar-society.

36. Anonymous, "Pilhaellŭm P'ik'ŭ taet'ongnyŏnggwa Chosŏn chŏnjae koa" [President Wilheim Pieck and Korean war orphans], *Rodong sinmun*, March 15, 1955: 1.

37. Anonymous, "Kim Ilsung susang uri nara chŏnjae koadŭrŭl kyoyuk kyoyanghanŭn hyŏngje kukka kyoyuk ilgundŭrŭl chŏpgyŏn" [Premier Kim Il Sung greets the teachers who educated our war orphans], *Rodong sinmun*, September 13, 1959: 1. For Ch'oe Yonggŏn in Poland, see Anonymous, "Ch'oe Yonggŏn wiwŏnjang p'aran-e innŭn Chosŏn koadŭlgwa sangbong" [Premier Ch'oe Yonggŏn meets Korean orphans in Poland], *Rodong sinmun*, April 28, 1959: 1. For Kim Il and Pak Kŭmch'ŏl, see Anonymous, "Kim Il pususanggwa Pak Kŭmch'ŏl puwiwŏnjangŭl pirot'an tanggwa chŏngbu chidojadŭl Chungguk-esŏ kwigukhan uri nara chŏnjae koadŭrŭl kyŏngnyŏ" [Vice Premier Kim Il, Vice Minister Pak Kŭmch'ŏl, and Party-state leaders meet with war orphans returned from China], *Rodong sinmun*, July 1, 1958: 1. For a delegation to Mongolia, see Anonymous, "Uri chŏngbu taep'yodan Monggo-e innŭn chosŏn chŏnjae koadŭrŭi yayŏngjirŭl pangmun" [Our government delegation visits Korean war orphans' camp in Mongolia], *Rodong sinmun*, July 19, 1956: 2. For photos of Kim in Romania, see *Chosŏn nyŏsŏng*, August 1956: 3. For Ch'oe awarding visiting teachers, see Anonymous, "Ch'oe Yonggŏn wiwŏnjang uri nararŭl pangmunhan Ch'ek'o sŭllobak'iya kisulja, ŭiryo ilgun mit chŏnjae koa kyowŏndŭl-ege hunjang mit medarŭl suyŏ" [Premier Ch'oe Yonggŏn awards medals to visiting Czechoslovakian technicians and war orphan teachers], *Rodong sinmun*, May 4, 1959: 1.

38. Anonymous, "Chogugŭn hangsang uriŭi kasŭm sok-e issŭmnida" [The ancestral land is always in our hearts], *Rodong sinmun*, June 21, 1956: 1

39. Chang Ŭihwan, "Uri nara chŏnjae koadŭrŭl sŏngsim sŏnguiro yangyukhayŏ chun Chungguk inminŭi hyŏngjejŏk uae" [The brotherly love given heartfully in raising our national war orphans], *Rodong sinmun*, May 16, 1958: 3; Anonymous, "Chosŏn chŏnjaengkoadŭrŭl wihan hwansonghoe sŏngdaehoe chinhaeng" [Send-off celebrations held for Chosŏn war orphans], *Rodong sinmun*, June 19, 1958: 2; Anonymous, "P'yŏngyangsi hwansong taehŏe chinhaeng" [Holding welcoming celebrations in Pyongyang], *Rodong sinmun*, December 13, 1958: 4; Chin Posŏ "Chungguk ŏmŏnidŭrŭi puman-esŏ" [In the heart of Chinese mothers], *Chosŏn nyŏsŏng*, May 1954: 46–48.

40. Cho Ŭnjin and Ri Chŏngnyŏ, "Uri-ege nŏmgyŏ talla" [Hand them over to us], *Chosŏn nyŏsŏng*, September 1958: 24–25; Cho Ŭnjin, Ri Chŏngnyŏ, and Rim Pokcha, "Nambanbuŭi modŭn ryurang koadŭrŭl uri-ege nŏmgyŏ tara" [Hand over to us all of the South's homeless orphans], *Chosŏn nyŏsŏng*, September 1958: 24–25.

41. Kang Yŏngja, "Uriŭi sonŭro yuch'iwŏn han'gaerŭl" [With our own hands, one nursery], *Chosŏn nyŏsŏng*, February 1965: 38.

42. Anonymous, "Pult'anŭn nyŏmwŏn" [Burning desire], *Chosŏn nyŏsŏng*, February 1965: 39.

43. Personal tragedy, of course, was a long-held theme. Anonymous, "Kukjejŏk pŏtdŭrŭi p'umsok-esŏ" [In the hearts of our international friends], *Chosŏn nyŏsŏng*, June 1953: 56–59.

44. Editorial, "Aeguk ryŏlsa kajokdŭl-e taehan wŏnhosaŏbŭl chŏn inminjŏk undongŭro!" [Turning the task of supporting the patriotic martyr families into a nationwide movement!], *Rodong sinmun*, April 27, 1957: 1.

45. Paek Sangbŏm, "Ne nammaeŭi ŏmŏniin aeguk yŏlsaŭi anhae" [The wife of a patriotic martyr and mother of four children], *Rodong sinmun*, May 25, 1957: 3;

Kim Yŏnggŏl, "Ŏnjena ap'chang-e sŏsŏ" [Always standing at the vanguard], *Rodong sinmun*, June 6, 1957: 3.

46. Ch'oe Pobu, "5 nammaerŭl k'iumyŏnsŏ" [While raising five children], *Rodong sinmun*, March 8, 1957: 3.

47. Editorial, "Aeguk ryŏlsa kajokkwa hubang kajoktŭl-e taehan sahoejok wŏnhorŭl tŏuk kanghwahaja" [Let's strengthen the social support for the families of patriotic martyrs and rearguard families], *Rodong sinmun*, January 15, 1958: 1. See also Editorial, "Aeguk ryŏlsa kajogŭl-e taehan wŏnho saŏbŭl chŏn inminjŏk undongŭro" [Toward making the task of supporting patriotic martyr families a nationwide movement], *Rodong sinmun*, April 27, 1957: 1.

48. Pak Chongae, "Sahoejuŭi kŏnsŏl-esŏ nyŏsŏngdŭrŭi yŏkharŭl nop'igi wihan sasang saŏbŭl kanghwahal te taehayŏ" [To strengthen the ideological enterprise in order to raise the role of women in socialist construction], *Rodong sinnmun*, April 12, 1957: 2–3.

49. Anonymous, "Yŏsŏt koaŭi ŏmŏni" [A mother of six orphans], *Chosŏn nyŏsŏng*, April 1954, 44.

50. Ch'oe Dalgon, *PukHan Honinbŏp* [North Korean marriage law] (Seoul: Koryŏ taehakkyo ch'ulp'anbu, 1977), 17–23.

51. Cho Ilho, *Chosŏn kajokpŏp* [Korean family law] (Pyongyang: Kyoyuk tosŏ ch'ulp'ansa, 1958), 13.

52. Ibid., 67.

53. Translation by Suzy Kim, *Everyday Life in the North Korean Revolution, 1945–1950*, 185.

54. Ibid., 186–187.

55. David L. Hoffman, *Stalinist Values: The Cultural Norms of Soviet Modernity, 1917–1941* (Ithaca, NY: Cornell University Press, 2003); Eric Naiman, *Sex in Public: The Incarnation of Early Soviet Ideology* (Princeton, NJ: Princeton University Press, 1997); Richard Stites, *The Women's Liberation Movement in Russia: Feminism, Nihilism, and Bolshevism, 1860–1930* (Princeton, NJ: Princeton University Press, 1978); Wendy Z. Goldman, *Women, the State, and Revolution: Soviet Family Policy and Social Life, 1917–1936* (Cambridge: Cambridge University Press, 1993).

56. Suzy Kim, *Everyday Life in the North Korean Revolution, 1945–1950*, 186–187.

57. Yun Miryang, *PukHanŭi yŏsŏng chŏngch'aek* [North Korean policies on women] (Seoul: Hanul, 1991), 211–227.

58. Cho Ilho, *Chosŏn kajokpŏp*, 126.

59. Ibid.

60. Ibid., 129.

61. Ibid., 135.

62. Ibid., 133.

63. Anonymous, "Namnyŏ p'yŏngdŭnggwŏn pŏmnyŏng palp'o 15chunyŏn" [The proclamation of the gender equality laws fifteen years later], *Chosŏn nyŏsŏng*, July 1961: 2–3.

64. Anonymous, "Namnyŏ p'yŏngdŭnggwŏn pŏmnyŏng 10chunyŏnŭl mat'ihayŏ" [Welcoming the tenth anniversary of the proclamation of the gender

equality laws], *Chosŏn nyŏsŏng*, July 1956: 1–2. Note that this story, despite not mentioning Kim Il Sung, included a side illustration by Pak Kyŏngnan of Kim at the center of an imagined scene of the proclamation.

65. Indeed, mention of divorce rights was already left out as early as 1956: already, in the year that the Party-state eliminated mutual consent, divorce was not part of the commemoration in the magazine. Anonymous, "Namnyŏ p'yŏngdŭnggwŏn pŏmnyŏng 10chunyŏnŭl mat'ihayŏ."

66. Anonymous, "Namnyŏ p'yŏngdŭnggwŏn pŏmnyŏng 15chunyŏn kinyŏmhoe-esŏ han Pak Chŏngae tongjiŭi pogo" [Comrade Pak Chŏngae's Report at the fifteenth anniversary commemorative meetings for the gender equality laws], *Rodong sinmun*, July 30, 1961: 2.

67. Kim Kyŏngsuk, "Wae rihonharyŏ haetdŏnga?" [Why did you want to divorce?], *Chosŏn nyŏsŏng*, October 1956: 24–25.

68. For an article of a similar tone, specifically labeled as received from a male reader, see Ro Yangguk, "Urijip saramŭn ch'ach'a choa chimnida" [My wife is gradually improving], *Chosŏn nyŏsŏng*, June 1956: 14–16.

69. Kim Kyŏngsuk, "Wae rihonharyŏ haetdŏnga?," 25.

70. Cho Ilho also published articles, including "Kyŏrhon-e taehaesŏ urinara pŏmnyŏng'ŭn ŏttŏge kyujŏnghago innŭnga?" [How is marriage administered by our country's laws?], *Ch'ŏngnyŏn saenghwal*, August 1956: 17–21.

71. Anonymous, "Haengbokhan kajŏng" [Happy family], *Chosŏn nyŏsŏng*, January 1959: 30–32, 30.

72. See the collection of essays, including Kim's speech, published after the congress: Chosŏn nyŏsŏngsa, ed., *Chŏn'guk ŏmŏni taehoe: munhŏnjip* [All-Nation Congress of Mothers: Document collection] (Pyongyang: Chosŏn nyŏsŏngsa, 1962).

73. Not everyone thought the birth rate was sufficient. Kim Wŏnsŏk, "Sahoejuŭiŭi kŏnsŏrŭi piyakchŏk paljŏnwa roryŏk munje" [The labor problem and rapid development of socialist construction], *Kŭlloja* 156 (November 1958): 31–35.

74. Ch'oe Kyŏngse, "Imsinjungŭi wisaeng" [Hygiene during pregnancy], *Chosŏn nyŏsŏng*, February 1957: 34–35.

75. Ri Sich'ae, "Haesanjŏn chunbiwa haesan si wisaeng" [Preparations before birthing and hygiene during birthing], *Chosŏn nyŏsŏng*, April 1965: 125–127.

76. Ri Sich'ae, "Yusangwa kŭŭi yebang" [Miscarriage and its prevention], *Chosŏn nyŏsŏng*, March 1965: 116–117.

77. Anonymous, "Airŭl pogi choge ŏbŭryŏmyŏn" [If you want to carry and see your baby], *Chosŏn nyŏsŏng*, February 1964: 75.

78. See the journal *Pediatrics and Obstetrics* (*Soa sanbuingwa*).

79. Editorial, "Imsinhan mosŏngdŭrŭn nyŏsŏng sangdamgwarŭl ch'aja kasipsio" [Pregnant mothers—please go visit the women's counseling services], *Chosŏn nyŏsŏng*, July 1956: 12–13.

80. Anonymous, "Ŏmŏni hakkyo" [Mother school], *Rodong sinmun*, March 11, 1957: 3.

81. Anonymous, "Sangdamsil" [Meeting room], *Chosŏn nyŏsŏng*, February 1965: 105.

82. Editorial, "Ŏrinidŭrŭi haengbogŭl wihayŏ" [For the happiness of children], *Rodong sinmun*, June 1, 1956: 2. This postwar celebration of childhood happiness was also common in South Korea; see Na Sil Heo, "Rearing Autonomous Children in Cold War Korea: Transnational Formations of a Liberal Order, 1950s–1960s" (PhD dissertation, University of Toronto, 2020).

83. Anonymous, "Ahop nammaeŭi ŏmŏni" [A mother of nine children], *Rodong sinmun*, July 1, 1955: 3; Sim Myŏngja, "Ilgop changbyŏngŭi ŏmŏni" [A mother with seven soldiers], *Chosŏn nyŏsŏng*, January 1963: 22–23.

84. Ri Ponggŭm, "Haengbok" [Happiness], *Chosŏn nyŏsŏng*, March 1959: cover.

85. See Elaine Tyler May, *Homeward Bound: American Families in the Cold War Era* (New York: Basic Books, 1988: 1–12).

86. Nicholas Eberstadt and Judith Banister, *The Population of North Korea* (Berkeley: Institute of East Asian Studies, University of California, 1992), 21.

87. Cho Ilho, *Chosŏn kajokpŏp*, 135–136.

88. Kim Il Sung, "Chanyŏ kyoyang-esŏŭi ŏmŏnidŭrŭi immu" [The duty of mothers in childhood education], in Chosŏn nyŏsŏngsa, ed., *Chŏn'guk ŏmŏni taehoe: munhŏnjip*.

CHAPTER SEVEN

1. Susan E. Reid, "Communist Comfort: Socialist Modernism and the Making of Cosy Homes in the Khrushchev Era," *Gender and History* 21.3 (2009): 465–498. On comfort more generally, see Charles Rice, *The Emergence of the Interior: Architecture, Modernity, Domesticity* (London: Routledge, 2007); John E. Crowley, "The Sensibility of Comfort," *The American Historical Review* 104.3 (1999): 749–782.

2. Kim Yŏngsuk, "Saenghwarŭl kaesŏnhagikkaji" [Until I improved my life], *Chosŏn nyŏsŏng*, January 1960: 34–35.

3. Ibid., 35.

4. Editorial, "Uri nyŏsŏngdŭrŭn sahoejuŭi kŏnsŏrŭi midŭmjikhan yŏkkunida" [Our women are a socialist construction worth believing in], *Rodong sinmun*, March 8, 1958: 2.

5. Pak Chŏngae, "Sahaejuŭi kŏnsŏl-esŏ nyŏsŏngdŭrŭi yŏkharŭl chegohal te taehayŏ" [On raising the role of women in socialist construction], *Chosŏn nyŏsŏng*, April 1959: 5–7.

6. Anonymous, "Nyŏsŏngdŭurŭn tang-e taehan ch'ungsilsongŭro kyoyanghaja!" [Let's nurture women with loyalty to the Party], *Chosŏn nyŏsŏng*, July 1959: 1–2.

7. Anonymous, "Kŭngjirŭl katke toelttaekkaji" [How long in your corner?], *Chosŏn nyŏsŏng*, October 1958: 8.

8. This trope received special attention when it was repeated in Kim Il Sung's speech to the Congress of Mothers. See Chosŏn nyŏsŏngsa, ed., *Chŏn'guk ŏmŏni taehoe: munhŏnjip* [All-Nation Congress of Mothers: Document collection] (Pyongyang: Chosŏn nyŏsŏngsa, 1962), 1–35.

9. Anonymous, "Ŏnjekkaji chikchangŭl korŭlgŏsinga?" [How long before you choose a workplace?], *Chosŏn nyŏsŏng*, October 1958: 8.

10. Anonymous, "Igŏsŭn rodong kyegŭptaun haengdongi anida" [This is not working-class behavior], *Rodongja*, December 1958: 36.

11. Ra Chaeguk, "Rodong ilgaŭi kippŭmŭl chŏnhamnida" [Passing along the happiness of one working family], *Rodong sinmun*, January 1, 1957: 3.

12. Kim Il Sung, "Nyŏmaeng chojiktŭrap-e nasŏnŭn myŏtkaji kwaŏp-e taehayŏ" [On several tasks arising in the Women's Federation), *Collected Works*, vol. 35 (September 2, 1965): 415–426.

13. Kim Osŏp, "Ilsang saenghwal-esŏ chŏryak wŏnch'ŏnŭl ch'anŭn sat'aek nyŏmaengwŏndŭl" [Women's Union members finding the source of savings in everyday life], *Chosŏn nyŏsŏng*, February 1957: 27.

14. Anonymous, untitled cartoon, *Chosŏn nyŏsŏng*, February 1961: 31.

15. Anonymous, "Haengbokhan kajŏng" [Happy family], *Chosŏn nyŏsŏng*, January 1959: 30–32, 32.

16. Editorial, "Sahoejuŭi kŏnsŏlgwa nyŏsŏng munje" [Socialist construction and the woman issue], *Rodong sinmun*, November 13, 1965: 2–3.

17. Kim Kuiryŏn, "Ŏmŏniŭi maŭm: haengbok" [The heart of a mother: Happiness], *Chosŏn munhak*, March 1955: 112–113.

18. Editorial, "Konghwaguk nyŏsŏngdŭrŭi yŏngye" [The glory of the republic's women], *Rodong sinmun*, March 8, 1955: 1.

19. Anonymous, "Ŏmŏnidŭrŭi moksorirŭl tŭrŭra!" [Listen to the voices of mothers!], *Rodong sinmun*, July 7, 1955: 1.

20. For one contemporary reproduction of his speech, see Chosŏn nyŏsŏngsa, ed., *Chŏn'guk ŏmŏni taehoe: munhŏnjip*, 1–35.

21. Anonymous, "Inminŭi naemuwŏn" [A servant of the people], *Chosŏn nyŏsŏng*, July 1957: 8

22. For one exception, see photograph by Kim Chongyun, "Sŏl maji chunbi" [Preparations for the new year], *Chosŏn nyŏsŏng*, December 1956: front cover.

23. Chu Hyŏngdo, "Puŏk'-esŏ haebangdoeŏtta" [Liberated from the kitchen], *Chosŏn nyŏsŏng*, April 1959: 20–21.

24. Ch'oe Changsik, "Saengsan munhwarŭl hwangnip" [Establishing production culture], *Rodongja sinmun*, October 28, 1962: 4.

25. Anonymous, "Saengsan munhwarŭl kŭpsokhi chegohaja" [Let's quickly establish production culture], *Rodongja*, May 1954: 56–57.

26. Ri T'aekkki, "Wisaeng saŏbŭl saengsangwa miljŏphi; saengsan munhwarŭl hwangnip" [Hygiene goes hand in hand with production; let us establish production culture], *Rodong sinmun*, May 16, 1959: 5.

27. For one translation, by A.Essŭ.Makkarenkko [A. S. Makarenko], see "Pumorŭl wihan ch'aek" [A book for parents], *Chosŏn nyŏsŏng*, November 1958: 40.

28. Anonymous, "Kimch'i tamgŭnŭn pŏp" [The way to prepare kimch'i], *Chosŏn nyŏsŏng*, October 1962: 40; Anonymous "T'ang myŏtkaji" [Various soups], *Chosŏn nyŏsŏng*, January 1965: 114–115.

29. Anonymous, "Yŏrŭmbŭrahŭsŭ" [Summer blouses], *Chosŏn nyŏsŏng*, May 1959: 38; Anonymous, "Kangaji" [Puppy], *Ch'ŏllima*, August 1963: 149; Anonymous, "Panŭjirŭi kibon" [The basics of sewing], *Chosŏn nyŏsŏng*, January 1965: 125–129; Hong Ŭnsuk, "Wŏnp'isŭ myŏtkaji" [Several one-piece outfits], *Chosŏn nyŏsŏng*, January 1965: 100–101, 122–24; Kim Yŏngsuk, "Panghanyong changgapkwa mahura ttŭnŭn pŏp" [The way to make winter gloves and muffler], *Chosŏn nyŏsŏng*, October 1956: 38.

30. Kim Insŏn, "Chosŏn'ŏt" [Korean dress], *Chosŏn nyŏsŏng*, January 1956, 38–39; for a toddler's dress, see Kim Insŏn, "Nyŏabok" [Little girl's dress], *Chosŏn nyŏsŏng*, June 1956, 39.

31. Hŏ Ryŏnsuk, *Kajŏng saenghwal tokbon* [A reader for family living] (Pyongyang: Chosŏn nyŏsŏngsa, 1959). Not all the collections of remedies were from the Women's Union; see the Chosŏn Academy of Medicine, Eastern Medicine Research Center's collection of popular remedies, as advertised in "Saero naol ch'aek: mingan ryobŏpchip" [Upcoming books: A collection of popular remedies], *Naegwa* 6 (June 1965). Ri Hongjong, *Nyŏsŏngdŭrŭi kongsanjuŭi p'umsŏng* [The communist character of women] (Pyongyang: Chosŏn nyŏsŏngsa, 1960); Chosŏn nyŏsŏngsa, *Ŏmŏni hakkyo kyojae: kajŏng kwalli chisik* [A motherhood school reader: Knowledge for home management] (Pyongyang, Chosŏn nyŏsŏngsa, 1963); Chosŏn nyŏsŏngsa, *Nyŏsŏng ch'ŏllima kisudŭl* [Female thousand-mile horse riders] (Pyongyang: Chosŏn nyŏsŏngsa, 1960).

32. Chosŏn nyŏsŏngsa, *Arŭmdaun nyŏsŏngdŭl* [Beautiful women] (Pyongyang: Chosŏn nyŏsŏngsa, 1963); Nam Kunman, *Pulgŭn nyŏsŏngdŭl* [Red women] (Pyongyang: Chosŏn nyŏsŏngsa, 1960); Pak Sŭngsu and Kim Sŏngnak, *Chosŏnŭi ŏmŏni, 3* [Korean mothers, part 3] (Pyongyang: Chosŏn nyŏsŏngsa, 1960); Chosŏn nyŏsŏngsa, *Chogugŭi chayuwa tongnibŭl wihayŏ ssaunŭn Chosŏn nyŏsŏng* [Korean women fighting for our ancestral land's freedom and independence] (Pyongyang: Chosŏn nyŏsŏngsa, 1954).

33. Ivan Paris, "Between Efficiency and Comfort: The Organization of Domestic Work and Space from Home Economics to Scientific Management, 1841–1913," *History and Technology* 35.1 (2019): 81–104.

34. Pak Pongok, "Kajŏng sallimŭl kaesŏnhago" [Improving domestic life], *Chosŏn nyŏsŏng*, October 1959: 29.

35. Kim Chŏnghye, "Kajŏng sallim-esŏ kyehoekchŏk chich'urŭn chungyohan irida" [In domestic housekeeping, planning expenses is important], *Chosŏn nyŏsŏng*, August 1957: 31–32.

36. For one example, see Sonia Ryang, *Reading North Korea: An Ethnological Inquiry* (Cambridge, MA: Harvard University Asia Center, 2012): 40–84.

37. Anonymous, "Roryŏk yongŭn—Pak Tosul tongmu" [Labor hero—Comrade Pak Tosul], *Ch'ŏllima*, July 1964: 48. Untitled photograph of Comrade Kim ingman's family by Kim Wŏnguk, *Rodongja*, December 1960: back cover photo.

38. Kang Hyosun, "Abŏjiwa adŭl" [Father and son], *Sae sedae*, April 1956: 12–16.

39. Chŏn Yŏng, "Kŏnsŏljangŭi abŏjiwa adŭl" [A construction site father and his son], *Rodong sinmun*, November 30, 1955: 3; Paek Chongjin, "Cheyŏmso-esŏ ilhanŭn

abŏjiwa adŭl" [A father working at the saltworks and his son], *Rodong sinmun*, December 2, 1955: 3; Kang Hyosun, "Abŏjiwa adŭl."

40. Chŏn Minu, "Onammae k'iunŭn abŏjiŭi kamsarŭl" [The thanks of a father who raised five children], *Rodong sinmun*, November 1, 1958: 4; Hong Sŏngbŏp, "Abŏji-ege tŭrinŭn p'yŏnji" [A letter to my father], *Rodong sinmun*, December 25, 1954: 3.

41. Chosŏn nyŏsŏngsa, ed., *Ch'ŏn'guk ŏmŏni taehoe: munhŏnjip*, 18–19.

42. For one such usage, see Ri Sansun, "Tang-e ch'ungsilhan mosŏng rodongja" [A mother-worker loyal to the Party], *Chosŏn nyŏsŏng*, February 1956: 5–7.

43. Cartoonists frequently played up the differences between pre-marriage promises and post-marriage actualities. Anonymous, "Kyŏrhon chŏnhu" [Before and after marriage], *Ch'ŏngnyŏn saenghwal* 81 (June 1956): 6–7; Cho Ilho, "Kyŏrhun-e taehaesŏ urinara pŏmnyŏngŭn ŏttokye kyujŏnghago innŭnga?" [What are our country's laws about marriage?], *Ch'ŏngnyŏn saenghwal*, August 1956: 17–21.

44. Kim Pong, "Namp'yŏndŭldo iyagi toeyŏya handa" [We must speak about husbands], *Ch'ŏllima*, June 1962: 130–133.

45. Ibid., 130.

46. Ibid., 131.

47. Anonymous, "Inminban saenghwal" [Inminban life], *Chosŏn nyŏsŏng*, June 1959: 18–19.

48. Kim In'gŏl, "Ch'ogŭp tang tanch'edŭr-esŏ pidangwŏndŭlkwaŭi saŏbŭl ŏttŏgye hal kŏsinga" [How should primary Party cells proceed with non-Party members?], *Tangganbudŭl-ege chunŭn ch'amgo charyo*, October 1960: 20–25.

49. For Hamhŭng, Kim Suhyŏn, "Inminbanŭi sallimgundŭl" [The frugal housewives of an inminban], *Ch'ŏllima*, July 1964: 56–57; Haeju, "Namp'yŏndŭl-ege hago sip'ŭn mal" [Words I want to say to my husband], *Ch'ŏllima*, February 1965: 82–87; Sinŭiju, Kim Sangsŏn "Iuttŭri han kajŏngŭro" [Neighbors as one family], *Chosŏn nyŏsŏng*, April 1965: 54–55.

50. Ri Unbong, "Hwamokhan tae kajŏng" [A big harmonious family], *Ch'ŏllima*, January 1964: 72–74.

51. Anonymous, "Kkotp'inŭn iminban t'agaso" [An inminban day care flourishing like a flower], *Chosŏn nyŏsŏng*, May 1965: 64–66.

52. Kim Pyŏngnin, "Ilt'owa chut'aegŭl tŏuk arŭmdapke" [Making workplaces and home more beautiful], *Rodong sinmun*, April 23, 1960: 3.

53. Kim In'gŏl, "Ch'ogŭp tang tanch'edŭr-esŏ pidangwŏndŭlkwaŭi saŏbŭl ŏttŏgye hal kŏsinga," 20.

54. Anonymous, "Inminban-esŏ pibŏpchŏk sang haengŭiwaŭi t'ujaengŭl kanghwahaja" [Let's strengthen the struggle against illegal commercial behavior in inminban], *Sŏndongwŏn such'ŏp* 5.2 (March 1958): 25–26.

55. Kim Sŏnghwan, "Hyŏngmyŏngjŏk kyŏnggaksŏngŭl nop'ira" [Raise our revolutionary awareness], *Chosŏn nyŏsŏng*, January 1956: 14–15.

56. Anonymous, "Pan'ganch'ŏp t'ujaeng chŏllamhoe kaegwan" [The opening of the anti-spying campaign exhibition], *Rodong sinmun*, July 27, 1957: 2.

57. For Im Hwa, see Kim Myŏngsu, "Miguk kanch'ŏbŭi munhak" [The literature of an American spy], *Chosŏn nyŏsŏng*, April 1956: 14–15. For Pak Hŏnyŏng, see Kim Sŏnghwan, "Hyŏngmyŏngjŏk kyŏnggaksŏngŭl nop'ira."

58. Anonymous, "Kyŏnggaksŏng nop'ŭn nyŏsŏngdŭl" [Highly vigilant women], *Chosŏn nyŏsŏng*, September 1957: 30–31, 31.

59. Anonymous, "Hyŏngmyŏngjŏk kyŏnggaksŏngŭl nop'ija" [Let's raise our revolutionary awareness], *Sŏndongwŏn such'ŏp* 15 (August 1957): 36.

60. Anonymous, "Kŏju chilsŏwa sukpak kyuryurŭl ŏmsuhayŏya handa" [We must strictly observe the order of residences and the discipline of staying over], *Sŏndongwŏn such'ŏp* 15 (August 1957): 32–33; Anonymous, "Pan'ganch'ŏp t'ujaengŭn inmindŭrŭi ch'amga ha-esŏ man sŏnggwaitke chinhaeng toel su itta" [The anti-spy struggle can only achieve results with the participation of the people], *Sŏndongwŏn such'ŏp* 17 (September 1957): 19.

61. Anonymous, "Panhyŏngmyŏng punjadŭlgwaŭi t'ujaengŭl kanghwahaja" [Let us strengthen the struggle against antirevolutinary elements], *Sŏndongwŏn such'ŏp* 19 (October 1957): 14–16.

PART FOUR

1. Paul Betts and Katherine Pence, eds., *Socialist Modern: East German Everyday Culture and Politics* (Ann Arbor: University of Michigan Press, 2008); Susan E. Reid and David Crowley, eds., *Pleasures in Socialism: Leisure and Luxury in the Eastern Bloc* (Evanston, IL: Northwestern University Press, 2010).

2. Anonymous, untitled photograph, *Sangŏp*, May 1964: back cover.

3. For the logic of a furniture exhibition announcement, see Anonymous, "Chŏn'guk kagu chŏllamhoe chinghaeng" [Holding a national exhibition of furniture], *Rodong sinmun*, December 8, 1959: 3; Anonymous, "Uriŭi sahoejuŭi gongŏp-e ŭihayŏ chejaktoen sae chakpumdŭl" [New products produced by our socialist industry], *Rodong sinmun*, June 17, 1958: 4.

CHAPTER EIGHT

1. Laura C. Nelson, *Measured Excess: Status, Gender, and Consumer Nationalism in South Korea* (New York: Columbia University Press, 2000).

2. Editorial, "Inmin chŏgŭm undong-esŏ tŏ nop'ŭn sŏnggwarŭl chaengch'uihaja" [Let's achieve even greater results in the national savings movement], *Rodong sinmun*, May 15, 1957: 1.

3. O Kyurae, "Chŏryak—inŭn aeguksimŭi p'yohyŏn ida" [Savings—this is a sign of patriotism], *Rodong sinmun*, December 16, 1964: 2–3.

4. For one listing of rates, put up just when workers were receiving their bonuses, see Anonymous, "Chŏgŭmŭro saenghwarŭl tŏuk hyangsang sik'ija" [Let's raise living standards by saving], *Rodong sinmun*, December 28, 1956: 3.

5. Pak Chudong and An Sŭngo, "Kakchi kŭllojadŭrŭi chŏgŭmyŏl" [The savings fever of workers around the country], *Rodong sinmun*, April 21, 1957: 1.

6. Anonymous, "Up'yŏn chŏgŭm ch'wigŭp" [Post office deposits], *Rodong sinmun*, July 19, 1957: 4.

7. See the table of rates and terms issued by banks in Anonymous, "Chŏgŭmŭro saenghwarŭl tŏuk hyangsang sik'ija."

8. Anonymous, "Up'yŏn chŏgŭm ch'wigŭp."

9. Pak Chudong and An Sŭngo, "Kakchi kŭllojadŭrŭi chŏgŭmyŏl," 1; Ri Chuyŏn, "Inmin chŏgŭm saŏbŭi kaesŏn kanghwarŭl wihayŏ" [For the improvement and strengthening of the people's savings], *Rodong sinmun*, September 25, 1957: 3.

10. Paek Chongjin, "T'ikkŭl moa t'aesan" [Specks of dust, collected, make large mountains], *Rodong sinmun*, February 18, 1955: 3; Ri Yangsŏp, "T'ikkŭl moa t'aesan" [Specks of dust, collected, make large mountains], *Rodong sinmun*, October 19, 1960: 4.

11. Anonymous, "T'ikkŭl moa t'aesan" [Specks of dust, collected, make large mountains], *Chosŏn nyŏsŏng*, September 1960: 36–37. See also Ri Taeho, "T'ikkŭl moa t'aesan," *Hwasal* 104 (June 1959): 6.

12. The radio cartoon: Ri Ch'unsu, "Irŏn chŏmŭn koch'ipsida" [Let's correct these points], *Chosŏn nyŏsŏng*, February, 1959: 40; the water cartoon: Sŏng Tuwŏn, "Irŏn saramdŭrŭn ŏmnŭnga?" [Aren't there people like this?], *Ch'ongnyŏn saenghwal*, November 1958: 47.

13. Anonymous illustrator, "Pip'an-e taehan 'hŏsimhan chŏmsu'" [Judging criticism with an "open mind"], *Rodongja*, August 1955: 61.

14. Anonymous, "Ingŭm insang mit mulga inhawa kwallyŏnhan kukka kyehwoek wiwŏnhoe wiwonjang ŭi tamhwa" [Conversations with the national planning commissioner about the rise of income and the decline of prices], *Rodong sinmun*, August 14, 1956: 1.

15. Chosŏn minju nyŏsŏng tongmaeng chungang wiwŏnhoe, *Nyŏsŏngdŭrŭn munhwa sujunŭl nop'ija* [Women, let us raise our cultural levels] (Pyongyang: Chosŏn nyŏsŏngsa, 1956), 31–34.

16. The first sentence of his chapter on clothing captured the tone: "Some comrades think that you are only fashionable if you wear expensive clothes." Hwang Yŏngsik, *Saenghwarŭi kŏul* [A guide to living] (Pyongyang: Sahoejuŭi rodong ch'ŏngnyŏn tongmaeng ch'ulp'ansa, 1965), 30.

17. Kim Il Sung, "Kongsanjuŭi kyoyang-e taehayŏ" [On communist cultivation], *Rodong sinmun*, December 9, 1958: 2–3.

18. Christina Kiaer, *Imagine No Possessions: The Socialist Objects of Russian Constructivism* (Cambridge, MA: MIT Press, 2005), 1–40, esp. 30–31.

19. Ibid., 5–6.

20. Anonymous, "Uri saenghwalkwa sanŏp misul" [Our living and industrial design], *Ch'ŏllima*, October 1964: 84, 106.

21. Karl Gerth, *Unending Capitalism: How Consumerism Negated China's Communist Revolution* (Cambridge: Cambridge University Press, 2020).

22. Yiching Wu, *The Cultural Revolution at the Margins: Chinese Socialism in Crisis* (Cambridge, MA: Harvard University Press, 2014).

23. Chosŏn rodongdang, *Kyŏngje sangsik: kongŏp, nongŏp, sangŏp* [A primer on economics: Industry, agriculture, commerce] (Pyongyang: Chosŏn rodongdang ch'ulp'ansa, 1960).

24. *Nyŏwŏn*, December 1962, as quoted in Chŏn Changsŏk, *Miguksik saenghwal yangsikkwa namChosŏn-e mich'in kŭ hugwa* [American-style living and its effect on South Korea] (Pyongyang: Chosŏn rodongdang ch'ulp'ansa, 1965), 81–82.

25. Kim Unch'ŏl, "NamChosŏn-e taehan mijeŭi sasang munhwa ch'imnyak chŏngch'aek" [The American policy of ideological and cultural penetration of South Korea], in *NamChosŏn munje nonmunjip* (Pyongyang: NamChosŏn munje ch'ulp'ansa, 1965), 134–154.

26. P'yŏngyang Hyangt'o Sa P'yŏnch'an Wiwŏnhoe, ed., *P'yŏngyang chi* [Pyongyang records] (Seoul: Han'guk Munhwasa, 1999).

27. Pak Yong and Hyŏn Tongun, "Tugajŏng" [Two families], *Rodongja sinmun*, February 13, 1959: 3.

28. Yŏl Panghwa, *Rodongja sinmun*, October 21, 1959: 4.

29. Pak Inja, "Ch'amŭl su opta" [Can't stand it anymore], *Rodongja sinmun*, July 26, 1959: 3.

30. Ŏm Byŏnghwa, untitled cartoon, *Hwasal* 126 (May 1960): 7.

31. For a photograph of the bonus envelopes being distributed to the workers of the Chosŏn Beer Factory and an explanatory article, see Anonymous, "Nyŏnmal sanggŭmŭl pannŭn Chosŏn Maekchu Kongjang rodongjadŭl" [Chosŏn Beer Factory workers receiving their year end bonus], *Rodong sinmun*, December 28, 1954: 3.

32. Ri Chŏngja, "Nyŏnmal sanggŭm" [Year-end bonus], *Rodong sinmun*, December 26, 1954: 3. There was similarly a long-standing genre of workers writing in to newspapers to thank the party for wage increases; see Anonymous, "Tanggwa chŏngbu-e simsimhan kamsarŭl tŭrimnida" [I am sincerely grateful to the Party and government], *Rodong sinmun*, December 7, 1956: 3

33. Anonymous, "Nyŏnmal sanggŭmŭro sŏl maji" [Greeting the new year with a bonus], *Rodong sinmun*, December 30, 1954: 3.

34. Sŏk Yŏng, "Saejip" [New home], *Minju Chosŏn*, November 22, 1956: 3.

35. "Pyongyangho" [Pyongyang model], *Ch'ŏllima*, January 1964: 68. For a full-page advertisement of the preceding model, celebrated as domestically produced, see Anonymous, "Kungnaesan pidulgi p'yo chaebonggi taryang ipha" [Domestically produced Pigeon brand sewing machines arrive in quantity], *Sangŏp*, May 1958: front inset.

36. Gerth, *Unending Capitalism*.

37. Sheila Fitzpatrick takes the former position in her book *Everyday Stalinism: Ordinary Life in Extraordinary Times: Soviet Russia in the 1930s* (Oxford: Oxford University Press, 1999), 91.

38. For advertisements with different logics, see "Kŭn'gan yego" [Recent publication notice], *Chosŏn nyŏsŏng*, December 1955: 23; "Kungnip kŭkchang kongyŏn" [Public performances at the national theater], *Rodong sinmun*, September 12, 1956: 4. For a young woman pictured with alcohol, see "Samnoju" [Samno Alcohol], *Chosŏn* 42 (January 1960): 15.

39. For a 1955 Soviet example, see "Report, Embassy of Hungary in North Korea to the Hungarian Foreign Ministry (December 16, 1959)," History and Public Policy Program, MOL, XIX-J-1-j Korea, 11. doboz, 24/b, 001660/1960, translated for NKIDP by Balàzs Szalontai, https://digitalarchive.wilsoncenter.org/document/116302 and https://digitalarchive.wilsoncenter.org/document/113404.

40. P'i Ch'angnin, "Maegaegun-e p'yŏnggyun 4-5gae isang kongjangŭl kŏnsŏlhayŏttda" [Each county has built on average at least four or five factories], Sŏndongwŏn such'ŏp 21 (November 1958): 14–15.

41. Editorial, "6wŏl chŏnwŏn hoeŭi kyŏljŏngŭl chŏkkŭkchŏgŭro silch'ŏnhaja" [Let's implement the June conference decisions enthusiastically], Rodong sinmun, July 11, 1958: 1; see also Editorial, "6wŏl chŏnwŏn hoeŭi kyŏljŏngŭi kwanch'ŏrŭl muŏsi chŏaehanŭn'ga" [On implementing the decisions of the June all-member meeting], Rodong sinmun, August 10, 1958: 1.

42. Editorial, "Taejungŭi angyangdoen kiserŭl tongwŏnhayŏ sobip'um saengsan-esŏ saeroun chŏnhwanŭl irŭk'ija" [Let's create a new turning point in the production of consumer goods and mobilizing the spirit of the masses], Rodong sinmun, January 16, 1964: 1.

43. Editorial, "Inmin pongniŭi kailch'ŭngŭi chŭngjinŭl wihayŏ" [For advancing further the people's welfare], Rodong sinmun, June 7, 1958: 1.

44. Editorial, "Ilyongp'umgwa singnyo kagongp'umŭi p'umjong hwaktaerŭl wihayŏ" [For increasing the production of everyday and processed food goods], Rodong sinmun, March 13, 1960: 1.

45. Sim Pŏmjun, "5 kaeŭi kongjangŭl saero kŏnsŏl" [Five newly opened factories], Rodong sinmun, August 27, 1958: 3; Editorial, "Inmin pongniŭi kailch'ŭngŭi chŭngjinŭl wihayŏ."

46. Kang Chunghan, "Inmin sobip'um saengsanŭi hwaktaewa chibanggongŏbŭi kisuljangbiŭi kanghwa" [The increase in production of the popular consumer products and the strengthening of local industrial technology], Rodong sinmun, January 10, 1964: 2.

47. Kim Sangdo and Kang Walgŭn, "Saenghwal p'ilsup'um saengsan-esŏ Hamhŭngsiŭi mobŏmŭl ttarŭja" [When it comes to the production of life necessities, let's follow the model of Hamhŭng], Rodong sinmun, February 19, 1964: 2.

48. For one attempt to compile postwar prices and wages, see Robert Scalapino and Chong-sik Lee, Communism in Korea: Part I, The Movement, and Part II, The Society (Berkeley: University of California Press, 1972), esp. chapter 14.

49. Song Kunch'an, "Inmindŭrŭi muljil munhwa saenghwal kaesŏnŭl wihan tanggwa chŏngbuŭi ilgwanhan paeryo" [The care of the Party and government for improving the people's cultural and material living], Rodong sinmun, April 16, 1956: 2

50. Anonymous, "Hyangsangdoenŭn uriŭi saenghwal" [Our improving life], Chosŏn nyŏsŏng, December 1956: 22–23.

51. Memo from K. Koval to the CPSU CC, "Concerning the main issues of the economic situation of the DPRK (April 1956)," History and Public Policy Program, RGANI Fond 5, Opis 28, Delo 412, translated by Gary Goldberg, https://digitalarchive.wilsoncenter.org/document/120799.

52. "Memorandum of a Conversation with DPRK Ambassador to the USSR Ri Sang-jo on 16 June 1956 (June 21, 1956)," History and Public Policy Program, RGANI, Fond 5, Opis 28, Delo 412, Listy 238–241, obtained for NKIDP by Nobuo Shimotomai and translated for NKIDP by Gary Goldberg, https://digitalarchive.wilsoncenter.org/document/114133.

53. Kim Sebong, "Sangp'um konggŭp saŏbŭl kaesŏnkanghwahagi wihayŏ" [For improving and strengthening the provision of commercial goods], *Rodong sinmun*, April 13, 1964: 2.

54. Anonymous, "Chut'aek mit hapsuk saenghwarŭl munhwajŏkŭro" [To make home and dormitory life cultural], *Rodongja sinmun*, August 21, 1957: 3.

55. Editorial, "Inmin chŏgŭm undong-esŏ tŏ nop'ŭn sŏnggwarŭl chaengch'uihaja."

56. "Notes from a Conversation between the 1st Secretary of the PRL Embassy in the DPRK with Go Hui-man, Director of the Industry Department of the CC, on 13.I.1958 (January 13, 1958)," History and Public Policy Program, Polish Foreign Ministry Archive, obtained for NKIDP by Jakub Poprocki and translated for NKIDP by Maya Latynski, https://digitalarchive.wilsoncenter.org/document/111284.

57. Ch'oe Yŏnggŭn, untitled, *Hwasal* 125 (May 1960): 13.

58. Cho Myŏngsik, "Isanghan kŏul" [Funny mirrors], *Hwasal* 120 (February 1960): 5; Chang Hyŏnch'ae, "Hwanyŏng patchi mothanŭn chep'um" [Unwelcome products], *Hwasal* April 1959: 4.

59. Kim Ryong, "T'ŭkchep'um" [Special products], *Hwasal* 125 (May 1960): 12.

60. Ch'oe Yŏnggŭn, "Sae 'p'umjong'" [New "products"], *Hwasal* 125 (May 1960): 13.

61. Ch'oe Hanjin, "Kanhok irŏn ilto ittda" [Perhaps this too happens], *Chosŏn nyŏsŏng*, April 1959: 29.

62. Ri Ch'unsu, "Yŏmsaegŭi chirŭl nop'ija" [Let's improve the quality of dye], *Chosŏn nyŏsŏng*, March 1959: 40.

63. Another realm of criticism was of the service—or lack thereof—in stores. See the journal *Commerce (Sangŏp)* for regular treatment of this issue, such as the round-table held by Song Yugyun, "Che 1 kugyŏng paekhwajŏm kogaek hyŏbŭihoe-esŏ" [At the No. 1 department store's consultation meeting with customers], *Sangŏp*, February 1956: 50–53. In the national press, see Anonymous, "Pongsasŏngŭl nop'igi wihayŏ" [To raise the level of service], *Rodong sinmun*, May 18, 1959: 3; Yang Sŏngnyŏp, "Sangjŏmdŭri chumindŭl-ege tŏuk p'yŏllihage kkuryojigo ittda" [Stores are arranging to become more convenient for residents], *Rodong sinmun*, August 8, 1965: 3.

64. Hong Ingap, "Tokchadŭrŭi p'yŏnji-esŏ: pirŭl makchi mothanŭn piot" [From readers' letters: Raincoats that can't stop the rain], *Rodong sinmun*, September 1, 1956: 2.

65. Anonymous, "Chiri najŭn taejung sobip'um-e taehan ŭikyŏni manta" [Plenty of opinions about the low quality of mass consumer goods], *Rodong sinmun*, October 8, 1956: 2.

66. Anonymous, "Tokchadŭrŭi p'yŏnji-esŏ: ilyongp'umŭi chirŭl tŏuk nop'ira" [From readers' letters: Raise the quality of daily necessities], *Rodong sinmun*, May 29, 1958: 2.

67. Chŏng Myŏngsuk, "T'aol p'anmei-esŏ" [The selling of towels], *Sangŏp*, December 1956: 20.

68. Ch'oe Kwanhwa, "Tokchadŭrŭi moksori: kudu rŭl chiham p'ojanghan taero p'al kŏsŭl yoguhanda" [Readers' voices: Demands to guarantee the quality of shoes for sale], *Rodong sinmun*, September 24, 1956: 2.

69. Ch'oe Kŭmok, "Kogaegŭi moksori" [Voices of customers], *Sangŏp*, November 1956: 24.

70. Krisztina Fehervary, "Goods and States: The Political Logic of State-Socialist Material Culture," *Comparative Studies in Society and History* 51.2 (2009): 426–459.

71. Editorial, "Taejung sobip'um saengsan mit konggŭp saŏbŭi kaesŏn kanghwarŭl wihayŏ" [Toward improving and strengthening the supply and production of mass consumer goods], *Rodong sinmun*, December 6, 1956: 2.

72. Editorial, "Inmin pongniŭi kailch'ŭngŭi chŭngjinŭl wihayŏ."

73. Anonymous, "70 yŏchongŭi kajŏngyong yuri chep'umi saengsandoenda" [More than 70 types of household glass products produced], *Rodong sinmun*, January 12, 1958: 2.

74. Chang Ujong,"Ilyongp'um p'umjongŭi hwaktaerŭl wihayŏ" [For the increased production of everyday necessities], *Rodong sinmun*, July 2, 1958: 3.

75. Anonymous, "Uriŭi modŭn himgwa chihyerŭl tongwŏnhayŏ inmin sobip'um saengsan-esŏ ildae chŏnhwanŭl irŭk'ija!" [Let's achieve a generational change in the production of people's consumer goods by mobilizing all our strength and wisdom!], *Ch'ŏllima*, November 1963: 26–29; Pak Sŭngjŏng, "P'yŏngyang sangp'um" [Pyongyang products], *Ch'ŏllima*, January 1964: 66–68.

76. Anonymous, "Inmin sobip'um saengsan-esŏ ildae chŏnhwanŭl irŭk'ija!" [Let's bring about a turning point in the production of the people's consumer goods], *Rodong sinmun*, January 4, 1964: 1.

77. Chosŏn chungang t'ongsinsa, *Chosŏn chungang nyŏn'gam, 1965* [Korean national yearbook, 1965] (Pyongyang: Chosŏn chungang t'ongsinsa, 1965), 481.

78. For sewing repair cooperatives, see Anonymous, "Kajŏng pongsaban" [House sewing team], *Chosŏn nyŏsŏng*, January, 1961: 11.

79. Michael Kim, "Industrial Warriors: Labor Heroes and Everyday Life in Wartime Colonial Korea, 1937–1945," in Alf Lüdtke, ed., *Everyday Life in Mass Dictatorship: Evasion and Collusion* (New York: Palgrave Macmillan, 2016), 126–146.

80. Anonymous, "Sahoejuŭi kŏnsŏl-esŏ nyŏsŏngdŭrŭi yŏkharŭl tŏuk nop'ija" [Let's raise the role of women in socialist construction], *Chosŏn nyŏsŏng*, February 1962: 2–3; Kim Oksun, "Kajŏng puindŭrŭn kanae chagŭp-e chŏkkŭk ch'amgahaja" [Let housewives enthusiastically participate in household labor], *Chosŏn nyŏsŏng*, April 1960: 12–13.

81. For one ideal account in a photo spread that blurred household and factory labor, see *Chosŏn* 56 (March 1961): 20–21.

82. Kim Kyŏnghŭi, "Kanae kongŏp-e taehan tangŭi chŏngch'aegŭl ch'ŏljŏhi kwanch'ŏlsik'imyŏ nyŏsŏngdŭrŭi sasang chŏngch'i ŭisik sujunŭl tŏuk nopikettda"

[To thoroughly implement the Party's policy on household industry, raise even higher the consciousness levels of women's political ideology], in Chosŏn nyŏsŏngsa, ed., *Ch'ŏn'guk ŏmŏni taehoe: munhŏnjip* [All-Nation Congress of Mothers: Document collection] (Pyongyang: Chosŏn nyŏsŏngsa, 1962), 161–184.

83. Anonymous, "Puyang kajokturi kongjang kanae kongŏppan-e mangna" [Inside a household production team], *Rodongja sinmun*, March 23, 1960: 1.

84. Anonymous, "Taejungjŏk ch'angbalsŏngŭi pitnanŭn yŏlmae—dayanghan chibang kongŏp chep'um" [The bright fruits of mass initiative—the wide variety of products from local industry], *Rodong sinmun*, October 11, 1959: 4; "50 chongŭi ilyongp'umŭl saengsan" [Producing fifty types of daily necessities], *Rodong sinmun*, March 27, 1960: 2.

85. Ch'oe Pyŏngch'un, "Tongdang tanch'e saŏp-esŏ chegidoenŭn myŏt kaji munje" [Several problems arising in neighborhood party units], *Tangganbudŭl-ege chunŭn ch'amgo charyo*, November 1960: 20–24; Kim Tongch'un, "Sŏro topko iggŭlmyŏnsŏ" [Mutually helping and leading], *Chosŏn nyŏsŏng*, May 1961: 8.

86. Chu Hannyul, "On siga sobip'umŭl saengsanhada" [The entire city produces consumer goods], *Rodong sinmun*, August 13, 1964: 2.

CHAPTER NINE

1. For women's fashions, see Kim Suk-Young, *Illusive Utopias: Theater, Film, and Everyday Performance in North Korea* (Ann Arbor: University of Michigan Press, 2010): 205–259.

2. For a photo of the interior of the games room of the Sŏngjin Ironworks, see "Myŏngnyanghan yagan hyuyangso" [Bright outdoor recreation spots], *Rodong sinmun*, March 27, 1955: 3.

3. Anonymous, "P'ehŏ u-e irŏsŏn yŏngung tosi—Pyongyang" [A heroic city arising out of the ashes of war—Pyongyang], *Rodong sinmun*, July 27, 1957: 4.

4. Anonymous, "Ch'ŏllimaŭi kisangŭl an'go ilttŏsŏn uriŭi tosiwa maul" [With the embrace of Ch'ŏllima spirit, our cities and villages rise up], *Rodong sinmun*, August 14, 1959: 5; Hwang T'aegyun, "Kŏnsŏldoenŭn Hamhŭngsi" [Hamhŭng under construction], *Chosŏn*, October 1956: 16–17. For a hand-illustrated example, see Rim Yonghwang, "Charangsurŏun choguk" [A nation worthy of pride], *Rodong sinmun*, September 8, 1957: 3.

5. More often than not, such articles had no accompanying photographs. See Chŏng Kiho, "Haengbokhan pubu kyowŏn" [A happy teachers couple], *Rodong sinmun*, January 14, 1956: 3.

6. Chu Hyŏngdo, "Sŏl maji" [Greeting the new year], *Chosŏn nyŏsŏng*, December 1956: 18; see also Paek Sangbŏm, "Kirŭnŭn ŏmŏniŭi chŏngsŏng" [A caring mother's best wishes], *Rodong sinmun*, February 19, 1956: 3.

7. Anonymous, "Chibanŭl munhwajŏguro kkurija" [Let's arrange our rooms culturally], *Chosŏn nyŏsŏng*, December 1958: 15.

8. Tomás Maldonado, "The Idea of Comfort," tr. John Cullars, *Design Issues* 8.1 (1991): 35–43; Kristin Ross, *Fast Cars, Clean Bodies: Decolonization and the Reordering of French Culture* (Cambridge, MA: MIT Press, 1996).

9. The relation between wall pictures and children's aesthetic and emotional development had, by this point, been discussed briefly in articles about child rearing. For a slightly earlier example, see Hong Chŏngsu, "Chanyŏdŭl-ege arŭmdaun kamjŏngŭl killŏjuja" [Let's nurture beautiful emotions in our children], *Chosŏn nyŏsŏng*, June 1958: 34–35.

10. For example, see an article with a title nearly identical to "Let's Arrange Our Rooms Culturally," and from the same year, which never makes even the briefest mention of décor: Anonymous, "Kajŏngŭl munhwajŏguro kkurija" [Let's arrange our homes culturally], *Sŭndongwŏn such'ŏp* 20 (October 1958): 24–25.

11. Chu Hyŏngdo, "Kyehoek-e ŏpttŏn ch'walyŏng" [An unplanned photo shoot], *Chosŏn nyŏsŏng*, February 1959: 20–21.

12. As cited in Andrew Gordon, *Fabricating Consumers: The Sewing Machine in Modern Japan* (Berkeley: University of California Press, 2012), 107.

13. As cited in Michael Robinson, "Broadcasting, Cultural Hegemony, and Colonial Modernity in Korea, 1924–1945," in Gi-wook Shin and Michael Robinson, eds., *Colonial Modernity in Korea* (Cambridge, MA: Harvard University Asia Center, 1999), 60.

14. Rim Tŏbo, "Inmin'gun changbyŏngdŭl-ege chŏn inminjok yŏngyewa chon'gyŏngŭl ponaenda" [Sending the entire nation's glory and respect to the people's soldiers], *Chosŏn nyŏsŏng*, February 1956: front inset; see also Ri Ponggŭm, untitled photo, *Chosŏn nyŏsŏng*, January 1958: 41.

15. See cartoon by Ch'oe Hanjin, "Yang Unbong kwalli wiwŏnjang-i kŏrŏ on kil" [The route walked by administrator Yang Unbong], *Chosŏn nyŏsŏng*, March 1961: 21; and photograph by Anonymous, "Roryŏk yŏngungŭi anhae" [The wife of a worker hero], *Chosŏn nyŏsŏng*, October 1958: 28–29.

16. Anonymous, "Kŭdŭrŭi kajŏngŭl ch'aja" [Visiting their homes], *Sinsaenghwal* 54 (1961): 34–35.

17. Anonymous, untitled illustration, *Wisaeng munhwa*, December 1959: front cover; Ch'oe Pyŏngsŏ, "Nanŭn haengbokhada" [I'm happy], *Sinsaenghwal* 53 (1961): 58; Chang Sŏgyŏng, "Pongŭppŭl patkosŏ" [After receiving wages], *Chosŏn*, December 1956: 18–19; Anonymous, "Imgŭmi tto orŭnda" [Wages rise again], *Rodongja*, November 1958: 18–19; Anonymous, untitled illustration, *Kyŏngje chisik*, June 1960: back cover.

18. An illustration accompanies a story by Son Myŏngja, "Sidaeŭi hŭrŭm-e match'wŏ" [Following the flows of the era], *Ch'ŏllima*, February 1965: 86. See also Yu Chŏngok, "Ch'ŏllima kisudŭrŭi kajŏngŭl ch'ajasŏ" [Finding the home of Ch'ŏllima riders], *Ch'ŏllima*, August 1962: 82–85.

19. Anonymous, "Nyŏsŏngdŭlsok-esŏ kyegŭp kyoyangŭl kanghwa haja" [Let us strengthen class education among women], *Chosŏn nyŏsŏng*, June 1963: 26–27.

20. Mun Ho, "Olmana mŏgŭl kŏsinga?" [How much should one eat?], *Ch'ŏllima*, September 1964: 68–70.

21. Hygiene remained part, for example, of the Three Chores Movement. Anonymous, "Segaji undongŭl tŏ simhwasik'ijamyŏn" [If we pursue more fervently the Three Chores moment], *Chosŏn nyŏsŏng*, February 1963: 22–26.

22. Rooms symbolically prepared for Koreans from Japan were also pictured as empty, as if awaiting their return. Ri Ch'unyŏng, "Kidarinŭn maŭm" [With a waiting heart], *Chosŏn nyŏsŏng*, December 1959: 16–17, 17.

23. Anonymous, "Pangan kkurigi" [Room decorating], *Ch'ŏllima*, April 1965: 145–146, 146. For another black-and-white illustration, see Anonymous, "Panganŭl munhwajŏgŭro kkurijamyŏn" [If we arrange a room culturally], *Rodongja*, February 1965: 36.

24. Anonymous, "App'at'urŭl ch'ajasŏ" [Finding apartments], *Sinsaenghwal* 55 (January 1962): 8–11, 9.

25. For a rural example, see Anonymous, "Nongch'ŏn munhwa chut'aegŭl ŏttŏgye kkurinŭn kŏsi choŭlgayo?" [How best to decorate rural cultural homes?], *Chosŏn nyŏsŏng*, March 1964: 72–74. For how furniture emerged as a criterion of rural good living, see Ri Pyŏnghun, "Kagu-e taehan saenggak" [Some thoughts on furniture], *Ch'ŏllima*, July 1963: 30.

26. Anonymous, "Pangan kkurigi," 145.

27. See the six-part serialized article on Chosŏn material culture beginning with Rim Chongsang, "Rijo sigiŭi munhwa, 1" [The culture of the Yi Dynasty period, part 1], *Ch'ŏllima*, December 1963: 64–67. See also the two-page photo spread "Kongye" [Handicrafts], *Ch'ŏllima*, May 1964: 104–105.

28. Rim Chongsang, "Rijo sigiŭi munhwa, 4" [The culture of the Yi Dynasty period, part 4], *Ch'ŏllima*, March 1964: 104–108.

29. For a picture of the ribbon-cutting ceremony and a story about this factory, see Anonymous, "P'yŏngyang mokchae kagu kongjang chop" [Pyongyang wood furniture factory], *Rodong sinmun*, October 23, 1957: 1–2. Earlier that year, a plywood factory had also been completed with Soviet assistance; see Anonymous, "Ssoryŏnŭi wŏnjoro kŏnsŏldoenŭn Kilchu happ'an kongjang" [The Kilchu plywood factory being constructed with Soviet assistance], *Rodong sinmun*, March 16, 1957: 2. See two photos from inside this factory in Anonymous, "Inmindŭrŭi kiho-e matke" [Suiting the people's tastes], *Chosŏn nyŏsŏng*, November 1957: 22.

30. See the photographs by an anonymous photographer that are part of the four-page spread cited above, Anonymous, "App'at'urŭl ch'ajasŏ," 8–11.

31. Ri Wŏnin, "Chohwadoen arŭmdaumŭl tugo ..." [For harmonized beauty...], *Ch'ŏllima* May 1964: 60–61.

32. For one use, see Anonymous, "Urisidaenŭn munhwhajŏgin in'ganŭl yoguhanda" [Our era demands a cultural humanity], *Ch'ŏllima*, May 1963: 5–7.

33. Anonymous, "Kagu" [Furniture], *Ch'ŏllima*, April 1964: unnumbered pullout.

34. Ri Wŏnin, "Chohwadoen arŭmdaumŭl tugo," 61.

35. See an article by the furniture designer Ho Kŭmch'ol, "Tŏuk paljŏnsik'il yoksimi nanda" [My desire to make improvements is even greater], *Ch'ŏllima*, May 1964: 46.

36. For practicality and beauty in desk design, see ibid. See also Susan E. Reid, "Cold War in the Kitchen: Gender and the De-Stalinization of Consumer Taste in the Soviet Union under Khrushchev," *Slavic Review* 61.2 (2002): 211–252.

37. Anonymous, "Pangan ch'ijang" [Room décor], *Chosŏn nyŏsŏng*, January 1965: 134.

38. Pang Ch'iwŏn, "Kagui mi" [The beauty of furniture], *Ch'ŏllima*, May 1965: 87; "Kagu" [Furniture], *Ch'ŏllima*, April 1964: two-page pullout. For a treatment of the design and aesthetic challenges as understood by architects, see Hong Kŭmch'ŏl, "Kŏnch'ukkwa kagu" [Architecture and furniture], *Kŏnch'ukkwa kŏnsŏl*, June 1962: 30–33.

39. Anonymous, "Nongch'on sallimbangŭl ŏttŏge kkuril kŏsin'ga" [How to arrange living rooms in villages], *Ch'ŏllima*, April 1964: 66–67; Kye Tongwan, "Saenghwal p'ilssup'umgwa saekkal" [Everyday necessities and color], *Ch'ŏllima*, July 1964: 81. For flower vases, see Anonymous, "Tŭl kkotkwa kkot pyŏng" [Wild flowers and flower vases], *Ch'ŏllima*, May 1964: 75.

40. Florian Urban, *Tower and Slab: Histories of Global Mass Housing* (London: Routledge, 2012).

41. Anonymous, "Ch'angmun" [Windows], *Chosŏn nyŏsŏng*, May 1964: 52–53.

42. For a similar type of argument about apartment entrance ways, see Anonymous, "Hyŏn'gwan" [Entranceways], *Chosŏn nyŏsŏng*, February 1965: 90.

43. Ina Merkel, "Working People and Consumption under Really-Existing Socialism: Perspectives from the German Democratic Republic," *International Labor and Working Class History* 55 (1999): 92–111; Ina Merkel, "Consumer Culture in the GDR, or How the Struggle for Anti-modernity Was Lost on the Battleground of Consumer Culture," in Susan Strasser, Charles McGovern, and Matthias Judt, eds., *Getting and Spending: European and American Consumer Societies in the Twentieth Century* (Cambridge: Cambridge University Press, 1998): 281–300.

44. Kim Chinsŏng, "Sallim'bangŭi saekkal" [The colors of the living room], *Ch'ŏllima*, May 1964: 62; Anonymous, "Pangan ch'ijang."

45. Anonymous, "Alttulhan pang" [A frugal room], *Ch'ŏllima*, February 1963: 90.

46. Kim Unbong, "Ottŏn chŏm-e koryŏrŭl torryŏya hanŭnga?" [What points should I be concerned about?], *Ch'ŏllima*, May 1964: 61.

47. Ri Wŏnin, "Chohwadoen arŭmdaumŭl tugo," 60.

48. Anonymous, "App'at'urŭl ch'ajasŏ," 10.

49. On rotating vases depending on the flower, see Anonymous, "Tŭl kkotkwa kkot pyŏng [Wild flowers and flower vases], *Ch'ŏllima*, May 1964: 75; on production of porcelain, see Chŏn Yŏng, "Tayanghago chil chŏun tojagirŭl tŏ mani saengsanhagi wihayŏ" [To produce more types and better quality of porcelain], *Rodong sinmun*, November 27, 1959: 3. For an upbeat article about six Pyongyang porcelain factories, see Anonymous, "Pyongyang tojagi" [Pyongyang porcelain], *Chosŏn nyŏsŏng*, November 1964: 72. Articles praising porcelain production started appearing immediately after the war; see, for example, "Chil chŏun tojagirŭl saengsan" [The production of good-quality porcelain], *Rodong sinmun*, September 20, 1954: 3.

50. *Chosŏn nyŏsŏng* was one of the few magazines that released its circulation numbers, printed on the back page of every issue, until it stopped doing so at the end of 1960.

51. Anonymous, "Uri saenghwalgwa san'ŏp misul" [Our lifestyles and commercial art], *Ch'ŏllima*, October 1964: 84–85.

52. Anonymous, "Chaebongch'im" [The art of sewing], *Ch'ŏllima*, February 1964: pullout.

53. Chang Chŏngin, "Anŭkhan pang ch'arim" [Cozy room décor], *Chosŏn nyŏsŏng*, November 1964: 100–101.

54. Ibid., 100.

55. Kim Chinsŏng, "Sallim'bangŭi saekkal," 62.

CONCLUSION

1. Mary Fulbrook, *The People's State: East German Society from Hitler to Honecker* (New Haven, CT: Yale University Press, 2005), 11.

2. Lankov believes that this statistic is on the low side, given that many purges were secret. Andrei Lankov, *From Stalin to Kim Il Sung: The Formation of North Korea, 1945–1960* (New Brunswick, NJ: Rutgers University Press, 2002), 82.

3. For a classic example of this approach, see Bonnie C. Koh, "North Korea and Its Quest for Autonomy," *Pacific Affairs* 87.4 (2014): 765–778.

4. Benjamin R. Young, *Guns, Guerillas, and the Great Leader: North Korea and the Third World* (Stanford, CA: Stanford University Press, 2021); Moe Taylor, "One Hand Can't Clap: Guyana and North Korea, 1974–1985," *Journal of Cold War Studies* 17.1 (2015): 41–63; Moe Taylor, "Discipline, Education, and Mass Games: Ideological Exchange and Sports Diplomacy between North Korea and Guyana during the Cold War," *World History Bulletin* 36.2 (2020): 7–11; Vicki Sung-yeon Kwon, "Guyanese Mass Games: Spectacles That 'Moulded' the Nation in a North Korean Way," *Inter-Asia Cultural Studies* 20.2 (2019): 180–203.

5. Kim Kwangun, *PukHan chŏngch'isa yŏn'gu 1: kŏndang, kŏn'guk, kŏn'gunŭi yŏksa* [North Korean political history: A history of the construction of the Party, the state, and the military] (Seoul: Sŏnin, 2003).

6. For some anthropological accounts, see Sonia Ryang, "Anthropology as Method: North Korea at a Distance," *Journal of Korean Studies* 26.2 (2021): 187–203; Sonia Ryang, *Reading North Korea: An Ethnological Inquiry* (Cambridge, MA: Harvard University Asia Center, 2012); Heonik Kwon and Byung-ho Chung, *North Korea: Beyond Charismatic Politics* (Lanham, MD: Rowman and Littlefield, 2012).

7. For a discussion of how the historiography on state socialism establishes Euro-America as the norm for modernity, see Paul Betts and Katherine Pence, eds., *Socialist Modern: East German Everyday Culture and Politics* (Ann Arbor: University of Michigan Press, 2008), introduction.

8. Andre Schmid, "Historicizing North Korea: State Socialism, Population Mobility, and Cold War Historiography," *The American Historical Review* 123.2 (2018): 439–462.

9. Suzy Kim and Cheehyung Harrison Kim argue for a Korean socialist modernity. Suzy Kim, *Everyday Life in the North Korean Revolution, 1945–1950* (Ithaca, NY: Cornell University Press, 2013); Cheehyung Harrison Kim, *Heroes and Toilers: Work as Life in Postwar North Korea, 1953–1961* (New York: Columbia University Press, 2018).

10. Anonymous, "Kim Il Sŏng sŏnjip che 2 p'an che 1 kwŏn palhaeng" [The first volume of the second edition of Kim Il Sung's selected works is published], *Rodong sinmun*, January 4, 1964: 1.

11. Anonymous photo accompanying Ri Ch'unyŏng, "Kidarinŭn maŭm" [With a waiting heart], *Chosŏn nyŏsŏng*, December 1959: 16–17, 17. For a photo that shows a Kim photo hanging prominently on the wall of a Pyonyang Textile Factory worker's home, see Kim Wŏnguk, "Haengbok" [Happiness], *Rodongja*, January 1959: back cover.

12. For the classic guide to these changes in English, see Dae-sook Suh, *Korean Communism, 1945–1980: A Reference Guide to the Political System* (Honolulu: University of Hawai'i Press, 1981).

13. For a discussion of these follow-up reports, see Ri Hongdŏk, "Kongsanjuŭi kyoyanggwa sinmun bodo" [The cultivation of communism and newspaper reports], *Chosŏn kija*, March 1959: 20–22.

14. Kim Oksun, "Chosŏn minju nyŏsŏng tongmaeng chungang wiwŏnhoe saŏp ch'onghwa-e taehayo" [On reviewing the tasks of the central commit of Korean Democratic Women's Union], *Chosŏn nyŏsŏng*, September 1965: 19–45.

15. Kim Il Sung, "Nyomaeng chojiktŭrap'-e nasŏnŭn myŏtkaji kwaŏp-e taehayŏ" [On several tasks facing the future of the Women's Union organizations], *Collected Works*, vol. 35 (September 2, 1965): 415–426.

16. Brian Myers, "The Watershed That Wasn't: Re-evaluating Kim Il Sung's 'Juche Speech' of 1955," *Acta Koreana* 9.1 (2006): 89–115; Brian Myers, "Ideology as Smokescreen: North Korea's Juche Thought," *Acta Koreana* 11.3 (2008): 161–182. Some other English-language studies on Juche: Sergei O. Kurbanov, "North Korea's Juche Ideology: Indigenous Communism or Traditional Thought?," *Critical Asian Studies* 51.2 (2019): 296–305; Shine Choi, "The Art of Monument Politics: The North Korean State, Juche, and International Politics," *Asian Studies Review* 45.3 (2021): 435–453; Jae-Jung Suh, ed., *Origins of North Korean Ideology: Colonialism, War, and Development* (Lanham, MD: Lexington Books, 2013).

17. Wada Haruki, *PukChosŏn: yugyŏktae kukka-esŏ chŏnggyugun kukkaro* [North Korea: From guerrilla to garrison state], tr. Sŏ Tongman and Nam Kijŏng (Seoul: Tolbegae, 2002). This interpretation was picked up on in J. E. Hoare and Susan Pares, *North Korea in the 21st Century: An Interpretative Guide* (Kent: Global Oriental, 2005). For an alternative understanding of the origins of the revolution in Manchuria, see Hyun Ok Park, *Two Dreams in One Bed: Empire, Social Life, and the Origins of the North Korean Revolution in Manchuria* (Durham, NC: Duke University Press, 2005).

18. Hyŏn P'ilhun, "Sahoejuŭi kŏnsŏrŭi kojowa ch'ulp'an podo ilgundŭrŭi kwaŏp" [The high tide of socialist construction of publishing-sector workers], *Chosŏn kija*, December 1958: 15; Ri Paekham, "Yuch'iwŏngi adongdŭr-e taehan hyŏngmyŏng chŏnt'ong kyoyang" [Teaching the revolutionary tradition during a child's day care years], *Inmin kyoyuk*, February 1960: 30–34.

19. Mun Mira, "1950–1960 nyŏndae PukHanŭi 'hyŏngmyŏng chŏnt'ong' hwangnip kwajŏnggwa yŏksa insikŭi pyŏnhwa" [The process of establishing North Korea's "revolutionary tradition" and shifts in historical understanding during the 1950s and 1960s], *Yŏksawa hyŏnsil* 119 (March 2021): 237–271.

20. For another treatment of naming practices, see Fyodor Tertitskiy, "The Ascension of the Ordinary Man: How the Personality Cult of Kim Il Sung Was Constructed (1945–1974)," *Acta Koreana* 18.1 (2015): 209–231.

21. Anonymous, "Kakto saengsanp'um Pyŏngyang ryŏnhap chingmaejŏm kaejŏm" [Pyongyang cooperative wholesale store with provincial products opens branch], *Rodong sinmun*, August 15, 1958: 4.

22. Alan Taylor, "Kim Jong Un Looking at Things," *The Atlantic*, February 1, 2012, https://www.theatlantic.com/photo/2012/02/kim-jong-un-looking-at-things/100237/.

23. Kwon and Chung, *North Korea: Beyond Charismatic Politics*, 18–25.

24. Min Pyŏnggyun, "Chosŏnŭi ŏmŏni" [Korean mother], *Chosŏn nyŏsŏng*, April 1960: 16–17. This expression was not reserved only for Kang but has a broader currency, as seen in Pak Sŭngsu and Kim Sŏngnak, *Chosŏnŭi ŏmŏni, 3* [Korean mothers, part 3] (Pyongyang: Chosŏn nyŏsŏngsa, 1960). For mother poems more generally, see Kim Chŏngguk, "Ŏmŏnisiyŏ!" [Mother!], *Rodongja sinmun*, September 27, 1959: 3; Kim Kuiryŏn, "Ŏmŏniŭi maŭm" [The heart of a mother], *Chosŏn munhak*, March 1955: 112–113; Chu T'aesan, "Chosŏnŭi ŏmŏni" [Korea's mothers], *Rodong sinmun*, March 8, 1955: 3. In Kang's case, this evocative expression received the lyricism of poetry.

25. Ri Myŏngwŏn, *Kŏnsŏl chagŏppanjangŭi sugi* [A construction brigade leader's memoir] (Pyongyang: Minch'ŏng ch'ulp'ansa, 1961), 142–154.

26. Such first encounters with Kim became standard fare in the print media, often written in poetry. See three poems composed on this theme by Kwak Mal-llyak, Ro Sa, and Chŏnhan in *Rodong sinmun*, November 30, 1958: 3.

APPENDIX

1. I have written a more extensive article on sources as an introduction to a special issue on North Korea. See Andre Schmid, "Introduction," *Journal of Korean Studies* 26.2 (2021): 169–186.

2. See the massive collection, already at 130 volumes for the nine years between 1945 and 1954, Kim Kwang-un, ed., *PukChosŏn sillok: nyŏnp'yowa saryo* [The veritable records of North Korea: Chronology and historical materials] (Sŏul T'ŭkpyŏlsi: Kyŏngnamdae, PukHan Taehagwŏndae, Korea Data Project, 2018).

3. For a critique of the effects of securitization, see Sonia Ryang, ed., *North Korea: Toward a Better Understanding* (Lanham, MD: Lexington Books, 2009); Hazel Smith, *North Korea: Markets and Military Rule* (Cambridge: Cambridge University Press, 2015).

4. The beer figure is from Chosŏn chungang t'ongsinsa, *Chosŏn chungang nyŏn'gam, 1961* [The Korean national yearbook, 1961] (Pyongyang, 1962), 235.

5. For a more general treatment of gender and sources, see Yi Onjuk, "Yŏsŏnggwa kajŏng saenghwal," in Son Pongsuk, Yi Kyŏngsuk, Yi Onjuk, and Kim Aesil, eds., *PukHanŭi yŏsŏng saenghwal: irongwa silje* [The lives of North Korean women: Theory and reality] (Seoul: Nanam, 1991), ch. 2.

6. See the cartoons in *Rodongja*, November 1955: 52.

7. "Samnoju" [Samno alcohol], *Chosŏn* 42 (January 1960): 15.

8. Hwang Toyŏn, "Kyesan—tonggye kyuyurŭi ŏmgyŏkhan chunsunŭn inmin kyŏngje paljŏnŭi p'ilsujŏk chogŏnida" [Strict adherence to displined calculations and statistics is a necessary condition for the development of the people's economy], *Kyŏngje kŏnsŏl*, June 1955: 13–23.

9. Kim Sŏnghwan and Rim Sanguk, "Kyŏrŭiwa silch'ŏngan-e koriga ittda: 'Hambuk ilbo' p'yŏnjipkuk saŏp-esŏ" [There's a gap between pledges and achievements: On the work of the *Hambuk Daily*'s editorial office], *Chosŏn kija*, March 1959: 39–43; Kim Myŏnghwan, "Chumindŭrŭi sangp'um suyo yŏn'gu pangbŏp" [Methods of researching product needs of residents], *Kyŏngje chisik*, December 1960: 64–68.

10. For a treatment of these challenges for grain production, see Sŏ Tongman, "1950 nyŏndae PukHanŭi kongmul saengsanryang t'onggye-e kwanhan yŏn'gu" [Research on 1950s North Korean statistics on grain production], in *PukChosŏn yŏn'gu* [Research on North Korea] (Seoul: Ch'angbi, 2010), 19–48.

11. Chosŏn chungang t'ongsinsa, *Chosŏn chungang nyŏn'gam, 1958* [The Korean national yearbook, 1958] (Pyongyang: Chosŏn chungang t'ongsinsa, 1958), 203.

12. Anonymous, "Kungnae chŏnggi kanhaengmul che3gi yeyak annae" [Guide to reserving domestic serials in the third term], *Rodong sinmun*, April 1, 1955: 4.

13. For one illustration of a political study session sponsored by the Workers' Federation, underway in a factory reading room, see Kim Yunjae, untitled illustration, *Rodongja sinmun*, October 21, 1959: 4.

14. See the call by *Women of Korea* published in *Rodong sinmun*, "'Chosŏn nyŏsŏng' ch'anggan 10 chunyŏn kinyŏm chakp'um hyŏnsang mojip" [Call for literary works commemorating the tenth anniversary of the opening of *Women of Korea*], *Rodong sinmun*, September 3, 1956: 4.

15. Kim Chunggap, "Saehae-edo nanŭn chapch'irŭl aedok hagetta" [I will devotedly read the magazine in the coming year too], *Chosŏn nyŏsŏng*, January 1957: 30.

SELECTED BIBLIOGRAPHY

The information in this book is largely derived from the newspapers and periodicals listed at the beginning of this bibliography. Due to the number of articles cited, full bibliographic information for all print media sources appears only in the endnotes. For a discussion of these print media sources, please see the appendix.

NORTH KOREAN PERIODICALS

Choguk powirŭl wihayŏ [For the defense of the ancestral land]

Ch'ŏllima [Thousand-mile horse]

Ch'ŏngnyŏn saenghwal [Youth life]

Chosŏn kija [Korean reporter]

Chosŏn nyŏsŏng [Women of Korea]

Chosŏn yŏnghwa [Korean film]

Hwalsal [Life and death]

Hwasal [Arrow]

Inmin pogŏn [Popular public sanitation]

Kŏnch'ukkwa kŏnsŏl [Architecture and construction]

Kŏnsŏl [Construction]

Kŏnsŏlja [Builder]

Kŭlloja [Laborer]

Kyŏngje chisik [Economic knowledge]

Kyŏngje kŏnsŏl [Economic construction]

Kyŏngje yŏn'gu [Economic research]

Malgwa kŭl [Speech and writing]

Minju Chosŏn [Democratic Korea]

Munhwa yusan [Cultural heritage]

Naegwa [Internal medicine]

NamChosŏn munje [South Korean problems]

Rodong sinmun [Worker daily]

Rodongja [Worker]

Rodongja sinmun [Workers' newspaper]

Sae sedae [New generation]

Sangŏp [Commerce]

Sinsaenghwal [New living]

Soa sanbuingwa [Pediatrics and obstetrics]

Sŏndongwŏn such'ŏp [Notes for propaganda workers]

Tangganbudŭl-ege chunŭn ch'amgo charyo [Reference materials for party cadres]

Wisaeng munhwa [Hygiene culture]

BOOKS, JOURNAL ARTICLES, AND REPORTS

Althusser, Louis. "Ideology and Ideological State Apparatuses: Notes toward an Investigation." Translated by Ben Brewster. In *Lenin and Philosophy and Other Essays*, 127–196. New York: Monthly Review Press, 1968.

Appy, G. Christian, ed. "Introduction." In *Cold War Constructions: The Political Culture of United States Imperialism, 1945–1966*. Amherst: University of Massachusetts Press, 2000.

Barraclough, Ruth. "Red Love and Betrayal in the Making of North Korea: Comrade Hŏ Jŏng-suk." *History Workshop Journal* 77 (Spring 2014): 86–102.

Betts, Paul, and David Crowley, eds. "Domestic Dreamworlds: Notions of Home in Post-1945 Europe, Introduction." *Journal of Contemporary History* 40.2 (2005): 213–236.

Betts, Paul, and Katherine Pence, eds. *Socialist Modern: East German Everyday Culture and Politics*. Ann Arbor: University of Michigan Press, 2008.

Brazinsky, Gregg A. "Remembering Ŏmŏni: Using Chinese Memoirs to Understand Sino-North Korean Interactions during the Korean War." *Journal of Korean Studies* 26.2 (2021): 251–270.

Brown, Wendy. *States of Injury: Power and Freedom in Late Modernity*. Princeton, NJ: Princeton University Press, 1995.

Buck-Morss, Susan. *Dreamworld and Catastrophe: The Passing of Mass Utopia in East and West*. Cambridge, MA: MIT Press, 2000.

Castillo, Greg. *Cold War on the Home Front: The Soft Power of Midcentury Design*. Minneapolis: Minnesota University Press, 2009.

Central Statistical Board under the State Planning Commission of the DPRK. *Statistical Returns of National Economy of the Democratic People's Republic of Korea, 1946–1960.* Pyongyang: Foreign Languages Publishing House, 1961.

Chandra, Vipan. *Imperialism, Resistance, and Reform in Late Nineteenth-Century Korea.* Berkeley: Institute of East Asian Studies, University of California, 1988.

Chang Sehun. "Han'guk chŏnjaenggwa nambukHanŭi tosihwa: Sŏulgwa P'yŏngyangŭi chŏnhu pokku kwajŏngŭl chungsimŭro" [The Korean War and the urbanization of North and South Korea: With a focus on the postwar recovery process of Seoul and Pyongyang]. *Sahoewa yŏksa* 67 (2005): 237–238.

Chatterjee, Partha. *Nationalist Thought and the Colonial World: A Derivative Discourse.* Minneapolis: University of Minnesota Press, 1993.

Cheng, Yinghong. *Creating the "New Man": From Enlightenment Ideals to Socialist Realities.* Honolulu: University of Hawai'i Press, 2008.

Cho Hyŏng and Pak Myŏngsŏn. "PukHan ch'ulsin wŏlnaminŭi chŏngch'akkwajŏngŭl t'onghae pon nambukHan sahoegujoŭi pyŏnhwa" [Changes in North and South Korean society as seen through the settlement process of refugees from North Korea]. In *Pundan sidaewa Han'guksahoe* [The division period and Korean society]. Seoul: Kkach'i, 1985.

Cho Ilho. *Chosŏn kajokpŏp* [Korean family law]. Pyongyang: Kyoyuk tosŏ ch'ulp'ansa, 1958.

Cho, Sanghun. "Memory as Propaganda: The Molding of Official Memory of the Korean War and Its Employment in the DPRK from 1953 to 1958." MA thesis, University of Toronto, 2007.

Ch'oe Chinuk. *Hyŏndae PukHan haengjŏngnon* [Contemporary North Korea's bureaucracy]. Seoul: Myŏngin munhwasa, 2007.

Ch'oe Talgon. *PukHan Honinbŏp* [North Korean marriage law]. Seoul: Koryŏ taehakkyo ch'ulp'anbu, 1977.

Choi, Hyaeweol. *Gender and Mission Encounters in Korea: New Women, Old Ways.* Berkeley: University of California Press, 2009.

———. *New Women in Colonial Korea: A Sourcebook.* New York: Routledge, 2013.

———. "Transpacific Aspiration toward Modern Domesticity in Japanese Colonial-Era Korea." *Journal of Women's History* 30.4 (2018): 60–83.

Choi, Shine. "The Art of Monument Politics: The North Korean State, Juche, and International Politics." *Asian Studies Review* 45.3 (2021): 434–453.

Chŏn Changsŏk. *Miguksik saenghwal yangsikkwa namChosŏn-e mich'in kŭ hugwa* [American-style living and its effect on South Korea]. Pyongyang: Chosŏn rodongdang ch'ulp'ansa, 1965.

Chŏn Namil, Yang Sehwa, Hong Hyŏngok, and Son Segwan, eds. *Han'guk chugŏŭi sahoesa* [A social history of South Korean housing]. P'aju: Tol Pegae, 2008.

Chŏn Sŏnggŭn. *Nyŏsŏngdŭrŭi kongsanjuŭijŏk ryeŭi todok* [The communist etiquette and morality of women]. Pyongyang: Chosŏn nyŏsŏngsa, 1963.

Chŏng Yŏngch'ŏl. "PukHanhagŭi hyŏnhwanggwa chŏnmang" [The current situation and outlook for North Korean studies]. *Hwanghae munhwa* 57 (December, 2007): 304–325.

Chosŏn chungang t'ongsinsa. *Chosŏn chungang nyŏn'gam, 1958* [The Korean national yearbook, 1958]. Pyongyang: Chosŏn chungang t'ongsinsa, 1959.

———. *Chosŏn chungang nyŏn'gam, 1961* [The Korean national yearbook, 1961]. Pyongyang: Chosŏn chungang t'ongsinsa, 1962.

———. *Chosŏn chungang nyŏn'gam, 1964* [The Korean national yearbook, 1964]. Pyongyang: Chosŏn chungang t'ongsinsa, 1965.

Chosŏn minju nyŏsŏng tongmaeng chungang wiwŏnhoe. *Nyŏsŏngdŭrŭn munhwa sujunŭl nop'ija* [Women, let us raise our cultural levels]. Pyongyang: Chosŏn nyŏsŏngsa, 1956.

Chosŏn nyŏsŏngsa. *Arŭmdaun nyŏsŏngdŭl* [Beautiful women]. Pyongyang: Chosŏn nyŏsŏngsa, 1963.

———. *Chogugŭi chayuwa tongnibŭl wihayŏ ssaunŭn Chosŏn nyŏsŏng* [Korean women fighting for our ancestral land's freedom and independence]. Pyongyang: Chosŏn nyŏsŏngsa, 1954.

———, ed. *Ch'ŏn'guk ŏmŏni taehoe: munhŏnjip* [All-Nation Congress of Mothers: Document collection]. Pyongyang: Chosŏn nyŏsŏngsa, 1962.

———. *Nyŏsŏng ch'ŏllima kisudŭl* [Female thousand-mile horse riders]. Pyongyang: Chosŏn nyŏsŏngsa, 1960.

———. *Omŏni hakkyo kyojae: kajŏng kwalli chisik* [A motherhood school reader: Knowledge for home management]. Pyongyang, Chosŏn nyŏsŏngsa, 1963.

Chosŏn rodongdang. *Chunggŭp haksŭppan ch'amgo charyo* [Reference materials for mid-level study classes]. Pyongyang: Chosŏn nodongdang ch'ulp'ansa, 1957.

———, ed. *Kim Ilsŏng chŏnjip* [The collected works of Kim Il Sung]. Pyongyang: Rodongdang ch'ulp'ansa, 1995.

———. *Kyŏngje sangsik: kongŏp, nongŏp, sangŏp* [A primer on economics: Industry, agriculture, and commerce]. Pyongyang: Chosŏn rodongdang ch'ulp'ansa, 1960.

Chungang t'onggyeguk, ed. *Chosŏn minju inmin konghwaguk inmin kyŏngje mit munhwa paljon, t'onggyejip, 1946–57* [The DPRK statistical report on economic and cultural development]. Pyongyang: Kungnip ch'up'ansa, 1958.

CIA Intelligence Memorandum. *North and South Korea: Separate Paths of Economic Development.* General CIA records, May 1, 1972. https://www.cia.gov/readingroom/document/cia-rdp85t00875r001700030082-7.

Cliff, Tony. *State Capitalism in Russia.* London: Pluto Press, 1974.

Clinton, Maggie. *Revolutionary Nativism: Facism and Culture in China, 1925–1937.* Durham, NC: Duke University Press, 2017.

Collins, Robert. *Marked for Life: Songbun, North Korea's Social Classification System.* Washington, DC: The Committee for Human Rights in North Korea, 2012.

Connell, Robert W. "The State, Gender and Sexual Politics: Theory and Appraisal." In H. Radtke and H. Stam, eds., *Power/Gender*, 136–173. London: Sage, 1994.

Corner, Paul, and Jie-Hyun Lim, eds. *The Palgrave Handbook of the History of Mass Dictatorship.* London: Palgrave Macmillan, 2016.

Crowley, John E. "The Sensibility of Comfort." *The American Historical Review* 104.3 (1999): 749–782.

Cumings, Bruce. *The Origins of the Korean War, vol. 1: Liberation and the Emergence of Separate Regimes, 1945–47.* Princeton, NJ: Princeton University Press, 1981.

Department of Public Health and Welfare, Bureau of Vital Statistics. *Population of South Korea, by Geographical Divisions and Sex.* Seoul: U.S. Army Military Government in Korea, 1946.

Deuchler, Martina. *The Confucian Transformation of Korea: A Study of Ideology and Society.* Cambridge, MA: Harvard University Press, 1992.

Duncan, John. *The Origins of the Chosŏn Dynasty.* Seattle: University of Washington Press, 2000.

Eagleton, Terry. *Ideology.* London: Routledge, 2013.

Eberstadt, Nicholas, and Judith Banister. *The Population of North Korea.* Berkeley: Institute of East Asian Studies, University of California, 1992.

Engels, Friedrich. *The Origin of the Family, Private Property and the State.* New York: International Publishers, 1893.

Esposito, Roberto. "Totalitarianism or Biopolitics? Concerning a Philosophical Interpretation of the 20th Century" [translated by Timothy Campbell]. *Critical Inquiry* 34.4 (2008): 633–644.

Fehervary, Krisztina. "Goods and States: The Political Logic of State-Socialist Material Culture." *Comparative Studies in Society and History* 51.2 (2009): 426–459.

Ferguson, Kathy E. *The Feminist Case against Bureaucracy.* Philadelphia: Temple University Press, 1984.

Filatov, Victor Pavlovich. *Lenin's 'What Is to Be Done?'* Moscow: Progress Publishers, 1987.

Fitzpatrick, Sheila. *Everyday Stalinism: Ordinary Life in Extraordinary Times: Soviet Russia in the 1930s.* Oxford: Oxford University Press, 1999.

———, ed. *Stalinism: New Directions.* New York: Taylor & Francis, 2000.

Foreign Languages Publishing House, ed. *Kim Il Sung: Works.* Pyongyang: Foreign Languages Publishing House, 1980.

Forgacs, David, ed. *The Gramsci Reader: Selected Writings, 1916–1935.* New York: NYU Press, 2000.

Foucault, Michel. *The Birth of Biopolitics: Lectures at the Collège de France, 1978–1979.* Translated by Michel Senellart. New York: Picador, 2008.

———. *Discipline and Punish: The Birth of the Prison.* New York: Vintage Books, 1979.

———. *The History of Sexuality, vol. 1: An Introduction.* Translated by Robert Hurley. New York: Vintage Books, 1978.

———. *Society Must Be Defended: Lectures at the Collège de France, 1975–76.* Translated by David Macey. New York: Picador, 2003.

Frank, Rüdiger. "Lessons from the Past: The First Wave of Developmental Assistance to North Korea and the German Reconstruction of Hamhŭng." *Pacific Focus* 23.1 (2008): 46–74.

Fujitani, Takashi. *Race for Empire: Koreans as Japanese and Japanese as Americans during World War II.* Berkeley: University of California Press, 2013.

Fulbrook, Mary. *The People's State: East German Society from Hitler to Honecker.* New Haven, CT: Yale University Press, 2005.

Gabroussenko, Tatiana. *Soldiers on the Cultural Front: Developments in the Early History of North Korean Literature and Literary Policy.* Honolulu: University of Hawai'i Press, 2010.

Gerth, Karl. *Unending Capitalism: How Consumerism Negated China's Communist Revolution.* Cambridge: Cambridge University Press, 2020.

Goldman, Wendy Z. *Women, the State, and Revolution: Soviet Family Policy and Social Life, 1917–1936.* Cambridge: Cambridge University Press, 1993.

Gordon, Andrew. *Fabricating Consumers: The Sewing Machine in Modern Japan.* Berkeley: University of California Press, 2012.

Grinker, Roy Richard. *Korea and Its Futures: Unification and the Unfinished War.* New York: St. Martin's Press, 2000.

Han Sŏnghun. *Chŏnjaenggwa inmin: PukHan sahoejuŭi ch'ejeŭi sŏngnipkwa inminŭi tansaeng* [War and people: The establishment of the North Korean socialist system and the birth of the people]. Tolbegae: Kyŏnggi-do P'aju-si, 2012.

Harootunian, Harry. *Overcome by Modernity: History, Culture, and Community in Interwar Japan.* Princeton, NJ: Princeton University Press, 2000.

Harris, Steven E. *Communism on Tomorrow Street: Mass Housing and Everyday Life after Stalin.* Baltimore: Johns Hopkins University Press, 2013.

Harsch, Donna. *Revenge of the Domestic: Women, the Family and Communism in the German Democratic Republic.* Princeton, NJ: Princeton University Press, 2007.

Hellbeck, Jochen. *Revolution on My Mind: Writing a Diary under Stalin.* Cambridge, MA: Harvard University Press, 2006.

Henry, Todd A. *Assimilating Seoul: Japanese Rule and the Politics of Public Space in Colonial Korea, 1910–1945.* Berkeley: University of California Press, 2014.

Heo, Na Sil. "Rearing Autonomous Children in Cold War Korea: Transnational Formations of a Liberal Order, 1950s–1960s." PhD dissertation, University of Toronto, 2020.

Hershatter, Gail. *The Gender of Memory: Rural Women and China's Collective Past.* Berkeley: University of California Press, 2011.

Hŏ Ryŏnsuk. *Kajŏng saenghwal tokbon* [A reader for family living]. Pyongyang: Chosŏn nyŏsŏngsa, 1959.

Hoare, J. E., and Susan Pares. *North Korea in the 21st Century: An Interpretative Guide.* Kent, UK: Global Oriental, 2005.

Hoffman, David L. *Stalinist Values: The Cultural Norms of Soviet Modernity, 1917–1941.* Ithaca, NY: Cornell University Press, 2003.

Hoganson, Kristin. "Cosmopolitan Domesticity: Importing the American Dream, 1865–1920." *The American Historical Review* 107.1 (2002): 55–83.

Hong, Intaek. "North Korea's War Orphans: Trasnational Education and Post-war Society." *Sources and Methods: A Blog of the History and Public Policy Program,* June 18, 2020. https://www.wilsoncenter.org/blog-post/north-koreas -war-orphans-transnational-education-and-postwar-society.

Hong Sunwŏn. *Chosŏn pogŏnsa* [A history of Korean public health]. Hambuk: Kwahak, paekkwasajŏn ch'ulp'ansa, 1981.

Hong, Tŏkki. *Tasan Chŏng Yaggyongŭi t'oji kaehyŏk sasang* [The land reform thought of Tasan Chŏng Yagyong]. Kwangju: Chŏnnam taehakkyo ch'ulp'anbu, 2001.

Hong Yang-hee. "Debates about 'A Good Wife and Wise Mother' and Tradition in Colonial Korea." *The Review of Korean Studies* 11.4 (2008): 41–60.

Hong Yanghŭi. "Singminji sigi hojŏk chedowa kajok chedoŭi pyŏnyong" [Colonial-era changes in the family registration and family systems]. *Sahak yŏn'gu* 79 (2005): 167–205.

Hong, Young-Sun. "Through a Glass Darkly: East German Assistance to North Korea and Alternative Histories of the Korean War." In Quinn Slobodian, ed., *Comrades of Color: East Germany in the Cold War World*. New York: Berghan Books, 2015.

Hwang Yŏngsik. *Saenghwarŭi kŏul* [A guide to living]. Pyongyang: Sahoejuŭi rodong ch'ŏngnyŏn tongmaeng ch'ulp'ansa, 1965.

Jones, Mark. *Children as Treasures: Childhood and the Middle Class in Early Twentieth-Century Japan*. Cambridge, MA: Harvard University Asia Center, 2010.

Jung, Youngoh. "The History of Conscientious Objection and the Normalization of Universal Male Conscription in South Korean Society." MA thesis, University of Toronto, 2014.

Kal, Hong. *The Aesthetics of Korean Nationalism: Spectacle, Politics, and History*. New York: Routledge, 2011.

Kang Chŏnggu. "Haebanghu wŏllaminŭi wŏllam tonggiwa kyegŭpsŏng-e kwanhan yŏn'gu" [Research on the motivations and class character of people who crossed south after liberation]. In Han'guk Sahoe Hakhoe, ed., *Han'guk chonjaenggwa Han'guk sahoe pyŏndong* [The Korean war and changes in Korean society]. Seoul: Pulp'it, 1992.

Kantola, Johanna. *Feminists Theorize the State*. London: Palgrave Macmillan, 2006.

Kawashima, Ken C. *The Proletarian Gamble: Korean Workers in Interwar Japan*. Durham, NC: Duke University Press, 2009.

Kelly, Catriona. *Refining Russia: Advice Literature, Polite Culture, and Gender from Catherine to Yeltsin*. Oxford: Oxford University Press, 2001.

Kelly, Phyllis M., and Caroline Shillaber. *International Bibliography of Prefabricated Housing*. Cambridge, MA: MIT Press, 1954.

Kiaer, Christina. *Imagine No Possessions: The Socialist Objects of Russian Constructivism*. Cambridge, MA: MIT Press, 2005.

Kiaer, Christina, and Eric Naiman, eds. *Everyday Life in Early Soviet Russia: Taking the Revolution Inside*. Bloomington: Indiana University Press, 2006.

Kief, Jonathon. "Reading Seoul in Pyongyang: Cross-Border Mediascapes in Early Cold War North Korea." *Journal of Korean Studies* 26.2 (2021): 325–348.

Kim Chaeŭng. *PukHan ch'ejeŭi kiwŏn: inminwiŭi kyegŭp, kyegŭpwiŭi kukka* [The origins of the North Korean system: Class above people and state above class]. Kyŏnggi-do Koyang-si: Yŏksa pip'yŏngsa, 2018.

Kim, Cheehyung Harrison. *Heroes and Toilers: Work as Life in Postwar North Korea, 1953–1961*. New York: Columbia University Press, 2018.

Kim Hyegyŏng and Chŏng Chinsŏng. "Haekkajok nonŭiwa singminjijŏk kŭndaesŏng: singminji sigi saeroun kajokkaenyŏmŭi toipkwa pyŏnhyŏng" [Debates on the nuclear family and colonial modernity: The introduction and transformation of new concepts of the family in the colonial era]. *Han'guk sahoehak* 35.4 (2001): 213–244.

Kim, Janice C.H. *To Live to Work: Factory Women in Colonial Korea, 1910–1945.* Stanford, CA: Stanford University Press, 2009.

Kim Keong-il. "Alternative Forms of Marriage and Family in Colonial Korea." *The Review of Korean Studies* 11.4 (2008): 61–82.

Kim Kwangun. *PukHan chŏngch'isa yŏn'gu 1: kŏndang, kŏn'guk, kŏn'gunŭi yŏksa* [North Korean political history: A history of the construction of the Party, the state, and the military]. Seoul: Sŏnin, 2003.

———, ed. *PukChosŏn sillok: nyŏnp'yowa saryo* [The veritable records of North Korea: Chronology and historical materials]. Sŏul T'ŭkpyŏlsi: Kyŏngnamdae, PukHan Taehagwŏndae, Korea Data Project, 2018.

Kim, Michael. "Industrial Warriors: Labor Heroes and Everyday Life in Wartime Colonial Korea, 1937–1945." In Alf Lüdtke, ed., *Everyday Life in Mass Dictatorship: Evasion and Collusion*, 126–146. New York: Palgrave Macmillan, 2016.

———. "Sub-nationality in the Japanese Empire: A Social History of the Koseki in Colonial Korea, 1910–45." In David Chapman and Karl Jakob Krogness, eds., *Japan's Household Registration System and Citizenship: Koseki, Identification and Documentation*, 111–126. New York: Routledge, 2014.

Kim Namsik. *PukHan kongsanhwa kwajŏng yŏn'gu* [Studies on the communization process of North Korea]. Seoul: Tonga ch'ulp'ansa, 1972.

Kim Pyŏngno. "Han'guk chŏnjaengŭi injŏk kŭ sonsilgwa PukHan kyegŭpchŏngch'aegŭi pyŏnhwa" [Human losses in the Korean War and changes in North Korean class policy]. *T'ongil chŏngch'aek yŏn'gu* 9.1 (2000).

Kim Sŏngbo [Seong Bo]. *NambukHan kyŏngjegujoŭi kiwŏngwa chŏn'gae: PukHan nongŏpch'ejeŭi hyŏngsŏngŭl chungsimŭro* [The origins and development of the North Korean economic structure: With a focus on the formation of North Korea's agricultural system]. Seoul: Yŏksa pip'yŏngsa, 2000.

———. "PukHan hyŏndaesa yŏn'guŭi sŏnggwa kwa chaengjŏm" [The results and disputed points of North Korean contemporary history research]. *Yŏksa munje yŏn'gu* 13 (December 2004): 15–44.

Kim Suk-Young. *Illusive Utopias: Theater, Film, and Everyday Performance in North Korea.* Ann Arbor: University of Michigan Press, 2010.

Kim, Sungjo. "The Countryside and the City: A Spatial Economy of the New Village Movement in 1970s South Korea." PhD dissertation, University of Toronto, 2015.

Kim, Suzy. *Among Women across Worlds: North Korea in the Global Cold War.* Ithaca, NY: Cornell University Press, 2023.

———. *Everyday Life in the North Korean Revolution, 1945–1950.* Ithaca, NY: Cornell University Press, 2013.

————. "Revolutionary Mothers: Women in the North Korean Revolution, 1945–1950." *Comparative Studies in Society and History* 52.4 (2010): 742–767.

Kim Tuhŏn. *Han'guk kajok chedo yŏn'gu* [Studies of the Korean family system]. Seoul: Sŏul Taehakkyo ch'ulpanbu, 1968.

Kim Unch'ŏl. "NamChosŏn-e taehan mijeŭi sasang munhwa ch'imnyak chŏngch'aek" [The American policy of ideological and cultural penetration of South Korea]. In *NamChosŏn munje nonmunjip*, 134–154. Pyongyang: NamChosŏn munje ch'ulp'ansa, 1965.

Kim Yŏnch'ŏl. *PukHanŭi sanŏphwawa kyŏngje chŏngch'aek* [North Korea's industrialization and economic policies]. Seoul: Yŏksa pip'yŏngsa, 2001.

Kim Yonghyŏn. "1950–60nyŏndae PukHan kyŏngjeŭi kunsahwa" [The militarization of the North Korean economy in the 1950s and 1960s]. *Saehoe kwahak yŏn'gu* 9.1 (2003): 164–183.

Ko, Sunho. "Food for Empire: Wartime Food Politics on the Korean Homefront 1937–1945." PhD dissertation, University of Toronto, 2018.

Koh, Bonnie C. "North Korea and Its Quest for Autonomy." *Pacific Affairs* 87.4 (2014): 765–778.

Kornai, János. *The Economics of Shortage*. Amsterdam: Elsevier North-Holland, 1980.

————. *The Socialist System: The Political Economy of Socialism*. Oxford: Clarendon, 1992.

Kotkin, Stephen. *Magnetic Mountain: Stalinism as Civilization*. Berkeley: University of California Press, 1995.

Kraus, Richard. *Class Conflict in Chinese Socialism*. New York: Columbia University Press, 1981.

Krylova, Anna. "Stalinist Identity from the Viewpoint of Gender: Rearing a Generation of Professionally Violent Women-Fighters in 1930s Stalinist Russia." *Gender and History* 16.3 (2004): 626–653.

————. "The Tenacious Liberal Subject in Soviet Studies." *Kritika* 1.1 (2000): 119–146.

Kukka kyehoek wiwŏnhoe chungang t'onggyeguk, ed. *1946–1957 Chosŏn minjujuŭi inmin konghwaguk inmin kyŏngje mit munhwa paljŏn t'onggyejip* [1946–1957: The Democratic People's Republic of Korea's statistics collection on the national economy and cultural developments]. Pyongyang: Kungnip ch'ulp'ansa, 1958.

Kurbanov, Sergei O. "North Korea's Juche Ideology: Indigenous Communism or Traditional Thought?" *Critical Asian Studies* 51.2 (2019): 296–305.

Kwak, Nancy. *A World of Homeowners: American Power and the Politics of Housing Aid*. Chicago: University of Chicago Press, 2015.

Kwon, Heonik, and Byung-ho Chung. *North Korea: Beyond Charismatic Politics*. Lanham, MD: Rowman and Littlefield, 2012.

Kwon, Tai-Whan. *Demography of Korea*. Seoul: Seoul National University Press, 1977.

Kwon, Vicki Sung-yeon. "Guyanese Mass Games: Spectacles That 'Moulded' the Nation in a North Korean Way." *Inter-Asia Cultural Studies* 20.2 (2019): 180–203.

Lankov, Andrei. *From Stalin to Kim Il Sung: The Formation of North Korea, 1945–1960.* New Brunswick, NJ: Rutgers University Press, 2002.

Lee, Soo-Jung. "Making and Unmaking the Korean National Division: Separated Families in the Cold War and Post–Cold War Eras." PhD dissertation, University of Michigan, 2006.

Li, Jie. *Shanghai Homes: Palimpsests of Private Life.* New York: Columbia University Press, 2014.

Lim, Jie-Hyun, and Karen Petrone, eds. *Gender Politics and Mass Dictatorship: Global Perspectives.* London: Palgrave Macmillan, 2010.

Lim, Sungyun. *Rules of the House: Family Law and Domestic Disputes in Colonial Korea.* Oakland: University of California Press, 2019.

Lüdtke, Alf, ed. "Introduction." In *The History of Everyday Life: Reconstructing Historical Experiences and Ways of Life.* Princeton, NJ: Princeton University Press, 1995.

MacKinnon, Catharine A. *Toward a Feminist Theory of the State.* London: Harvard University Press, 1989.

Maldonado, Tomás. "The Idea of Comfort" [translated by John Cullars]. *Design Issues* 8.1 (1991): 35–43.

Matveeva, Natalia. "Building a New World: The Economic Development Strategies of the Two Koreas in the Cold War, 1957–1966." PhD dissertation, School of Oriental and African Studies, London, 2021.

May, Todd. *The Philosophy of Foucault.* London: Routledge, 2014.

Merkel, Ina. "Consumer Culture in the GDR, or How the Struggle for Antimodernity Was Lost on the Battleground of Consumer Culture." In Susan Strasser, Charles McGovern, and Matthias Judt, eds., *Getting and Spending: European and American Consumer Societies in the Twentieth Century,* 281–300. Cambridge: Cambridge University Press, 1998.

———. "Working People and Consumption under Really-Existing Socialism: Perspectives from the German Democratic Republic." *International Labor and Working Class History* 55 (1999): 92–111.

Miller, Owen. "War, the State, and the Formation of the North Korean Industrial Working Class, 1931–1961." *Third World Quarterly* 37.10 (2016): 1901–1920.

Miller, Owen, ed. *State Capitalism and Development in East Asia since 1945.* Leiden, The Netherlands: Brill, forthcoming.

Mironenko, Dmitry. "A Jester with Chamelon Faces: Laughter and Comedy in North Korea, 1953–1969." PhD dissertation, Harvard University, 2014.

Miyoshi Jager, Sheila. *Narratives of Nation-Building in Korea: A Genealogy of Patriotism.* London: Routledge, 2003.

Moeller, Robert. *Protecting Motherhood: Women and the Family in the Politics of Postwar West Germany.* Berkeley: University of California Press, 1993.

Mun Mira. "1950–1960 nyŏndae PukHanŭi 'hyŏngmyŏng chŏnt'ong' hwangnip kwajŏnggwa yŏksa insikŭi pyŏnhwa" [The process of establishing North Korea's "revolutionary tradition" and shifts in historical understanding during the 1950s and 1960s]. *Yŏksawa hyŏnsil* 119 (March 2021): 237–271.

Mun Sojŏng. "Singminji sigi tosigajokkwa yŏsŏngŭi hyŏnsil-e kwanhan yŏn'gu" [Studies on the situation of urban families and women in the colonial period]. *Hyangt'o Sŏul* 70 (2007): 5–49.

Myers, Brian. *Han Sŏrya and North Korean Literature: The Failure of Socialist Realism in DPRK.* Ithaca, NY: East Asia Program, Cornell University, 1994.

———. "Ideology as Smokescreen: North Korea's Juche Thought." *Acta Koreana* 11.3 (2008): 161–182.

———. "The Watershed That Wasn't: Re-evaluating Kim Il Sung's 'Juche Speech' of 1955." *Acta Koreana* 9.1 (2006): 89–115.

Naiman, Eric. *Sex in Public: The Incarnation of Early Soviet Ideology.* Princeton, NJ: Princeton University Press, 1997.

Nam Kunman, *Pulgŭn nyŏsŏngdŭl* [Red women]. Pyongyang: Chosŏn nyŏsŏngsa, 1960.

NamChosŏn munje ch'ulp'ansa. *NamChosŏn munje nonmunjip* [Essays on the South Korea problem]. Pyongyang: NamChosŏn munje ch'ulp'ansa, 1965.

Neitzel, Laura L. *The Life We Longed For: Danchi Housing and the Middle Class Dream in Postwar Japan.* Honolulu: University of Hawai'i Press, 2016.

Nelson, Laura C. *Measured Excess: Status, Gender, and Consumer Nationalism in South Korea.* New York: Columbia University Press, 2000.

Pae, Yŏngsun. *Hanmal Ilche ch'ogiŭi t'oji chosawa chise kaejŏng* [Land surveys and tax reform in the Hanmal and early Japanese colonial period]. Taegu: Yŏngnam taehakkyo ch'ulp'anbu, 2002.

Pak Hyŏnsŏn. *Hyŏndae PukHan sahoewa kajok* [Contemporary North Korean society and family]. Seoul: Hanul ak'ademi, 2003.

Pak Kŭmch'ŏl. *Tangŭi t'ongilgwa tangyŏrul tŏuk kanghwahalde taehayŏ* [On strengthening the unity and solidarity of the Party]. Pyongyang: Chosŏn rodongdang ch'ulp'ansa, 1958.

Pak Kyŏngsuk. "Singminji sigi (1910–1945) Chosŏnŭi in'gu tongt'aewa kujo" [Colonial (1910–1945) Korea's population movement and arrangement]. *Han'guk inguhak* 32.2 (2009): 29–58.

Pak Myŏngnim. *Han'guk 1950: Chŏnjaenggwa pyŏnghwa* [1950 Korea: War and peace]. Seoul: Nanam, 2002.

Pak Sŭngsu and Kim Sŏngnak. *Chosŏnŭi ŏmŏni, 3* [Korean mothers, part 3]. Pyongyang: Chosŏn nyŏsŏngsa, 1960.

Pak Sunso, ed. *Taejung chŏngch'i yongŏ sajŏn* [Popular dictionary of political terms]. Pyongyang: Chosŏn rodongdang ch'ulp'ansa, 1964.

Pak Yŏngja. "PukHanŭi namnyŏ p'yŏngdŭng chŏngch'aegŭi hyŏngsŏnggwa kuljŏl" [The formation and shifts in North Korea's gender equality policy]. *Asia yŏsŏng yŏn'gu* 43.2 (2004): 305–307.

———. "PukHanŭi 'saengch'ejŏngch'i'" [North Korean "biopolitics"]. *Hyŏndae PukHan yŏn'gu* 7.3 (2005): 97–149.

———. "PukHanŭi yŏsŏng chŏngch'i: 'Hyŏksinjŏk nodongja—hyŏngmyŏngjŏk ŏmŏni'roŭi chaegusŏng" [North Korea's gender politics: Remaking the reformed worker-revolutionary mother]. *Sahoekwahak yŏn'gu* 13.1 (2005): 356–389.

Palais, James B. *Confucian Statecraft and Korean Institutions: Yu Hyŏngwŏn and the Late Chosŏn Dynasty.* Seattle: University of Washington Press, 1996.

Paris, Ivan. "Between Efficiency and Comfort: The Organization of Domestic Work and Space from Home Economics to Scientific Management." *History and Technology* 35.1 (2019): 81–104.

Park, Alyssa M. *Sovereignty Experiments: Korean Migrants and the Building of Borders in Northeast Asia, 1860–1945.* Ithaca, NY: Cornell University Press, 2019.

Park, Hyun Ok. *The Capitalist Unconscious: From Korean Unification to Transnational Korea.* New York: Columbia University Press, 2015.

———. *Two Dreams in One Bed: Empire, Social Life, and the Origins of the North Korean Revolution in Manchuria.* Durham, NC: Duke University Press, 2005.

Park, Kyung Ae. "Women and Revolution in North Korea." *Pacific Affairs* 65.4 (1992/1993): 527–545.

Parr, Joy. *Domestic Goods: The Material, the Moral and the Economic in the Postwar Years.* Toronto: University of Toronto Press, 1999.

Pateman, Carole. "The Patriarchal Welfare State" [1988]. In Amy Gutman, ed., *Democracy and the Welfare State.* Princeton, NJ: Princeton University Press, 1998: 231–260.

Person, James F. "Narrating North Korean History through Socialist Bloc Archives: Opportunities and Pitfalls." *Journal of Korean Studies* 26.2 (2021): 229–249.

———. "'We Need Help from Outside': The North Korean Opposition Movement of 1956." *Cold War International History Project, Working Paper 52* (2006): 28–35.

Poole, Janet. *When the Future Disappears: The Modernist Imagination in Late Colonial Korea.* New York: Columbia University Press, 2014.

PukHan yŏn'gu sent'ŏ, ed. *Chosŏn nodongdangŭi oegwak tanch'e* [North Korea's extra-Party organizations]. Paju City: Hanul ak'ademi, 2004.

P'yŏngyang Hyangt'osa P'yŏnch'an Wiwŏnhoe, ed. *P'yŏngyang chi* [Pyongyang records]. Seoul: Han'guk Munhwasa, 1999.

Reid, Susan E. "Cold War in the Kitchen: Gender and the De-Stalinization of Consumer Taste in the Soviet Union under Khrushchev." *Slavic Review* 61.2 (2002): 211–252.

———. "Communist Comfort: Socialist Modernism and the Making of Cosy Homes in the Khrushchev Era." *Gender and History* 21.3 (2009): 465–498.

———. "The Khrushchev Kitchen: Domesticating the Scientific-Technological Revolution." *Journal of Contemporary History* 40.2 (2005): 289–316.

Reid, Susan E., and David Crowley, eds. *Socialist Spaces: Sites of Everyday Life in the Eastern Bloc.* New York: Berg, 2002.

———, eds. *Pleasures in Socialism: Leisure and Luxury in the Eastern Bloc.* Evanston, IL: Northwestern University Press, 2010.

Ri Hongjong. *Nyŏsŏngdŭrŭi kongsanjuŭi p'umsŏng* [The communist character of women]. Pyongyang: Chosŏn nyŏsŏngsa, 1960.

Ri Myŏngwŏn. *Kŏnsŏl chagŏppanjangŭi sugi* [A construction brigade leader's memoir]. Pyongyang: Minch'ŏng ch'ulp'ansa, 1961.

Ri Sungön. *Chut'aek soguyŏk kyehoek* [Residential neighborhood planning]. Pyongyang: Kungnip könsöl ch'ulp'ansa, 1963.

Rice, Charles. *The Emergence of the Interior: Architecture, Modernity, Domesticity.* London: Routledge, 2007.

Robinson, Michael. "Broadcasting, Cultural Hegemony, and Colonial Modernity in Korea, 1924–1945." In Gi-wook Shin and Michael Robinson, eds., *Colonial Modernity in Korea.* Cambridge, MA: Harvard University Press, 1999.

Rogaski, Ruth. *Hygienic Modernity: Meanings of Health and Disease in Treaty-Port China.* Berkeley: University of California Press, 2004.

Ross, Kristin. *Fast Cars, Clean Bodies: Decolonization and the Reordering of French Culture.* Cambridge, MA: MIT Press, 1996.

Ryang, Sonia. "Anthropology as Method: North Korea at a Distance." *Journal of Korean Studies* 26.2 (2021): 187–203.

——. "Gender in Oblivion: Women in the Democratic People's Republic of Korea (North Korea)." *Journal of Asian and African Studies* 35.3 (2000): 323–349.

——, ed. *North Korea: Toward a Better Understanding.* Lanham, MD: Lexington Books, 2009.

——. *Reading North Korea: An Ethnological Inquiry.* Cambridge, MA: Harvard University Asia Center, 2012.

Sanchez-Sibony, Oscar. *Red Globalization: The Political Economy of the Soviet Cold War from Stalin to Khrushchev.* Cambridge: Cambridge University Press, 2014.

Sand, Jordan. *House and Home in Modern Japan: Architecture, Domestic Space, and Bourgeois Culture, 1880–1930.* Cambridge, MA: Harvard University Asia Center, 2004.

Scalapino, Robert, and Chong-sik Lee. *Communism in Korea: Part I, The Movement,* and *Part II, The Society.* Berkeley: University of California Press, 1972.

Schmid, Andre. "Comrade Min, Women's Paid Labor, and the Centralizing Party-State: Postwar Reconstruction in North Korea." In Alf Lüdtke, ed., *Everyday Life in Mass Dictatorship: Evasion and Collusion,* 184–201. London: Palgrave Macmillan, 2016.

——. "Historicizing North Korea: State Socialism, Population Mobility, and Cold War Historiography." *The American Historical Review* 123.2 (2018): 439–462.

——. "Introduction." *Journal of Korean Studies* 26.2 (2021): 169–186.

——. "'My Turn to Speak': Criticism Culture and the Multiple Uses of Class in Postwar North Korea." *International Journal of Korean Studies* 21.2 (2016): 121–153.

Shin, Gi-wook, and Michael Robinson, eds. *Colonial Modernity in Korea.* Cambridge, MA: Harvard University Press, 1999.

Shin, Gunsoo, and Inha Jung. "Appropriating the Socialist Way of Life: The Emergence of Mass Housing in Post-war North Korea." *The Journal of Architecture* 21.2 (2016): 159–180.

Sinsaenghwal undong chungang ch'ongbonhoe. *Uriŭi sinsaenghwal sŏlgyesŏ* [A planning guide for our new living]. Seoul: Chinsaenghoe, 1952.

Slobodian, Quinn, ed. *Comrades of Color: East Germany in the Cold War World.* New York: Berghan Books, 2015.

Smith, Hazel. *North Korea: Markets and Military Rule.* Cambridge: Cambridge University Press, 2015.

Sŏ Tongman. "1950 nyŏndae PukHanŭi chŏngch'i kaldŭnggwa ideollogi sanghwang" [The situation of political conflict and ideology in 1950s North Korea]. In *PukChosŏn yŏn'gu* [Research on North Korea], 122–168. Seoul: Ch'angbi, 2010.

———. "1950 nyŏndae PukHanŭi kongmul saengsanryang t'onggye-e kwanhan yŏn'gu" [Research on 1950s North Korean statistics on grain production]. In *PukChosŏn yŏn'gu* [Research on North Korea], 19–48. Seoul: Ch'angbi, 2010.

———. *PukChosŏn sahoejuŭi ch'eje sŏngnipsa, 1945–1961* [The history of the establishment of the North Korean socialist system, 1945–1961]. Seoul: Sonin, 2005.

———. "PukChosŏnŭi yugyodamron-e gwanhayŏ" [On North Korean Confucian discourse]. In *PukChosŏn yŏn'gu* [Research on North Korea], 269–331. Seoul: Ch'angbi, 2010.

Son Pongsuk, Yi Kyŏngsuk, Yi Onjuk, and Kim Aesil, eds. *PukHanŭi yŏsŏng saenghwal: yiron'gwa silje* [The lives of North Korean women: Theory and reality]. Seoul: Nanam, 1991.

Stites, Richard. *Revolutionary Dreams: Utopian Vision and Experimental Life in the Russian Revolution.* New York: Oxford University Press, 1989.

———. *The Women's Liberation Movement in Russia: Feminism, Nihilism, and Bolshevism, 1860–1930.* Princeton, NJ: Princeton University Press, 1978.

Strasser, Susan, George Charles McGovern, and Matthias Judt, eds. *Getting and Spending: European and American Consumer Societies in the Twentieth Century.* Cambridge: Cambridge University Press, 1998.

Suh, Dae-sook. *Korean Communism, 1945–1980: A Reference Guide to the Political System.* Honolulu: University of Hawai'i Press, 1981.

Suh, Jae-Jung, ed. *Origins of North Korean Ideology: Colonialism, War, and Development.* Lanham, MD: Lexington Books, 2013.

Szalontai, Balàzs. *Kim Il Sung in the Khrushchev Era: Soviet-DPRK Relations and the Roots of North Korean Despotism, 1953–1964.* Stanford, CA: Stanford University Press, 2005.

Taylor, Moe. "Discipline, Education, and Mass Games: Ideological Exchange and Sports Diplomacy between North Korea and Guyana during the Cold War." *World History Bulletin* 36.2 (2020): 7–11.

———. "One Hand Can't Clap: Guyana and North Korea, 1974–1985." *Journal of Cold War Studies* 17.1 (2015): 41–63.

Tertitskiy, Fyodor. "The Ascension of the Ordinary Man: How the Personality Cult of Kim Il Sung Was Constructed (1945–1974)." *Acta Koreana* 18.1 (2015): 209–231.

Tikhonov, Vladimir. "Korea in the Russian and Soviet Imagination, 1850s–1945: Between Orientalism and Revolutionary Solidarity." *Journal of Korean Studies* 21.2 (2016): 385–342.

Tyler May, Elaine. *Homeward Bound: American Families in the Cold War Era.* New York: Basic Books, 1988.

Urban, Florian. *Tower and Slab: Histories of Global Mass Housing.* London: Routledge, 2012.

Viola, Lynne. "Introduction." In *Contending with Stalinism: Soviet Power and Popular Resistance in the 1930s.* Ithaca, NY: Cornell University Press, 2002.

Volkov, Vadim. "The Concept of *Kul'turnost'*: Notes on the Stalinist Civilizing Process." In Sheila Fitzpatrick, ed., *Stalinism: New Directions.* New York: Taylor & Francis, 2000.

Wada Haruki. *The Korean War: An International History.* Lanham, MD: Rowman and Littlefield, 2018.

———. *Puk Chosŏn: yugyŏktae kukka-esŏ chŏnggyugun kukkaro* [North Korea: From guerrilla to garrison state]. Translated by Sŏ Tongman and Nam Kijŏng. Seoul: Tolbegae, 2002.

Wang, Zheng. *Finding Women in the State: A Socialist Feminist Revolution in the People's Republic of China, 1949–1964.* Oakland: University of California Press, 2017.

Watt, Lori. *When Empire Comes Home: Repatriation and Reintegration in Postwar Japan.* Cambridge, MA: Harvard University Press, 2009.

Workman, Travis. *Imperial Genus: The Formation and Limits of the Human in Modern Korea and Japan.* Oakland: University of California Press, 2017.

Wu, Yiching. *The Cultural Revolution at the Margins: Chinese Socialism in Crisis.* Cambridge, MA: Harvard University Press, 2014.

Yi Chuch'ol. *Chosŏn rodongdang tangwŏn chojik yŏn'gu, 1945–1960* [Studies of the Korean Workers' Party's membership and organization, 1945–1960]. Seoul: Sŏnin, 2008.

Yi Migyŏng. "PukHanŭi mosŏngideollogi: 'Chosŏn nyŏsŏng' naeyong punsŏgŭl chungsimŭro'" [North Korea's motherhood ideology: A study of the content of *Women of Korea*]. *Han'guk chŏngch'i woegyosa nonch'ong* 26.1 (2004): 391–422.

Yi Onjuk. "Yŏsŏnggwa kajŏng saenghwal" [Women and domestic life]. In Son Pongsuk, Yi Kyŏngsuk, Yi Onjuk, and Kim Aesil, eds., *PukHanŭi yŏsŏng saenghwal: iron'gwa silje* [The lives of North Korean women: Theory and reality]. Seoul: Nanam, 1991: 37–93.

Yi Taegŭn. *Chosŏn Nodongdangŭi chojik ch'egye* [North Korean Workers' Party's organizational system]. In Sejong yŏn'guso PukHan yŏn'gu sent'ŏ, ed., *Pukhanŭi tang, kukka kigu, kundae* [North Korea's Party, state organizations, and military]. Seoul: Hanŭl, 2007.

Yi Yonggi. "Yisangajok yŏn'gu ŏdikkaji wanna?" [How has the state of research on separated families developed?]. *Yŏksa pip'yŏng* 44 (1998): 252–269.

Yoo, Theodore Jun. *The Politics of Gender in Colonial Korea: Education, Labor, and Health, 1910–1945.* Berkeley: University of California Press, 2008.

Yoshiaki, Yoshimi. *Comfort Women: Sexual Slavery in the Japanese Military during World War II*. Translated by Suzanne O'Brien. New York: Columbia University Press, 2000.

Young, Benjamin R. *Guns, Guerillas, and the Great Leader: North Korea and the Third World*. Stanford, CA: Stanford University Press, 2021.

Young, Louise. *Japan's Total Empire: Manchuria and the Culture of Wartime Imperialism*. Berkeley: University of California Press, 1998.

Yu Yŏngik. *Kabo kyŏngjang yŏn'gu* [Studies on the Kabo reforms]. Seoul: Ilchogak, 1990.

Yun Haedong. *Singminji kŭndaeŭi p'aerŏdoksŭ* [The paradox of colonial modernity]. Seoul: Hyumŏnisŭt'ŭ, 2007.

Yun Miryang. *PukHanŭi yŏsŏng chŏngch'aek* [North Korean policies on women]. Seoul: Hanul, 1991.

Yuval-Davis, Nira. *Nation and Gender*. London: Sage, 1997.

INDEX

advertisements, 183; position in socialism, 188; Pyongyang sewing machine, 188–189, 195; Samno ginseng alcohol, 245
advice literature, 12, 41, 42–62, 66–70, 73, 76, 82, 84, 95, 96, 99, 145, 153, 155, 167–168, 173, 175, 180–181, 225; "comradely," 67; décor advice, 203–220; Kim Il Sung's on-the-spot guidance, 237; silence on consumption, 183–185
affect, 238–240
alcohol(ism), 43; and historical sources, 244–245; disorderly, 70–71; in worker dormitories, 74; masculinized, 185–187; on production line, 69–70; Samno ginseng alcohol, 245
All-Nation Women Socialist Builders Meeting, 161
An Chaebok, 27
Anju, 70
anti-revolutionary elements: "hidden in cracks," 11, 49; *sŏngbun,* 27
anxieties, 1, 16; about apartments, 158, 159–160, 201; about criticism, 66; about socialist transition, 21–41; changing gender relations, 41; Cold War, 75; domestic interiors, 158–159; geopolitical, 11; male, 55, 150; political economic, 22, 75, 76, 159; Workers Federation, 75–76
apartments: as primary space of consumption, 19; as revolutionary narrative, 107–111, 235; assigned, 213; biopolitics, 46, 133; building campaign, 77; cityscape, 133; communal, 134–135; crisis,

133; design, 133–136; designed for families, 158; feminization of interiors, 9, 131, 165, 172, 180, 211; household factories, 196–200; ideological threat of interiors, 159–164; *inminban,* 134, 175; isolating effect, 133–134; media representation of, 108, 201–203; moving-in day, 140–141; popular stakes in, 9, 141, 235; political economy of, 79–128; prefabricated construction, 116–123; propaganda competition with the south, 109–111; Pyongyang campaign, 124–128; quality problems, 124–125; seen as unproductive, 131, 163, 196–197, 201; size, 119; socialist theory of, 134; statistics, 245. *See also* interior décor
architects, 81, 85; and housing crisis, 117; Chinese influence, 133; communal designs, 135; criticized, 119, 121; design divisions among, 119–121, 133; mocked in cartoons, 119; participation in socialist conferences, 118, 133; Soviet influence, 133. See also *ondol*

Banister, Judith, 156
banks, 207; Bank of Chosŏn, 100–101; saving certificates, 183
Barraclough, Ruth, 138
biopolitics, 45–48; apartment living, 141; as part of criticism culture, 68; Cold War setting, 25; collective property, 48; colonialism, 46; continuities of, 8–9; family registration, 146–147, 175; lack of

biopolitics *(continued)*
gendered critique, 8–9, 14; participation of housewives, 160; Party-state power in local social worlds, 146; popular desire and statist purpose, 46; production culture, 165–166; pro-natalism, 155; transcendent to regime type, 45–46, 48. *See also* Foucault, Michel

bourgeois: architects, 121–122; colonial period, 45; comparison to uses in China, 184; elimination of (1958), 94; film industry, 49; heteronormative nuclear family and, 138, 141; historical dialectic, 13; housewives, 162; in South Korea, 49, 185, 215; Japanese thought, 66; label, 50, 121–122, 220; literary world, 49; remnants, 8, 11, 24; reunification, 185; threat of, 71–72, 206, 215; values, 238

Brown, Wendy, 13

Budapest, 143

bureaucratism, 36, 121, 126–127

buses, 43–44, 52; lining up, 43, 63

capital shortage, 22, 79, 81; aggregate labor reserve, 94; collectivization and, 29; competition, 30; demographic crisis, 27; Fordism and, 8, 28–33; heavy industry priority, 28; independent capital, 58; labor reserves of women, 104, 196, 200; labor shortage and, 32; light industries, 196; relation to devolution, 199–200; savings drive, 182–183; socialist allies' assistance, 28–29, 179, 189, 224

cartoonists, 223, 231; alcohol, 186, 245; anxieties, 22; architects, 119; avoiding hygiene inspection, 46–47; Chinese, 45, 112–114; consumer challenges, 192–193, 237; criticism culture, 183; diligence, 84; domestic abuse, 186–187; efficiency, 79–80; flashes of criticism and, 14; "hating work," 162; housewives, 163; husbands, 177–178; ill-mannered rubes, 42; *kijunnyang*, 89; limits, 73, 194; material incentives, 112–114; mocking officials, 67, 126–127; orderly bus lines, 44; production secret, 89–90; representations of the south in, 110–111; self-

sufficiency, 30–31; sense of era's rapid change, 21–22; slovenly men, 39; spies, 176; urban visual culture, 53. *See also* flashes of criticism, *individual cartoonists by name*

central planning, 4; alcohol production, 185–186; collectivization of commerce, 32; construction objectives, 124; contradictions in, 200; investment priorities, 194; *kijunnyang*, 85, 89; limits of, 82; material incentives, 113; retail, 195; undermined, 30, 33, 91; urban preference of, 52; wage-working women and, 81, 196; wartime, 33. *See also* devolution; heavy industry; light industry; wages

Chang Chŏngin, 218–220

Chatterjee, Partha, 140

China, 63, 94; acceptance of war orphans, 142–143; architectural design, 114–115, 134–135; class categories, 10, 184; collectivization, 29; comparative approach, 10; flashes of criticism, 227; historiography of foreign relations, 228; housing, 134–135; "Hundred Flowers" campaign, 10; Japanese invasion of, 23, 46; Juche narratives and, 228; labor supply, 94; linguistic decolonization from, 56–57; Mao on population, 155; Maoist ideological commitment, 113; marriages with Koreans, 31; masculinization of women thesis, 54; media, 112–114; New Living in, 5; nostalgia for countryside, 52; PLA work projects, 28; post-revolution class formation and consumption, 184; postwar assistance, 28; purges, 121; return of PLA soldiers, 11; shared terminology, 5; translation of Chinese cartoons, 45, 112–114; translation of Mao's speech, 36; views on material incentives, 112–114. *See also* People's Liberation Army, Chinese

Cho Ilho, 145–158

Ch'oe Hanjin, 177–178, 192

Ch'oe Kŭmok, 194

Ch'oe Kwanhwa, 194

Ch'oe Pobu, 144

Ch'oe Tŏkkil, 69

Ch'oe Wanho, 55, 60

Ch'oe Yonggŏn, 142
Ch'oe Yŏnggŭn, 110–111
Choi, Hyaeweol, 137, 138
Ch'ŏllima campaign, 81, 115, 174, 190, 197, 202
Ch'ŏllima radios, 218
Chŏn Sŏnggŭn (cartoonist), 40
Chŏn Sŏnggŭn (historian), 40
Chonch'ŏn Match Factory, 194
Chŏng Chŏnghyŏp, 106–107
Chŏng Ch'oru, 125
Chŏng Yagyong, 241
Ch'ŏngjin, 70, 109; Ch'ŏngjin Rubber Factory, 70; Ch'ŏngjinTextile Factory, 74, 102, 103
Ch'ŏnnaeri Cement Factory, 90
Chosŏn dynasty, 5, 45, 140, 157, 229; family formation, 136–137; furniture, 213
Chu Hwanju, 70
Chu Hyŏngdo, 202–205
CIA, 30, 242
class, 71, 123, 225; advice literature and, 48; antibourgeois rhetoric, 8, 11, 13, 49–50, 206; architectural design and, 134–135; as an emancipatory subject, 13; colonial era, 45; compared to Europe, 24; consumption and, 180, 184–185, 206; critique, 8–9, 48, 138, 141, 206, 226; depoliticization of, 4, 10–12, 14, 41, 48–50, 121, 131, 180, 210, 218–220; domesticity, 134, 136; enemies, 26, 27, 75, 144, 163, 176; lack of empirical data about, 11, 61; legitimation of, 63–65, 226; modern family and, 5, 134–135, 138–139, 255; on contradictions, 36–37; Party-state time, 6; postwar formation, 11, 184–185, 22; remnants, 8; reunification and, 49; sŏngbun system, 26–27; struggle, 11, 49; upward mobility, 34; working-class lifestyles, 43, 206. See also social stratification
Cold War: apartments, 133; archives, 242; as part of Korea's long twentieth century, 6; blurring of boundaries between capitalism and socialism, 16; commonalities across Cold War divide, 29, 52, 55, 76, 133; historiography, 109, 229–230; kitchen debate, 109; labeling practices,

16; Party-state and, 76; rhetoric, 75; rivalry between north and south, 25
collective: consciousness, 72, 134; ideals, 10, 35; *inminban* and, 173; living relationships, 141; transition to socialism, 39
collective property, 15, 29; advice literature and, 48, 61; biopolitics, 48; Cold War, 76; comparison to the South, 49; dormitory facilities, 40, 72–77, 135, 206; farm, 53
collectivization: agriculture, 27, 29, 33; capital flows, 19–20; elimination of private commerce, 32; of the material means of production, 1958 completion, 11; Party self-assessment, 6–7; recruitment of Party member through, 34, 53–54; working class and, 13, 29–30
comfort women, 24
commodity fetish, 221–222
communist morality: Kalinin on, 44; Kim Il Sung speech on, 231–232; manuals about, 166
Confucianism, 50; as explanation for personality cult, 229; family and, 134, 137
conservatism (*posujuŭi*), 71, 121, 123
consumption, 179–222; and class, 206; conspicuous, 207, 208; demand for, 190; devolution, 188–196; purchasing power, 191–192; relation to cultural levels, 180, 217; resolution of clothing, food, and housing problem, 190, 202; shortage of goods, 192–195; silence on norms of, 183–185, 201, 202. See also furniture; interior décor; light industry; sewing
cooking, 167
cost of living, 191
cranes, 9, 85, 108, 123, 127; as more than decorations, 79; efficiency and, 79–80
criticism culture, 65–72, 96, 223, 244. See also "My Turn to Speak"
cultural levels (*munhwa sujun*), 58, 59, 64, 75, 165; as justification for hierarchies, 14, 44, 61, 169–170; consumption and, 217; depoliticization, 10, 180; domesticity and, 131, 153, 168, 172, 174; feminine language and, 59–62, 217; individuating impulse, 71, 154, 173, 214; interior décor

cultural levels *(continued)*
and, 180–181, 201, 216–217; low levels
and ideological danger, 65, 76; Party-
state time and, 58, 125, 166, 199; privileging of city, 54; socialism and, 48, 99, 131,
161, 168
cultural living, 39–41, 69, 177, 202; as
means of justification, 70, 99, 220;
colonial history of, 45, 138
culture, 19; advice literature, 42–50; as
distinct from discourse and ideology, 7;
consumption and, 206, 244; cultural
approaches in historiography, 219–220;
cultural revolution, 52, 122, 125, 184;
"culturedness" *(munhwasŏng)*, 43, 180,
201, 210, 216, 218, 201; depoliticization,
131–132, 173; emphasis on individual, 10,
208; food culture, 209; hygiene and,
203–204; male anxieties and, 55; masculinist norms, 170; national culture, 229;
non-uniformity of, 17–18; official use
with ideology, 7; "outmoded," 49–50;
Party-state time and, 8, 10, 160; personality cult, 238; political culture, 58, 224;
"production culture" *(saengsan
munhwa)*, 165–166, 173; proletarian
consciousness, 41; publishing culture,
231; reading culture, 246; transnational
socialist culture, 30, 45, 112; uncultured,
74; visual culture, 21, 43, 53, 54, 95, 126;
writing culture, 96. *See also* criticism
culture; cultural levels *(munhwa sujun)*;
division culture; ideology
Culture Palace, 239
Cumings, Bruce, 24

Dark Shadow (*Kŏmŭn kŭrimja*), 70
day care, 69, 105–107, 161; devolution of
responsibility, 99, 105, 106; during work
campaigns, 128; inadequate supply, 105;
inminban and, 174; Manchurian history, 234; media criticism about, 105;
quality problems, 106; self-provision,
106–107, 128; teachers of, 234; women's
paid labor and, 69, 105–107, 161
decolonization: and male social power, 14;
Cold War and, 25; linguistic decolonization, 55–57

demography: crisis, 22–27, 31, 154–155;
fragmented families, 142–145; pro-
natalism, 154–158; urban growth, 51–52
"dependent family members" *(puyang
kajok)*, 98–100, 160
depoliticization, 4, 41, 96, 131–132, 218, 220,
226; class, 11–12, 14; comparative
approach to, 10; consolidation of Party-
state power, 4; consumption, 206;
definition of, 10; displaced to south,
185–186; emphasis on individual and,
10–16; gender, 12–14, 77, 173; interior
décor and, 210, 220; use of family for,
76–77
developmentalist narrative/time, 9, 244;
comparison to Party-state time, 234;
contradiction of central planned economies and, 179; day care and, 105; defer-
ral of women's liberation and, 14;
delayed gratification, 95; heavy industry,
179; Kim Il Sung's abandonment of,
238–240; New Living and, 235; Party-
state and, 9; popular internalization of,
9, 234–235; promise of equality, 206;
public cafeterias and, 104
devolution, 30, 94, 131, 199, 218; criticism
and, 106; day care and, 105–107; Kim Il
Sung and, 237–238; light industry and,
188–196; politics of blame, 190, 192, 194;
without financing, 107
discourse, 20, 45, 48, 50, 184; as multivocal,
17–18, 227, 243; class, 11; femininities,
226; home décor, 210, 217–218; in contrast to Party definitions of ideology and
culture, 7; indeterminacy of, 19, 244–
246; Juche, 234; Kim Il Sung, 230–232
division culture: anxieties and, 22; family
separation, 25; historical analysis and,
230; military conscription, 31; north-
south propaganda competition, 109–111,
230; romanization and, xi; security and
ideological anxieties, 75–76
division of labor, gendered, 12, 71, 131, 208;
as seen in photographs, 102; depoliticization of, 84, 98; lack of statistics about,
245–246; Ri Myŏngwŏn's use of,
97–98; undertheorized, 9, 102. *See also*
light industry

divorce: child custody and, 146; Cho Ilho's "true divorce," 150; colonial debates about, 137; criticism of legal changes in, 14, 131, 151–154, 226; freedom of, 148; gender equality laws and, 148; Kim Il Sung and, 157–158, 233; politics of reproduction, 145–158; pro-natalism and, 155–157; South Korea and, 185; Soviet experience, 149–150; termination of mutual consent, 149

dormitories, 65, 72–77, 134, 191, 244; as collective property, 40, 73, 135, 206; gendered segregation, 73; ideological dangers of, 75–76; model stories of, 74; surveillance of, 41, 65, 72–77, 230

Dresden, 142

Eberstadt, Nicholas, 156

efficiency, 79–107, 116–117; household management and, 167–168, 219; labor allocation, 31; speed of construction, 124–125

Engels, Friedrich, 134

"equalism" (*py'ŏnggyunjuŭi*), 11

everyday life, 223, 238; and commodities, 184; as category of analysis, 3; as problems, 103; *byt*, 44; in 1920s Japan, 45

familialism (*kajokchuŭi*), 139

family law, 12, 145–158

famine, 98, 104, 133

fashion, 209; femininities and, 54–57; purses, 221–222

fathers, 105, 107, 149, 170–173, 186; husband-father, 188

feminine speech, 41, 54–62, 74; cultural levels and, 217

femininities: dormitories, 73–74; hierarchies and, 226; idealized, 50, 217; nationalized, 54; representations of, 14, 210; speech, 59–62. *See also* fashion; masculinities

Five-Year Plan (1957–61), 85, 189

flashes of criticism, 14–15; as critique, 226–227; as indicating discursive breadth, 15, 19; individual flashes, 36–38, 63–64, 112–114, 177–178

food, 142, 167, 178, 186, 209; circulation and distribution problems, 104, 194; cooking lessons, 174; famine (1955), 98, 104; growing expectations, 190; homefront preparation of, 197; industrialization, 102, 104, 167; *inminban* and, 174; "resolution" of food problem, 104, 190, 202

Fordism, 8–9; gendered political economy, 28–33; lack of gendered critique, 14

forestry, 90

formalism (*hyŏngsikchuŭi*), 71, 121

Foucault, Michel, 46, 48, 50. *See also* biopolitics

fragmented families, 142–145

Fujitani, Takeshi, 46

Fulbrook, Mary, 214

furniture, 190; advice on arrangement, 210–215; apartments, 202, 204–205; consumer hopes for, 190; cultural levels and, 217; day care, 106; photographs for consumers of, 179–180; politics of, 206, 218; Pyongyang Wood Furniture Factory, 28, 213, 218, 228; styles, 213–215. *See also* interior décor

gender equality laws: cover for masculinist Party-state, 12, 170; divorce and, 148–151; hollowed out by family law, 145; "modesty" and, 61; proliferation of femininities and, 226; promulgation and celebration of, 12, 74; use of, 96–97; women's paid labor and, 54

General Federation of Trade Unions, 35; cartoons criticizing leaders, 183; house newspaper, 67; responsibility for dormitories, 72–77; stripped of power, 14

Germany (East), 28, 134, 142, 224

Haeju, 109, 174, 198

Hamhŭng, 28, 109, 171, 174, 191, 228

Han Chŏngjik, 56

happy family: couple, 170–171, 172, 202; trope of, 19, 129–132, 188, 202, 205, 209, 223

Harootunian, Harry, 6, 45

heavy industry, 189, 192, 227; contradiction within, 179; labor shortage and, 104; Party member recruitment from, 34; prioritization of, 28, 30, 179

Hŏ Chungsuk, 138
Hŏ Sŏngmun, 68
home décor. *See* interior décor
Hong Chongho, 30, 127
Hong Ŭngun, 69
household factories, 197–200, 208; Kim Il
    Sung and, 233; labor statistics and, 246
household management, 73, 130; double
    burden and, 169; global ideas of, 159;
    interior décor and, 210, 219; Kang
    Pansŏk and, 238; relation to economic
    production, 168–169, 181; scientific
    management, 203, 217
housewives (*kajŏng puin*), 127; demeaning
    expression for, 163; housewife-mothers,
    100, 128, 197, 199; non-routinized labor
    of, 127; photographs of self-study, 165;
    pressures to participate in paid labor,
    162–163; shopping, 194; trope of unhap-
    piness, 159–163
housing. *See* apartments
husbands, 73; bland criticism of, 96;
    demeaning comments, 163; dependent
    family members and, 99; divorce, 152–
    154; domestic violence and, 186; gen-
    dered slant of critique, 171; husband-
    fathers, 170, 171–172, 188; ideal of
    cooperative, 14, 164–172; Kim Il Sung
    and, 158; "new type of husband"
    (*saehyŏngŭi namp'yŏn*), 171, 177–178;
    Pak Chŏngae and, 161–162; widows and,
    144–145, 146
Hwang Pongsu, 101
Hwang Yŏngsik, 42–45, 48–50, 63–64
Hyesan, 109
hygiene, 7, 48, 67; alcoholism and, 244;
    criticism of superiors on, 69; dormito-
    ries and, 73–75; home inspection,
    46–47, 161, 166, 173, 220; *inminban*
    and, 174; interior décor and, 203–205;
    neighborhood committees, 35, 74, 173;
    production and, 166–167; pro-natalism
    and, 155; Pyongyang rebuilding cam-
    paign, 124

ideology, 2, 16–19, 129; as distinct from
    culture and discourse, 7; discourse and,
    17–18; gender and, 13; husbands, 177–

178; indeterminacy of, 7, 49; inminban,
    174; Juche, 233–234; "Kim Il Sung
    Thought," 7, 228; masculinization of,
    75–76; mass line, 127; non-uniformity
    of, 227, 244; official categories, 244;
    official use with culture, 7; "outmoded,"
    49; Party self-assessment of, 6; Party-
    state time and, 6, 10, 71, 94, 161, 188;
    politics of blame, 7, 75, 93, 99, 106, 154,
    161, 163, 190, 192–195, 225, 237, 244;
    primacy of, 115, 122–123, 202, 228;
    rebuilding Pyongyang campaign, 116,
    122; relation to economic growth, 81, 93,
    115, 122; relation to language in advice
    literature, 58–59; self-consciousness,
    243; socialist morality, 63–64; threat of
    interiors, 159–164; versus material
    incentives, 112–114; versus structural
    obstacles, 94, 131–132, 161–162, 169. *See
    also* culture; discourse; Juche
Im Hwa, 175
India, 140
inminban (neighborhood committees), 186;
    as primary local organization, 35; as
    provider of social welfare service, 174;
    black marketeering and, 175; functions
    of, 173–176; neighborhood work, 220;
    registration, 175; spies and, 175–176;
    surveillance by, 174–175
Instruction for the Inner Chamber (*Nae-
    hun*), 63
interior décor, 180, 201–220; and cultural
    levels, 201, 214, 216–217; and Kim's
    portrait, 231; as a fantasy, 217; photo-
    graphs of, 201–206

Japan, 2, 8, 23, 24, 25, 26, 46, 136, 143;
    anti-Japanese partisan movement, 36,
    108, 174, 234, 235; colonial vestiges, 66;
    comparison of living standards with
    colonial era, 31; emperor system, 229;
    linguistic decolonization and, 55–56;
    migrants from, 231; neologisms, 45, 137
Jones, Mark, 45
Juche, 50; development of, 231; domestic
    discursive context for, 50, 233–234;
    geopolitical explanations for, 228; Kim
    Il Sung's first usage, 233–234

collectivization, 29, 54; factory construction in, 30; limits of central state power over, 34–35; media representation of, 52; migration from, 27–33, 51, 98, 175, 229, 230; private homes in, 125; registration, 27; retired soldiers, 35; rural-urban disparities, 51–52, 59, 61, 104, 207; similarity to South Korean capital flows, 51; wartime loss of men, 23

Russo-Japanese War, 23

Ryang, Sonia, 170

Sand, Jordan, 137

Sariwŏn, 109; Sariwŏn Co-op Factory, 192

savings certificate, 182–183, 191

Scandinavian design, 179, 213

Scott, James, 8

self-criticism, 41, 65–72, 172

self-help, 167–168

Seoul, 15, 24, 49, 50, 111, 138, 143, 242; comparative housing propaganda, 109–111

Seven-Year Plan (1961–70), 85

sewing, 167

sewing machines, 19, 102, 188–190, 195, 215, 218, 219; brand names of, 218; political meanings of, 206–209; Singer brand, 206

Sim Chŏngsun, 152–154

Sin Chaehyo, 213

Sin Kŭmok, 171–172

Sinch'on County, 23

single-manager system, 85, 92; lack of education of, 90–94

Sinŭiju, 102, 109, 174

Slobidian, Quinn, 30

Small Manners for Scholars (Sasajŏl), 63

Sŏ Tongman, 29, 35, 229

Sŏ Yŏngbŏm, 68

social stratification, 84, 225; advice literature and, 43; cultural justification for, 14, 41; depoliticization and, 206; feminine speech and, 61; interior décor, 180; lack of empirical data about, 11. *See also* class

social welfare facilities, 161; *inminban* and, 174; public cafeterias, 104; rural medical clinic, 51; shortage of, 167, 172, 224. *See also* day care

socialism: anxieties of, 21–35; apartment interiors and, 131, 160; domestic labor, 131, 164, 166, 168; future generations, 145; household factories, 199; ideal socialist subject and, 82–83, 224–225, 240; Juche and, 234; Kim Il Sung's abandonment of, 240; New Living and, 4; outmoded thought and, 49–50; Party self-assessment, 6; prefab construction and, 117; rebuild Pyongyang campaign and, 125–126, 128; transition to, 239. *See also* Party-state time

socialist bloc: archive, 242; intra-bloc cultural circulation, 44–45, 118

socialist industrial design, 213

socialist modernity, 3, 15, 229, 230; South Korea as a norm for modernity, 15. *See also* state capitalism

socialist subject, 39–41, 225, 246; consumption and, 184; Juche and, 234; reassertion of masculinity, 14, 225, 246. *See also* Foucault, Michel

socialist work competitions, 86–90, 113, 239

Song Siyŏp, 79

sŏngbun, 41, 50, 144, 146, 224; and labor shortage, 32; class formation and, 11; implementation of, 26–27

Sŏngjin Steel Factory, 195

sources, 16–19, 241–247

Soviet Union (USSR), 94, 223; acceptance of orphans, 142; ambassador, 237; anti-Kulak purges, 10; apartment construction, 159; architectural design, 134–135; as source of models, 26, 35, 44–45, 83, 85, 99, 192, 235; class categories in, 10; collectivization, 29; commodity design, 184; communal architecture, 114–115; diplomatic reports, 16, 30; divorce, 148–149; elite politics and, 122, 228; historiography of, 9, 228; interiors, 214; labor supply, 94; "Learn from the Soviets" slogan, 36, 45, 231; linguistic decolonization, 57; material incentives, 113; non-critique of biopolitics, 48; occupation, 24, 148; parenting handbooks, 167; postwar assistance, 28, 213; purges, 121; Ri Myŏngwŏn's memoir

Soviet Union *(continued)*
 and, 86; wartime allies, 10. *See also*
 Khrushchev, Nikita; Stalin(ism)
Stalin(ism), 10, 44; de-Stalinization, 37,
 159, 228
state capitalism, 15–16, 252n35
Sunch'ŏn, 102, 274n67; paper factory, 30
surplus value, 15, 86, 112–114, 227
surveillance, 225; dormitories, 41, 72–77,
 230; *inminban,* 174–176; New Living
 and, 19; over media, 18–19; shared with
 South Korea, 76; spies, 175–176

TaeAn Electric Factory, 163
Taylorism, 230
Three-Year Plan (1954–56), 28, 84
tourism, 52–53
Trotsky, 15

United States of America: "American-style
 living" 185; baby boom, 155–156; bombing campaign and effects, 23, 33, 51, 135,
 142, 191; cartoons and, 111; CIA report,
 30; Cold War knowledge, 242; introduction of nuclear weapons, 11; Korean
 War, 3, 26, 143; missionaries, 137; occupation, 24; postwar turn to families, 2;
 sŏngbun and, 26, 32; troops in South
 Korea, 11; spies, 176
urbanization, 41, 51–53, 209

wages: bonuses, 83, 113, 187–188;
 diplomatic reports on, 191; "equalism"
 (*py'ŏnggyunjuŭi*), 11, 102; higher
 urban wages, 33; inequities, 84, 97,
 102–103; material incentives, 83, 112–
 114; surplus value, 112–113; *togŭpche*
 system (wage rankings), 58, 83. *See also*
 consumption; division of labor, gendered; *kijunnyang;* socialist work
 competitions
Watt, Lori, 24
West Pyongyang Railway Company, 92
widows, 23, 26, 136, 142–146
"Wise Mother, Good Wife," 137
Wŏn Kwangsu, 21
Wŏnsan, 80, 109
Workman, Travis, 45

Yi Chuch'ŏl, 33
Yi Poksil, 99
Yi Pulban, 53
Yi Sŭngman (Syngman Rhee), 176
Yi T'aejun, 66
Yi Tongsŏp, 69
Yu Hyŏngmok, 118
Yun Haedong, 23
Yun Miryang, 149
Yun Ponggu, 144

zoo, 52

www.ingramcontent.com/pod-product-compliance
Lightning Source LLC
Chambersburg PA
CBHW020454270326
41926CB00008B/600